EXPLORING
THE TALMUD

EXPLORING
THE TALMUD

Volume I

EDUCATION

Edited by

HAIM Z. DIMITROVSKY

KTAV PUBLISHING HOUSE, INC.
NEW YORK
1976

Library of Congress Cataloging in Publication Data
Main entry under title:

Exploring the Talmud.

Includes bibliographical references.
CONTENTS: v. 1. Education.
1. Talmud—Addresses, essays, lectures. 2. Jews—Education—History—Addresses, essays, lectures. 3. Jewish
learning and scholarship—History—Addresses, essays,
lectures. I. Dimitrovsky, Hayim Zalman.
BM500.2.E88   296.1 2   76-7449

MANUFACTURED IN THE UNITED STATES OF AMERICA

CONTENTS

Section Three—TEACHER AND STUDENT

Section Four—THE TEACHING PROCESS

Section Five—SCHOOLS AND ACADEMIES

ACKNOWLEDGMENTS

The editor is deeply grateful to the publishers of the following for their generosity in granting permission to reprint the articles in this volume:

"Several Sidelights of a Torah Education in Tannaite and Early Amoraic Times" by Judah Goldin, *Ex Orbe Religionum*, vol. 1, 1972 (pub. by E.J. Brill).

"Pukhovitzer's Concept of Torah Lishmah" by Norman Lamm, *Jewish Social Studies*, vol. 30, 1968.

"Two Principles of Character Education in the Aggadah" by Bernard Mandelbaum, *Judaism*, vol. 21, 1967.

"Fundamental Principles of Jewish Education in the Light of Halachah" by Z.E. Kurzweil, *Judaism*, vol. 16, 1967.

"Towards a Rabbinic Philosophy of Education" by David M. Gordis, *The Samuel Friedland Lectures*, The Jewish Theological Seminary of America, New York, 1974.

"Education among the Jews" by Henry M. Leipziger, *Educational Monographs*, vol. 3, 1890.

"The Sage is More Important than the Prophet" by Abraham I. Kook, translated by Ben Zion Bokser, *Judaism*, vol. 21, 1972.

"The Wise Man in Rabbinic Judaism and Stoic Philosophy" by Nathaniel L. Gerber, *Yavneh Review*, vol. 2 , 1969.

"Rabbis and Community in Third Century Babylonia" by Jacob Neusner, *Religions in Antiquity, Essay in Memory of E.R. Goodenough*, ed. J. Neusner, Leiden: E. J. Brill, 1968.

"Abba, Father" by Kaufmann Kohler, *Jewish Quarterly Review*, original series, vol. 13, 1901.

"Is the Title 'Rabbi' Anachronistic in the Gospels" by Hershel Shanks, *Jewish Quarterly Review*, new series, vol. 53, 1963.

"A Reply" by Solomon Zeitlin, *Jewish Quarterly Review*, new series, vol. 53, 1963.

"Origins of the Title 'Rabbi' " by Hershel Shanks, *Jewish Quarterly Review*, new series, vol. 59, 1968.

FOR
SHALOM SPIEGEL
איש האשכולות

PREFACE

It is the purpose of this volume, and of the volumes that I hope will follow it, to put into the hands of both the student of Judaic tradition and the general reader a comprehensive collection of articles relating to talmudic literature. The educational, social, historical, folkloristic, linguistic, and literary aspects of the Talmud will be dealt with. The areas of law and theology in the Talmud have already been the subject of considerable attention in a number of other collections. In dealing with these subjects the present anthology will focus mainly on the relevance of the Talmud for contemporary religious and social problems.

The Talmud is mainly a religio-nomological compilation. Its development, however, was intimately tied to everyday life. It grew out of the daily experiences of all the strata of the Jewish people, learned and simple, sophisticated and naive, rich and poor, urban and rural, aristocratic and common. Given the wide social spectrum that prevailed during the talmudic period (100 B.C.E.–500 C.E.), it is obvious why an endless variety of problems arose. The conflicts of interest and approach were numerous—wealthy landlords versus their tenants, priests versus laymen, the religious practices and ways of worship of the highly sophisticated city-dwellers versus the simple and superstitious beliefs of those who lived in the remote rural areas of the country, such as the Galilee or Edom, to mention but a few.

The academies, the centers of learning in Palestine and Babylonia in which the talmudic literature was created and compiled, were attuned and attentive to the problems and needs of all the elements of the Jewish people. With an abundance of good will they tried to work out the best solutions available within the framework of the Torah and tradition. They were especially well suited to the tasks they faced. From the beginning of the first century C.E., and especially after the establishment of the center at Jabneh following the destruction of the Temple (70 C.E.), the rabbinic institutions of learning were open to all segments of the population alike. All who possessed the necessary intellectual ability and will to learn could become students in the academies, and eventually scholars in their own right. As a result, virtually all segments of Jewish society were represented in the academies. All groups had spokesmen who knew at first hand the problems they faced, and who could be consulted on the best ways to handle these problems. It is true that, being human, even the scholars of the academies could not free themselves of their backgrounds, and consequently tensions frequently flared up among them. Nevertheless, notwithstanding these differences, the genuine piety and deep sense of commitment toward the needs of the people as a whole, that prevailed among the sages, enabled them to pave the talmudic way of life.

This series of anthologies will include the following five divisions: (1) education, (2) social sciences and history, (3) realia and folklore, (4) linguistics and philology, (5) the study of the Talmud, both traditional and scholarly. A supplementary volume will include a general index and a comprehensive analytic bibliography of Talmudic scholarship. The present volume, the first of the series, deals with education at all levels, elementary, middle and higher.

The main goal of this series is to bring together as much information as is available about the subjects under consideration. Accordingly, articles that enrich the descriptions of these topics, even if popular rather than scholarly, have been included. Moreover, even where the editor has had reservations about the conclusions drawn, he has made only a short comment to this effect in the introductory remarks and has refrained from a detailed critical analysis.

Unfortunately, a few additional articles that should have been included in this first volume were omitted because of difficulties in reaching agreement with the original publishers.

Last but not least, I am deeply grateful to my dear wife, Lilly, for all her help, encouragement, and patience in completing the preparation of this volume.

Dec. 1, 1975

HAIM Z. DIMITROVSKY
Judge Lieberman Professor
of Talmudic Exegesis,
The Jewish Theological Seminary
of America

INTRODUCTORY REMARKS

An anthology, by its very definition a collection of materials and articles selected and arranged according to a preconceived plan, cannot aspire to present as systematic a description of the subject on which it focuses as a monograph written by a single author. The editor of an anthology must choose from material that is already available, and often this material does not cover all aspects of the subject under consideration. Moreover, since the individual articles may have been written at different times—in the case of the present volume, over a period of close to a century—they may reflect methods of scholarship and analysis different from those currently in use, as well as ignorance of sources that became available only later. Nevertheless, despite these shortcomings, there are great advantages to the anthological method of presentation, for it can vividly demonstrate how research on the subject under consideration has developed, how views were revised, why new interpretive trends came into being, and the bases upon which present research has reached its conclusions. In short, it can clearly show the ways in which contemporary scholarship is an outgrowth of earlier research.

The present volume does not claim to give a consistent and systematic description of talmudic education. However, an attempt has been made to present as complete a picture as possible of both the theoretical and practical aspects of the subject, including its aims, aspirations, and ideals, as well as the institutions and personnel instrumental in accomplishing the educational work.

I

The basic character of Western education is its subordination to its social and cultural environment. As has been noted, "Education is a collective technique which a society employs to instruct its youth in the values and accomplishments of the civilization within which it exists" (H. I. Marrou, *A History of Education in Antiquity* [New York, 1956]), p. xiii). As a result, Western education follows closely in the footsteps of its mother society. When social and political conditions are good, learning and knowledge grow and flourish; conversely, under adverse conditions education declines. In short, social development and educational achievement waxed and waned in parallel curves.

By way of contrast, Jewish education, as understood by the talmudic sages, was entirely different in nature. According to them its plan was conceived by supernatural wisdom prior to the existence of organized Jewish society. It therefore followed that once the principles of education were pronounced in the Torah, they were immutable, regardless of the conditions faced by the Jewish people. This conception of Jewish education was already clearly formulated at the beginning of the postexilic era, and thus those responsible for the creation of Jewish institutions of learning took part in a process that was the reverse of that in which Western educators were involved. For the Jewish educators society was subordinate to the educational system, and not its cause. The achievements of Jewish education were particularly remarkable during periods of national distress, when, according to the Western concept, Jewish education should have come to an end. Instead, the rabbis succeeded in keeping educational ideals and institutions alive, and in this way they created a new Jewish society powerful enough to survive within even the most hostile of environments.

To be sure, the rabbis' concept was somewhat utopian, and perhaps never was fully realized. Throughout, however, the sages remained loyal to its goals as originally conceived. They aimed not simply to prepare the young to successfully join the ranks of their elders, but to create an ideal society conducted according to absolute theological and moral principles. By educating the young the sages hoped to raise the entire nation to the ideal heights of a utopian dream.

II

In the first section, "Jewish Education: Its Program and Goals," a wide range of ideas and techniques concerning Jewish education is presented. Three major themes emerge as outstanding in importance. The first of these is the notion of the centrality of the individual and his link to God as the focus of education. It becomes clear that the immediate aim of Jewish education is the establishment of a well-balanced relationship between each individual and his creator. The emphasis throughout is upon the individual, for God is seen as having a relationship with individual man, not with the world as a whole. When the world stands in judgment before its maker, it is the sum total of the deeds of all individuals that counts. Each man bears the burden of responsibility, for even a single good deed may tip the scales of the world for the good, and, conversely, a bad deed may do the reverse. Accordingly, each person must be instructed on every action in his life, big or small. Since human feelings and desires are as an open book before God, importance is also attached to thoughts, feelings, and beliefs. Just as one must discipline his actions, so must he guard his thoughts from evil, from jealousy, bitterness, and haughtiness. Ideally, a constant sense of the presence of God should be created.

The second major theme is that of the obligation to educate. The responsibility rests first with the parents. However, it is not limited to them, and extends on the one hand to the community as a whole, and on the other to the individual himself. If a person was not educated during his youth, it is his obligation to become educated during his maturity, no matter what his financial status. Two major concepts leading to the accomplishment of talmudic education were developed, *Yediat haTorah* and *Yegiat haTorah*—the knowledge of the Torah, and the toil of the Torah. The first of these, which ideally means a vast and comprehensive knowledge of the written as well as the oral Torah, is a lofty aspiration. Few can reach this aim. "One in a thousand . . . makes it" (See Goldin, pp. 4, 12). Only he to whom Providence has granted the talent and intellectual ability to became a *talmid ḥakham,* a learned man, bears the responsibility of achieving this goal, the pinnacle of Jewish educational accomplishment. However, no one, no matter how limited his intellectual capacity, can free himself from the responsibility of the toil of the Torah, from the labor of studying Torah.

The third major theme is that of the importance of study per se. The study of Torah should not be used as a means of achieving status for the individual; nor even does its primary significance lie in the fact that it is necessary for the training of teachers, rabbis, and judges for the community. Rather it is a goal in and of itself. Each Jew is inaugurated into the study of Torah as soon as he is able to pronounce syllables, and he should continue to study until the day of his death. One cannot graduate from the study of Torah, and at no point did talmudic students complete their course of studies. Unlike the Western institutions of higher learning, the talmudic academies never had a study program leading to a degree, and as a result they never graduated their students. It is true that in each generation some of the most outstanding students in turn became heads of academies. However, they achieved such status not by virtue of having received official recognition in the form of higher academic degrees, but rather because of their wide knowledge and their reputation as great scholars. Although ordination (*semikha*) was practiced in the Palestinian academies, it was not a degree awarded for scholarly achievement or rank. Rather it was a judicial title, which granted its recipients jurisdiction in certain specific areas. As far as ritual laws, worship, and religious issues were concerned, it was assumed that all who had the relevant knowledge were entitled to make the necessary decisions.

It should be noted that the obligation of total involvement with the study of Torah created a religious and social conflict regarding the question of the possibilities for survival for a society entirely involved in study. A glimpse at some of the answers provided by the sages can be found on page 39. (See also E. E. Urbach, *The Sages,* Jerusalem 1975, p. 606 N. 81)

III

The nature of the type of religious leader that appeared on the Jewish scene with the close of the era of the prophets is an intriguing topic, dealt with in Section II. Our knowledge of his image and traits is meager. From the vague, fragmentary, and legendary sources that are available, the impression is conveyed that he was often of aristocratic or priestly origin, both a religious and a social expert, and well versed in legal and human problems. His function appears to have been more that of judge and legislator than of a teacher dedicated to his students and the Book. (See E. E. Urbach, *Proceedings of the Israel Academy of Sciences and Humanities,* Jerusalem 1968, vol. 2, p. 44 ff.).

With the passage of time a new kind of Jewish leader emerged. More and more his worldly and practical occupations gave way to involvement with scholastic and spiritual activity. The wise man described in the wisdom literature as the consultant to kings, who feels at home in the royal court and comfortable in the company of princes, was gradually replaced by the person of deep piety who delves into the Torah in search of answers to all his problems.

The turning point in this development occurred at the end of the first century B.C. with the establishment of the early tannaitic academies, and reached its climax with the founding of the center at Jabneh shortly after the destruction of the Temple (70 C.E.). It would seem that it was with the change in the nature of the hakham that the title *rabbi* was created (see pp. 164-186). However, despite this change, traits reminiscent of the leader of the past remained within the personality of the new rabbinic master, especially in the first half of the tannaitic period. During this time the Jewish scholars showed a notable interest in Greek and Roman culture and intellectual trends, and evidence of the influence of their contact with the outside world is apparent. There are, on the one hand, striking parallels between the teachings of the rabbis and the thinking of the gentile philosophers. For example, both searched for moral maxims and for the good way of life. On the other hand, there are still more impressive differences that separate them. Thus, for instance, the pessimism and passivity of the Stoic philosophers stand in marked contrast to the active optimism of the rabbis, which vividly expressed itself in their efforts to strike a balance between the contradictory forces and passions that cause restlessness and disturbance in man.

The image of the rabbi, as compared with the non-Jewish philosopher of his time, is discussed in Berger's article (p. 105). Goldin's article (p. 357) affords us a glimpse into the tannaitic academy and its handling of philosophical problems. For further reading on related issues, the reader is referred to H. A. Fischel's *Rabbinic Literature and Greco-Roman Philosophy* (Leiden, 1973). A fascinating description of the ideal image of the talmudic personality, its unique way of thinking and perception of all aspects of life, is presented in Rabbi J. B. Soloveitchik's monograph *Ish haHalakha* [The man of Halakha] (*Talpioth,* vol. 1, p. 651, N. Y. 1944).

The status of the sages is an additional subject of great interest. The degree of influence held by the rabbis varied in different communities and at different periods. In Palestine, where, since the establishment of the center at Jabneh, all authority had been concentrated in the hands of the head of the Sanhedrin, and where there had been no division between the religious and lay leadership, the rabbis had a profound and all-encompassing influence on virtually all aspects of Jewish communal life. Despite the fact that the heads of the Sanhedrin and the rabbis were at times involved in a struggle for power, with the relationship between them tense and strained, their religious and educational backgrounds and outlooks were similar.

By way of contrast, in Babylonia the situation closely resembled that prevailing in Palestine prior to the destruction of the Temple, where the political and social administration was controlled by the Hasmonean dynasty, and later by Herod and his descendants, while the sages aspired to leadership in religious and intellectual areas. The administration of the Babylonian Jewish community, as far back as we can account for, was in the hands of a lay leader. Thus, when the disciples of Rabbi Akiba and Rabbi Ishmael immigrated to Babylonia in the aftermath of Bar Kokhba's rebellion (135 C.E.), they found a deeply rooted tradition of lay leadership, and it was undoubtedly not easy for them to attain a position of authority in the community. Beginning in the latter half of the second century C.E., when the lay leader begins to figure in talmudic sources as a real personality, with the title *resh galuta* (exilarch), the rivalry between this lay authority and the sages emerges even more clearly. During the course of the next thousand years there was a continuous struggle, at times overt and at times concealed, between the exilarch and the sages. The nature and intensity of this struggle often depended on the temperament, education, and attitude toward the Torah of the exilarch, as well as the degree of determination of particular sages. However, it seems clear that the exilarch, as a result of his political status and the recognition he was granted by the government, consistently maintained the upper hand in this struggle.

An additional factor affecting the status and influence of the sages in Babylonia was the attitude of the Jewish masses toward them. Although different Jewish sects existed in Palestine, each of these had religious and halakhic traditions which developed along their own course. This was not the case in Babylonia. While the names of a few sages who lived there in the first and second centuries C.E. are known to us, we have no information concerning prevalent religious practices, theological concepts, and the attitudes of the Babylonian Jews toward the Pharisaic halakha. Moreover, it seems reasonable to assume that if the Babylonian Jews turned to the authorities in Jerusalem and the Temple for guidance in earlier times, and it seems certain that they did, the instructions they received undoubtedly sometimes differed from the Pharisaic halakha, for often the Sadducees were the ruling party in the Sanhedrin. (This may be the rationale for the Karaite claim that they had in their possession halakhic compilations of Sadducean origin.) Moreover, even instructions in the Pharisaic tradition that had been received from Jerusalem were not identical with the Jabnaic decisions that the Palestinian sages brought to Babylonia. In view of this, it would appear more than likely that when the Palestinian rabbis brought their teachings to Babylonia, they found themselves opposing a halakhic and religious tradition claiming its authority from the Temple in Jerusalem. In addition, we may also assume that they confronted local customs practiced in the ancient Babylonian synagogues, places of worship that were believed to have been founded by the exiles from Judea after the destruction of the First Temple. Folk customs reflecting the influence of the rural environment were also deeply rooted in the people of the provinces.

This was the background against which the talmudic establishment in Babylonia came to maturity in the third century c.e. By the end of the first half of the third century, all the public institutions playing a role in the life and administration of the Babylonian Jewish community, including the office of the exilarch and the great academies presided over by the most distinguished scholars, had already evolved. Moreover, a certain balance had been achieved between them.

The rabbis were especially active in the areas of teaching and the judiciary. As far as teaching was concerned, they were completely independent. The *yeshivot* were the domain of the sages, and there they did what they pleased. Obviously the people associated with the *yeshivot* recognized the Torah as the highest authority in Jewish life. For them the heads of the academies gradually began to take precedence over the exilarch, notwithstanding the sentimental attachment to the latter because of his claim to Davidic descent. The judicial area, by way of contrast, was the domain of the exilarch, and the rabbis who acted as judges were his delegates, making judgments and enforcing their decisions by his authorization. In the few instances in which rabbis appear to have achieved a status of judicial independence, this would appear to have been by way of a concession on the part of an exilarch who felt close to the academies and wanted to please the sages.

The rabbis appear to have been most reluctant to exert their influence in the area of worship and synagogue practice, where old customs and local traditions seem to have retained a strong hold. They appear to have tolerated these customs, although they did not approve of them. For their part, the sages tended to worship and pray in the *yeshivot* rather than the synagogues, asserting that a place where Torah is studied has greater importance than one reserved only for prayers. It is worthy of note in this connection that the position of rabbi as we know it today did not exist in the talmudic period. The duties of the rabbi of today were divided among different functionaries—the judge, the preacher, whose main expertise was in Bible and Aggada, the *archisynagogos,* and the *parnas.* Responsibility for synagogue practice lay in the hands of these functionaries, and this may have been the reason why the Babylonian rabbis retired to the academies for prayer.

Although the Babylonian rabbis did not mingle with the people in prayer, they took a very active part in the economic life of the community, especially in such areas as farming, trade, and finance. As they interacted with the people they attracted them with the power of their personalities. They also impressed them with their knowledge, which encompassed subjects as diverse as medicine, astronomy, and what would today be known as psychology. Legend attributing miraculous attributes to the sages began to arise. In addition to J. Neusner's article in this volume (p. 128), which deals mainly with third-century Babylonia, the reader interested in a more general discussion of this subject is referred to E. E. Urbach's article, "The Talmudic Sage—Character and Authority" (Journal of World History, vol. XI, 1–2, 1968, p. 116–147). For information on the activities of the Babylonian sages in areas outside the academies, the reader is referred to M. Beer's *Amorai Bavel* (Tel Aviv, 1974).

The last two articles in this section deal with the origins of the honorary titles commonly used in talmudic literature. Kohler's intriguing explanation of the title *abba* (p. 150) is in line with the scholarly trend of searching for ancient halakhic elements differing from the Pharisaic tradition, which was begun by A. Geiger in the nineteenth century. The refutation by Urbach (in the *Proceedings of the Israel Academy of Sciences and Humanities,* Jerusalem 1968, vol. 2, p. 54, note 36) of Kohler's conclusion that *abba* was originally an Essenian title is not completely convincing. It seems clear that it was an honorary title used only in pietistic and mystic circles (see Berakhot 16b; J. N. Epstein's *Mavo Lenusach Hamishna,* vol. 2, pp. 1302–3; and S. Lieberman's *Tosefta Ki-Fshuta,* pt. 5, p. 1062, n. 68), and not in common use as Urbach claims. The evidence that *abba* predates the destruction of the Temple also has bearing on the question of the date of origin of the title *rabbi* (see p. —). Obviously, if this title was already in use prior to the destruction, it cannot be claimed that at that time the sages were addressed by name only. It is noteworthy in this connection that the Qumran sect called its teacher by the title *moreh,* and, as Kohler has pointed out (see p. 150), the three titles *abba, rabbi* and *moreh* are found side by side in the Talmud.

V

As shown in a number of articles[1] in this volume (p. 77 ff.; 192 ff.), a great deal is known about the nature and structure of the elementary schools of ancient Israel. Even such details as the location at which teaching took place (the teacher's home or the synagogue), the hours of instruction, the curriculum, the nature of the relationship between the teacher and the students, the income of the teachers, and the techniques of teaching generally in use are clear (see p. 7 ff.; 193 ff.). Imber's conjecture[2] that the compilation entitled *The Letters of Rabbi Akiba* served as a primer for teaching children the Aleph Bet should be mentioned here. While the book in its present form can hardly be called a primer, version B of this compilation appears to incorporate parts of a primer, and it is reasonable to assume that these parts are similar in format to other such manuals in use at the time. As support for this assumption,

---

[1] Although Ginzberg's article, p. 287, deals largely with the post talmudic period, it was included in its entirety because it presents so vivid a description of the rabbinic elementary school through the generations.

[2] N. H. Imber, The Letters of Rabbi Akiba, or the Jewish Primer as it was used in the Public Schools Two Thousand Years Ago. Report of the commissioner of education for 1895-96, chapter 14. Washington, 1897.

the story of the young children who came from the elementary school
to the *bet midrash* (academy) and expounded on the letters of the
alphabet should be mentioned here (B. Shabbat 104a). They are
quoted as explaining the shape and form of the letters in terms of
teachings concerning ethics, morals, charity, and good behavior.
This is, of course, a combination suitable for small children, and it
seems to be the original material used in elementary schools. (Compare also this story as told in Genesis Rabba I, 11).

Our information regarding the schools of higher learning, on the
other hand, is relatively limited. We know of the existence of two
academies in ancient Israel prior to the destruction, the House of
Shammai and the House of Hillel. However, we know very little
about the curriculum and methods of teaching in use at these academies. We know that shortly after the founding of the center at
Jabneh a number of additional academies were established in other
cities, but we do not know whether this occurred in response to local
social and intellectual demand, or, as Allon[3] has proposed, as a result
of dissension between leading scholars and the head of the Sanhedrin at Jabneh. We have quite detailed information about the form
of instruction at Jabneh, but know little concerning this at other
academies. Did they also follow the elaborate rituals of the seating
order and the presentation of the "lesson" as these were practiced at
Jabneh?
A question of particular interest relates to the curriculum and
study texts used at the various academies. We know that a mishnaic
text was the formal study material used in the academy of the president at Jabneh, but do not know whether a text of this kind was
also studied in the other academies. There is convincing evidence of
the existence of a mishnaic collection known as the "Mishna Ris-
hona" [The First Mishna], which, according to well-established
claims, dates back to the pre-Jabnaic period. It might be claimed
that this was a text used in the tannaitic *yeshivot*. However, we also
know that Rabbi Akiba arranged collections of Midrash and Mish-

---

[3] See G. Allon, *Meḥkarim Betoledot Yisrael*, vol. 1, p. 255 ff.

nah. His pupils did the same, Rabbi Meir compiling a comprehensive mishnaic collection, Rabbi Nehemia a collection known as Tosefta, and Rabbi Yehuda and Rabbi Shimon midrashic collections. One must wonder about the cause and purpose of this sudden proliferation of new collections. Was it perhaps that the sages heading the various academies compiled these original collections as study texts for their own *yeshivot?*

We know that the academy at Jabneh had a large number of students, but know nothing about how many students there were in the local academies. It suffices to mention the legend that there were either twelve thousand or twenty-four thousand students in the *yeshiva* of Rabbi Akiba. It is intriguing to speculate about the size of the other tannaitic *yeshivot*. Rabbi Akiba's wife, Rachel, labored to support her husband while he attended primary school. We know very little about how pupils, or for that matter even some teachers in the higher schools of learning, supported themselves. We do know that some sages earned their livelihood in various trades, but we do not know whether this was true of all the rabbis. Finally, it should be noted that as little as we know about tannaitic academies in ancient Israel, we know even less about those in Babylonia. Indeed, it is not even certain that there were tannaitic academies in Babylonia.

To go back to the pre-Jabnaic period, it seems beyond doubt that Midrash occupied a central place in the curriculum and instruction at the academies. However, nonmidrashic material must also have been taught. Thus, it is interesting to note that in the abundance of material attributed in talmudic sources to the Houses of Hillel and Shammai, and to sages that lived at least part of their lives before the destruction (i.e., R. Eliezer, R. Joshua, and R. Tarfon), we find little midrashic material and an abundance of mishnaic material.

Talmudic scholarship has struggled to fill some of these gaps in our knowledge of the academic and material aspects of life in the *yeshivot*. Clearly, questions concerning the ways in which the oral tradition was transmitted are of central importance. Two major theories concerning this crucial issue have been proposed. According to J. N. Epstein[4], whose theory is based on the detailed analysis of internal evidence in the talmudic literature, redacted mishnaic collections existed prior to the destruction of the Temple. Individual sages, such as R. Yoḥanan ben Zakkai, R. Eliezer ben Hyrcanus, and R. Joshua, compiled collections of Mishna even during the pre-Jabnaic period. This process of compilation continued throughout tannaitic times, until Judah the Prince compiled his Mishna, which soon achieved primary status in most of the academies and became known as "The Mishna." With great erudition Epstein attempted to identify in "The Mishna" elements of the mishnaic compilations of all of the distinguished tannaim, as well as of the pre-Jabnaic compilations. If this theory is correct, it may shed light on the curriculum and instruction in the tannaitic academies. Thus, if, as is well established, Judah the Prince compiled his Mishna as a study text, it seems reasonable to assume that the other mishnaic collections were also compiled for the same purpose, and that each *yeshiva* used its own mishnaic collection as a study text. In this way Epstein's theory supplies us with the materials that may have occupied the central place in the programs of study of the tannaitic academies.

The second major theory concerning the ways in which the oral tradition was transmitted has been most fully presented by H. Albeck[5] According to him, the first mishnaic collection was the original recension of *Mishna Eduyot* at Jabneh. Prior to this the content of the oral tradition was neither edited nor organized within any literary framework. While laws, rulings, and ordinances existed before, these were not organized or grouped according to subject matter. Moreover, they were not formulated in a fixed style, and thus only their content was transmitted, and their exact language was not. It was only in the Jabnaic period that this amorphous material became a formulated literature. This approach leaves us with the puzzling problem of what was taught in the academies prior to the Jabnaic period. Although Goldin's interesting description of the "philosophical session" (p. 357) suggests that study in the tannaitic academies

---

[4] J. N. Epstein, *Mevoot Lesifrut Hatannaim,* Jerusalem, 1957.

[5] H. Albeck, *Mavo Lamishna,* Tel Aviv, 1959; p. 63 ff.

sometimes took the form of a free dialogue unrelated to text, it seems highly unlikely that the "halakhic session" followed the same pattern. It also seems improbable that all of the instruction was associated with the biblical text. Furthermore, while the approach expounded by Epstein allows time for the development of the mishnaic literary style, that of Albeck assumes the sudden birth of new literary forms.

The theory of literary development so painstakingly expounded by Epstein had one weak point. It left open the question of how a substantial and constantly expanding literature could be faithfully transmitted orally over a period of hundreds of years. The answer to this question has been supplied by B. Gerhardsson. In his book *Memory and Manuscript* (Uppsala, 1961), he has presented a detailed description of all the teaching techniques and processes mentioned or indirectly alluded to in rabbinic literature. He has also added a new dimension to scholarship in this area by introducing the analytical and critical methods used in the modern study of early Christian and other oral traditions into the field of research in talmudic literature. To be sure, while Gerhardsson assumes the existence of a substantial oral mishnaic and midrashic literature, he does not really attempt to prove the existence of this literature. For such proof he seems to rely entirely on the work of Epstein and his predecessors. His major effort is directed to the clarification of the ways in which this literature could have been preserved, transmitted, and taught.

Gerhardsson's book has aroused a good deal of criticism. The main thrust of this criticism has been directed against the assumption of the existence of a formulated oral rabbinic literature. Controversy on this issue has helped generate new studies of the ancient rabbinic literature. It is noteworthy that the resulting research is largely based on form criticism and comparative methods of the very kind used by Gerhardsson himself. A more comprehensive description of this new trend in research will be presented in the last division of the present anthology.

Finkelstein's article (p. 241) is probably the first attempt to explain the evolution of different versions (as distinguished from variants, or changes attributable to copyists) from one primary text. The idea that the different versions are the result of the teaching processes prevalent in the various schools has far-reaching implications and is worthy of further research.

As far as the amoraic period is concerned, considerably more is known about the administration of elementary and higher education, methods of instruction, and curriculum. However, this material has not yet been exhaustively studied, and no comprehensive work on the amoraic institutions of learning is available.[6] The present volume includes all the articles dealing with this area available in English. The articles by Lauterbach and Gandz are striking examples of the guesswork to which scholars are at times inclined to resort in their attempts to explain obscure talmudic terms. While these articles contain important information concerning the amoraic schools, they fail to solve the specific problems to which they address themselves. Greenfield's article, by way of contrast, is based on sound comparative philological methodology.

---

[6] As the present volume went to press, David M. Goodblatt's *Rabbinic Instruction in Sasanian Babylonia* (Leiden: E. J. Brill, 1975) appeared in print.

Section One—

JEWISH EDUCATION:
ITS PROGRAM AND GOALS

SEVERAL SIDELIGHTS OF A TORAH EDUCATION
IN TANNAITE AND EARLY AMORAIC TIMES

BY

J. GOLDIN

New Haven, Conn.

In his magisterial way, as he summarizes the laws of *Talmud Torah*, of Torah study, Maimonides writes : "Every Jew (*kl 'yš myśr'l*) is obliged to study Torah, be he poor or rich, enjoying good health or in pain, young or so old as to be failing in strength—even if he is so poor as to be dependent on charity and (in his begging) must make the rounds from one house to another; and even if he is a family man with wife and children (to support), he must set aside fixed times for study of the Torah, day and night... Until when must one study ? Until the day he dies..." [1]

Of course Maimonides is not inventing, much as this view is doubtless congenial to his temperament. He is stating in concentrated form (that's why it sounds so apodictic) what is either stated explicitly or implied in several places of the Talmud. As the commentators observe, what Maimonides has in mind here is very likely such passages as the *baraita* (*tnw rbnn*, the tannaite statement) in B. Yoma 35b, that on the Day of Judgment neither the poor man nor the rich man nor the philanderer will have a real alibi for having neglected to study—the poor man was no poorer than Hillel was, when he first settled in the Holy Land; the rich one did not own as much real estate and other properties to take up all his time and thoughts, as Rabbi Eleazar ben Ḥarsom owned; and the philanderer [2] had no more lusty an appetite or better opportunities than Joseph had in Potiphar's house.

---

[1] Maimonides, Code, Book of Knowledge, Hilkot Talmud Torah, 1:8, 10. See also the reaffirmation in Joseph Karo's Code, Yoreh De'ah, 246:1, 3. And note how Rabban Yoḥanan ben Zakkai is quoted in Midrash Tannaim, 58. Is the last clause really R. Yoḥanan's, or is it the addition of the compiler of Midrash ha-Gadol ? Even if it should be the latter, the compiler of the Midrash ha-Gadol has caught Yoḥanan's emphasis correctly. See *ARNA*, 58, top.

[2] That's what *rš'* means in that passage.

3

That many talmudic scholars were poor and supported themselves by menial occupations, Maimonides also asserts : [1] of course, again, on the basis of talmudic records. So too, he manages to persuade us that until the day of death one must study, by a neat exercise of biblical exegesis; for it is said in Deuteronomy 4:9, " Take utmost care and watch yourselves scrupulously' " lest the (divine) " '*dbrym* fade from your mind as long as you live'; and so long as one does not engage in study, he *does* forget". Hence, to call a halt to study before one dies is to transgress.[2]

Needless to say, what such statements reflect is an ideal, perhaps in truth so lofty an ideal, that even most of those who would assent to it cheerfully, would be unable to fulfill it. The significant thing, however, is that so extreme or hyperbolic a demand is not a priori dismissed as a manifest impossibility and therefore not to be taken seriously, or therefore to be excluded from codified programs for human conduct. A man's reach must exceed his grasp, or what's the Talmud for. In other words, the significant thing about the talmudic views which Maimonides adopts and organizes is that they do serve as ideals, that they are regarded as *feasible*.

And it's not as though talmudic sages are ignorant of what's really going on in the world. "Here's the way it is (*bnwhg šb'wlm*)", they tell us; "of the thousand who start out with an education in Scripture, only a hundred go on further; of the hundred studying Mishnah, only ten go on further; of the ten studying Talmud, only one comes forth (to become an authority)".[3] One in a thousand therefore makes it—if that, we may add, not because we are cynical, but because *we* are not called upon to interpret the verse in Ecclesiastes (7:28), "I found only one human being in a thousand, and the one I found among so many was never a woman".[4]

What really takes place, then, is much less spectacular than what one might be tempted to derive from Maimonides' imperatives or some rococo haggadot. Nevertheless, only such imperatives make

---

[1] *Op. cit.*, 1:9.

[2] *Cf.* Haggahot Maimoniyyot on Hilkot Talmud Torah 1:10; Naḥmanides on Deut. 4:9. See also the statement by R. Jonathan in B. Shabbat 83b, on "never" staying away from the *bet midrash*, even in the hour of death. On the moving story of R. Akiba continuing to teach as *his son* was dying, see Semaḥot VIII (ed. Zlotnick), 63.

[3] Lev. R. 2:1, ed. Margulies, p. 35; *cf.* Eccl. R. 7:28, and *here* we read, "(only) one of them comes forth to become an authority (*lhwr'h*)."

[4] See Five Megilloth and Jonah (introductions by H. L. Ginsberg [Philadelphia, 1969]), p. 69.

12

comprehensible a number of halakic and haggadic passages in the midrashic-talmudic sources. For example : The Mishnah [1] declares that if one goes to recover something his father had lost and something his teacher had lost, he is first to recover what the teacher lost; only thereafter does he go to recover what his father lost : "for his father brought him (only) into this world; his teacher on the other hand brings him to the life of the world to come". Again, if one's father and one's teacher were taken captive, first to be ransomed is the teacher; only after that is the father ransomed.

Talmudists will be quick to remind us that this is far from the last word on the subject,[2] and that already the Mishnah itself, on the spot, introduces a qualification or two. True enough. But the basic principle here involved—that my first responsibility is to him that teaches me Torah—is unmistakable. Does not the Mishnah in still another treatise [3] admonish me that *mwr' rbk kmwr' šmym*, that towards my teacher I must feel the same awe as I feel toward Heaven ?

Or, an even bolder example : "Do thou toil away over the words of Torah", says a well-known treatise,[4] "and do not engage in idle matters". Then by way of explaining this proposal, the treatise continues as follows : "Once as Rabbi Simeon ben Yoḥai went about visiting the sick, he came upon a man, laid up with an affliction of bowel sickness, uttering blasphemies against the Holy One, blessed be He.

" 'Racca (wretch) !' Rabbi Simeon cried, 'you should be beseeching mercy for yourself; yet you utter blasphemies !'

"Said the man, 'May the Holy One, blessed be He, remove the sickness from me and lay it on you !'

"(Thereupon) Rabbi Simeon exclaimed : 'Well has the Holy One, blessed be He, done with me, for I neglected the words of Torah and engaged in idle matters' ".

Even Solomon Schechter was baffled by this anecdote.[5] Who in the world of the talmudic sages would call an act of lovingkindness

---

[1] Baba Mesi 'a 2:11. Cf. M. Keritut, end. See also Diogenes Laertius, V, 19.

[2] See Maimonides, Hilkot Talmud Torah, 5:1, and Kesef Mishneh and Leḥem Mishneh *ad loc.*

[3] Pirqe 'Abot 4:12; cf. C. Taylor's commentary (Sayings of the Jewish Fathers) *ad loc.*

[4] 'Abot de-Rabbi Natan, ed. Schechter, Version A, 130.

[5] *Cf.* J. Goldin, *Fathers According to Rabbi Nathan* (New Haven, 1955), 219.

like visiting the sick [1] "idle matters" ? Schechter therefore emended the text, and unwittingly almost made a barbarian out of Simeon ben Yoḥai. Simeon ben Yoḥai is often enough hard to take even without conjectured textual emendations. He is the man who felt (not altogether mistakenly) that Torah was for manna-eaters or those with guaranteed private incomes [2] who didn't have to work for a living. This reminds one of Breasted who, I'm told, when asked by a student, How does one become an Egyptologist, replied, "First, he must marry a rich woman". The correct reading of our talmudic story is fortunately preserved in the Oxford manuscript and first edition of 'Abot de-Rabbi Natan. And what the story tells us is that Simeon ben Yoḥai once had an experience which emphasized for him that so important is Torah study, that, compared to it, even as meritorious an act as visiting the sick may be regarded as an "idle matter". Which is exactly what I would expect from Simeon ben Yoḥai.[3] So also, a father was not wrong when he complained to his son, "Look here, I sent you away to college to study, and not to spend your days piling up virtues. For that, we have plenty of corpses to bury in our own town"! [4] At all events, the value judgment expres-

---

[1] "Whose fruits one eats in this world, while the stock is laid up for him in the world to come"; cf. Baer, Seder 'Abodat Yiśrael (Schocken, 5697), 38 f.

[2] Mekilta, Wa-Yassa', III (ed. Lauterbach, II, 104). On Simeon ben Yoḥai discouraging scholars from physical labors, cf. Sifre Deut., 42, ed. Finkelstein, 90. See also Rosenthal, *Knowledge Triumphant* (Leiden, 1970), 296.

[3] Even in amoraic times, and in Babylonia, note what Raba said about R. Hamnuna taking a long time at *prayer*! B. Shabbat 10a. See also the perfectly intelligent question raised in B. Berakot 32b about the reported conduct of the "early saints."

[4] Literally, "R. Abbahu sent his son R. Ḥanina to study Torah" (yzky, cf. Qorban ha-'Edah *ad loc.*) "in Tiberias. (Some people) came and reported to him that (R. Ḥanina) was occupying himself with acts of lovingkindness. (R. Abbahu thereupon sent the following message to his son : 'Is it for lack of burial places in Caesarea that I sent you to Tiberias ?' " P. Pesaḥim 3:7. The parallel passage occurs in P. Ḥagigah 1:7. See further S. Lieberman, Hayerushalmi Kiphshuto (Jerusalem, 1934), 425 f.

I am unable to suppress the following (which is not entirely irrelevant even to our theme; cf. G. F. Moore, *Judaism*, II, 247), especially since I must acknowledge indebtedness in any event. The anecdote about R. Abbahu and his son I knew from some earlier studies, though I did not remember that it had to do with Abbahu. However, when I came to draw up the present footnotes, I could not recall where the story occurred, though I rummaged high and low. After four days of futile efforts, I finally telephoned Professor Lieberman long distance, and had only begun the anecdote when he interrupted with, "It's in Yerushalmi Pesaḥim 3:7, 30b; the parallel is in Yerushalmi Ḥagigah 1:7. Be sure to consult Ibn Shuaib's Derashot which has an interesting reading. See my Yerushalmi Kiphshuto." Now cf. George Foot Moore again. And on the importance of reviewing in order to remember, see also *ARNA*, 76. How terrible it is to forget, cf. R. Gamaliel, *ibid.*, 76.

6

sed by our story about Simeon ben Yoḥai, even if one were to take
exception to it, is comprehensible only in terms of the injunction,
Every Jew must study Torah till the day he dies. No wonder an ancient
commentary on the saying, "Let all your deeds be for the sake of
Heaven" has it that "for the sake of Heaven" equals "for the sake
of Torah".[1] More radical still is God Himself. "Would they had for-
saken Me", He says, "but kept My Torah".[2]

So much for the rhetoric in praise of Torah and Torah study,
although on this theme one can go on seemingly endlessly; see, for
example, the long chapter of talmudic and midrashic passages
(174 pages) devoted to the theme of *Talmud Torah* in Volume III
of H. G. Enelow's edition of *Menorat ha-Ma'or* (New York, 1931)
by the 14th century martyr Israel ibn Al-Nakawa.

If we move on now to passages *descriptive* of learning, primary
and higher, as it was actually carried on, only sidelights are granted
us. That is to say, no systematic account or even outline of the course
of higher learning is preserved. Nor are we too much better off in
regard to primary schooling. Our sources are much too often quiet
where we wish they'd been more talkative, and maybe the reverse
is also true. The kind of questions asked by S. D. Goitein,[3] for example,
in connection with learning and education in late geonic and early
post-geonic centuries, as reflected by the Genizah documents, is
valid also for the tannaite and early amoraic times in Jewish Palestine : What was the curriculum? How was instruction carried on?
How were students tested? Where and in what ways were so-called
secular subjects taught : mathematics, astronomy, zoology, aspects
of human physiology—subjects which had to be studied if only to
understand, or to determine, the halakah in pressing, practical,

---

[1] *ARNA*, 66.

[2] Lam. R., Petiḥta 2, ed. Buber, 1b-2a, and *cf.* Buber's n. 12 (the correct reading
is *hš'wr*).

Of course I do not mean to leave the impression that acts of lovingkindness were
uniformly treated as of inferior status to the obligation to study Torah. Contrast, for
example, the conduct of R. Judah bar 'Il'ai when a bridal procession passed by as he
was teaching : *ARNA*, 19, *ARNB*, 22. Significantly, however, it seems that R. Judah
feels called upon to explain his decision to his disciples (will they otherwise not understand?), and that his model was nothing less than God's conduct! (Lovingkindness,
however, one always learns from God : B. Soṭah 14a, and *cf.* S. Schechter, *Some Aspects
of Rabbinic Theology*, N. Y., 1936, pp. 202 f.).

[3] Sidre Ḥinuk (Jerusalem, 1962), 143 ff.; *cf.* 46 f.

problems of living : the calendar, for example; [1] permitted and forbidden foods; conditions of likely impurity when husbands and
wives must keep apart from each other; bodily blemishes which
disqualified a marriage[2]; and so forth.

For some of these questions there are some and partial answers.
In the elementary school, for instance, the *bet ha-sefer*, the first things
taught apparently were the recitation of the Shema and the Tefillah,
and the Grace blessings—the *birkat ha-mazon*.[3] One also learned to
write there, and presumably practised writing the alphabet forwards
and backwards on a pinax— [4] which is somewhat reminiscent of
primary Hellenistic education in Roman times, when "it was not
enough to know the alphabet from alpha to omega. It had to be
learned backwards, from omega to alpha and then both ways at
once, $A\Omega$, $B\psi$, ΓX, ... MN".[5]

In his History of Education in Antiquity from which I have just
now quoted, H. I. Marrou describes [6] how after learning the alphabet,
"the pupil went on to syllables; and, with the same passion for system,
he was taught a complete list of them, in their proper order. No words
were attempted until all the syllables had been combined in every
possible way. The simplest came first : βa, $\beta\epsilon$, $\beta\eta$, $\beta\iota$, βo, $\beta\upsilon$,
$\beta\omega$ ... ; γa, $\gamma\epsilon$, $\gamma\eta$ ... up to ψa, $\psi\epsilon$, $\psi\eta$, $\psi\iota$, ψo, $\psi\upsilon$, $\psi\omega$; and these
apparently were not simply pronounced according to their sound
but by the name of each individual letter first and then as joined
together—thus : beta-alpha-ba; beta-ei-be; beta-eta-be ..." Even
today, there are men who surely had such first lessons in learning
to read Hebrew from a textbook called *Reshit Da'at* and the opening
pages of an edition of the traditional Jewish Prayerbook : [7] אָ, בָּ,
בַּ, גִ, דֵ, הֻ, וֹ, זִ, and so on. Perhaps such instruction is still going on;
my wife tells me that this is how she was taught to read, English,
close to fifty years ago in Tulsa, Oklahoma. There is even a Yiddish
folk song nostalgically referring to this method of learning,[8] and I

---

[1] Note M. Rosh ha-Shanah 2:8 for the visual aids Rabban Gamaliel II had in his attic.

[2] See, for example, M. Ketubot 7:7-10.

[3] Note the question put by Yoḥanan ben Zakkai to Eliezer ben Hyrcanus when the
latter appeared in Yoḥanan's school, *ARNB*, 30.

[4] See *ARNA*, 29.

[5] H. L. Marrou, *History of Education in Antiquity* (N. Y., 1956), 151. On some
additional features, see M. Schwabe in Tarbiz, XXI, pp. 112-23.

[6] *Ibid.*

[7] Siddur Śefat 'Emet he-Hadash, ed. A. Hyman (N. Y., 1936).

[8] I don't know the title of the song, but the relevant lines go, "*kometz aleph aw,
kometz bes baw, kometz gimmel gaw.*"

8

think the mood it wishes to create is, Ah, those were the days! The
method was doubtless common in the ancient Palestinian elementary
school.[1]

For the child—the boy, that is—[2] formal elementary education
began when he was about 5,[3] or 6 or 7;[4] and it was an immediately
relevant, functional education : that is, the child learned the principal
prayers he had to recite every day of his life; he learned Scripture
which taught him his history, not for the sake of learning history
in the abstract, but to teach him whose descendant he was and what
were the values and goals to be pursued in life, what was expected
of him;[5] by the Pentateuch especially, but not exclusively, he was
informed of the mandatory, the permitted, the forbidden. It was
clearly the practice for children to memorize : "Tell me the verse
you've learned by heart",[6] an adult might say to a child. This was
also excellent practice for the memorizing he would later do when
and if he progressed to study of the Oral Law. It is possible that the
boy spent as much as five years on biblical studies, till the age of 10 [7]
when *ideally* he began the study of Mishnah. Until then, however,
and with the preliminaries out of the way, he learned his Bible thoroughly. The scroll he learned from probably was not a copy of the
best editions;[8] nevertheless, as we've said, he learned his Bible
thoroughly. Even in St. Jerome's time (4th century) one could not
help being impressed by the stunt of some Jews "to recite all the

---

[1] *Cf.* also what is reflected by the halakic problem in M. Shabbat 12:3 ff.

[2] On the education of girls, see T. Perlow, *L'Éducation et l'Enseignement chez les
Juifs à l'Époque Talmudique* (Paris, 1931), 98-101. In sixteenth century Safed we hear
of special teachers for women (and children) to teach them the liturgy and the prescribed
benedictions : *cf.* S. Schechter, "Safed in the Sixteenth Century," *Studies in Judaism,*
Second Series (Phila., 1908), 242 and n. 98 *ad loc.* S. D. Goitein, *op. cit.*, 70, tells of a
woman who knows part of Scripture by heart. On European (Ashkenazi) practice,
see I. Twersky in 'Enṣiqlopedia Ḥinukit, IV (the volume on the history of education),
260 f. : a woman lectures even on Talmud. (For something similar in 12th century
Baghdad, *cf.* S. Asaf, *Tequfat ha-Geonim* [Jerusalem, 1955], 116 and 129.)

[3] PA 5:21, but the figures in that Mishnah may be schematized.

[4] B. Baba Batra 21a.

[5] Note what are the first things to teach the child when he begins to speak : note 2, p.
186 below. In Sifre Zuta, 288, it is said that in addition a father must teach his son Hebrew, *lešon ha-qodeš.*

[6] *Cf.* B. Ḥagigah 15a-b. See also the interesting example of this in Esther R. 7:13, 13a.

[7] PA 5:21.

[8] *Cf.* S. Lieberman, *Hellenism in Jewish Palestine* [hereafter HJP] (N. Y., 1962), 22 f.

generations from Adam to Zerubbabel with such accuracy and facility, as if they were simply giving their names".[1]

One began as a rule with the Book of Leviticus; [2] what order was followed thereafter is nowhere indicated, I think. Yet a bright boy was evidently at home in all parts of the Bible; what is more, he knew how to turn a biblical verse or clause into gracious response. When,[3] on a visit to Rome, Rabbi Joshua ben Hananiah was told of a good-looking Jewish boy who had been taken captive, from Jerusalem possibly, he approached the lad and called out in the words of Isaiah (42:24), "Who gave up Jacob to the spoiler, and Israel to the robbers?" The lad replied promptly with the latter half of the verse, "Was it not the Lord, against whom we have sinned, in whose ways they would not walk, and whose Torah they would not obey". To round out the story let me add that Joshua ransomed the boy and brought him home; and, according to some, the boy is supposed to be none other than Ishmael ben Elisha, a leading Tanna of the first half of the 2nd century.

The thorough mastery of Scripture which was aimed at will explain in part a fact to which Professor S. Lieberman has called attention

---

[1] *Cf.* S. Krauss cited in L. Finkelstein, *The Jews*[3], 171 and 212, n. 23, and see also HJP, 52.

[2] Lev. R. 7:3, p. 156. E. Ebner (*Elementary Education in Israel*, N. Y., 1956, 78 f.) writes : "In the opinion of this author (i.e. Ebner) the practice to begin the study of the Bible with Leviticus is based upon nationalistic-religious sentiments that crystallized in the era following the destruction of Temple and state. The leaders of Jewish life were anxious to lead the people away from despair and resignation by holding out to them the promise of future glory. The Temple would be rebuilt and the priestly service reinstituted. In the meantime the attachment to Israel's past eminence had to be kept alive. To that end they introduced several customs designed to impress the memory of the Temple upon the people, like R. Johanan ben Zakkai's ordinance to repeat the service of the Lulab for seven days, as it was done in the Temple, or the custom to eat on the Seder night unleavened bread together with herbs 'in memory of Hillel at the time of the Temple.' One other such custom was the practice to let the school boys begin the study of the Pentateuch with Leviticus, the Priestly Code. And since this was meant merely as an expression of faith, it was not necessary to study the book of Leviticus till its end and thus unduly tax the learning capacity of the student. The purpose was well served by studying only the first part. Hence R. Judah's permission to edit special children's scrolls containing only the first eight chapters of Leviticus. Thereafter the boy would return to Genesis and study the Torah in the proper order. Many years later, after the people had long made its adjustment to existing conditions, this custom had lost its original urgency. But because it was so well established it was continued and R. Assi advanced another reason to justify its perpetuation."

[3] Lam. R. 4:2, ed. Buber, 72a, and *cf.* Buber's notes *ad loc.* See also Diogenes Laertius, IV.

in connection with some of his researches,[1] namely, that we find the
talmudic rabbis quoting from all books of the Scriptures with complete
familiarity, we find them noting with punctilio various peculiarities
of the biblical texts; but nowhere is there so much as a suggestion
that they had dictionaries or concordances to consult or to help
them out. They knew their Bible inside out, and could put its sentences
to halakic use and aggadic exhortation whenever the need arose.
For a student of Midrash this remains a perpetual source of wonder.

I am personally convinced that like their counterparts in the general
Hellenistic schools, Jewish boys were taught aphorisms (χρεῖαι).[2]
While the Greek boy learned and memorized aphorisms commonly
attributed to Diogenes, the Jewish boy learned and quoted Hillel,
for instance, "Moreover he saw a skull floating on the face of the water.
He said to it : 'For drowning others wast thou drowned; and in the
end they that drowned thee shall be drowned' ". In the Jewish primary and secondary schools—and not necessarily in the advanced
schools—they heard *exempla* which were a delight and a lesson in
good conduct—like the story of Hillel who refused to lose his temper,
or the story of the irascible Shammai and the patient and witty
Hillel : a model for all good boys who hoped someday to win over
strangers to the study and love of Torah; or the stories of how the
poor Akiba became a great scholar, how the rich Eliezer ben Hyrcanus
acquired his great learning.[3]

Although there are still other bits and pieces of information regarding primary education—for example, on the proper size of a class;[4]
on children's responsive recitations with a *pasoqa*,[5] a person who
simply starts the children off with the first words of a verse and they
continue merrily on their own; on the proper ways to punish a child
("Smack him down at once or hold your peace and say nothing")—[6]
everywhere in the ancient world discipline was brutal, and even Aristotle was persuaded that "amusement does not go with learning—

---

[1] HJP, 52.

[2] *Cf.* J. Goldin, "The End of Ecclesiastes : Literal Exegesis and Its Transformation,"
in A. Altmann (ed.), *Biblical Motifs* (Cambridge, Mass., 1966), 136-138. See now too
H. A. Fischel in *Religions in Antiquity* (Leiden, 1968), 372 ff.

[3] On Hillel and Shammai, *ARN*, 60-62; on R. Akiba and R. Eliezer, *ibid.*, 28-33.

[4] See B. Baba Batra, *loc. cit.*

[5] See S. Lieberman, *Tosefta Ki-Fshutah on Shabbat*, 10 f.

[6] *Cf.* Šemaḥot (ed. Zlotnick), 232.

μετὰ λύπης γὰρ ἡ μάθησις (for learning is a painful process)"—[1]
although, as I say, more can be said about elementary education,
in the little space that remains let us examine a few of the sidelights
of secondary and advanced Torah education. It is not always easy,
by the way, to draw a hard and fast line between them, despite the
mishnaic "At ten, the study of Mishnah... At fifteen, the study of
Talmud".[2]

Even among those who studied as children, not all were able to go on
to advanced learning (as we were told above by the Midrash on the
verse in Ecclesiastes), and even among those who did go on, not all
were the teacher's comfort. Rabban Gamaliel the Elder had a habit
of classifying disciples, students, in terms of fish, and was not overly
fond of the poor fish (nor, by the way, like Mark Twain, did he think
much of the Jordan, or, to be precise, of fish from the Jordan).[3]
There were (according to some old lists) four kinds of disciple, four
kinds of those frequenting the *bet midrash*, four kinds of those in
attendance when the recognized Sages lectured (*ywšbym lpny ḥkmym*);[4]
in each instance, the fourth kind is not to be envied. Like the debate
in Hellenistic circles over whom one ought to admit to higher education, in Jewish circles too there were opponents of the Hillelite
policy which encouraged teaching even the poor and those of humble
origin.[5] Despite idealistic protestations that Torah was intended
for all, that the crown of Torah was to be had for the toiling, there
very definitely were favorites, like the *bny ḥkmym*, scholars' sons,
whose privileged position the late Gedaliah Allon analyzed so finely.[6]

---

[1] Politics, VIII, 1339a, 28 (Loeb Classics, 1932, 651)—I owe this reference to Marrou, 159.

[2] PA 5:21, and see Taylor's *Sayings of the Jewish Fathers*, 97 f.

[3] *ARNA*, 127 : "On the subject of disciples Rabban Gamaliel the Elder spoke of four kinds : An unclean fish, a clean fish, a fish from the Jordan, a fish from the Great Sea.

"An unclean fish : who is that ? A poor youth who studies Scripture and Mishnah, Halakah and Aggadah, and is without understanding.

"A clean fish : who is that ? That's a rich youth who studies Scripture and Mishnah, Halakah and Aggadah, and has understanding.

"A fish from the Jordan : who is that ? That's a scholar who studies Scripture and Mishnah, Midrash, Halakah, and Aggadah, and is without the talent for give and take.

"A fish from the Great Sea : who is that ? That's a scholar who studies Scripture and Mishnah, Midrash, Halakah, and Aggadah, and has the talent for give and take."

[4] *Cf. ARN*, 126 f.

[5] *Cf.* J. Goldin in *Harvard Theological Review*, 58 (1965), 365, n. 5.

[6] Meḥqarim, II (Tel Aviv, 1958), 58-73. *Cf.* Mid. Tan., 212 f.

I would not call their schools democratic; but then there are very
few schools I would call democratic; and I would say for those in
ancient Jewish Palestine that they did what they could to make
education widespread,[1] because learning was commanded by Him
who is the Commander of all.[2] And yet, and yet... Bastards, for
instance, had a tough time of it.[3] For until the devastations of the
Great War (66-73), the leading schools were in Jerusalem; and what
appears to be an old homily admonishes men against illicit relations
by warning that the boy born as a result of such an affaire de cœur
will not be able to accompany his school mates beyond Ashdod,
as they proceed to Jerusalem, for "a bastard may not enter Jerusalem
under any circumstance".[4] Maybe such expostulations did discourage
infidelity. In any event, though a bastard *tlmyd ḥkm* takes precedence
or is superior to an ignoramus high priest,[5] he still can't get into the
top schools. [Incidentally, Ashdod must have been quite a town,
located by the sea south of Jabneh (of all places!). At least it had
a synagogue with a nice inscription, ἀγαθὸν καὶ εὐλογίαν, שלום].[6]

In the secondary and advanced schools the curriculum revolved
around the Oral Law, what one might (and did) call Mishnah. That
study is to be *oral*, that learning is to be from the teacher's word of
mouth rather than from books, was already emphasized by the middle
of the third century B.C.[7] The Oral Law in turn seems to have been
composed of three parts, Midrash, Halakot, and Aggadot.[8] As a
matter of fact, those who advocated that a man find himself one
teacher to study with and not run from teacher to teacher, saw in their

---

[1] Contrast this with the conception of culture as a privilege of the governing classes
spoken of by C. J. Gadd, *Teachers and Students in the Oldest Schools* (London, 1956),
23-25—but this was of course of much much earlier times—and by Marrou, 295 f.

[2] The first "words" to be taught a child when he begins to speak are "Moses charged
us with the Torah, the heritage of the congregation of Jacob" (Deut. 33:4) and "Hear,
O Israel! The Lord is our God, the Lord alone" (*ibid.* 6:4). *Cf.* Maimonides, Code, Talmud
Torah, 1:6. The reason Deut. 33:4 says *"Moses* charged us with, commanded us, the
Torah," when the Commander is really God, is that Moses gave his life for the Torah
(Mid. Tan., 212, and *cf.* Mekilta, ed. Lauterbach, II, 3 f.).

[3] *ARNA*, 53, and see also *ARNB*, 54 (though this latter text is poorly preserved).

[4] There are difficulties with the meaning of this statement. See S. Bialoblotzki
in Alei Ayin, p. 40.

[5] M. Horayot 3:8.

[6] Sefer ha-Yishuv, I (Jerusalem, 1939), s.v.

[7] *Cf.* "End of Ecclesiastes" (above p. 184, n. 2), 142 ff.

[8] See, for example, *ARNA*, 34 f., 127, and *cf.* above p. 185, n. 3.

counsel this distinct advantage : [1] if by chance the master had failed to make something clear in the course of Midrash lessons, he could take care of that during the subsequent study of Halakot; if something were left unclear in the course of Halakot study, it could be cleared up during the Aggadah sessions. In some respects, Rabbi Meir felt that one teacher rather than several was best for a man; [2] but if we can depend on our sources, there were occasions when Rabbi Meir also felt as did others, that a man ought to study under more than one teacher.[3] An ideal faculty for an advanced student was made up of three scholars the like of Eliezer ben Hyrcanus, Joshua ben Hananiah, and Ṭarfon (or, possibly, Akiba).[4]

A word about the tripartite division of the Oral Torah. Midrash seems to refer to more complex forms of interpretation of Scripture than were undertaken in the elementary schools (where emphasis for the most part may have been on memorizing), perhaps with emphasis on the employment of hermeneutic rules, such as the seven rules of Hillel [5] or the thirteen rules of Rabbi Ishmael, or perhaps the principles favored by Nahum of Gimzo and his disciple Akiba.[6] There are several chapters devoted to "rabbinic interpretation of Scripture" in Professor S. Lieberman's *Hellenism in Jewish Palestine* [7] which will reward any student of biblical exegesis, regardless of how many times he rereads them.

Halakot is a term that is used for collections or statements of laws,

---

[1] *ARNA*, 35 f., but the text is not completely clear; even more garbled is the reading in *ARNB*, 39.

[2] *ARNA*, 36.

[3] *ARNA*, 16.

[4] *ARNA*, ibid.; *ARNB*, 39; *cf. Harvard Theological Review*, 58 (1965), 379 ff. And now see also S. Lieberman, *Siphre Zutta* (N. Y., 1968), 89 f., (in n. 54).

[5] *ARNA*, 110 (and *cf.* Schechter's n. 12 *ibid.* for parallels). I would like to take this occasion to remark that while quite rightly it is nowhere even suggested that Hillel was the inventor of these rules, it seems to me significant that they are quoted as the rules Hillel used in his exegesis in the presence of the Bᴇᴀ Bathyra. To me this means that Hillel was known not as the author of these rules, but as a vigorous advocate of the use of these rules, as a well known *practitioner* of these rules. His resorting to them was neither a one-time affair, nor merely one more thing that characterized him. Hillel was *noted* as a constant advocate of their application.

[6] On what characterized the exegetical methods of the two principal schools, see the indispensable chapter in J. N. Epstein, *Mebo'ot le-Sifrut ha-Tannaim* (Jerusalem-Tel Aviv, 1957), 521-536.

[7] New York, 1962, pp. 20-82.

the kind of material we generally associate with the "Mishnah".[1]
Probably this included learning the laws and the reasons for them,
as well as their logical and extended consequences. Or a session might
be devoted to a student's questions and the master's answers. Thus,
even on his death bed,[2] for example (recall Maimonides' statement!),
Eliezer ben Hyrcanus was asked halakic questions, and he answered
them and continued teaching—at least so it was later reported;
his disciples, according to one of them, responded with greater enthusiasm to what they then learned from their teacher than to what
they had learned from him in his lifetime. They asked him : If a round
cushion, a ball, a shoe last, an amulet, or a phylactery, which was
torn, contracted uncleanness, what was the status of the substance
or stuff inside them? He replied : "It's unclean; be careful with such
objects and immerse them in an immersion pool as they are—for
these are established laws (hlkwt qbw'wt)[3] which were transmitted
to Moses at Sinai". As his close disciples kept putting questions to
him, he answered Unclean for the unclean and Clean for the clean—
and he breathed his last breath with the word "Clean" on his lips.

This then is an illustration—admittedly on the dramatic side—of
a session of Halakot study. We can get an idea of the frame of mind
accompanying such study in a remark once made by Rabbi Joshua
when he heard that a number of partly metallic wood objects were
declared to be susceptible to uncleanness : [4] "ועל כלן אמר ר' יהושע דבר
חדוש חדשו סופרים ואין לי מה אשיב With regard to all these objects which
the Sages had declared susceptible to uncleanness, Rabbi Joshua
said, 'The Scribes have invented someting novel, but I can think
of no adequate arguments against their view' ".

Or even more vividly : When [5] Rabbi Eliezer ben Hyrcanus was
once asked concerning a particular case of ceremonial impurity,
he declared that that particular plague was one of those whose victim
had to be shut up (ysgyr) by the priest. Why, the Sages asked him?

---

[1] Cf. Ch. Albeck, Mabo la-Mishnah (Jerusalem-Tel Aviv, 1959), 2.

[2] Cf. ARNA, 70 and 80 f.

[3] In ARNA, 80, hlkwt gdwlwt.

[4] M. Kelim 13:7, M. Ṭebul Yom 4:6. Note the reading in Codex Kaufmann for both
these sources. Cf. Albeck at Ṭebul Yom 4:6 who points out that Joshua has this feeling
about quite a number of additional laws where teachers arrived at a more lenient ruling
than he was comfortable with; and cf. Mishnah, ibid., pp. 458 and 602.

[5] M. Nega'im 9:3; cf. 11:7. And in M. 'Ahilot 16:1 (ed. A. Goldberg, 117) we come
upon Akiba also eager to confirm the view of the early Sages. See also the statement
by R. Meir (or, Rabbi) in M. Kil'aim 2:11 and the comment by Albeck ad loc.

What is more, they showed that they had good reason to reject Eliezer's view. When they cornered him with their arguments, he admitted he had no valid proofs for the correctness of his decision,
but the decision was nevertheless the one that had been handed
down to him, and he had no intentions of being an innovator.[1] Whereupon Judah ben Bathyra spoke up : "Master, may I say something
that I have learned in my studies ?" "You may", Eliezer replied,
"but only on condition that it is in support of the view of the earlier
Sages from whom I got my view". With that permission granted,
Rabbi Judah explained and defended the old view, presumably to
everyone's satisfaction. When he finished, Rabbi Eliezer declared,
"חכם גדול אתה שקימת דברי חכמים, You are a great scholar because you
confirmed the view of the (early) Sages".

In other words, in the study of Halakot, the inherited views are
the preferred views. Who is a great scholar (ḥkm gdwl) ? He who
knows how to justify the views of earlier sages. Note that it is not
only Rabbi Eliezer who leans in that direction— from Eliezer ben
Hyrcanus we would expect it; Rabbi Joshua too is uncomfortable
with debar ḥiddush, and regrets he is unable to think of a refutation.
Even a bold spirit like Akiba undertakes to confirm "the view of the
Sages", chafe at it as Rabbi Ṭarfon might. Allow me to quote Marrou
again,[2] this time in his description of secondary Hellenistic education,
because his remarks are apt also for much of the study of the Oral
Law, and the Halakot in particular : "Classical culture did not know
any romantic need to make all things new, to forget the past and
be original; it was proud of its inherited wealth, proud of its pedantry,
proud of being what our modern pedantry—whose only sign of progress seems to be that it has replaced literary scholarship by technical
science—would call the victim of a culture complex".

The third component of the Oral Torah was Aggadot. Intellectuals
were often tempted to slight it (although in tannaite centuries especially, the leading halakists were among the leading aggadists) :
and not only in geonic or medieval times.[3] We can tell that this is
so from the remark in the Sifre on Deuteronomy.[4] Beware lest you

---

[1] Cf. in another connection his exclamation in M. Yadayim 4:3.

[2] Op. cit., 170.

[3] Cf. 'Oṣar ha-Geonim, IV, Ḥagigah, 59 f., and cf. the quotations from Rišonim
(early medieval authorities) in S. Lieberman, Shekiin (Jerusalem, 1939), 82 f.

[4] Sifre Deut., 48, p. 113; cf. Mid. Tan., 43, 205, 262; Midrash 'Aśeret ha-Dibrot
(Bet ha-Midrasch, ed. Jellinek, I, 65).

say, I've studied Halakah and that's quite enough for me; on the contrary, one must go on and study Midrash and Aggadah too. In truth, this is the field in which the Creator of the universe is caught sight of and man adopts and cleaves to His ways.[1] The extent of the Aggadah was almost limitless; here individual speculation had if not complete freedom then at least ample space to try out ideas and the imagination's capabilities.

Lots more should be said about advanced study of the Oral Law : of the existence of various study circles—there were clubs (ḥbwrwt) [2] for Scripture study, clubs for Mishnah study, clubs for Talmud study, and Moses held an honorary appointment in all of them. Lots too can be said of the rabbinic objection to certain kinds of water-sports,[3] particularly in centuries when athletics still formed part, even if only a relatively small one, of the education of the cultivated man. This strong objection did not apply of course to swimming,[4] or to bathing in order to keep the body clean—*that* could actually be called a *miṣwah*, a religious act.[5] I wish there were room to say a little at least about the importance of *šmwš tlmydy ḥkmym*, attendance upon and close observing of the Master Scholar by his disciples as he went about his various tasks. Without this attendance and observing, one's education was bound to be deficient, and led at times to disastrous results.[6] In the classical world, paideia was not held to be a book enterprise principally. It is instructive too to learn of the way men specialized, some hoping to get a reputation as experts in Halakah (רעותיה מתקרי בר הלכן) or experts in Midrash (רעותיה מתקרי בר מכאלא) or as Talmud experts, רעותיה אתקרי בר אולסן[7]. And more besides : Of those of them who studied Greek, for example : who were their teachers ? And what exactly did they study ? [8] Homer ? [9] Anything

---

[1] Sifre Deut., 49, p. 115. Such characterization itself testifies to the vigorous recommendations Aggadah required.

[2] Sifre Deut., 355, p. 418.

[3] *Cf.* M. Makširin 5:1 and S. Lieberman in Sinai, IV, 54 ff. On the significance of athletics even after the decline of gymnastics set in in the Hellenistic world, *cf.* Marrou, *op. cit.*, 130 ff.

[4] A baraita in B. Kiddushin 29a; *cf.* T. Kiddushin 1:11 and Mekilta (Pisḥa XVIII), I, 166.

[5] *ARNB*, 66.

[6] See *ARNA*, 56, Šemaḥot, 225.

[7] Lev. R. 3:1, pp. 54 f.

[8] *Cf.* HJP, 105, 113.

[9] *Cf.* M. Yadayim 4:6.

else ? Let me conclude, however, with a quotation that can serve
at the same time as one answer to the question that inevitably must
rise at some point : What did Torah study achieve ? Of what use was
it ? There are several eloquent answers, and they keep being referred
to by every Talmud anthologist. But there is one which is a favorite
of mine, although it too is probably wellknown.[1] "ג' נתמעטו משריבה ת''ת.
Three began to diminish when Torah-study increased : נתמעטו המזיקים,
demons went on the decrease, נתמעטה מהומה [2], pandemonium declined,
נתמעטו עושי רע, (and the number of) evil-doers diminished. And some
say : The same applies to the planting of cucumbers". This is no
mean achievement, in any age. I should explain, of course, that
planting of cucumbers was a form of magic, and Rabbi Eliezer ben
Hyrcanus was singularly expert in it. He could fill a whole field with
them by saying one word ; so too by one word he could empty a field.[3]
What a pity that the word has not come down to us !

---

[1] *ARNB*, 130.

[2] I think the reading in ed. Schechter requires a minor correction (not *ntm'ṭ ḥmhwmh*
but *ntm'ṭh mhwmh*) : it's probably a typographical mistake.

[3] *ARNA*, 81, B. Sanhedrin 68a.

PUKHOVITZER'S CONCEPT OF *TORAH LISHMAH*

By Norman Lamm

The study of Torah is one of the most fundamental commandments in Judaism; it outweighs all the other precepts.[1] The question of what should be the motivation for such study depends upon how one defines the talmudic concept of *Torah lishmah*,[2] usually translated as "Torah for its own sake." The definition of this teleology of study is, in turn, usually contingent upon one's general orientation to Jewish values: the role of the intellect as against ethical and ritual performances, inwardness vis-à-vis external acts, and so on. Moreover, the degree to which one insists upon pure motivation, *i.e.*, study *lishmah*, depends upon the significance one attaches to the study of Torah as such: the more one esteems the act of study, the less one is disposed to demand *lishmah*, however one interprets the term; and the less one's relative emphasis on the study of Torah, the more likely is his insistence upon *lishmah*.[3]

The various definitions of the term *Torah lishmah* can generally be grouped in three categories, with the understanding that they are not mutually exclusive:

a. *The Functional Definition.* Torah must be studied for the sake of the commandments under consideration. *Lishmah* thus means for the sake of the precepts dealt with in the Torah text being studies. This theme is often expressed as *lilmod al menath la'asoth*, to study in order to do (*i.e.*, perform the commandment being studied).[4]

b. *The Devotional Definitions.* Torah must be studied "for the sake of Heaven";[5] for the love of God (rather than. fear);[6] or to attain certain mystical ends;[7] or to achieve *devequth* (communion) with God experientially.[8]

---

[1] Thus, *Peah* 1:1—"The study of Torah excels them all," and elsewhere throughout the entire literature.

[2] Sifre (ed. Friedman) *Eqev*, 48; *Avot* 6:1; *Nedarim* 62a, etc.

[3] The documentation for this assertion is too extensive for, and essentially irrelevant to, the purposes of this article. An elaborate discussion and appropriate references may be found in my heretofore unpublished doctoral dissertation, *The Study of* Torah Lishmah *in the Works of Rabbi Hayyim of Volozhin*, (submitted at Yeshiva University, 1966), chaps. v-viii. All that follows in this article concerning the general theme of the study of Torah, and especially study *lishmah*, is based upon sources discussed in greater detail in the above work.

[4] Sifre, *loc. cit.*: *Ber.* 17a.: J. T.. *Ber.* 1:5: *Sefer Ḥasidim*, ed Margoliot (Jerusalem 1950), No. 944; R. Elijah de Vides, *Reshith Ḥokhmah* (Jerusalem-New York 1958), Introduction, pp. 2a, 3b; R. Isaiah Halevi Horowitz, *Shene Luḥoth ha-Berith* (Jerusalem 1959), pp. 99–101.

[5] *Ber.* 5b; *Midrash Tehillim* (ed. S. Buber), 31:9; pp. 240f.; all through *Seder Eliyahu*, see Introduction by Friedman to his edition of this work, pp. 109–113.

[6] Sifre (ed. Friedman) to *Wa-ethanan*, 32, p. 73a; *Sotah* 31a; J. T. *Ber.* 9:7 and *Sotah* 5:5; Maimonides, Commentary to the Mishnah, end of *Makkot*, and Code, *Hil. Teshuvah*, 10:4, 5; *Sefer Ḥasidim*, No. 289; Nahmanides, Commentary to the Pentateuch, to Dt. 6:5; Crescas, *Or Adonai*, 2:6, chaps. i and ii.

[7] *Zohar Ḥadash, Tiqqunim*, p. 63a, b; R. Hayyim Vital, *Peri Ets Ḥayyim*, beginning of *Shaar Hanhagath ha-Limmud*.

[8] *Keter Shem Tov*, p. 19c; R. Pinhas of Korzec (Koretz), *Liqqutim Yeqarim*, p. 4b; R.

c. *The Cognitive Definition*. Study for the sake of knowing and understanding the Torah. In this definition, made famous by R. Hayyim of Volozhin (1749–1821), *lishmah* means *leshem ha-torah*, for the sake of the Torah itself.[9]

In this context, it is interesting to analyze the writings on the study of Torah *lishmah* by R. Yehudah Leib Pukhovitzer, a late seventeenth-century rabbi and preacher whose books reflect the kabbalistically oriented piety of his times.[10] As a representative of this period, his works tell us something about the religious spirit and views of seventeenth-century Polish Jewry and about its religious and educational institutions and problems. This analysis is made particularly necessary because of some recent assertions about Pukhovitzer's concept of *Torah lishmah* which this writer considers highly questionable.

Relying mostly on kabbalistic sources, Pukhovitzer fully subscribes to the functional definition of *Torah lishmah*:

> He who studies *lishmah* merits both this world and the world-to-come, as is written in the Zohar. . . . The reason for this is that Torah (i.e., study) without [the performance of] the commandments is as nothing. Therefore one [who studies Torash *lishmah*] merits two worlds: one for his Torah and one for his commandments.[11]

He then cites, approvingly, two interpretations of the dictum of R. Meir, that "whosoever engages in Torah *lishmah* merits many things,"[12] by R. Elijah de Vides, the first of which defines *lishmah* as studying with the intention of putting into practice that which is studied.[13] Clearly, therefore, to study *lishmah* means to study Torah in order better to perform the commandments of the Torah.

This is no isolated passage in the works of Pukhovitzer. Elsewhere[14] he supports the definition of *lishmah* by R. Isaiah Halevi Horowitz[15]—to carry out what God has commanded us. He considers this definition the *peshat* or literal signification of the term.[16] Other such references to the functional definition of the *lishmah* concept abound throughout his works.

Pukhovitzer also anticipates the cognitive definition of study *lishmah* that was later to be elaborated and popularized by R. Hayyim of Volozhin:

> There are those who intend, by their dialectical skill (*pilpul*), to boast, as if to say, "What a wise man I am, how brilliant! I can, by my dialectical acumen,

Jacob Joseph of Polonne, *Toledoth Yaaqov Yosef* (Lwow, 1863) to *Wa-yetsei*, p. 28d, and to *Shelah*, p. 123d; R. Yosef Yitzhak of Lubavitch, *Liqqutei Dibburim*, Vol. III, No. 22, pp. 890–892; cf. Scholem, Gershom, "Devekuth, or Communion with God," *Review of Religion*, vol. xiv, no. 2 (January 1950), p. 125.

9 R. Hayyim of Volozhin, *Nefesh ha-Ḥayyim*, 4:3, based on *Ned.* 62a and commentary of R. Asher, *ad loc.*; cf. *Avot de R. Nathan* (Version A) to *Avot* 2.12.

10 Pukhovitzer, who died in Palestine in the 1680's, was the author of four works, mostly collections of sermons and some halakhic material. They are: *Divre Ḥakhamim, Qeneh Ḥokhmah, Derekh Ḥokhmah,* and *Kevod Ḥakhamim*. Information about him, which is quite sparse, may be obtained from Herman (Ḥayyim) Michael, *Or ha-Ḥayyim*, p. 464, *Jewish Encyclopedia*, vol. x, p. 92, q. v.

11 *Qeneh Ḥokhmah*, p. 18c.
12 *Avoth* 6:1.
13 *Reshith Ḥokhmah*, p. 3b.
14 *Derekh Ḥokhmah*, p. 24b.
15 *Shene Luhot ha-Berith*, pp. 99–101.
16 *Derekh Ḥokhmah*, p. 24b and d; *Divre Ḥakhamim*, Part I (*Shaar ha-Avodah*, chap. v), p. 43a.

discover forty-nine ways of proving 'creeping things' ritually pure," and thus become famous and praised amongst people, as happens so unfortunately often in our generation. Thus [do people study Torah] for other, ulterior motives which are unacceptable to the Lord. Rather, the main intent of discourse [in Torah] should be to arrive at the halakhic truth, to elucidate the truth; for by means of debate and dialectics is the truth elucidated.[17]

Although, in this particular passage, he does not explicitly identify the cognitive motive of study as *lishmah,* nevertheless the context clearly implies it, this section coming immediately after a description of Torah *not* studied *lishmah.*

Interestingly, Pukhovitzer's view of the relationship between Torah as such and its individual commandments prefigures the concept of Torah and *mitswoth* by R. Hayyim. The latter maintained that not only is Torah more significant than the other commandments, but it is totally inclusive; Torah is the whole of which the *mitswoth* are the individual parts. Whereas the general halakhic assumption is that Study is but one aspect of Practice (in that the commandment to study Torah is one amongst 613), R. Hayyim shows that Practice is only one aspect of Study. The *mitswoth* are individual *organs*; Torah is the hypostasized mystical *organism.*[18] This conception, which undergirds the cognitive interpretation of *lishmah,* is adumbrated by Pukhovitzer as follows:

> So one who engages in [the study of] Torah augments light and brings great effluence into all of its individual commandments, for all of them derive from the root and essence of the spirituality of the Torah; for it (Torah) includes them all, and they branch out from it, as is well known. However, one who engages in only one commandment (other than Torah) contributes power and light only to it alone and fills it with the capacity to draw upon the inner essence of Torah . . . for the whole sustains the parts, whereas the parts do not sustain the whole.[19]

Thus far we have seen that there is nothing exceptional in Pukhovitzer's writings on *lishmah.* He repeats the functional definition which has roots in tannaitic times, and anticipates the severely halakhocentric definition offered by the mitnagdic theoretician, R. Hayyim of Volozhin, as an alternative to hasidic *devequth.*

However, a problem arises with regard to Pukhovitzer's references to the second definition of *lishmah,* what we have called the devotional definitions, especially the kabbalistic. Or, to be more accurate, the problem does not really arise of itself at all, but has been raised for us by a distinguished contemporary historian who has professed to find in Pukhovitzer a reinterpretation of *Torah lishmah* and, with it, certain far-reaching social consequences.

Prof. Jacob Katz, describing the changing position of the kabbalist, writes: "A good deal of the prestige enjoyed by the scholar who pursued the study of Torah *lishmah* now passed to the man whose learning found expression not in public leadership, halakhic decisions, and the teaching of Torah, but in studying the Kab-

---

[17] *Derekh Hokhmah,* p. 25b.
[18] See *Nefesh ha-Hayyim,* 1:6 and 5:30, end. This stands in contrast to the hasidic view that because God is uniformly immanent in all the commandments, Torah included, they comprise an essential unity, such that all of them and each of them provides access to God; so the Baal Shem Tov, quoted by R. Jacob Joseph, *Toledoth Yaakov Yosef* to *Yithro,* p. 55a.
[19] *Divre Hakhamim,* Part I, p. 42c.

balah and in performing the *mitzvot* in accordance with its dictates, a skill which only initiates were capable of appreciating."[20] This enhanced prestige of the kabbalist, according to Katz, resulted in "propaganda for the founding of schools for individuals who study Torah *lishmah*. . . . " More significantly, he maintains that "*lishmah* is occasionally defined not as unselfish personal intention, but as engaging in mystical studies. We also know of the founding of such schools and of the support of scholars of this cloistered type."[21] Katz here adds in a footnote that "R. Yehudah Leib Pukhovitzer prefers the founding of schools for the study of *Torah lishmah* over support for students of the Yeshivah."[22] If Katz is right, then we have not only a completely new interpretation of *lishmah* with the most significant theoretical consequences, but the institutionalization of this new conception in the form of separate schools dedicated to this idea.

A careful analysis of the sources Katz cites will reveal, however, that they do not support his theory. We find no mention of such exclusive schools. And the writings of R. Yehudah Leib Pukhovitzer yield nothing as radical as the identification of *Torah lishmah* as the study of Kabbalah.

We have seen that Pukhovitzer repeatedly refers to the functional view of *lishmah* and also speaks of the cognitive definition. However, he also writes favorably of the kabbalistic definition of *lishmah*. He cites the Zohar's forceful condemnation of self-interest in the study of Torah: scholars who study because of the desire for reward, whether in this world or the next, are like barking dogs who cry out, "give, give"; such people are blind and heartless. Why then should one study? What is the proper motivation? The object should be redemptive: the classical kabbalistic ambition of releasing the *Shekhinah* from its exile and reuniting it with its "husband," the Holy One. Study *lishmah* means study for the purpose of contributing thereby to the unity of the World of the *Sephiroth*.[23] On the basis of this passage, Pukhovitzer fortifies his statement, previously mentioned,[24] that study without *lishmah* causes man to merit only this world, whereas study *lishmah* brings him the blessings of both worlds: "By means of study *lishmah* one unites the *Shekhinah* up above, and thus the purpose of his study is to perform the work of his Master (*i.e.*, to serve God's purpose); whereas those who study but not *lishmah*, all their effort is to sustain this world, and thus they serve themselves."[25]

Pukhovitzer often quotes later kabbalists for support in his denunciations of those who study Torah *she-lo lishmah*, i.e., for selfish reasons. He clearly describes what he means by *she-lo lishmah*—and he by no means intends those who fail to study the Kabbalah. Thus, in one lengthy passage, he cites R. Isaac Luria and R. Hayyim Vital as his authority for castigating those "who have made the Torah a spade to dig with, . . . who study in order to receive reward and additional stipends,

---

20 Katz, Jacob, *Masoret u-Mashber* (Jerusalem 1958), p. 258. References will be to this original Hebrew edition, which contains full notes. Translations in this article are based mostly on the English edition, *Tradition and Crisis* (New York 1961) pp. 223f.
21 *Ibid.*, in the Hebrew; the paragraph is missing in the English.
22 *Ibid.*, n. 23, referring to Pukhovitzer's *Derekh Ḥokhmah*, p. 26a.
23 *Zohar Ḥadash, Tiqqunim*, p. 63a, b. See too *Reshith Ḥokhmah, loc. cit.*
24 *Supra*, n. 11.
25 *Qeneh Ḥokhmah*, p. 18d.

and also to be included amongs the heads of the Yeshivot and judges in the court, so that their names and reputations will cover the earth."[26]

It is clear beyond doubt that what Pukhovitzer has suggested is nothing new or startling; he is within the mainstream of normative Jewish piety. The kabbalistic definition of *lishmah,* which Pukhovitzer adopts along with the other two, is quite clear: the study of the classical texts, biblical and rabbinic, with a kabbalistic purpose in mind. It does not imply the study of kabbalistic texts. The mystical element in study *lishmah* has reference merely to the intention, not the content or subject matter. Were Pukhovitzer to propose anything as novel as the theory Katz attributes to him, he would have stated so explicitly. Furthermore, if Pukhovitzer had meant to define *lishmah* as the study of Kabbalah, and to imply along with it the social and institutional exclusiveness Katz speaks of, he would have emphasized this definition of *lishmah* as a way of reenforcing the element of exclusiveness. The fact is that he gives it no more prominence than he does to the functional and cognitive definitions, especially the former.

What might possibly be the cause of misunderstanding is the following:

> This matter [the study of Torah *she-lo lishmah*] causes him to propose novellae which are not true (*emeth*), as is mentioned in the writings of Luria . . . "Each deed of a man causes an angel to be created, and therefore the angel will correspond to the deed. If one studies Torah *lishmah,* without any ulterior motive at all, so the angel created therefrom will be very holy, lofty, and faithful in all ways. So if he studies Torah without any errors, the angel will be without errors and mistakes. But if that Torah [studied] contained some evil thought, *she-lo lishmah,* or some errors or mistakes, so will the angel created therefrom possess an admixture of evil, for it will have been created from two elements, good and evil, and therefore [the angel] will not be faithful in all ways." And therefore that angel will bring him to [propose] novellae which do not accord with the truth (*emeth*).[27]

The source of possible confusion here is the term *emeth,* truth. It often refers to the Kabbalah; it is so used regularly, for instance, by Nahmanides. It would, however, be stretching the imagination too far to attribute this symbolic signification to the word as used in the context of this passage. The term here unmistakeably means "truth" in its ordinary sense: ideas which correspond to the actual meaning of the material studied. Pukhovitzer here uses the word *emeth* quite pointedly as the opposite of *ta'uth weshibbushim,* error and mistakes.[28]

The solitary reference to plumbing the "secrets of Torah" (the usual euphemism for esoteric knowledge) that I have been able to find in Pukhovitzer's works in connection with *lishmah* means only that mystical graces are the consequence of

---

[26] Quoted by Pukhovitzer, *Derekh Ḥokhmah,* p. 24d, from Vital's Introduction to his *Ets Ḥayyim.*
[27] *Derekh Ḥokhmah,* p. 25a.
[28] This was also the understanding of the unknown author of *Ḥemdath Yamim* who plagiarized Pukhovitzer and copied the passages mentioned with only slight modification, indicating that he too understood them in the conventional, non-mystical sense; see *Ḥemdath Yamim,* Part III, p. 50. On this work, *see* Yaari, Abraham, *Taalometh Sefer* (Jerusalem 1954); the article by Scholem in *Behinot* (1955), no. 8, pp. 79–95; and the three exhaustive articles by I. Tishbi in *Tarbitz,* vols. 24–25, and his *Netive Emunah u-Minuth* (Ramat Gan 1964).

but not the contents of studying *lishmah*.[29] R. Hayyim too refers to mystical illumination as the result of studying Torah *lishmah*;[30] but in the case of both writers, the subject matter of the Torah study remains the classical texts.

Having established that Pukhovitzer accepts all three standard definitions of *lishmah* in rabbinic literature and proposes no new understanding of the concept, it is important to follow through on Katz's thesis to see where his notion has led him. In doing so we shall discover that this one error in the interpretation of Pukhovitzer perforce results in invalid conclusions based upon it.

Having identified *lishmah* with the study of Kabbalah, and attributed this occupation to an emerging coterie of kabbalists—among whom he counts the Gaon of Vilna[31]—who held themselves aloof both from ordinary people and traditional halakhic scholars, Katz then claims the discovery of a new attitude towards the public support of scholars:

> The support of the scholar is no longer considered an ordinary *mitzvah* for which there is ready reward, but a means to achieve *devekut* with the Shechinah—something of which the ignoramus is incapable, but which the scholar achieves in the course of his study and contemplations. It is clear that the intention here is to the Kabbalah scholar, to whom the concept of *devekut* applies in its mystical meaning.[32]

However, what might seem significant were we to accept the idea of a reinterpretation of *lishmah*, no longer appears important at all. Pukhovitzer's description of how attachment to the scholar is a form of *devequth* with the *Shekhinah*[33] has nothing new to add to the theme of "support" for scholars, and hence no social or economic significance. It is merely his formulation of a relationship already proposed in the Talmud,[34] to which Katz himself refers,[35] in terms of the kabbalistic idea of the threefold soul. This very interpretation is attributed by Pukhovitzer to R. Elijah de Vides. It is, therefore, nothing more than a restatement in kabbalistic idiom of a well known talmudic idea, and has no relation to a new definition of *lishmah* as the study of Kabbalah.

Prof. Katz's assertion that this supposedly new idea was institutionalized in the form of special schools exclusively devoted to the study of Kaballah as *lishmah* is even more astonishing. To support his contention that such special schools were organized, Katz points to the "Kloiz" in Brody of which at least some members studied the Kabbalah.[36] He refers to an article by Gelber.[37] In this study, the author

---

29 *Divre Ḥakhamim*, p. 43b, c. Note in this passage the use of the conjunction "also": *Gam al yede zeh yukhal lizekoth le-limmud raze Torah*. This unequivocally implies the non-identity of the revelation of esoteric mysteries with the actual study of *Torah lishmah*.

30 *Nefesh ha-Ḥayyim* 4:21.

31 Katz, *op. cit.*, p. 258, n. 23, relying on Klausner, *Vilna bi-Tequfath ha-Gaon* (Jerusalem 1942), pp. 16–20. This conventional view of the Gaon has, however, been challenged by Moshe Shmuel Shapiro-Shmukler. *See* his "Li-Demuth ha-Gaon mi-Vilna" in *Hadoar* (no. 33, 1926), recently reprinted in *Reb Mosheh Shmuel we-Doro*, published by Shapiro-Shmuklers sons and friends (New York 1964), pp. 30, 100f.

32 Katz, *op. cit.*, p. 259.

33 *Ibid.*, n. 25; *Kevod Ḥakhamim*, p. 46b.

34 *Ketuboth* 111b.

35 *Loc cit.*

36 *Ibid.*, n. 23.

37 Gelber, N. M., *Toledoth Yehude Brod* in *Arim we-Imahoth be-Yisrael*, vol. vi, pp. 62f.

writes of the famed "Kloiz" and the "Sages of the Kloiz of Brody." This hall, right next to the Great Synagogue of Brody, was a meeting place and magnet for some of the most distinguished scholars of the age. In addition to Halakhah, there were those who studied Kabbalah as well. This small group, Gelber writes, had for their private use a small chamber attached to the "Kloiz" where only the prominent kabbalists prayed, using the Prayerbook of Luria. Only people over the age of thirty were permitted to join them in their studies, and only the kabbalists themselves were entitled to wear white garments on Sabbath and holidays.

However, all this proves nothing more than that those interested in Kabbalah tended to move in small, intimate circles; and this fact is of no significance at all either to the study of this period or the understanding of the concept of *lishmah*. Kabbalists always inclined towards their own societies, as witness the medieval German Hasidim and the Safed Brotherhood—indeed, the exclusive and elite group of which the Zohar itself speaks. Further, there is no mention here or elsewhere of these mystical studies as *lishmah*. In addition, the article by Shochet to which Katz further refers in this note[38] begins with a description of the various societies (*haburoth*) in the fifteenth century founded both for mystical and non-mystical studies. There is thus nothing startling or original about the mystics attached to the "Kloiz" in Brody. Gelber, in the article mentioned above, refers to special privileges for the students of Kabbalah in the "Kloiz" but also maintains that those over thirty, ostensibly non-Kabbalists, were permitted to join them in prayer. Shochet, describing the adult study groups in Safed, quotes a letter from a German Jew writing from Safed in 1607 and admiring the fact that the Safed kabbalists would, twice daily, after morning and evening services, break up into five or six classes and study such subjects as Talmud, Zohar, Maimonides, Bible, etc.[39] Thus neither the Safed nor the Brody mystics were as isolated, ingrown, and self-contained as Katz would have us believe.

Nor is Katz's assertion that Pukhovitzer urges the establishment of schools for the study of Torah *lishmah* (i.e., for Kabbalah, according to Katz's view) over and above the support of Yeshivah students[40] any more valid. In a discourse or *derashah* devoted to the support of Torah, after promising and threatening in the fashion of the times, Pukhovitzer specifically castigates rabbis and communities for neglecting poor scholars. Once, he complains, even poor people would seek out rabbis who would disseminate the teachings of Torah, and would support needy students; today only the children of the wealthy are taught Torah because they can afford to pay for it.[41] Rather than cater to the rich and the self-seeking, Pukhovitzer suggests that in order to do one's duty, it is best, if one can afford it, to support one Torah student who studies for the sake of Heaven, either by lodging him or providing for him in the student's own home . . . for if, Heaven forfend, there are no kids, there will be no goats.[42] This last metaphor, as well as his use of the term *bahurim* in

---

[38] "Study groups in the 17th and 18th centuries in Palestine, Poland, Lithuania, and Germany" (Hebrew), in *Ha-Ḥinnukh* (1957), pp 404–418.
[39] *Ibid.*, p. 405.
[40] Katz, *op. cit.*, p. 258, n. 23; *Derekh Ḥokhmah*, p. 26a.
[41] *Derekh Ḥokhmah*, p. 26b.
[42] *Ibid.*

the passage before it, indicates that he is speaking of youngsters, not accomplished kabbalists. He then bemoans the fact that most who study *she-lo lishmah* do not continue beyond the age of fifteen; who knows, therefore, if they will ever really study Torah *lishmah* and if they will remember what they learned.[43] Very simply, he feels that youngsters "graduate" too early from their courses of study, that they have never learned to study out of an appreciation of study itself and, hence, perhaps the whole educational system is a failure. Pukhovitzer therefore recommends the establishment in each community of regular schools not only for the young, but also for the more mature who are already gainfully occupied and will attend courses of Torah study after working hours, and who will study *lishmah*, i.e., not in order to receive stipends as do the "professional" scholars.[44] His emphasis on study for those over the age of fifteen is, far from urging mystic contemplation, an attempt to increase higher and adult education, and—shades of modernity!—not leave the study of Judaism to little children. This is an eminently practical *derashah*.

R. Yehudah Leib Pukhovitzer is, hence, a typical rabbinic scholar and preacher of his period, drawing heavily on kabbalistic sources, in the fashion then prevailing, in order to persuade his audience of his noble but unexceptional ethical and religious preachments. His view of the study of *Torah lishmah* runs the whole gamut of acceptable, normative definitions of the concept, and he deserves credit for anticipating the approach of R. Hayyim of Volozhin by about a century and a half. But there is nothing in what Pukhovitzer writes to warrant the conclusion that he advocates schools for mystics, or that he identifies the study of Kabbalah as yet another definition of the term "the study of Torah *lishmah*."

[43] *Ibid.*
[44] *Ibid.* Cf. *Divre Ḥakhamim*, p. 43c.

Two Principles of Character Education in the Aggadah

BERNARD MANDELBAUM

The Role of Aggadah

Aggadah IS USUALLY DEFINED AS THE MORAL and ethical teachings of Rabbinic literature, in contrast to *halakhah* which is the law and the legal decrees. A. A. Halevi, in his *Shaarei Haaggadah,* ascribes a different reason for the names given to the principal categories of Rabbinic literature, relating them to the external form of the literature rather than their contents: *mishnah* is so named for "stating or repeating" the law and lore; *talmud* is the further "learning and explication" of it; *mikra* is the "written tradition" which is read, and *aggadah* is the total, expanded "oral" tradition. As the developing oral tradition, *aggadah* is more than a specific category of ideas. It reflects the reality of continuing Jewish history and experience. *Aggadah,* in this definition, then, is the *total oral tradition* (i.e. including both *halakhah* and *aggadah*) in contrast to *mikra* which is the written Torah that is read. As the "spoken" tradition, *aggadah* records the dialogue between wise men as they confronted *mikra* with the changing circumstances of history, and derived insight, purpose and strength for human life and their own existence as Jews. The organic process of developing these values and rulings, usually referred to as *midrash,* with *aggadah* as its end product, is more than a literary achievement. It incorporates an approach to life which combines continuity and change, commitment and flexibility, ideas and action.

In Willa Cather's *Obscure Destinies,* the hero, Mr. Rosen, provides an interesting metaphor which throws light on the ultimate achievement of *aggadah* in the mind of the Jew throughout history. "All countries were beautiful to Mr. Rosen. He carried a *country* of his own in his mind and was able to unfold it like a tent in any wilderness." (italics mine) For "country" substitute "*aggadah*"; for "wilderness" substitute the "vicissitudes of daily life" or "the values of a surrounding world" and you see the unique power of the *aggadah* to be unfolded in any wilderness to raise the Jew above the ephemeral and attach him to the purposeful and eternal.

Further insight into the power of *aggadah* is suggested by the definition of myth presented in "The Religious Philosophy of the Jews" by Samuel Hirsch who "finds himself in complete agreement with the Bibli-

27

cal story. He does not hesitate to characterize the story as mythical, but myth for him is not (as is true of rationalistic interpretations of history) a poetic fabrication. It is *'the presentation of an inner event in the dress of an outer occurrence which fully presents this content free of all contingency.'* " (italics mine) [1]

Aggadah, or myth (in Hirsch's definition), is the repository of inner ideas which shape the outer behavior of Jews. Many of them have ultimately shaped the course of western civilization. Alfred North Whitehead described this reality of history when he wrote: "Thoughts lie dormant for ages, and then almost suddenly, as it were, find that they have embodied themselves in institutions." Ideas vital for the good society are often ignored and resisted because they demand the sacrifice of temporary advantages for long range goals, but the ideas that underlie these meaningful goals are not dormant. The major ones have been kept alive by *aggadah,* in the tradition of Judaism, "until their time has come."

Without minimizing the creative role of other traditions and cultures in shaping Western civilization, the historic role of Judaism in establishing the goals of a good society is evident in many vital areas, as can be illustrated in the way *aggadah* keeps alive two principles of education in character.

The Role of Study in Fashioning Human Character

The failure of contemporary education is traceable to at least two causes: the absence of concentration on education in character, and a fumbling ignorance about how to achieve it even when the concern is there. This is especially true on the college level and is expressed poignantly in the following passage from J. D. Salinger's *Franny and Zooey.* Franny is speaking:

> What happened was, I got the idea in my head—and I could not get it out—that college was just one more dopey, inane place in the world dedicated to piling up treasure on earth and everything. I mean treasure is treasure, for heaven's sake. What's the difference whether the treasure is money, or property, or even culture, or even just plain knowledge. . . .
> I don't think it would have all got me quite so down if just once in a while—just once in a while—there was at least some polite little perfunctory implication that knowledge should lead to wisdom, and that if it doesn't it's just a disgusting waste of time! But there never is! You never even hear any hints dropped on campus that wisdom is supposed to be the goal of knowledge. You hardly even hear the word "wisdom" mentioned! Do you want to hear something funny? Do you want to hear something—and this is the absolute truth—in almost four years of college, the only time I can even remember the expression of "wise man" being used was in my freshman year, in Political Science! It was used in reference to some weird old poopy elder Statesman who'd made a fortune in

---

1. Julius Guttman, *Philosophies of Judaism,* trans. David Silverman (New York: Holt, Rinehart and Winston, 1964), p. 316.

the stock market and then gone to Washington to be an advisor to President Roosevelt. Honestly now! Four years of college, almost! I'm not saying that it happens to everybody, but I just get so upset when I think about it I could die.[2]

Wisdom, as understood in Judaism, is the wisdom of good action. It is the goal of all learning and fundamental to any theory of education. A man's character, his moral quality, is shaped by the method of study kept vividly alive and at the very center of concern by *aggadah*. The classical discussion of this relationship between study and good action took place in the Academy of Lydda between Rabbi Tarfon and Rabbi Akiba:

> Rabbi Tarfon and the Elders were once reclining in the upper story of Nitza's house in Lydda, when the question was raised before them: Is study greater or practice? Rabbi Tarfon answered, saying: Practice is greater. Rabbi Akiba answered, saying: Study is greater for it leads to practice. Then they all answered and said: Study is greater for its leads to action.[3]

As pointed out by Isaac Weiss Hirsh,[4] this discussion reflected a practical problem facing the Jewish people in a specific historic situation. During the Hadrianic persecutions, both study and the practice of the commandments were forbidden, and the leaders of the generation had to decide which was the greater risk. However, from the point of view of *aggadah*, that discussion deals with the more permanent issue of the role of study in shaping a person's character, as we see from the statement which precedes it in the same paragraph of the *Sifre*:

> "Study them and observe them faithfully" (*Deuteronomy* 5:1), this verse tells us that action depends upon study.[5]

A Theory of Education—First Principle

The special role of study in determining the ethical behavior of a person and shaping his character is described in the opening statements of one of the most popular portions of the *mishnah* studied most frequently by the masses, *Pirkei Avot*, which is usually translated aptly, though not literally, as "The Ethics of the Fathers." Each of the first four Rabbinic teachings deals with an aspect of the role of study and ideas in the development of character. They outline two basic principles which are the cornerstones of any meaningful theory of education. The first stresses the powerful role of a teacher and the example of his behavior as an influence of the student.

> They (the Men of the Great Assembly) said three things: be slow in judgment, raise many wise men and make a hedge about your words.[6]

---

2. J. D. Salinger, *Franny and Zooey* (New York: Bantam Books, 1964), pp. 146–147.
3. *Sifre, Deuteronomy*, 41; *Kiddushin*, 40B.
4. *Dor Dor Vedorshav* II, p. 25.
5. *Sifre, Deuteronomy*, 41.
6. *Pirkei Avot*, 1:1.

Explaining the relatonship among these three assertions, Dr. Finkel-stein describes the role of a teacher in effective instruction:

> The hedge required by the instructors was not for the Torah, but for the words of the judge. His audience was entitled not merely to specific decisions, but also to an *explanation* of his decisions. The argument enabled hearers to *emulate his manner of analysis and thus to apply Torah to the details of their lives.* . . .
> In its original meaning, the injunction to make a hedge about one's words naturally led to the dictum, "and raise many wise men." The wisdom to which the saying refers is the Hasidean and Biblical *wisdom of knowing right from wrong and pursuing it.* Through slowness in judgment. (i.e., great care in what and how one says things) local judges instruct disciples and help rear a generation of wisdom . . . the judicial and *pedagogic functions* of the scholar become inseparable in the Hasidean tradition. (italics mine) [7]

Aggadah stresses the role of serving the learned (in Torah—*shimush ḥakhamim*) as a major force in character education. The student learns from what a teacher says, but particularly from his daily acts. Rabbi Yoḥanan dramatically demonstrated the priority of learning for his disciple, Rabbi Ḥiya son of Abba:

> Rabbi Yoḥanan was going from Tiberias to Zippori and was leaning on the shoulder (of his disciple) Rabbi Ḥiya bar Abba. When they passed (a particular) field, (Rabbi Yoḥanan) said: "This field once belonged to me but I sold it because I preferred busying myself with the study of Torah." They then passed a vineyard and Rabbi Yoḥanan said: "This vineyard belonged to me and I sold it in order to concentrate more on the study of Torah." (Later) they passed an olive orchard and Rabbi Yoḥanan said: "This orchard belonged to me but I sold it so as to spend more time on the study of Torah." Rabbi Ḥiya began to cry. "Why do you cry?" (Rabbi Yoḥanan asked). He answered: "I am crying because you don't seem to have left yourself anything for your old age." Rabbi Yoḥanan answered: "Ḥiya, my son, was it really a silly thing to sell something (i.e., material things) which took only six days to be given to us (by God) and to acquire that (namely Torah) which was given to us after forty days and forty nights?" [8]

Such instruction, the careful observing of the ways of a sage, reached into every detail of life:

> Rabbi Yoḥanan further said in the name of Simeon son of Yoḥai, the service of Torah is ever greater than its study. For it is said: "Here is Elisha the son of Shafat, who poured water on the hands of Elijah" (2 Samuel 7:10). It is not said "who learned," but "who poured water." This teaches that the service of Torah is greater than its study. [9]

In serving his master, Elijah, Elisha was taught elements of cleanliness and good manners. Nothing in the action of the teacher was too miniscule for observance as a source of instruction by example.

> It has been taught: Rabbi Akiba said, "Once I went in after Rabbi Joshua to a privy and I learnt from him three things" . . . said Ben Azzai to him:

---

7. *On the Ethics of Pharisaism,* an unpublished paper, pp. 36–38.
8. *Pesikta de Rav Kahana,* p. 402.
9. *Berakhot,* 7B.

"Did you dare to take such liberties with your master?" He replied: "It was a matter of Torah, and I had to learn. . " Rabbi Kahana once went in and hid under Rab's bed. He heard him chatting (with his wife) and joking and doing what he required. . . He said to him: "Kahana, are you there? Get out because it is rude." He replied: "It is a matter of Torah, and I have to learn."[10]

A student could best learn the application of the law to life by "observing his teacher in his daily routine, at prayer, at meals, even in the privy, and especially in the academy, answering questions and deciding cases, the desired result being a disciple trained to study and to teach and qualified to render proper decisions."[11]

Closer to our times, the role of acts of kindness was indelibly impressed upon the disciples of the *Ḥatam Sofer* who guided his personal action by the values inherent in the following *aggadah:*

Rabbi Lulyani of Rome taught in the name of Rabbi Judah the son of Simon. The Holy One blessed be He stated there are four members of your household and four in Mine. Your four are your son, your daughter, your manservant and maidservant. The four members of My household are the Levite, the stranger, the orphan and the widow. And all four are referred to in one verse: "Rejoice in your festivals—you, your son and daughter, your manservant and maidservant, the Levite, the stranger, the orphan and the widow" (*Deut.* 16:14). Said the Holy One blessed be He, you rejoice the members of My household and those of your household on the festivals that I gave you. If you do this, I, too, will bring happiness to your household as to Mine.[12]

For the *Ḥatam Sofer* this spelled itself out in a commitment to specific moral responsibilities. Before each festival, he would send his disciples with provisions to the homes of the widows in the town. Furthermore, he celebrated the wedding of each of his children by providing the dowry for an orphan who was being married. Since God was providing joy for his household, his response was to provide for the widow and orphan of the Almighty's household.

Each of us can probably recall the influence of a great teacher, which is also the role played by parents. The power of their personal example, illustrating the ideas of their instruction, made the real impact on our lives. That basic principle of education, implied by the Men of the Great Assembly in this first statement of the *Pirkei Avot,* is expanded in the fourth one:

Yossi son of Yoezer teaches: "Let thy house be a meeting place for the wise and sit in the very dust of their feet and thirstily drink in their words."

The commentary of Rabbi Joseph, son of Joseph Naḥmias, explains Yossi son of Yoezer's principle of learning as "attending upon learned men."

10. *Berakhot,* 62A.
11. Dov Zlotnick, *The Tractate "Mourning,"* (New Haven: Yale University Press. 1966), p. 22, note 106.
12. *Pesikta de Rav Kahana,* p. 173.

This is an exhortation to us to attend upon the sages, for attendance is even more instructive than study.[13]

Education is viewed as much more than the accumulation of facts and ideas. Its essential goal is the wisdom to choose between right and wrong. The wise man, the good teacher, is the expert in such behavior. Observing his ways carefully, learning from his method of relating reason to action, the disciple can integrate into his own character the teacher's approach to human problems. For the wise man, ethical decision-making involves rigorous effort, approaching a science, in the study of alternatives among the actions that are possible for man. And, like a student in the laboratory who assiduously observes every step of the instructor's experiments, a disciple of the wise has the opportunity, in "attending upon learned men," to learn from the habits, the reasoning and the art of human relations of his teacher.

The calamity of today's university in this regard need not be detailed here. The "publish or perish" syndrome, faculty experts preoccupied with private research and extra-curricular assignments for government and industry—these realities militate against any meaningful faculty-student contact. The ideal method of education, as taught by aggadah—the lasting influence of great men by intimate contact with them, observing their ways of thinking and acting—has been missing from American education.

But to some extent there has been an awakening to an appreciation of this pivotal role of the wisdom and conduct of the learned man. Recently, it was projected as a goal in a study by *Life Magazine* on the inadequacies of American education.

> In the midst of the blare of commercial success we must recapture an *honest respect for learning and learned people.* Abandoning that basic virtue in the first place was never meant to be part of modern education and is part of no theory. . . .
> If we are going to start insisting upon honest respect for learning, hard work and good conduct, *most of us will have to get tough with ourselves* as well as with our children and our schools.[14] (italics mine)

A Theory of Education—Second Principle

The first principle of a theory of education is, then, the influence and example of a teacher. The second principle involves the subject matter of study. It is the concern of *aggadah* to put ethics into the curriculum. This second principle is developed in the second and third Rabbinic statements of the *Pirkei Avot.*

> Simeon the Righteous was one of the last members of the Great Assembly. He used to say: On three things the world stands: on the Torah, on Temple Service and on acts of kindness.

---

13. Based on statements in *Berakhot,* 7B and *Tosafot* on *Ketubot,* 17A.
14. "It's Time to Close our Carnival," *Life Magazine,* March 24, 1958.

The commentaries explain Torah as "the study of Torah," which teaches man the way of relating himself to God ("Temple Service"), which, in turn, is the basis for his proper relationship to this fellow man ("acts of kindness").

The statement is given a focus of ethical concern in *The Fathers, According to Rabbi Nathan:*

> Once, as Rabbi Yoḥanan ben Zakkai was coming forth from Jerusalem, Rabbi Joshua followed after him and beheld the Temple in ruins. "Woe unto us," Rabbi Joshua lamented, "that this, the place where the iniquities of Israel were atoned for, is laid waste."
> "My son," Rabbi Yoḥanan said to him, "be not grieved; we have another atonement as effective as this. And what is it? It is acts of loving-kindness, as it is said, 'For I desire mercy and not sacrifice'" (Hosea 6:6).[15]

Sensitivity to ethics is further illustrated by the comment of the *Mahzor Vitry:*

> The rabbis taught, acts of kindness are greater than charity in three ways: Charity is something a man does with his wealth, acts of kindness he carries with his wealth and by means of his person; charity affects the poor only, acts of lovingkindness affect the poor and the rich; charity applies only to the living, acts of lovingkindness apply to the living and the dead.[16]

The way *aggadah* builds mounting insights of ethical concern, as stated by Simeon the Righteous, points to Judaism's view of it as the essential subject of education. The comment of *Mahzor Vitry* points to one of the results of proper study, as leading to good action for its own sake, which is the mark of a man of character. It is also the meaning of the very next statement in *Pirkei Avot:*

> Antigonus of Sokho received (the tradition) from Simeon the Righteous. He used to say: Be not like servants who serve their master for the sake of their allowance. Be rather like servants who serve their master with no thought of an allowance—and let the fear of heaven be upon you.

On the face of it, the metaphor is unconvincing. In *The Fathers According to Rabbi Nathan,* one of the disciples of Antigonus of Sokho raises this very question: "Is is possible that a laborer should do his work all day and not receive his reward in the evening?"[17] However, what Antigonus teaches is explained by the Meiri:

> Let not your service of God in carrying out His commandments be motivated by the desire for reward—as is the case of a child who does not appreciate the value of wisdom and will not study until you have bribed him with trinkets or money. . . . *One must study for the sake of wisdom and Torah . . .* (italics mine)[18]

---

15. *Avot de Rabbi Natan* (A) Chapter 4—Translation by Judah Goldin in *The Living Talmud: The Wisdom of the Fathers.*
16. Based on the passage from *Sukkah*, 49B.
17. *Avot de Rabbi Natan* (A) chapter 5.
18. See note 15.

The goal of study, according to *aggadah,* is the acquisition of that knowledge which molds a man's character, so that he can approach the image of God in himself and acquire the capacity to be a creative partner with the Almighty in helping fashion a better world.

A Similar Goal for American Education

Robert Hutchins has frequently described the failure of contemporary education in terms which echo this view of *aggadah:*

> The demands of this new world, like the political community, are first of all demands that we think and learn. We face them ill prepared in a world that depends upon what people think. . . .[19]

Consider the remarkable parallel between the subject matter of *aggadah* in developing the Jewish ethos and its way of cultivating the man of character and Hutchins' description of the method which developed the American character:

> The Founding Fathers meant us to learn. . . . The Constitution is to be interpreted, therefore, as a charter of learning. We are to learn how to develop the seeds the fathers planted under the conditions of our own time. This political botany means that nothing we have learned and no process of learning could be unconstitutional. What would be unconstitutional would be limitations or inhibitions on learning. . . . Learning is a rational process. Law is an ordinance of reason, directed to the common good. The process of reaching a judicial conclusion is to be criticized in terms of its conformity, not to local or popular custom, but to universal standards of reasonableness. If the Constitution is to teach us, and we are to learn under its instruction, the dialogue that goes on about its meaning must be about what is *reasonable and unreasonable, right and wrong, just and unjust. The question is not what interests are at stake,* not what are the mores of the community, not who has the power or who is the dominant group, not what the courts will do or the legislature has done, *but what is reasonable, right and just.* . .[20] (italics mine)

Such an approach to the education of man has been kept alive through the ages by *aggadah* and is the greatest need of our society. It is reflected in this statement of Hutchins and others who criticize[21] American education for its almost total preoccupation with preparation for a profession and making a living (the "allowance" in the statement of Antigonus). The purpose of education is the fashioning of a life governed by the wisdom which is the possession of the man of good character.

In summary, then, the theory of education kept alive by *aggadah* stresses two basic principles:

(1) The role of a teacher's example, its influence on his student through adequate contact between the two, and the overriding interest of the teacher in the development of his disciple's character.

19. *Conference on American Character,* sponsored by the Center for the Study of Democratic Institutions.
20. *Ibid.*
21. See, for example, Irving Kristol, *New York Times Sunday Magazine,* Dec. 8, 1968.

(2) A curriculum of study consisting of wisdom literature, such as *aggadah,* which is not a prescribed code of ethics, but reflects the continuous reasoning, effort and persistence that are involved in ethical decision-making and the development of character.

We know of the almost insurmountable obstacles in contemporary society to raise the status and improve the training of gifted, dedicated teachers. Our experience with many research programs in Jewish education gives us sufficient awareness of the almost equally trying task ot Yet it is self-deceiving to think that there are shortcuts or any other way. The extent to which our tradition succeeded in training character in our ancestors reflected their single-mindedness of purpose and the highest priority placed on those goals as the greatest need of man in their time or at any time.

To achieve these goals in our time, for our schools and for our children, demands unrelenting effort and struggle. Yet the reward makes it worthwhile. In the words of the Rabbis:

> Good people must experience travail. If they accept it as part of life, they can enjoy the blessing of seeing children who live long (and meaningful) lives of Torah.[22]

---

22. *Berakhot,* 5A.

Fundamental Principles
Of Jewish Education
In the Light of Halachah

Z. E. KURZWEIL

WHEN SPEAKING OF JEWISH EDUCATION, I REFER to an education which aims at the perpetuation of Judaism through the transmission of Jewish culture from generation to generation. By the terms "Judaism" and "Jewish culture," I mean the unbroken chain of Jewish tradition as it reigned supreme from its beginnings down to the Emancipation, as well as the continuation of this tradition, albeit somewhat transformed, within the various streams and interpretations of Judaism in the Diaspora of our time. Hence, to some extent at least, my evolution of the principles of Jewish education is related to the three main streams of Judaism today—Orthodox, Conservative and Reform.

My first observation is that Jewish education does not operate in a quasi-Halachah-free zone, but is subject to Halachic rulings which have left their imprint on Jewish education and have helped to establish its specific character. The thesis of this article is that these Halachic rulings concerning Jewish education have on the whole been interpreted with leniency and flexibility, providing leeway for the considerable diversification which results from individual and idiosyncratic opinion, and which is determined to no small degree by the specific exigencies and circumstances of the Jewish communities both in Israel and the Diaspora. Naturally I am aware that in the course of Jewish history there have been manifestations of a narrow and unenlightened interpretation of these perennial principles; but when taking a wider view and surveying the whole panorama of Jewish education throughout the ages, I cannot but be impressed by the wisdom and farsightedness with which these principles have been interpreted and applied to concrete situations.

I shall now endeavor to expound these principles which in my opinion are five in number. They occurred to me while I was sifting through those sources of Judaism relating to education. It is these principles that have created the framework and, also, established the limits within which any Jewish education deserving that name has been transmitted.

I

THE FIRST PRINCIPLE IS that Jewish education aims at the realization and observation of *mitzvoth*. It is always an education towards commitment, and never pure instruction. Its purport is to "learn and teach, to heed to do and to fulfil in love all the words of instruction in Thy Law."[1] Jewish education maintains that observance (action) and not mere instruction is its main concern. It takes seriously the well-known verse in *Joshua* 1:8: "This book of the Law shall not depart out of thy mouth, but thou shalt meditate therein day and night, that thou mayest *observe to do according to all that is written therein.*"

This principle is a mere corollary to and function of the specific character of historic Judaism, which, if I may borrow a concept usually associated with Christian theological thought, believes in salvation through "works," dissociating itself from any religious doctrine which puts faith or contemplation at the top of its scale of values. In simpler terms, it might be said that since Halachah forms an integral part of Judaism (Judaism being in fact completely impregnated with its spirit), and since it is the task of Jewish education to pass on the Jewish heritage from generation to generation (illuminated, enhanced and enriched as well as related to the spirit of the time), there can be no Jewish education without Halachah, i.e. without commitment to the Jewish way of life. Indeed, this principle has been accepted by the three main streams of Judaism today, Orthodox, Conservative and Reform, with the considerable distinction that the two latter streams assume a more selective approach to the adoption of Halachah than the former. I am not trying to gloss over other fundamental distinctions of a theological nature that exist between these three streams of Judaism; I simply claim that there is no school of thought in Judaism today which would completely delete the principle of Halachah from Judaism and hence from Jewish education.

It follows from what has been said so far that in Jewish education the approach to the sources of Judaism cannot be purely literary, i.e. it is not their historical, archaeological, philological, aesthetic or folkloristic aspects which are of primary importance to the teacher. The Bible and the Oral Tradition are not to be taught like Homer and Shakespeare. They demand the learner's identification with their moral precepts and ideas which have to be accepted as a source of orientation.

Yet we find rabbinical authorities of unimpeachable Orthodoxy who have not anathematized forms of Jewish education that are non-committal in point of Halachah. They have judged Jewish education according to the circumstances of the time and in terms of "better" and "poorer" rather than issue an outright condemnation and prohibition of conceptions of Jewish education which do not conform to the principle of commitment here propounded as the first to characterize Jewish education. I base this observation particularly on the attitude adopted by Orthodox rabbinical authorities to *Religionsunterricht* in

1. The *Ahava Rabba* Prayer.

the post-Emancipation period in Central Europe, and to "Jewish consciousness" as taught in the schools of Israel today.

By *Religionsunterricht* I mean the religious instruction given to Jewish children in non-Jewish primary and secondary schools. It must be remembered that in Western Europe there is no complete separation between State and Church as is the case in America today, and hence it is legitimate to give denominational religious instruction to school children within the precincts of the school, i.e. separate Catholic, Protestant and Jewish instruction. Religion is regarded like any other school subject, and in view of the generally small number of Jewish children involved it is neither opportune nor even possible to differentiate between the various forms of Judaism in which these children are nurtured at home. Hence the type of religious instruction given to the Jewish children in non-Jewish schools is uniform for all, and more often than not non-Orthodox. It is the rabbi with the more liberal approach who appeals to the non-Jewish school authorities and who can move freely in Gentile society. Yet the Orthodox rabbinate—at least during the *last two centuries*—has not condemned outright this type of religious instruction, though the instruction is generally non-committal, on the point of *kiyum mitzvoth*, being informative rather than formative, confining itself more often than not to the teaching of the Jewish faith in catechism fashion: the teaching of the Ten Commandments, the Thirteen Creeds, and those portions of the Bible with a mainly historical content; and in the higher grades, a somewhat critical interpretation of the Bible.

Rabbi S. R. Hirsch's attitude to *Religionsunterricht* (as reflected in his article on this subject[2]) bears out the point I have made. Hirsch leaves no doubt in the reader's mind that he views *Religionsunterricht* as a poor substitute for genuine Jewish education, but his attitude is one of gentle mockery ("Is it religion that you take down for dictation in your copybooks out of which you afterwards make paper trumpets?") rather than one of outright condemnation. Of course he considered *Religionsunterricht* completely inadequate, but he tolerated it on condition that the pupils also received what he considered a genuine Jewish education either at home or through private teachers. I myself am an alumnus of the S. R. Hirsch School in Frankfurt which catered for children only up to the age of 16, and in continuing my studies in the top grades of a non-Jewish *Oberreal-Schule* participated in *Religionsunterricht* together with other pupils of a similar background, and it was never suggested that we should withdraw from these lessons.

The rabbinate in Israel has adopted a similar attitude to the teaching of Jewish consciousness in Israeli general schools. Elsewhere I have

---

2. "Judaism Eternal," *Selected Essays from the Writing of Rabbi Samson Raphael Hirsch*, edited by Dr. I. Grunfeld, Soncino Press, London 1956.

dealt at some length with the subject of "Jewish consciousness,"[3] and so I shall here confine myself to a few brief remarks. This subject was incorporated into the school program of "General" schools in Israel in view of the indifference shown by the majority of Israeli youth to Jewish tradition and their failure to recognize their bond with the heritage of the Jewish past. To remedy this state of affairs, Jewish instruction was made compulsory, that is to say, a certain minimum knowledge concerning Judaism is being imparted, in particular knowledge of Jewish liturgy, Sabbath and Festival observance, and other laws and customs. However, this instruction is merely informative and non-commital. It acquaints the Israel child with the prayerbook without making it incumbent upon him to pray. Thus it does not conform to the specific character of Jewish education. In fairness to the initiators of the Jewish consciousness program, it must be said that they aimed at something more than instruction; they wanted the children to imbibe the atmosphere and spirit of a traditional Jewish way of life, to be influenced by it and adopt an attitude of reverence to it. But beyond this they refused to go. In other words, they did not demand commitment. Yet there has been no outcry on the part of the Orthodox rabbinate against the teaching of "Jewish consciousness," no doubt because they feel that "Jewish consciousness" instruction is better than none at all.

II

THE NEXT PRINCIPLE I should like to discuss is the insistence of Jewish education on the preparation of young people for an active life, that is to say, the pursuit of a calling which provides a livelihood. Jewish education has been most insistent on this point and there are many quotations from Rabbinic sources to bear it out. There is the well known saying in the *Ethics of the Fathers* (II:3) that "all learning which is not combined with work is destined to failure." Then there is the striking Talmudic injunction: "Let no man say 'I am a priest' or 'I am a learned man,' for a man should rather flay a carcass in the street than cease to earn his bread with his hands."[4]

It may be appropriate to view this problem within a wider historical setting. It arose for the first time in ancient Greek philosophy, Plato and Aristotle taking divergent views on this issue. Plato was the originator of the conception of the philosopher-king, thus viewing the good life as a combination of contemplation and professional or political activity, while Aristotle considered contemplation preferable to politics or any other activity, because it allows for leisure which is essential to the happiness of man. Moreover, Aristotle held that by being contempla-

3. Z. E. Kurzweil, *Modern Trends in Jewish Education*, Thomas Yoseloff, New York, 1964.
4. *Pesachim* 113a.

tive, man shares in the divine life, for "the activity of God, which sur-
passes all others in blessedness must be contemplative";[5] hence, in being contemplative man is most God-like.

In Jewish tradition, this problem has been presented in somewhat
different terms. I would adduce the famous discussion between Rabbi
Tarphon and Rabbi Akiba in the presence of the Elders in the garret
of Matizah in Lydda.[6] There they were asked which took preference,
learning (*limud*) or action (*ma'aseh*), and the opinions were divided.
Rabbi Tarphon favored action, and Rabbi Akiba learning. But the
majority decision was that learning is "greater" because it leads to action. In that context "action" would appear to mean charitable works
and concern for public welfare.[7] Learning leads to action in that only
a learned person realizes his duties towards God and his fellow human
beings, for an ignoramus cannot be pious.

The same problem was posed again in a more radical fashion, with
the question as to what was preferable, a life devoted to Torah study
or to professional work.[8] Here again there was a divergence of views.
Rabbi Shimon bar Yochai (a pupil of Rabbi Akiba) expressed himself
in favor of a life devoted to study neglecting worldly pursuits (most
probably in reaction to the prohibition of the study of Torah decreed
at that time by the Romans). Rabbi Ishmael, on the other hand, held
that Torah study combined with a professional occupation was preferable. Commenting on this controversy, the Talmud observes that many
followed Rabbi Ishmael's example and succeeded, whereas those
who followed Rabbi Shimon bar Yochai's ideal failed. The "failure"
occurred because those who chose a life of study only were dependent
on charity for their subsistence, and this led to loss of respect and self-
esteem, whereas those who followed Rabbi Ishmael thrived because they
earned an honorable livelihood and were independent of society's support.

There can be no doubt that the general tenor of Talmudic opinion
is in favor of a combination of learning and work, so much so that this
conception may indeed be regarded as a characteristic of Jewish education. Nevertheless, the Talmud seems to allow also for exception to
this principle and does not negate altogether a life entirely consecrated
to learning. On the contrary, it makes it incumbent upon society to support those scholars whose sole occupation is study of the Torah. Maimonides codified this principle in a passage which is worth examining
closely. In his *Mishne Torah*, at the end of *Hilchot Shmittah Veyovel*,
he pointed out that after the destruction of the Temple it was the Jew-

5. Quoted in *History of Western Philosophy*, by Bertrand Russell, Simon & Schuster,
N.Y., p. 181.
6. *Kiddushin* 40b.
7. See H. Z. Raines, *Torah U-Mussar*, Mossad Harav Kook. Jerusalem, 1954, p. 71.
8. See *Berachot* 35b.

ısh scholars who were to be viewed as the successors of the Priests and Levites of former times, particularly those scholars who forsook professional activity, turning their backs upon the petty struggles, strivings and burdens of everyday life in order to devote themselves wholly to spiritual devotion and study. He ended the relevant passage with the following prayer: "May the Lord be their portion and inheritance for ever and ever, and may He grant them in this world sufficient sustenance, as He granted to the Priests and Levites, as David—may his soul rest in peace—said: The Lord is the portion of my inheritance and my cup. Thou maintainest my lot."

It follows from the analogy drawn by Maimonides between the Priests and Levites on the one hand, and the Jewish scholars on the other, that in his opinion the latter should be supported by society as had been the Priests and Levites. Moreover, according to Maimonides, the study of supporting those who consecrate their lives to study and devotion applies to the world at large and not only to the Jewish people, because he speaks of "all those born into this world" (*kol ba'ei ha'olam*) who decide upon a life consecrated to learning.

We see from what has been said so far that, in accordance with the spirit of Judaism, Jewish education views the active life, which means *Torah U'melachah*, as the good life—but it does not rule out the contemplative ideal altogether. By refraining from uniform ruling and direction for all, Jewish education takes into account the wide diversification of human nature, and individual leanings and character traits.

III

I NOW TURN TO the third principle of Jewish education, namely, its attitude to Hellenistic culture (*Hochmah Yevanit*) and in a wider sense all non-Jewish culture. The basic source is Simon ben Gamaliel the Prince (second century) who reports that his father, Gamaliel the Second, had kept a school for one thousand pupils, five hundred of whom studied the Torah and the other five hundred Greek culture.[9] It remains an open question whether the two "trends" at Gamaliel's school were as clearly divided as it would appear, that is to say, that each trend confined itself exclusively to the fields mentioned; it would seem more likely that each included some element of the other. However that may be, the rationale of establishing a school to teach Hellenistic culture is quite obvious in view of Gamaliel's many contacts with the non-Jewish world, his journeys to Rome in the company of some of his colleagues, and his frequent disputations with various unbelievers and with representatives of the early Christian sect. Quite understandably he considered

---

9. Prof. Saul Lieberman leaves the question open whether *Hochmah Yevanit*, i.e. Hellenistic culture, meant art, philosophy and science, or whether it meant merely a superficial knowledge of all things Hellenistic.

these contacts important; hence it is also understandable that he wished to raise a cadre of young people, versed in Hellenistic culture, who would be capable of continuing these associations, and through whom the connection between the Jewish community and the outside world could be maintained.

I chose to begin my exposition of the problem of Judaism versus Hellenistic culture in its educational aspect with the above-mentioned source in order to soften right from the beginning the impact of the well-known dictum which appears elsewhere,[10] "Cursed be the man who teaches his son Hellenistic culture," reflecting as it does a prohibition of teaching Greek philosophy and science which was even extended to the study of Greek as a language. Professor Saul Lieberman makes the point[11] that this prohibition was never unreservedly accepted and he traces its institution in so far as it was enforced to two circumstances: firstly, a person versed in Greek or Roman culture tended to by-pass the Jewish legal authorities and have direct recourse to the Roman Pro-consul in matters of litigation between Jews, a fact which was damaging to the Jewish community as a whole; secondly, there was the apprehension that the study of Greek culture would be carried on at the expense of Torah study, which would be an infringement of the injunction, "Thou shalt meditate therein day and night."[12]

The conclusion to be drawn from these observations is that there was no objection to the study of Greek culture *per se*. The sources relevant to this problem display on the whole an attitude of tolerance, bearing in mind, as in the case of Gamaliel II, the requirements and interests of the Jewish people. As for the injunction, "Thou shalt meditate therein (*Torah*) day and night," this has been ingeniously interpreted as meaning not the whole day and night, but only once during the day with the donning of the phylacteries and the recital of the *Shema* prayer, and once in the evening by the recital of the *Shema* again.[13]

In our days it is of course not specifically Hellenistic culture we are concerned with, but the attitude of Jewish education to secular study in general. I claim that the relevant Jewish sources are on the whole tolerant of the pursuit of secular studies, particularly if these are required for professional purposes,[14] or if preoccupation with such studies is required for the welfare of the Jewish community as a whole. (This applies *a fortiori* to present-day Israel, which in view of its poverty in natural resources and its precarious political situation must aim at

---

10. *Breita, Sotah,* 49b.
11. *Yevanit ve-yevanut Be-eretz Yisrael,* Mossad Bialik, Jerusalem, pp. 19, 226.
12. *Joshua* 1:8.
13. *Menachot,* 99b.
14. Even a strict Halachist such as the late Rabbi Elchanan Wassermann concedes this in a responsa under the title, *Tshuva la'sho'el mi'medinah yeduah,* printed in *Sefer kovetz he'arot lemasechet yevamot,* New York, p. 157 ff.

maintaining a high professional standard in the fields of science and technology as well as in other areas.)

IV

THE FOURTH PRINCIPLE UPON WHICH I wish to elaborate is the distinction made in Jewish sources between the Jewish education of boys and girls. Plato in his *Republic* claims that education should be uniform and equal for both sexes. The Mishnah rules otherwise. There is the well-known saying of Rabbi Eliezer in Tractate *Sotah* (III, 4): "If anyone teaches his daughter Torah it is as if he taught her lewdness." However, there is also the opposite view expressed by Ben Azzai: "It is a man's duty to teach his daughter Torah, so that if she must undergo the ordeal of drinking (the bitter waters) she should know that the merit (of learning Torah) will hold her punishment in suspense" (and the bitter waters will not cause her to die, even if she has committed adultery).

I do not think it necessary here to elaborate upon the peculiar reasoning of Ben Azzai. Suffice it to say that in his opinion girls as well as boys have to study the Torah. And as for Rabbi Eliezer's pronouncement, the later codifiers, Maimonides and Joseph Caro, further mitigated its import by ruling that it holds good only for the Oral Law, but not for the Written Torah. In actual practice, this discrimination against girls in matters of Jewish education has been further watered down in accordance with the circumstances of the time. It may not be amiss to mention that the Jewish people have produced not only women Prophets and Judges, but also women versed in Jewish scholarship, and the Rabbis have not looked askance at this phenomenon. Nowadays, even in Orthodox schools, there is a uniform curriculum for boys and girls, the only exception being the study of the Talmud, which is reserved mainly for boys, although even this is no longer an absolute rule. It may be that since women are in any case precluded from pursuing the calling of rabbi, this last vestige of discrimination does not arouse serious opposition. It must also be borne in mind that although the emancipation of women has now been going on for many decades, there are certain fields of learning and art, such as mathematics, engineering, composition of music, etc., where women do not on the whole excel, and the same may very well hold good for the study of the Talmud. Yet it is interesting to note that it is a woman (Nechama Leibovitch) who has gained renown in Israel as a popular expounder of Torah, Commentaries and Rabbinic tales.

The Orthodox attitude to the education of girls is undergoing profound change, even in present-day Israel. Since the teaching profession nowadays is mainly in the hands of women—and this applies to religious as well as secular schools, Jewish and non-Jewish—the Jewish education of women has assumed great importance and the original reservations concerning the Jewish education of women are on the wane.

The same flexibility in the interpretation' of Halachic principles concerning Jewish education is discernible in the Diaspora regarding the problem of Israel-orientated education which stems from *mitzvat yishuv Eretz Yisrael*—my fifth principle. Throughout Jewish history, this *mitzvah* has not been interpreted as meaning that it is incumbent upon every Jew to emigrate to Israel because of the far-reaching implications of such a sweeping demand, though, as is well known, it was the aspiration of many Jews even before the rise of modern Zionism either to emigrate to the Holy Land or at the very least to end their lives on its sacred soil. With the creation of the State of Israel, there has arisen the possibility of furthering the cause of Israel from the Diaspora too, and therefore a spiritual orientation towards Israel is being substituted for an education directed towards *aliyah*. For the spiritual and intellectual leaders of Diaspora Jewry, there is of course the added consideration that the Jewish communities should not be deprived of leadership, but Jewish life should be fostered and strengthened wherever conditions permit.

Hence it is understandable that the Jewish people in the Diaspora (including their rabbinic leaders) are not inclined to accept the claim of Zionist ideologists that actual *aliyah* has to be the foremost aim of Jewish education in the Diaspora. Moreover, there are Orthodox, as well as Reform, rabbis who claim precisely the opposite, and who continue to regard it as the duty of Diaspora Jewry to stay on in Exile until the advent of the Messianic Age. Neither of these opinions has been accepted by the Jewish people at large, who hold fast to the principle of *mitzvat yishuv Eretz Yisrael*, but interpret it as implying political and economic support for Israel, the study of the Hebrew language and culture and the fostering of a feeling of identification with Israeli Jewry. Hence, both an education for *aliyah* and education for the Diaspora are legitimate possibilities.

V

ENOUGH HAS BEEN SAID SO FAR to bear out the thesis of this article, that Halachic principles concerning Jewish education are being interpreted in a most liberal way, and in accordance with the demands of the time. It would appear that Jewish education is a field in which Halachic rulings are most amenable to change, and subject to the requirements of what may be called *hora'at sha'ah*. In addition, I submit, that as education has so much bearing on a person's well-being, happiness and economic prosperity, it may in a wider sense be regarded as a matter comparable to *pikuach nefesh*, which would explain the hesitations of Jewish scholars of all times before rigidly circumscribing the field of education with hard and fast rules of perennial validity. I believe this observation to be in accordance with the spirit of Judaism, particularly in view of the fact that both the Torah and the Oral Tradition tend in certain circumstances to extend the principle of *pikuach nefesh* and make it applicable to mental states also (for instance that induced by rape), and the concept of *shefichut damim* has, as is well known, been made applicable in a figurative sense to publicly shaming a person and bringing disgrace upon him in the presence of others. However this may be, Jewish educators belonging to all streams of Judaism may feel reassured that their field leaves room for individual decisions concerning policy-making, syllabuses and other facets of practical education. Their decisions in these matters should be made in the spirit of Judaism and its Halachah, but need not be encumbered by strictly adhering to the forms and methods of past generations.

TOWARDS A RABBINIC PHILOSOPHY OF EDUCATION

David M. Gordis

Modern Jewish Education in the United States began with the arrival on the scene of a young Lebanese-born Jewish doctor named Samson Benderly, who deserted a promising career in medicine to enter the field of Jewish education out of a deep sense of commitment to the future of Jewish life in America. Benderly began his new career in the city of Baltimore where his innovations in the area of Jewish education earned him an invitation to move to New York and organize the efforts of the New York Kehillah to build a system of Jewish education for twentieth century Jewry.[1] When Benderly arrived in New York he found a large number of poorly-equipped and badly organized schools manned by inadequately-trained teachers, apparently without the necessary resources to improve and develop.

By the year 1916, Benderly had established in New York a Bureau of Jewish Education. It was the first agency created by a Jewish community in the United States designed to cope with the problem of Jewish education in a comprehensive, non-denominational communal setting. Benderly's innovations were many. He developed plants for testing new procedures. He originated programs and experimented with new ideas. His work directly influenced more than 200 schools, 600 teachers, and 35,000 students and indirectly many more. He moved in the area of curriculum development. He organized in-service study groups

46

for principals and teachers and began publishing text-books based on sound educational principles. He introduced comprehensive Jewish education for girls. He organized new students for leadership positions in Jewish education, and encouraged many young people to continue their studies at the newly founded Teachers Institute of the Jewish Theological Seminary. He attempted to place New York's Jewish education on a sound financial basis. He organized the Talmud Torah movement, stabilized a Sunday school program, instituted cooperation among congregational schools, institutional schools and some private schools in New York, and he conducted a department of information for reference and consultation by schools outside of the city. In addition, a program of mass education was attempted for those students for whom intensive education was not possible or was not available. Finally, he formulated an architectural plan and a successful pattern of organization for similar bureaus throughout the United States.[2] These were the accomplishments that Samson Benderly could look back on by 1916.

As we survey this pioneering career in modern Jewish life, from the vantage point of over half a century later, it may be appropriate to inquire, where have we come since Benderly's day? What have we accomplished in the last half century? How well have we implemented Benderly's program, and how effective has the program proved to be? While it is true that we have adopted some new programs and instituted some new procedures in Jewish education, including some important work in research and development, on the whole the directions that we have taken are the directions which Benderly mapped for us.

In all candor it must be admitted that with all our organizational successes, with all our progress in the direction of creating financial stability for Jewish education, despite the development of additional schools for research and the training of teachers, the proliferation of summer camps, and other programs in informal education, we are at the moment looking upon an operation which might be characterized as a "holding operation which isn't holding.'' The most hopeful sign in the field of Jewish education is the development of programs of Jewish studies on the college level which, ironically, are not under the formal auspices of the Jewish community at all. The situation is replete with paradox, for despite the oft repeated claim that we are failing because we are simply not getting the children into the schools, particularly at the secondary school level, it is clear that the roots of our failure must be sought much deeper than in problems of recruitment. Honesty compels us to admit that frequently it is just those young people who had faithfully attended our elementary Hebrew school programs and our secondary Hebrew school programs, who, when given a chance, make the most rapid escape possible from the confines of continuing Jewish education, while on the other hand it is frequently those young people who had been deprived of any elementary Jewish education or secondary Jewish education who come to us willingly at the college level seeking to satisfy their curiosity and to fill in the gaps. The obvious conclusion seems to be that we are not only failing to attract young people into our schools, but that there is something profoundly and fundamentally wrong with what we are doing with those who do find their way to us.

The current state of education is by no means an exclusively Jewish concern. Few would disagree with the assertion that the secular educational system in the United States, on every level, is currently crisis-ridden. Elementary schools are agonizing over the child-centered versus the subject-centered curriculum, and the open classroom as opposed to the traditional classroom. Secondary schools are plagued by a variety of philosophical and social problems, and colleges and universities face enormous economic pressures which in part, reflect a crisis of confidence in higher education, a disillusionment with the intellectual life and a disenchantment with the assumptions concerning the transmission of culture which heretofore had been accepted as axiomatic. The extensive literature which has been produced during the last

decade analyzing and criticising the educational establishment
serves as an index of anxiety and concern over the techniques and
objectives of our educational system.

Complex problems rarely allow for simple solutions, and that
is certainly the case with regard to the dilemmas which confront
both the Jewish and the general educational establishment. The
underlying assumption of the present paper is that the greater our
experience with the issues, the greater the likelihood of success
for the directions chosen, and conversely, to the extent that our
decisions ignore the experience of the past, the more limited their
chances of success. It is in the spirit of widening our experiential
data that I offer the present examination of some Rabbinic
sources on education. For the Jewish community, an education-
obsessed community, has throughout its history attempted to deal
with the issues of means and ends in education. The record of its
experience deserves our attention as we confront the very same
issues in a new age.

The record of Jewish experience is Jewish literature. It is a
heterogeneous record, embodying law and lore, comment and
commentary, dealing with matters ethical and ritual, economic
and social, theological, exegetical, physiological, and agricultural. At the center of post-Biblical Jewish literature is the Rabbinic
literature; the legal and ethical *Midrashim*, the *Mishnah* of R.
Judah the Prince, the *Tosefta*, the Talmuds of Babylonia and
Palestine, the Responsa literature, the Codes and Commentaries.
This staggering literature defies generalization and facile
classification. What can be said, however, is that in sum it
constitutes an account of the efforts of a people in time and space
to translate the eternal and universal ideals of Biblical-Prophetic
religion into the specific context of an economically and socially
developing society, in contact and confrontation with alien and
often hostile cultures.

A word of caution: we must not expect to find within Rabbinic
tradition a coherent and logically organized presentation of
educational goals and methods. This is not the nature of the

record which was left to us by the Rabbinic community. It is rather a tapestry which must be examined minutely both for what is explicitly stated and for what is suggested by implication. This record of the past cannot simply be read. Rather we must distill from it and extract from between its lines.

The Aims of Education

Originally, responsibility for educating the child revolved completely upon the father. The Talmud states that among the obligations of the father are to teach his son Torah and to teach him a livelihood.[3] At the very earliest stages of education it is clear that this responsibility was fulfilled by the father himself. Probably in response to the growing numbers of children whose fathers were unable for practical reasons to fulfill this role, the institution of communal education and the corollary notion of communal responsibility for education developed. The Talmud informs us that a certain Joshua ben Gamala established that elementary teachers be commissioned in every region and in every city, and that children of six or seven years of age were to be brought and placed in their care.[4] No dichotomy is suggested by the obligation of the father to teach his child "Torah" on the one hand and a livelihood on the other. Constantly reiterated in the sources is the unbreakable link between the theoretical and the practical. On one level some practical occupation is considered necessary to support and sustain independent and theoretical scholarship in such fashion that the latter not constitute a financial burden on the community. But the value of material and gainful employment far transcends the purely practical needs of self-support. The Rabbis state in a not atypical example of hyperbole that anyone who engages only in the study of the Torah resembles a person who has no God.[5] The Rabbis state also that a person's learning endures only when it is surpassed in extent by his good deeds.[6] Elsewhere, commenting on the statement of R. Josi "Anyone who says, 'I have no learning, has no learning (and receives no communal support)' the Talmud says, "obvious! rather understand the meaning to be 'He who says I have only learning is considered to have only learning'. Still obvious! Rather, he lacks even learning."[7] The implication is that studying Torah when detached totally from the area of the practical is not a desirable goal.

It is particularly interesting in this regard to contrast the role of the material in the Rabbinic view with its place in classical Graeco-Roman *paideia,* a term which embraces education as broadly conceived though it goes beyond it. Werner Jaeger describes the influence of Greek *paideia* on early Christianity in the following terms: "Philology and philosophy were tending in the same direction. They began their teaching with Homer but ended it with Plato, whose dialogues they read and explained. They led their pupils the way to that spirituality which was the common link of all higher religions in late antiquity. From this source of religious feeling all the traditions, pagan and Christian, were reinterpreted to make them acceptable to the man of the new age . . . Plato became the guide from material and sensual reality to the immaterial world in which the nobler minded of the human race were to make their home."[8] Though there do exist references in Rabbinic literature to the spiritual as distinguished from the material and sensual, with the former representing a higher level of human functioning, these sources do not represent the characteristic Rabbinic view. A classical medieval attempt to bridge the gap between the Graeco-Roman and Hebraic ideal is Maimonides' comment on the verse in Jeremiah, "Thus saith the Lord: Let not the wise man take pride in his wisdom, neither let the mighty man take pride in his might, let not the rich man take pride in his wealth, but for this shall he who takes pride pride himself: that he understands and knows me."[9] The verse seems to approximate the ideal of pure contemplation inherent in Greek *paideia.* Maimonides comments: "The prophets too have explained to us and interpreted to us the self-same notions—just as the philosophers have interpreted them—clearly stating to us that neither the perfection of possession nor the perfection of health nor the perfection of moral habits is a perfection of which one should be proud or that one should desire; the perfection of which one should be proud and that one should desire is knowledge of Him, may He be exalted, which is the true science."[10] This emphasis, however, would not have been acceptable to Rabbinic Judaism. The Rabbis emphasize the continuation of the verse in Jeremiah: "That I am the Lord who exercises Mercy, Justice and Righteousness in the world. For in these things I delight saith the Lord."[11] For example: R. Nathan comments: The law is pleasing to God, for he observes it and shows no favoritism. As is said: "That I am the Lord who exercises mercy, justice and righteousness in the world."[12] Similarly, commenting on the verse from Koheleth "And the wiser that Koheleth grew" (Koh.12.9) the Rabbis comment: "At the end of Koheleth it says: 'Koheleth sought desirable things' (12:10). Koheleth sought to understand the rewards of fulfilling the commandments."[13] Despite the demonstrated existence of mystical and speculative interests in the Rabbinic community, it is fair to say that in the mainstream of Rabbinic tradition, understanding and contemplation of God are meaningless when detached from the material and practical. We may in fact say that education in the Rabbinic period was principally an attempt to teach the developing child how to apply the abstract values inherent in prophetic religion to his daily life. It must be recalled, that in classical Greece the "nobler-minded" were free to engage in intellectual speculation only at the expense of an enslaved class which toiled to supply the needs of an aristocratic society. This is in stark contrast to the extensive rabbinic concern for the welfare of the slave both Jewish and gentile. Hellenistic education was the handmaiden of the aristocracy and an auxiliary of the state. It was an establishment tool. In the Jewish community education was an outgrowth of the family, deriving from the relationship of the father and his children. It was an auxiliary of the synagogue, and together with it constituted the great institutions of democratization in the Jewish community. Scholarship and learning became the ultimate source of decision-making power and authority, supplanting kingship, priesthood and sanctuary, the loci of power of an earlier era. And the role of education as an instrument of democratization was possible only because of the unbreakable link between the theoretical and the practical in the Rabbinic value system.

The Individual

Educational objectives in the Rabbinic community are of two fundamental types, the individual and the communal. Louis Ginzberg, in an essay on the Jewish primary school, pointed out that the characteristic feature of Jewish pedagogy was that the three chief ends of education for the individual were subsumed as a unity. Earliest instruction kept in view at once the intellectual, the moral and the religious thinking of the child.[14] It would be fair to say that the intellectual and religious components were subservient to the moral component. The great Babylonian sage, Rava, is reported to have said that the "aim of wisdom is repentance and good deeds."[15] The Talmud in an anonymous statement reports that the only effective antidote to the evil inclination is words of Torah.[16] The Midrash supplies a parable to illustrate the effectiveness of Torah, in countering the evil inclination. It is compared with a cupful of oil. If a drop of water falls into a cup which is overflowing with oil, then a drop of oil is forced out. So it is with Torah. If some matter of Torah enters the heart some corresponding foolishness is forced out. If some foolishness enters the heart it forces out some matter of Torah.[17] It should be recognized that the Rabbis were not asserting that knowing the correct way guaranteed moral conduct. They understood that decision making involves the constant struggle among conflicting inclinations. They felt, however, that the best guarantor of ethical behavior was for man to equip himself with the knowledge of Torah, which is the will of God.

53

Learning, together with wisdom which the Rabbis felt was its product, was considered the most desirable possession for the individual, the highest of all attainments. In the language of the *Midrash:* "If you lack knowledge, what have you attained? If you have attained knowledge, what do you lack?"[18] The importance of learning for the man who aspires to piety is perhaps summed up best in the famous Rabbinic dictum: *"lo am-ha-aretz chassid"* (the ignorant man cannot be truly righteous").[19] It is only by being immersed in the ways of God as revealed in his Torah, being knowledgeable concerning the reasons for observance that the Jew can attain to the highest level of piety.

Education and Society

Education as fundamental in the development of the individual represents only one side of the coin in the Rabbinic view. The community is the other side. One source asserts that each day an angel goes out from before the Holy One, blessed be He, intent upon destroying the world and returning it to its primeval formlessness. However, when the Holy One, blessed be He, looks upon the children in the schools and the scholars sitting in the academies, his anger is immediately turned into pity.[20] A popular source which occurs in the *Midrash* and is cited in the Palestinian Talmud tells of a delegation of three Rabbis who were sent on a mission to inspect educational facilities throughout Palestine. Coming to a place where there were no teachers, they asked the inhabitants to bring them to the protectors of the town. The townspeople responded by pointing to the military guard. The Rabbis replied, "These are not the protectors of the town, but its destroyers." The townspeople asked, "Who then are the protectors of the city?" The Rabbis' response was, "The teachers."[21] Education, then, has a vital social function in that it ensures the survival of the community. Education is the cement which holds the community together and gives it the strength to resist repeated onslaughts. The education of children may therefore be said to have both a personal goal and a patriotic one.

These two goals elevate education to a position of centrality among the Rabbis' concerns. Study is in one place described as of greater importance than the building of the Temple.[22] Elsewhere it is described as of greater importance than the priesthood and the throne.[23] A similar source reports that children's study may not be interrupted even for the sacred task of the building of the Temple.[24] And perhaps the clearest statement of this notion is that in the last three hours of the day the Holy One, blessed be He, occupies Himself in teaching children Torah.[25] The education of children and the vocation of scholars is therefore seen to be of the very highest importance in the hierarchy of values of the Jewish community. It attains to this importance first because it is a fundamental instrument in building character, and in developing an individual's ethical responsibility. And second, its role is crucial in guaranteeing the survival of the Jewish community. Torah is the protector of the city. Education and learning are the guarantors of survival.

Teacher and Student

Central to the process of education in the Rabbinic view, is the student-teacher relationship. It has been noted that the obligation to educate the child devolved originally upon the parent, and that as the school developed as a communal institution, it substituted in part for parental responsibility. What emerges most clearly from an examination of the sources is that the teacher functioned virtually as part of the child's family. He was in intimate contact with the child throughout the day and all through the year. This quasi-parental role of the teacher is articulated in many sources. Commenting on the verse: "And thou shalt teach them to thy children," the Rabbis state: "These are your students," and the comment is appended that generally one's students are called one's children.[26] A well-known source ascribed to Rabbi Samuel ben Nachman in the name of Rabbi Jonathan asserts that he who teaches the son of his friend Torah, Scripture credits him with the equivalent of having borne him.[27]

The intimate relationship between student and teacher had two sides to it: the student was under the constant scrutiny of the teacher, but the teacher was also under the constant scrutiny of the student. A teacher's behavior was constantly observed by his students. The sources stress the requirement of absolute moral excellence on the part of the teacher. All situations which may lead to moral laxity on the part of the teacher must be avoided in order to protect the student from exposure to a model which was not to be emulated. Moreover, absolute intellectual candor was the norm. On several occasions a teacher, having responded to a challenge by a sectarian in a way which satisfied the challenger but not the scholar's own students is challenged by them: "You've set him aside with a straw: What answer can you give us?"

Though in the Rabbinic view the process of education takes place only in part in the formal classroom environment, the classroom is, of course, of central importance. The Rabbis were aware of the developmental stages through which the child goes, and in this they anticipated some of the conclusions of contemporary developmental psychology.[29] They understood that at the younger ages children were most able to assimilate the various techniques which would allow them at a later time to explore the Jewish tradition in a profound way. For this reason, in the early stages of education great stress is placed upon the memory and the highest compliment for a student at this level is that everything is absorbed and assimilated and nothing is forgotten. A second emphasis at this stage is on development of language skills. This pattern of emphasizing technical skills first and only thereafter entering into more intensive study goes to the root of the Rabbinic view of the learning process. The Talmud states that a person should first assimilate superficially a large amount of data, and then he should enter into in-depth study of specific sources.[30] Rashi comments that a person should study with his teacher till the text of the Talmud and its superficial interpretation are absolutely familiar to him. Afterwards he may enter the matter in depth, questioning and comparing and seeking to resolve contradictions. In-depth study should be postponed in order that fullest advantage be taken of the presence of the teacher as a source of help on the technical level.[31] Developing familiarity with a great volume of material is in itself an important way of learning to deal with this material in depth. The Talmud states that after a person has covered a great deal of material he becomes secure in his knowledge and he is able to answer and solve difficult problems for himself.[32]

In the area of moral development, the Rabbis likewise anticipated some of the conclusions of contemporary psychology. They understood that discussions of ethical issues would only be comprehensible to the child if they were appropriate to his developmental level. "What is the nature of the evil inclination?" they asked. "For thirteen years the evil inclination is stronger than the good inclination. From before birth the evil inclination begins to grow and develop in a person. If he begins to violate the Sabbath, for example, the evil inclination does not prevent him from doing so. After the age of thirteen the good inclination develops. Thenceforth, if he begins to violate the Sabbath, the good inclination adjures him, "Foolish one, (you are violating the Sabbath!) Does not the Torah say 'he who violates the Sabbath must be put to death'?"[33] Inherent in this source is the awareness that during the period of adolescence a person's moral consciousness awakens. Throughout the pre-adolescent period, the child associates the rules of what he may or may not do with an external source of authority, usually the parent or the teacher. An act is viewed in terms of the authority's response in the form of pleasure or pain, reward or punishment. As he enters adolescence, the child moves away from this other-directedness, and towards inner-directedness. He begins to evaluate the abstract moral quality of behavior. He becomes intensely curious about the fundamental problems of right and wrong in the world, as his independence from outside authority grows. His confidence in his own judgment increases. He begins to evaluate moral causes for himself. The natural consequence of this insight concerning human development was the Rabbis' position that the years prior to the age of moral awareness were most efficiently utilized in developing language skills and emphasizing extensive rather than intensive study of texts. Dealing with more abstract and conceptual material came only after the child had reached the appropriate developmental level.

One additional point should be made in the area of curricular emphasis. Explicit and implicit in rabbinic sources is a stress on the importance of the Hebrew language in the total picture of Jewish education. The Mishna was compiled by Rabbi Judah the Prince at a time when the *lingua Franca* of the Jewish community was Aramaic, but the Mishna was written in a pure and refined Hebrew style, and it became the curriculum for all the academies of higher Jewish education in Palestine and Babylonia. In the Talmud itself, which is written in Aramaic, when an authority makes a legal assertion, as distinguished from an argumentative statement, in almost every case he chooses to make that statement in Hebrew. In commenting on the verse: "Thou shalt teach them to the children, and speak of them:" (Deut. 11:19) the Midrash comments that when a child begins to speak his father must speak with him in Hebrew, in the sacred tongue, and teach him Torah. If the father does not speak to his child in the sacred tongue and does not teach him Torah, then it is as if he were burying him.[34] The point of this hyperbole is clear; the teaching of Torah and the teaching of Hebrew are intimately related to each other: The objectives of studying Torah are, as we have shown, moral perfection and communal continuity. Study of Torah of the most meaningful kind cannot be accomplished unless the language of the texts themselves is understood. The full impact of the texts cannot be realized in translation. And furthermore, a familiarity with the tongue of the prophets is considered necessary for communal continuity. A Jew who is not conversant in Hebrew, who cannot read the Bible and the other sacred texts in the original, no matter how well educated he might be in other areas is to some extent still a stranger and an outsider.

On another level, the Rabbis were aware of diminishing returns in the educational process when class size was too large. They state that the maximum number of elementary school pupils in a single class should be twenty-five. If there are fifty students, the hiring of an additional teacher is required, and if class size reaches forty, some senior student should be engaged to assist the master teacher in his work.[35] This source reveals not only an awareness of the importance of individual attention for the student, but also the necessity of compromise when economic pressures or other exigencies make the hiring of an additional teacher impossible. The monotorial system, that is, the use of advanced students in lieu of professional teachers, a common practice in modern higher education, may have been a practical necessity, but it was clearly considered a compromise with the quality of education.

Summary

We may now attempt to summarize briefly the results of our excursion into some Rabbinic sources on education. In the Rabbinic view the theoretical and the practical were not to be detached from one another. Theoretical knowledge without practical application has neither survival value nor a beneficial effect on the development of the individual. In the Jewish view education involves no ascent up a ladder leading from the material through the spiritual to the theoretical, but involves rather a fusion of the material and the spiritual into a unity.

The goals of education in the Rabbinic view are two: first, developing a responsible and moral individual. The Rabbis did not pre-suppose a fundamentally sinful nature for man. The soul which God had implanted in man was pure, but man's life involved a series of struggles with conflicting inclinations, and education was the best equipment he could have to assist him in making correct decisions and judgments. The second goal of education is communal survival. If the community was to remain in existence, it had to effectively transmit the corpus of its tradition from one generation to the next.

Specific techniques in education were based on what would appear to be valid insights into the nature of the child's development. Curricula were planned for specific levels of development, with the early years devoted primarily to the techniques which can best be acquired at this level. Language skills, which were of particular importance in a society where books were scarce, training in memory, and the assimilation of large quantities of source material were stressed in this period. After the age of development of moral awareness, the attempt was made to enter into a higher speculative and conceptual level. This pattern was repeated in the training of textual scholars who were advised to study extensively before beginning intensive textual criticism. There is repeated stress on the fact that teachers were dealing with individuals whose inclinations, abilities, and interests were unique. The nature of the relationship between teacher and student was seen to be at least as important as the specific information being transmitted.

A few observations may be in order concerning the implications of the above for the contemporary dilemma. A recurrent theme in the Rabbinic sources is that no phase of the educational process can be viewed in isolation. Classroom and world, abstract and concrete, teacher and person, must not be seen as dichotomies but rather as unities. The educational enterprise is the integration of experience into a coherent view of the world. This integration requires both techniques and values, but techniques and values cannot be learned in isolation from one another.

It seems apparent that the Rabbis were convinced of the limitations of the classroom. If we are to draw the appropriate conclusion from their observations and their experience, we would move in the direction of stressing the informal aspects of education and we would attempt to overcome the notion of education delivered en masse to a consumer public. Our objective would be a pattern of education responsive to individual needs and stressing the relationships between student and model, placing far greater demands on teachers than is currently our practice. Furthermore, we ought not stress the isolation of the classroom from its world, but rather construct a curriculum in such a way as to convey the necessary techniques and information in the context of a community which is alive, at work, and involved in the problem solving and decision making for which the educational process is designed to prepare it.

For the Jewish community, the first and most obvious lesson to be learned is the priority of education within the community's hierarchy of goals. The recent upsurge of interest by the Jewish Federations in various parts of the country in the area of Jewish education represents the inclination to return education to its traditional place among the Jewish community's priorities. It should be encouraged.

A second important lesson to be learned is that Jewish education has two fundamental goals, one individual and one communal. The Rabbis were realists with regard to the potential of children at various developmental levels. It is of great importance to plan curricula appropriate to our children's developmental levels. Moreover, we must not delude ourselves concerning what can and cannot be accomplished in the classroom, particularly in view of the limited number of hours which most children devote to Jewish education. The six hour a week school is not going to accomplish a great deal in building character or creating ethical human beings. There is, in fact, generally some doubt about the effectiveness of all classroom character education programs. What is perfectly clear is that if Jewish education is to be limited to a few hours a week, and if the public school system insists as it properly does that it cannot and must not operate *in loco parentis,* then there is no alternative but to return to the home the primary responsibility for character training and moral development. The school can help in supplying material for discussion of various moral and conceptual problems. However, those of us who would assure ourselves that in six hours a week the child is going to be taught to be both an ethical person and a knowledgeable Jew are engaging in self delusion. Our schools must realistically evaluate what they can do. They must plan for the most efficient utilization of the hours spent in the classroom. At the primary level the emphasis should be on efficiently engendering knowledge of the Hebrew language, basic Jewish skills, and exposure to the most important sources of Jewish learning. Jewish education on a secondary level attains new importance. It comes at a time when moral awareness and sensitivity to moral decision making can lead to a sophisticated examination of concepts and ideas, and analysis of the nature of moral decision.

Furthermore, the second goal of rabbinic education must not be sacrificed to the first. Jewish education does not strive simply to create ethical human beings in a communal vacuum. It is the fundamental instrument for Jewish survival. There is a tendency in some of our schools to stress only the humanistic aspects of Jewish education. The Bible becomes a great work of literature which is analyzed for its moral lessons. Jewish history is taught in purely academic context. Jewish involvement, Jewish feeling, the specifically Jewish in Jewish education, including the Hebrew language; are not stressed. The result is that many students reach the conclusion that what is of value in the Jewish tradition can be expressed in purely humanistic terms, and consequently there is no need to define one's place within the Jewish commonweal. This should be a source of concern for the Jewish community.

In the rabbinic tradition the attainment of human excellence for the Jew is through the instrument of Jewish tradition. The values which Judaism has bequeathed to all civilized men are only part of the content of Jewish tradition. Jewish tradition supplies also the experience of a community applying standards and values to the specific situations which each individual confronts and a language refined to perfection by generations of experience, for expressing those ideals and those goals to which this community aspires. The Jewish experience since the age of the Enlightenment, and particularly in the twentieth century, is proof positive of the inadequacy of abstract moral platitudes detached from the concrete and devoid of an explicit and specific language for expressing moral standards and moral commitment.

Finally, in view of the increasingly limited period of time spent in formal Jewish training, a greater emphasis on informal Jewish education would appear to be absolutely essential. Greater resources must be allocated to summer camp programs and youth programs. Greater care must be exercised in selecting as teachers, counselors and advisors, models whom we would want our young people to emulate. Efforts must be redoubled in the area of teacher and leadership training and the development of scholars to assure that such models will be available. Institutional frameworks must be constructed which will facilitate education through exposure to a model to supplement formal educational programs.

In brief, we may conclude that those components of rabbinic education which suggest a re-evaluation of our methods and assumptions in Jewish education are: commitment to intellectual excellence, a realistic appraisal of the limited potential of the classroom, and the constantly reiterated commitment to a Jewish education which will be both an instrument for individual growth and development and the key to the survival of that people for which excellence in education has always been a primary goal.

Notes

1. Arthur A. Goren, *New York Jews and the Quest for Community*, New York, 1970) p. 96-f.

2. Nathan Winter, *Jewish Education in a Pluralist Society*, (New York, 1966) p. 84.

3. Babylonian Talmud, Kiddushin, 29a

4. B.T., Baba Bathra, 21a

5. B.T., Aboda Zara, 17b

6. Mishnah, Aboth, 3.9

7. T.B. Yabamoth, 109b

8. Werner Jaeger, *Early Christianity and Greek Paideia*, (Cambridge, 1961) p. 46

9. Jer. 9.22

10. Maimonides, *Guide for the Perplexed*, III, 54, (trans. by Shlomo Pines)

11. Jer. 9.23

12. Bereshith Rabbah, 30.16

13. Koheleth Rabbah, 12.10

14. Louis Ginzberg, "The Jewish Primary School," in *Students, Scholars and Saints*, (Philadelphia, 1928) p. 14

15. B.T., Berachot, 17a

16. B.T., Kiddushin, 30b

17. Song of Songs Rabbh, 1.28

18. Leviticus Rabbah, 1.6

19. Mishnah, Aboth, 2.5

20. Kallah Rabbati, II (82)

21. Palestinian Talmud, Hagigah, 1.7

22. B.T., Megillah, 16b

23. Mishnah, Aboth, 6.5

24. B.T., Shabbat, 119b

25. B.T., Horayoth, 13a

26. Sifre Deuteronomy, 34 (ed. Finkelstein, p. 61)

27. B.T., Sanhedrin, 19b

28. Genesis Rabbah, 8.9 and frequently

29. I have in mind in particular the researches of Jean Piaget and his followers.

30. B.T., A.Z. 19a

31. Rashi, *ad loc.*

32. B.T., Shabbat, 63a

33. *The Fathers According to R. Nathan,* 16.2

34. Sifre Deuteronomy, 46 (ed. Finkelstein, p. 104) See S. Baron Social and Religious History of the Jews, II, (New York and Philadelphia, 1952) p. 145

35. B.T., Baba Bathra, 21a

EDUCATION AMONG THE JEWS.

A Study in the History of Pedagogy.

Henry M. Leipziger

Although education and instruction are co-ordinate, still their methods are somewhat different. The education of a being, as of a nation, begins at birth ; instruction only after a certain degree of intelligence has been attained. Education has for its purpose the improvement of the condition of the human race and the attainment of human perfection. Instruction uses the material that has been handed down to us and that others have found of value in forming and elevating humanity.

Among the wonderful spectacles that the world's history presents, one of the most remarkable is the survival of the Jewish people despite the many vicissitudes it has encountered, and—what is of more interest to the student of education—is the maintenance of the high standard of intellectuality which marks the Hebrew race.

This intellectuality is due to a carefully devised system of training and education—a system without a parallel in the history of nations.

According to Prof. Dittes, "If ever a people has demonstrated the power of education it is the Hebrew people." What is remarkable about the system is that it is

66

adapted to every age and time. No step in the march of progress finds opposition among the Hebrews; but education is regarded as a process of evolution, a continual becoming.

Education, in a true system, depends upon the ideal that is held up for attainment. What is the perfect man? In Roman days it was the valiant soldier, capable of enduring fatigue, and stoical as to his fate. Among the Athenians the ideal man was one in whom physical and moral perfection were developed.

As a religion of practical morality Judaism did not create schools of philosophy, but erected schools for children, in which both sexes were trained in the teachings of duty and of love. "Go" said two great heathen thinkers to their contemporaries, " go to the Jewish schools where the children are trained in the observance of the moral law. There is the source of its strength—that is the secret of its indestructibility. If you would conquer them, you must attack these places."

The perfect man among the Hebrews was the virtuous man, the man who strove to be like God. Virtue was placed above everything.

And this ideal colored their system of education. God was their king, their teacher, and their judge, so that Hebrew education was particularly and specially religious. The union was not of church and state, but the more important one of religion and life.

Here, in early times before schools were regularly instituted, the parents were the first teachers. Parents felt an obligation to teach their children as a command of Jehovah, and every possible means was adopted to keep alive a lofty morality and to develop that national pride for God which has marked the Hebrew through all periods of his history.

The celebration of the anniversary of the exodus from Egypt illustrates one means of keeping alive this national love of God. On the Passover Evening symbols commemorating the great event were explained in each household to all the family, and the Talmud distinctly advised that questions should be encouraged. Even here we see the application of that pedagogic principle which favors direct observation and personal reflection as most desirable among children. But, strange to say, the contributions of the Jews to the science of education are but little known.

A study of the history of this race will show that very many of the new movements in education which mark our time have been anticipated by them centuries ago.

More than two thousand years ago they recognized the almost divine office of the teacher, established education for all upon the most democratic basis, displayed wise pedagogic knowledge in the arrangements of their schools and course of studies, and at all times favored the education of the hand in conjunction with the training of the intellect.

In the brief compass of this monograph I can give but a suggestion of the rich field that the student of pedagogy will find in the history of the Hebrew people. Certainly in the development of an American ideal, much can be learned from studying the methods which have won for the Hebrew race the following characterization : "Israel had a higher part assigned her in the drama of history, to which her secret instincts resistlessly drew her. Her predominant characteristic was an intense religiousness. Everything in the life of her people took on a serious and devout tone. Patriotism was identified with piety. Her statesmen were reformers, idealists, whose orations were sermons like the speeches of Gladstone in the Midlothian campaign, dealing with politics in the light of eternal principles. * * * The nation's ambitions were aspirations. Her heroes grew to be saints. The divine became to her not the true or the beautiful, but the good. She evidently had, as Matthew Arnold said of John Wesley, " a genius for godliness."

The character of Hebrew education during the Biblical period will be but briefly considered. The main portion of the essay will however be devoted to a view of Jewish theories and methods during the Talmudic times, which extend from Ezra's time until about the 5th century of the present era.

The Rabbis claim that systematic instruction dates from a very early period, but give no particulars as to the school. It is clear, though, from frequent references in the Bible, that all education was given at home—the parents being the first teachers. The child was not trained to be skilful in the use of weapons, or to become an artist, but a firm believer in God ; so that as soon as he could talk his lips whispered of God.

The laws of Moses require the fathers to " speak of Him when thou sittest in thy house, and when thou goest in thy way, and when thou sittest down, and when thou risest up."

That the higher classes at this time were cultured is admitted, but it seems certain, from the learning of men like Amos and Michah, that ability to read and write—as yet an unattained ideal among many peoples—was general. In the course of time there arose a class of men called Sopherim or Scribes who gradually supplanted the power of the priesthood, and who became the forerunners of the great Talmudic teachers.

In Samuel's time the schools of the Prophets came into existence. Some consider these schools as the originators of the cloister, others the first academies. In these schools religion, poetry and music were taught.

The first years of childhood were spent under the mother's care, later on the father took care of his son. Ethics was the staple of instruction. Short aphorisms were repeated by the young pupil and much instruction was conveyed in the form of parables and riddles. Religious observances exercised a great educational influence.

69

The ceremonial law, was so thoroughly interspersed with so many holy and wise teachings that it was a complete manual of study. Nor were natural phenomena permitted to occur without being brought into play in their system of religious training.

A prominent characteristic of the teaching at this period was the answering of children's questions. One comes constantly across passages as follows: "If your son should ask you the reason of this or that law or custom, then explain to him. Wait till a suitable opportunity occurs. Do not rest satisfied with the mere dry statement of the fact but let the practice precede the instruction and then will the law become his possession."

As soon as the child reached his third year he began to memorize verses from the Bible, and when old enough a tablet was given on which he learned to form the letters. At table the children were arranged in the order of their age, so that the older children exercised dominion over the younger.

The foundation of a system of schools among the Jews may be attributed to Simon ben Shetach, who lived 80 B. C. He felt the force of what Fichte afterwards said, "Whatever you would put in a nation's life you must put into its schools," and he enunciated the proposition— not yet universally assented to—that popular education is the best strength of a nation.

Troublous times occurred in Judea. The Holy City resounded with the tramp of the Roman soldier and the Temple was in ruins. Then Jochanan ben Sakkai obtained from the Roman Emperor Titus the privilege of establishing a school at Jamnia. And from this little spark the fire of education was enkindled—a fire which has steadily burnt among the Jewish people even until our day. During the period from the destruction of the Second Temple until about 500 of this era, the Talmud was in process of growth.

70

The Babylonian Talmud was for more than a thousand years the very essence of spiritual and intellectual activity of the Jews. Its very existence is an evidence of the influence of the schools. This wonderful work—this unique monument of lore—has been much misunderstood. "It is not a text book or a law book; it is a veritable encyclopedia."

Its influence on the Jewish people has been described as follows:

"The historical accounts contained in the Talmud fill a chasm in the history of the Jews and Judaism for which we might, else, in vain seek the bridge.

The Talmud, containing the literature of the Jews, and alluding to so many sciences, and requiring for its understanding several preparatory sciences and other acquirements, set an example and excited the Jews of the middle ages to literary pursuits, and thus gave rise to numbers of works, the variety and ingenuity of which extort, not unfrequently, marks of acknowledgment, even from the bitterest enemies of Judaism, and prevented the Jews from falling into the same ignorance which prevailed through centuries among European Christians. To the discipline of Talmudic study, requiring, as it does, such acuteness of perception and such subtlety of reasoning, may be attributed the success with which the Jews have, in all ages been enabled to extricate themselves from the snares and pitfalls which might else have been their destruction. Moreover, in those unhappy times when the Jews were compelled to live secluded from the rest of mankind, their spirit would have become entirely torpid for want of exercise, had the Talmud not kept alive their faculties, by offering to them so vast a field of mental exercise. Lastly, by rendering the Jews a literary nation, and by having thus continually sharpened and exercised their mental faculties, the Talmud made the possibility (nay, accounted for the fact) that in much less than a century, during which

71

the barriers have been struck down which excluded the
Jews from the remainder of European society, they have
exhibited a flexibility of intellect, which both in art and
science, produced so many great minds, as to exceed by
far all expectation."

And of this book, the great scholar Delitzsch says:

"The Talmud, that colossal Jewish religious code, in
which the Jew, educated in the lore of his nation, finds his
spiritual house, is to the educated in Christendom less
known than the Vedas of the Indians or the Avesta of
the Persians."

The Proverbs of Solomon contain sentences on education which were not for an age but "for all time;" while
in the apocryphal book of Sirach we find a "book rich
in pedagogical insight, which paints with master-strokes
the relations of husband and wife, parents and children,
master and servant, friend and friend, enemy and enemy,
and the dignity of labor as well as its division. This price-
less book forms a side-piece to the Republic of Plato and
his laws on ethical government."

We are not surprised that a race that had made two
such contributions to educational literature should in the
Talmud evolve a perfect pedagogic system. In its pages
will be found gems of educational wisdom. At a time
when the schoolmaster was despised, when intellectual
darkness reigned in all the European countries, the Jewish
rabbis carefully elaborated and practiced those wise pedagogic rules which are to-day slowly but surely coming in
vogue. Only within the present generation has England
established a national elementary school system. The
Jews established theirs twenty centuries ago. The Puritan
fathers only carried into practice sound Jewish teaching
when they insisted with Joshua ben Gamala that every
community should support a school. Truly it can be
said in the words of Isaiah, "Out of Zion shall go
forth the law, and the word of the Lord from Jerusalem."

We shall consider the subject under the following heads.
I.   Importance of Schools and Instruction.
II. Founding and Spread of Schools.
III. School Organization—including
    A. School house.
    B. Teachers.
    C. Schools.
    D. Material.
    E. Method.
    F. Regulations.

IMPORTANCE OF SCHOOLS AND INSTRUCTION.

The wise men of the Talmudic times had the highest conception of the value of schools and instruction ; the school was to them the long and short of life. The profession of teaching was regarded as the very highest, as one in which God himself was engaged. "What does God do in the fourth hour ?" is once asked in the Talmud. "He teaches little school children." The ancient history of other nations may be searched in vain for a single instance of regard of the high importance of the school, such as Rabbi Jehuda uttered in such distinct words when he said "The world is only saved by the breath of the school children."

The importance of the school and instruction, according to the Talmud, cannot be overrated. The very stability of the world, if it is to be the abode of intelligent beings, is connected with the school as effect is to cause.

"A city without schools should be destroyed or excommunicated." And "Jerusalem was destroyed because its people neglected the schools and school children."

As a consequence, the teachers and schools were regarded as the keepers and defenders of the city. For where spirituality dwells in a people or state, which permits all

73

circles of life, there the moral perfection of all its citizens is striven after, and the teachers of children take an honored place in society, and become the real defenders of the city; educating, training and elevating its citizens. " A President of the Academy" relates the Talmud "once sent several learned men from Palestine to aid the progress of instruction and establish schools where none existed. They came to a city where they saw no sign of a school nor could they find a teacher. They said to the citizens, ' bring the keepers of the city before us.' The magistrate and the chief police officials appeared. 'These are not the city's keepers!' the wise men exclaimed. 'Who then are?' asked the citizens in astonishment. ' The city's keepers are the teachers,' was the reply."

" When you see lovely gardens by the stream and the brilliant stars in heaven," says the Talmud, "then you have a picture of the true teacher, who takes care of the tender plants and sheds mild light on the dark world of growing childhood." The most beautiful ornaments of humanity are the teachers surrounded by children.

This conception arose from a natural feeling of *love* which they fostered. Each teacher felt it to be the most welcome task of his life to teach. The Talmud relates of Jochanan ben Sakkai that he spent a third of his life in teaching, and the Rabbi Akiba said to one of his disciples, "My son, the cow is more anxious to suckle than the calf to suck."

The classic nations of antiquity did not have the same regard for the dignity of the teacher as the Jews did. Among the Greeks and Romans the trainer of children was a man without standing, a veritable pariah in the community. The post of teacher was despised, and the teacher and servant were put on par.

This is what Plutarch says of the Roman pedagogue: "For if any of their servants be better than the rest, they dispose some of them to follow husbandry, some to navigation, some to merchandise, some to be stewards in their houses, and some lastly to put out their money to use for them. But if they find any slave that is a drunkard or a glutton, and unfit for any other business, to him they assign the government of their children ; whereas, a good peda- gogue ought to be such a one in his disposition as Phœnix, tutor to Achilles was."

The life of the teacher was closely bound to that of the scholar. Teacher and scholar were one and inseparable. Teachers and scholars shared each other's failures.

The disinterestedness with which they pursued their vocation indicates the love they had for their calling. The only reward which they were promised and which they desired, was to learn and then to teach. He who studies the law in his youth will use it in old age. He who has pupils in his youth will have them when he is old.

The father was no less convinced of the importance of instruction to the child. "A learned man," says the Talmud, "met a friend leading his son hurriedly to school."

"Why such haste" he asked him.

"Because," he replied, "the duty to lead the child to instruction precedes all other cares."

Another learned man did not eat his morning meal before his son was in school.

The esteem for the teacher and the love for him made instruction thus a pleasant duty.

Relating to teachers the Talmud says :

"He who has studied and does not teach resembles a myrtle in the desert."

But it was not the teacher alone who strove to awaken the intelligence of the child and to guide it in the right path ; the father was obliged to do his share. "Who is ignorant ? He who has sons and does not have them taught."

Many are the aphorisms to be found in the pages of the

Talmud on the importance of industry and perseverance
in study. "The day is short and the work great, the
workers are lazy, the reward is great, and the Master
praises." "It is not the same if one studies alone or with
a teacher." "Do not say 'When I get time, I will study.'
Perhaps you will not get time."

RISE AND SPREAD OF SCHOOLS.

It is to Joshua ben Gamala that the organization of the
Jewish school system is due. More then eighteen centuries ago he initiated it, carefully nursed it, and planted
the seed so thoroughly that even in the smallest village a
school became recognized as a necessity. It was he who
thus started that intellectual movement which has characterized the Jewish people down to the present day.

" Before Joshua ben Gamala," relates the Talmud, "the
father was the teacher of his children—and fatherless
children received no instruction. To supply the need,
children's schools were established in Jerusalem."

But things went on as before and only children who had
fathers to look after them attended these schools, while
the fatherless and uncared-for child as a rule did not go to
school.

Then a school was established in each community, which
was attended by scholars who had reached sixteen years
of age, who did not need the discipline of the child
and were left at their option. It was then that Joshua ben
Gamala appeared and ordered that in each town a school
should be established and that children from the age of
six upwards should be obliged to attend thereat.

From that time on, school instruction was a matter
conducted in real earnestness, as the ordinances established
sufficiently prove. After Rabbi Joshua's law was promul-
gated no one was permitted to take a child to school

from one city to another, the inhabitants of each city could be forced to maintain schools and teachers, and there was a stern prohibition against living in a town which was not provided with a school.

Rabbi Joshua's work was not temporary. Its effect was lasting. The spread of schools during his time was the most extensive that we can imagine. Schools sprung up everywhere and parents cheerfully brought their children to them. And if, perhaps, some of the Talmudic statements in reference to the number of schools, scholars and teachers appear at times exaggerated, still the fact remains that in every important city the school attendance was very great.

INNER ORGANIZATION OF THE SCHOOLS.

A. SCHOOLROOMS.

Space, Name, and Arrangement.

At the beginning of the Talmudic period it was the custom, in case no proper house was provided, to give instruction in some place in the open air. But from the time of Rabbi Jehuda Hanassi instruction was given in rooms specially arranged. These schools went under various names, such as Beth Hamedrath (House of Learning), *Yeshiba* (and sometimes under the Greek name "Skole)," Schools for children were held in what were termed Beth Ha-Keneseth. They were generally situated in the quieter parts of the city, so that the lessons might not be disturbed. Benches, stools, and cushions were only introduced into schools long after the schools themselves were established.

Maimonides furnishes a very correct picture of a school in practical operation.

"The teacher sat above, and the scholars surrounded him

77

as a crown the head, so that all could see and hear the teacher. The teacher did not sit on a chair while his scholars sat on the floor, but *all* sat either upon chairs or upon the floor. It was formerly the custom for the teacher to sit while the scholars stood, but shortly before the destruction of Jerusalem it was arranged that both scholars and teachers should sit. Children sat *in front* of their teacher so that they could see his face when he spoke, in accordance with the words of Isaiah 30 : 20, " Thine eyes shall see thy teacher."

The school houses were the favorites of the Jewish people. There they were wont to assemble. The house, the school and the synagogue formed a three-fold link which bound the race of the old book to the book of the ancient race. The school house was open all day.

B. THE TEACHER.

(a). *Choice of Teachers.*

On moral grounds no unmarried man or any woman could be a teacher. And among the number of those eligible to teachership only the best were chosen. The words of Rabbi Akiba are noteworthy in this regard. " Do you desire to hang yourself? If so, select a lofty tree," which, interpreted, means, " Learn from a distinguished teacher." The most experienced teacher was regarded as the most desirable, and when it came to a choice, always had the preference. " Instruction by young teacher " says the Talmud "is like sour grapes and new wine, while instruction by old teachers is like ripe grapes and sweet wine."

If however a less capable teacher had once been engaged, he was not set aside for a more competent, and for this reason. Perhaps the latter would be careless, since he would boast that he had no peer, and would not fear dismissal. The Talmud gives many "points" that should be considered in selecting teachers. In one place the teacher who gives his pupils much matter although he does not ground them in it is preferred, while in another place *thoroughness* is deemed most desirable. On the whole *thoroughness* was the chief point desired, because the Talmud lays great stress on the development of the understanding and the memory, and thoroughness is a great aid thereto.

(*b*). *Qualifications of the Teacher.*

Even temper and calmness, which do not permit of sudden anger, patience so that the teacher enters into the environment of the child and thinks with him,—these are the chief qualifications of the teacher. So Hillel said, "A hot-tempered man cannot be a teacher."

The Talmud says that "No child can ask too many questions from his teacher; he must repeat again and again so that he shall thoroughly understand what has been taught."

As additional qualifications, truth and exactness were demanded from the teacher. So highly impressed were the Talmudists with the sacredness of the teacher's work—for it is none other than humanizing the world—that school instruction was styled "God's work," so that according to Maimonides a careless teacher received the following severe criticism : " The teacher who permits his pupils to remain idle, or engage in other work during school time, or is careless about his instruction, belongs to those of whom it is said 'Cursed be those who manage the work of God basely.'"

Piety and culture are finally the indispensable requirements of a teacher.

(*c*). *Respect for the Teacher.*

Owing to the esteem with which instruction was regarded and to the responsibility placed upon the teacher, a deep respect for the teaching profession followed as a matter of course, for the teacher was considered as the expounder of the truth and the founder of human morals and well-being. Among the ancient Hebrews respect for teachers was identical with respect for God and his law. "Respect your teacher as you would God." Irreverence towards teachers was severely punished, and it was said that "Jerusalem was destroyed because the teachers of that city were deposed."

Teachers were even more respected than parents. "The teacher precedes the father ; the wise man, the King." If the father and teacher are both a prisoner, we should first free the teacher, then the father, for the one gives him only the temporary, the other eternal life.

A few examples of reverence, although intended more for advanced student schools, are still characteristic.

The scholar must not express his opinion in religious or ceremonial subjects in the presence of his teacher.

He must not walk at the right of his teacher.

He must not call his teacher by name.

He must not sit in his chair, nor pray before him nor behind his back, he must not go to bathe with him, he must not contradict him in his presence, etc.

All services that a servant must do for his master must a scholar do for his teacher except to take off and put on his shoes, etc.

When a scholar leaves his teacher's presence, he must not turn his face from him but gradually turn from him.

C. THE PUPIL.

(a). School-Age.

Recognizing the fact that systematic instruction before the sixth year would injure the bodily development of children and because they wished to foster a sound mind

in a sound body, the wise men of the Talmud fixed upon
the sixth year as the time for going to school. "He who
sends his son to school before his sixth year runs after him
and cannot catch him;" and this is interpreted to mean he
wants to strengthen and maintain him and cannot, because
the boy is doomed to die on account of weakness.

Still children were early taught the elements of religion.
" As soon as the child begins to speak" reads an old precept, "shall the father teach it the confession of God's
unity. 'Hear, O Israel, the Lord our God is one Lord.'"

(b).   *The Psychical Individuality of the Pupil.*

As attention was paid to the pupil's physical development, so too was his psychical individuality cared for.   He
was not rapidly hurried from one subject to another, but
led slowly and according to his ability to comprehend and
grasp it.   The subjects of instruction were adapted to
the age and mental ability of the pupil.   Until the tenth
year Biblical instruction was the chief study, so that at ten
years of age the pupil was thoroughly conversant with the
Bible.   From his tenth year upwards, the Mishna and
Gemara (divisions of the Talmud) were the special topics
of instruction.   With increasing mental power, subjects of
corresponding difficulty were introduced into the school
curriculum.

It is not always the case that as a child grows older his
mental grasp is strengthened, and therefore it is advised
that while at the beginning of instruction, when the mind
is still free, great attention should be paid, because what is
learnt as a child remains in the memory like ink written
on clean paper ; still if the child does not progress, great
forebearance should be exercised with him until his twelfth
year.   From that time he should be severely disciplined
because about the twelfth year the normal child attains
possession of his mental powers.

The ability to comprehend a subject and the love for
study appears in different children at different periods of

81

their lives. Some children readily remember and understand all that the teacher tells them. Some however
understand readily but do not remember. Others again
recollect the illustrations which a teacher uses but do not
understand the subject at all, and some are just the opposite.
These four classes of pupils are thus characterized in the
Mishna. " There are four kinds of scholars ; a sponge, a
funnel, a sieve, a winnow. The sponge absorbs everything, the funnel takes all in at one end and lets it out at
the other, the sieve lets the wine pass through and keeps
the lees, and the winnow removes the coarse meal and
keeps the fine."

These characterizations furnish a key to the manage-
ment of the various subjects of instruction, namely, that
the teacher must use a different method in dealing with
the different categories of pupils. With pupils of the first
and last classes the instruction can be broader and illustrated from collateral subjects, while with the other two
classes it is recommended to stick close to the topic and
to use simplest illustrations. Similar advice is given to
teachers with regard to the varying memory stages of the
pupil. Four qualities make their appearance among
pupils : Some understand readily and forget quickly ; here
the advantage balances the disadvantage. Some grasp
slowly and forget slowly. In this case the disadvantage
balances the advantage. Some grasp quickly and forget
slowly—that is a good quality ; and finally some learn
slowly and forget quickly—that is a bad trait. The teacher
can by various means overcome these difficulties—nor
will he complain about them, for these very weaknesses
compel him to think about ways and means of removing
them.

It was recognized that learning, in a narrow sense,
depends upon the activity of the memory as a preparation
for the other mental powers. Great stress was therefore
laid on the cultivation of the memory and it almost became

axiomatic that "Knowledge is won by aid of recollection, therefore train the memory." The development of the memory was attained in the following ways.

1. By practice, which was constant and gradual.
2. By discipline.
3. By thorough preparation of the subject.

(c). *Behavior of the Pupil.*

As Socrates did not accept as his pupil every one who applied to him but like his predecessor Pythagoras was affected by the outward appearance and demeanor of the scholar, so too did the Talmudic teachers in their high schools. Rabbi Gamaliel said, "every scholar whose deportment does not correspond to his inner aspirations should not attend the house of instruction." The same idea prevailed in elementary schools. As soon as a child proved himself incorrigible and liable to exert a baneful influence on his fellow pupils he was removed. "He who permits an unworthy pupil to remain in the school must be responsible for the evil consequences."

(d). *Honor of the Pupil.*

"Think as much of your pupil's honor as of your own ;" so reads a direction of the Talmud to teachers and educators in regard to the fostering of the feeling of honor in the child. This precept is of great pedagogic value, because if it is followed the foundation of a lofty feeling of honor will be early laid in the child. In every child there is feeling of self respect which is his dearest possession. This feeling evidences itself in many ways in the school room—perhaps as a keen appetite for study and a desire to be the head of the class, or in an endeavor to be the most modest and industrious pupil.

The cultivation of this feeling, then, becomes one of the most important duties of the teacher, and he was warned against hurting, particularly in any public way, the feelings of his pupil.

D. SUBJECTS OF INSTRUCTION.

(*a*). *National Literature.*

The subjects of instruction may be generally classed under the head, national literature, which includes the religious writings—the Bible and the Talmud. These subjects were so arranged that their study, as we shall see, covered nearly all known sciences.

The course of study was divided into three parts, 1st, Mikra (reading) ; 2nd, Mishna (repetition of the law) ; 3d, Gemara, (completion). The primary classes studied Mikra, and, according to Maimonides, the school session lasted all day. This may appear strange to us. It is probable that games were interspersed in the hours of instruction, and from time to time the teacher varied the exercises by relating parables or legends from the Talmud. (Hagada.)

The second division studied Mishna. Here the pupils ranged from 10 to 15 years. The teacher explained the oral law, or laws interpreting or explaining the Mosaic law, and which was put in form by Rabbi Judahin in the third century. Most of the instruction was oral.

The students from 15 to 18 years of age studied the Gemara. The oral laws form the subject of discussion and the students criticize the interpretations freely yet respectfully, and contrast two *Halachoth* (Rules). The teacher's duty is to refute the students' objections.

The various discussions embrace in their course natural history, anatomy, medicine, geometry and astronomy, all of which sciences were considered however only as the periphery of the true science, which was the law.

As soon as the child was able to read, the teacher began instruction in the Bible, and certain particular passages were preferred. The portions chosen for the beginning were either the 3d Book of Moses—containing the law for the priests, or the directions as to sacrifices. "Why," asked the wise men "should the first instruction in the Bible to children begin with the laws about sacrifices?" "Because little children are innocent and pure, and sacrifices are symbols of purity."

In the higher schools instruction was given in Talmudic subjects. The Gemara was only taught in the most advanced schools.

(b). *Foreign Languages.*

There are many facts to prove that in Talmudic times the Jews were well acquainted with foreign tongues; thus we find the query as to whether law could be read in distant lands in the language of the country.

Great value was attached to the study of languages as is shown by these remarkable words: "Holy Scripture says that God not only created heaven and earth but also language—because language creates a new world, the world of thought." All languages, even those of Israel's oppressors, were considered of great importance. Of all tongues, the Greek language was the favorite foreign speech of the Jews. "The law may be translated only into the Greek tongue because only that language can fully interpret it."

The Jews were always lovers of the beautiful and noble and the richness and pleasant sound of Greek particularly attracted them. Greek was considered the proper language for poetry. "Four languages," it is said, "which were spoken in and about Palestine possess each distinct attributes. Greek sounds sweet on account of its rhythm in song; Latin, on account of its sonorousness in battle; Syriac, by reason of its numerous voices in songs of lamentation and Hebrew on account of its distinctness in speaking." Instruction in Greek was general. This love for the Greek tongue remained for centuries among the

Jews. The President of the Academy in Nahardea was skilled both in Hebrew and Greek lore. In Spain, in Saragossa and Barcelona, Greek was earnestly studied, so much so that in the year 1304 the Jews of Spain felt obliged to forbid the learning of Greek before the 25th year. Although the Jews showed such a decided preference for Greek culture, still it did not prevent them from taking an interest in the languages and sciences suited to their time.

As in Palestine during the period of the second temple, the Hebrew tongue was gradually replaced by a Syriac idiom spoken by the neighboring peoples; as in Alexandria the Jews spoke and wrote Greek, so at the time of the destruction of the second temple the Jews appear as Latin poets and critics. Unprejudiced and willing, they went about their work, encouraged by their words. "Every word that proceeds from God's mouth is divided into seventy parts—i.e., into all the languages of the world;" meaning that no matter in what tongue an idea was expressed, it became a power for good, provided it was true and liberal.

(c). *Astronomy, Mathematics and Natural Sciences.*

The life of the old Hebrew was dedicated to the pursuit of religion; so the study of these sciences was not merely for intellectual purposes, nor for information that might lead to man's advantage or give him a loftier idea of the glory of God, but solely as an aid and help to religion. They were used as means for a deeper study of the law which formed to them the center of a circle as the sciences formed the periphery.

Many passages from the Talmud prove that these sciences were studied at this period. Rabbi Gamliel had in his study, charts and pictures of the moon. Samuel, a noted Rabbi, said he was as much at home in the streets of the heavens as he was in the streets of Nahardea.

Many of the Tractates of the Talmud show an extensive acquaintance with geometry. In another tractate a long list of plants and animals can be found. Still another furnishes information concerning animal anatomy.

It is doubtful whether these subjects were regularly taught in the elementary schools, but it is certain that the pupils of maturer age advanced far beyond the mere elements of these sciences.

(d). *Gymnastics.*

Gymnastics seems to have formed a part of divine worship in Mosaic times. It appears from the Bible that in David's days games with weapons and other forms of athletic skill were general. In Talmudic times the development of the body was advocated, partly as a personal benefit, partly also on religious grounds. This is shown by the command: "Every father must have his child taught to swim."

In the time of Antiochus Epiphanes, Greek gymnastics were introduced into Palestine, and the Hellenic party built a gymnasium in Jerusalem. At the time of the Roman rule in Judea, there were Roman circuses in many towns of Palestine, against visiting which Rabbi Meir warned the Jews, as destined to lead them to worship Roman gods.

But both intellectual and physical culture were considered only as accessories in Hebrew education, that which formed the principles of their teaching was morality and religion. So it was that, quite different from the old Spartans, physical deformity was not considered a crime in Hebrew eyes; and never were they guilty of that exposing of children which forms such a blot on the record of so many nations of antiquity. That, however, which they did regard with horror, and which they punished severely, was moral deformity, which might prevent the child from becoming an honest and moral man.

E. METHOD.

(a). *The Outward Bearing of the Teacher.*

In order to arouse the scholar's interest in his studies
the Talmud deemed it necessary that between pupil and
teacher feelings of mutual regard should exist. This
should be brought about by the teacher encouraging the
youthful tendency to cheerfulness, without however degen-
erating into frivolity. A distinguished teacher, relates the
Talmud, awakened the interest of his pupils by beginning
his lectures with a humorous anecdote, and then proceeded
to the subject in hand, to which the scholars gave most
earnest attention.

This cheerful earnestness should mark all intercourse
between pupil and teacher. It is highly important that
the teacher should listen patiently to the many questions
of the learner so that he may ward off that sense of false
shame which hinders so many children in their pursuit of
knowledge.

(b). *Knowing and Understanding.*

In the earliest stages of education, the Talmudists
advised that children first be furnished with subject matter
before they are ready for reflecting thereupon. "First learn
and then apprehend." For this reason it was forbidden to
give the children opportunity for unnecessary investigation
of things. "Take your children away from unnecessary
reflection."

Even for adults this rule held good, and therefore the
endeavor of all was for knowing to precede apprehension.

(c). *Memory Exercise.*

While it is advised that in the beginning acquaintance
with the subject matter should be the main point aimed at,
still it was not meant that the instruction should be

mechanical. On the contrary means were given to the teacher by which he should stimulate the thinking faculty and awaken the power of observation. Teachers were recommended to ask odd and queer questions in order to startle and then to concentrate the attention on the very opposite.

(*d*). *Form of Imparting Instruction.*

The subjects of instruction were divided into portions which had to be studied in a definite period. These periods were five years each and these were again subdivided into yearly periods, in order to render it possible for the pupils to grasp the entire subject. The existence of this plan shows that a *successive* method was employed. Instruction in the Bible and the Talmud did not go hand in hand, but the one followed the other; this being the principle, "If you lay hold of too much at once you get hold of nothing."

In order to aid the pupil's understanding, the teacher should not give too much matter at once, but give a little at a time and allow a period of rest. "God himself did not give Moses the Law all at once, but revealed it to him in several periods. How much more should this be done in human instruction."

Brevity is particularly recommended. The teacher should be sparing of his words, and express himself in the concisest manner possible. Learned digressions from the subject should be avoided and scholars should not be told in three words what could be said in one. "Always teach your pupils in the shortest possible manner."

(*e*). *Thoroughness in Instruction.*

The choice of the shortest method of instruction aids thoroughness, since too much can more readily injure than too little.

As means towards *thoroughness* the Talmud advises (1) careful and correct grounding, and (2) *practice* and *repetition*. Rabbi Akiba said, "The teacher must not only make the lesson clear to his pupils by means of illustrations and explanations, but must be untiring until they thoroughly grasp the contents of what he has taught." One Rabbi repeated a certain matter four hundred times to one of his scholars before he fully comprehended it.

Such methods were used (1) to prevent superficiality in learning, (2) to impress the knowledge acquired upon the memory, (3) to promote the acquisition of further knowledge.

The latter two points were stimulated by *viva voce* repetition of the pupil, and a system of mnemonics. (*a*) Vocal repetition of the learner fixes the matter in the memory. "Open your eyes" says the Talmud " so that you may keep your knowledge, and that it may be alive in you." (*b*) The old Greeks treasured and practiced an art of memory which was based on the law of association. The Jews, too, valued the system of mnemonics as a valuable help to memory. They used certain "catchwords" having sounds or letters which would remind them of the contents of the paragraph, or they used well known quotations from the Bible or Proverbs, or names of well known persons or places.

(*f*). *Other Methods.*

In order to sharpen the child's intellect it was considered advisable to change the school it attended in order that it might get the benefit of a new method or of greater ability in teaching. "Children should be taken from one school to another so that they may learn from the teachers who perhaps may have greater ability to give instruction." "He who learns constantly from the same teacher and gets only his opinion of the law, sees no sign

of the blessing." "A scholar who finds difficulty in learning should visit several schools."

Older pupils were advised to study in groups without
reference to the fact whether both were equally studious.
As a little piece of wood can light a large piece, so the
young and less capable pupils stimulate the large and
more developed ones. Iron sharpens iron, i.e., as one
piece of iron sharpens another so one scholar does the
other.

Disputation in debate is a most valuable aid to thoroughness, therefore the Talmud declares "Knowledge becomes
the property of the student by disputation, and elaborating
the phrase" *docendo discimus*, Rabbi Chanina said "I have
learnt much from my teacher, more from my fellow students, most of all from my scholars."

(g). *Connection between Instruction and Life.*

While the Jews believed in education for education's
sake, still they regarded the theoretical side of instruction
but as a preparation for practical life. The saying "Not
learning but doing is the principal thing," is proof that
the school was not the end in itself, but only a means and
a preparation for life and thus they evinced in their way
their belief in the principle, "Non scholae sed vitae
discimus."

The practice of the Law is more important than the
study. He who knows the theory but never practices is
an *am haarez* (ignoramus). Practice was acquired in
association with learned men or teachers. This was
considered very valuable, since the ordinary conversation
of wise men is profitable.

Without regard to social position in life, the Talmud
ordered that, besides study, a handicraft should be learned.
"As it is your duty to teach your son the law teach him
a trade." "Disobedience to this ordinance exposes one to

91

just contempt, for thereby the social condition of all was endangered." "He who does not have his son taught a trade prepares him to be a robber." "He who applies himself to study alone, is like him who has no God."

For the before-mentioned reasons and because one-sidedness in education was undesirable and partly for hygienic reasons, the greatest teachers of the Talmudic period were also workmen, who, while pulling the thread through the sole of the shoe or rolling their barrels to the market place, were meditating upon serious philosophical questions.

(h). *Influence of Instruction on Piety and Morality.*

The old Jews did not aim at intellectual progress only, but their principal endeavor was to develop the moral and spiritual side of man. Their endeavors were directed therefore not alone toward knowledge, but also toward love and reverence of God, and the development of the moral feeling and will. To think honestly and to act honestly must be the result of the study of the law. Abaji taught, it is said, "Thou shalt love the Eternal, thy God;" that means that, through you, God's name shall become beloved and glorified.

Thou shalt learn and mix with wise men, but all thy acts must be honest and thy words gentle, so that the people will say "Hail! to him, because he has studied the law; hail! his father, who permitted him to study; hail! his teacher, who taught him; woe to those who have learnt nothing! Look at him who has studied, how pleasant are his ways and how gracious his deeds!" But if you have studied and mixed with the wise, and your conduct toward your fellow men is not seemly, then will the people say, "Woe to him who has studied! woe to his father who had him instructed! woe to his teacher who has taught him! Look at him who has studied the law how corrupt are his acts and how hateful are his ways!"

The child must learn as early as possible to avoid pride and honestly to direct his better mind to study ; to show respect for his teacher, his superior, respect for all from whom he receives instruction, and above all respect for the elders, to imitate whom he must constantly strive.

"Only he possesses true knowledge who does not display it." "The law is not in heaven, where you must ascend, or on the other side of the sea," i.e., you will find it neither with him who in the extent of his thoughts resembles the ocean; nor will you find it among the proud or around merchants or pedlars; "Why," it is said in another place, "does the Book of the Law resemble water? For it is said 'Come ye that are thirsty, drink!'" Because the law, like the water which leaves its high position and chooses a lower spot for its slopping, has its seat among the humble in spirit. Another Rabbi asked, "Why does the scripture resemble water, wine and milk?" Because as these three drinks are kept in ordinary vessels, so are also the words of the law only in meek men."

The following story illustrates the point. The daughter of a Roman Emperor once asked Rabbi Joshua ben Chan-aujah, how it was that so gifted a man as he was so ugly. Without replying to her question he asked her, "In what kind of vessels are your father's finest wine kept?" "In earthen ones" she replies. "I am surprised at that" he said. "Wine for the royal table should be kept in gold-en vessels." And she told her father the Rabbi's opinion, and he had gold and silver vessels made for the purpose. But the wine turned sour. When the Emperor asked Rabbi Joshua his advice on this subject, he said his words were only a reply to his daughter's question.

SCHOOL REGULATIONS.
(a). *Classes.*

The perfection of school organization is attained when the scholars are arranged according to their mental stature and where each class is provided with proper instruction. In the Talmudic schools there were such divisions. The Beth Hamidrash or house of study was divided, as we have before said, into three great departments, each of which covered a course of five years, and each course was sub-divided in smaller courses, graded into lower and higher degrees. It was not possible for the same teacher to give instruction to a beginner and one who had already attended school for some time. In many of the classes there were monitors, generally the best scholar. He received his instruction with the rest of his classmates and then imparted his knowledge to the weaker pupils. The teacher was thus not hindered by the weaker pupils and they enjoyed the benefit of extra instruction. The pupils were accustomed to be seated, according to their rank, and the desire to be head of the class was certainly a great stimulus. In many of the classes too, instruction was given by a teacher who had a special knowledge either of the Bible or the Mishna or the Gemara.

(b). *Number of Scholars in a Class.*

How many children can a teacher, with advantage, instruct ? In our day when classes often contain more than sixty children, the teacher's duty seems to consist in getting " around the class once." The Talmud says " For one teacher there should be twenty-five scholars ; If there are fifty, there should be two teachers. If there are forty an assistant teacher should be appointed, and these teachers should be paid by the city." It may have been that these rules were adopted for sanitary reasons, for in a crowded room the vitiated atmosphere affects the physical condition of the children. Or perhaps too many children in a class make it difficult for the teacher to properly per-form his functions. The maximum of scholars for one teacher was fixed at twenty-five, for double that number there were two parallel classes each with a regular teacher. If the number of scholars was not sufficient however for the employment of an extra teacher the brighter scholars were called in to help. Both Bell and Lancaster adopted this monitorial system, although in Talmudic days it was not abused.

(*c*). *School Sessions.*

Punctuality in coming and going, in beginning and ending, is of great advantage in instruction. A fixed time for opening and closing the school. Instruction was commenced very early in the morning. According to Maimonides, the school period continued without interruption, and instruction was given every day in the week and all day long with the exception of a recess mid-day. The only holidays were the sabbaths and festivals. The interruption of school instruction was strictly prohibited. Nothing was important enough to supplant it. The Talmud says " The instruction of children may not be interrupted even on account of the building of the Temple." It may seem in our time impossible or unwise to continue the school session the whole year, but there is a tendency even in our time to use the vacations to the pupil's advantage by the study of nature, and by kindred means.

(*d*). *School Rules.*

The following are some of the Talmudic school rules :

a. Punctuality and regularity in attendance at school.

b. Pupils to be arranged according to their class standing.

c. No pupil was permitted to leave his seat without permission.

d. The scholar was not permitted to question the teacher immediately upon his entrance into the school room.

95

e. Questions not pertaining to the subject matter of instruction must not be asked.

f. Two scholars were not permitted to ask questions at the same time.

(*e*). *School Punishments and Rewards.*

The old Hebrews appealed in these respects more to the feeling than to the reason. He who gives instruction either to large or small pupils should not compel them to study by threats, or chastisement. The teacher should rather win the heart of the pupil, without however becoming too familiar with him. There should always exist on the part of the scholars a degree of reverence for the teacher. This advice is given to teachers, "Occasionally be very strict, without however being harsh." The Talmud says "Push away with your left hand, but bring back again with your right ; and do not do like the prophet Elisha, who pushed away his servant Gehazi with both hands and made him an apostate from his people." And again, "Pupils should be punished with one hand and caressed with two." This mild discipline was always effective when it appealed to the sense of honor of the pupil. In the case of small children, where the feeling is not yet developed, the Talmud recommends light corporal punishment and a deprivation of food. The grown up pupil however must not be punished corporally. In administering punishment the individuality of children should be considered. It thus can happen that two children guilty of the same offence would be punished in different ways ; or even one child should receive punishment and the other be sufficiently punished by the dread of it. If bodily punishment was given it was very light. The teacher was not permitted to hit with a stick for it might easily wound, but used a shoe-string instead. As punishment is a part of school discipline, so also is reward. It is said that one distinguished

Rabbi had in his elementary school, honey which he gave
as a reward to the children.   In the reward and the treatment of children there was one main rule of discipline and
that was the equality of all children before the teacher.
Therefore the Talmud disapproves of the conduct of Jacob
in preferring Joseph to his brothers, and regards that as one
of the reasons for the bondage in Egypt.

(f). School Dues.

The old Hebrews believed in the principle enunciated
by Socrates, that education and instruction were ends in
themselves.   They believed that the study and instruction
of the Law should be pursued without any other material
object.   Therefore there was a prohibition against taking
any fixed sum in payment for the services as a teacher.
"Do not make instruction a crown, to exalt yourself there-
with, nor a spade, with which to dig;" meaning thereby, do
not use your knowledge as a means of self-glorification, or
as a means of livelihood.   The care of the teachers was
however provided for in general either by gifts or special
aid.   The Talmud says.   "He who makes a present to a
learned man does as good a deed as though he brought
a first offering to the altar."

Maimonides in one of his commentaries writes: "We do
not find anywhere that our wise men strove for earthly
possessions.   They did not collect money for the schools,
for the judges and teachers.   But we find among them at
all times both the poorest and the richest."   Most of these
teachers, even if they were poor, could have had all the
money they needed for the asking, but they preferred to
support themselves by hard manual work.

The teachers of the very young children did receive
pay for caring for them, and the pay of these teachers
came from the general tax fund of the community.   The
schools were open to rich and poor alike, with the differ-

ence that the wealthier members of the community paid a special school tax while the poor, who were exempt from payment of all taxes, formed a class of free scholars.

IV. EDUCATION OF GIRLS.

Little is said in the Talmud about regularly organized schools for girls.

The instruction they received, was mainly what may be termed private instruction and consisted in the study of the Bible. That they must have been educated appears from the wisdom with which the Jewish mothers exercised their functions. The Talmud says the parents must aid their children in their studies, that is, the father and mother. The mothers often explained the lessons that the teacher could not make their pupils understand, so that though there were no schools their education was far from neglected. The education of girls was directed rather to the training of their feelings rather than the development of their understanding. Girls were not to become learned but rather intelligent mothers. The Talmud asks, "Where will you find true religion?" and answers by saying, "In a family where there is a good mother." In place of scientific training, the domestic virtues were cultivated. Household economy, dancing, music, and Greek (the polite language of ancient days), were the chief subjects of the education and curriculum of girls.

There were also many learned women in those times. Veruria wife of Rabbi Meir, was famous for her learning. In the 12th century a Jewess delivered lectures on the Talmud, and the daughter of Rabbi Meir wrote several scientific treatises.

V. MANUAL TRAINING.

While the Rabbis had differing views as to the influence

of foreign culture, or as to the extent to which the education of women should be carried, in one respect they were unanimous, namely, in their respect for labor. It was axiomatic in their teaching that every boy should learn a trade. It must certainly seem strange to the reader of history to find in our nineteenth century a race that has honored labor as no other race has, accused of despising manual work, and as being desirous of living on the producers, rather than producing. Nearly all the great teachers of the Talmudic times were workmen. Hillel earned money enough to attend the Academy by wood-cutting. Rabbi Joshua was a blacksmith, others were tanners, carpenters, millers. They practiced what they taught and their teachings are finding appreciation at a time when manual training is coming to the front. "Labor was truly worship with them." Here are a few of the Talmudic sayings about work.

"Great is labor ! it confers honor upon man, elevates the man who works, and brings support to the family."

"Choose any work and say not; 'I am a great man, a priest.'"

"The father who does not teach his children a trade, virtually brings him up to be a robber."

"The study of the law without occupation of labor will finally be interrupted and end in sin."

Work and study formed the principles of the educational system of the Talmudists. Study for the noblest purposes and not for money—work because it is man's duty. By this union was formed that intellectual force which we have said is a marked Hebrew characteristic.

There were no "middle ages" in Jewish history. While intellectual darkness prevailed in Christian lands, Hebrew Academies and schools for higher learning flourished in Toledo, Cordova, Narbonne, Padua and Rome.

The great Universities of France and Italy owe their existence to the Jewish doctors and philosophers who "contributed those elements of natural science and Greek philosophy which have increased in strength and volume in our modern academic life."

The school is in modern days still dear to the Hebrew. Párents feel it a sacred duty to have their children well educated and Jewish pupils are among the brightest in the schools and colleges of the world. In works of philanthropy and charity, the Hebrews are ever foremost and no movement of the advance guard "of educational workers finds more supporters than among that race truly styled the people of the Book."

Section Two—

THE RABBI

The Sage is More Important
Than the Prophet

ABRAHAM I. KOOK

Translated by BEN ZION BOKSER

AS A RULE, POETS KNOW HOW TO PORTRAY THE nobler side of life, its beauty, its dynamism and vitality. They also know how to describe the evils of life and to protest against them vigorously. But it is outside the competence of the imaginative faculty to probe the particular conditions which preserve life and safeguard it from any of the problems that are due to generate the most destructive consequences. This falls within the competence of a body of knowledge that deals with particulars. Here begins the work of physicians, economists, engineers, judges and all those who pursue practical wisdom.

This distinction has even wider application. Prophecy saw the great evil of idolatry in ancient Israel, and protested against it with all its might; it envisioned the majesty and delight associated with the belief in one God, and portrayed it in all its radiance. It saw corruption in moral depravity, in the oppression of the poor, in murder, adultery, and robbery, and it was infused with the spirit of God to offer help and to rectify these conditions through lofty and holy exhortations.

But the little lapses which forge the gross body of sin—these remained hidden from the eye of every prophet and seer. Similarly, it was not within the sphere of prophecy to grasp how the habitual performance and the study of commandments would, after a span of time, release their hidden inner graces, and a wholly divine influence would decisively vanquish the darkness of idolatry. Nor could it grasp how slow negligence, which disparages the performance of the commandments, with their inferences and elaborations, would start a process of erosion, destroying the vessels in which is stored the exalted spirit that causes human passions, the straying imagination which abounds in beautiful shoots outside, though in poisonous elements within, to become ever more ascendent, automatically.

It is true that this perception was granted to the prophecy of Moses, about which God is quoted as saying that He revealed it to him "from mouth to mouth" (Numbers 12:8), the prophecy of undimmed clarity that discerned simultaneously the claims of general principles as well as of the exacting demands of the particulars. But there never arose another like Moses, as we are told, "There never arose another prophet like Moses whom the Lord knew face to face" (Deut. 34:11). It was,

BEN ZION BOKSER *is the Rabbi of Forest Hills Jewish Center.*

necessary, therefore, to assign the enunciation of general principles to the prophets and of the particulars to the sages; and, as the Talmud declares, "the sage is more important than the prophet" (*Baba Batra*, 12a). And what prophecy, with its impassioned and fiery exhortations could not accomplish in purging the Jewish people of idolatry and in uprooting the basic causes of the most degrading forms of oppression and violence, —of murder, sexual perversity, and bribery,—was accomplished by the sages through the expanded development of the Torah, by raising many disciples and by the assiduous study of the particular laws and their derivative applications. " 'The eternal paths lead to Him' (Habakkuk, 3:6)—the term for 'paths,' *halikhot* may also be read as *halakhot*, and the text would then mean that the laws lead to Him" (*Niddah* 73a).

In the course of time, the concern with the work of the sages predominated over the work of the prophets and the institution of prophecy ceased altogether; after some time the general principles declined, they were immanent in the particulars but were not readily apparent. At the end of the present epoch, when the light of prophecy will begin to have its revival, as we are promised, "I shall pour out My spirit on all flesh" (Joel 3:1), there will develop, in reaction, a pronounced disdain for the particulars. This is alluded to in the Talmudic statement that, at the dawn of the messianic age, "the wisdom of the sages will become unsavory and those who live on the boundary (that is, the sages who define limits in the law) will turn from city to city without finding grace (*Sotah* 49b).

This will continue until the radiance of prophecy will re-emerge from its hiding and reveal itself, not as an unripe fruit, but as the first fruits full of vitality and life, and prophecy itself will acknowledge the great efficacy in the work of the sages, and in righteous humility exclaim: "The sage is more important than the prophet." This transcending of one-sidedness will vindicate the vision of unity expressed by the Psalmist: "Mercy and truth have met, justice and peace have kissed, truth will rise out of the earth and mercy will show itself from heaven: the Lord will also bestow what is good and our earth will bring forth its bounty" (Psalms 85:11). The spirit of Moses will then reappear in the world.

The Wise Man in Rabbinic Judaism and Stoic Philosophy

NATHANIEL L. GERBER

This paper seeks to compare the ideal of the wise man in Stoic philosophy as portrayed in the works of Epictetus, Seneca, and Marcus Aurelius, and the Rabbinic Jewish tradition as seen in פרקי אבות, and in the commentary אבות דרבי נתן. In both traditions, the wise man served as a bastion of strength from which the uninstructed might draw an example of virtue and wisdom. But a fundamental difference existed between these two philosophies and their respective conceptions of the ideal of the scholar, and this difference forms the underlying theme of my paper. Whereas Stocisim was individualistic and pessimistic with regard to the capacity of the wise man to effect change, Rabbinic Judaism was collectivist and optimistic; Rabbinic Judaism used as a criterion for the sage, not only his personal scholarship, but also, and perhaps more important, his enthusiasm and success in imparting the fruits of his study to his less knowledgeable followers. Whereas Rabbinic Judaism extolled the role of the wise man as the savior of society, the Stoic sage appeared as the last line of defense against the preponderant sense of purposelessness with which society had been pervaded.

40

Rabbinic philosophy as seen in פרקי אבות and אכות דרבי נתן was a post-Second Commonwealth phenomenon. With the destruction of the Temple, the house of learning became the focal point of the Pharisaic community, both in Palestine as well as in the Diaspora. The scribe, whose archetype was Ezra, replaced the cultic priest as the spiritual leader of the people. The study of Torah became the new means of achieving communion with God, through acquiring an understanding and appreciation of His Will. Thus it is said:

> But the study of Torah is more beloved by God than burnt offerings. For if a man studies Torah, he comes to know the will of God, as it is said, 'Then shalt thou understand the fear of the Lord and find the will of God.' Hence when a sage sits and expounds to the Congregation, Scripture accounts it to him, as though he had offered up fat and blood on the altar.[1]

For the Jew, the study of law became the source of his prescribed way of life, the only means of achieving continuity with the past of his people and assuring his just reward in the world to come. "Great is the Law, for it gives life to them that practice it both in this world and in the world to come."[2]

One striking characteristic of the post-Commonwealth Rabbinic society was its concern for security and permanence. The people turned to the never-ending *halakhic* discussion as a source of permanence and a link with the past, for the Law, unlike the Temple, was independent of locale and could be observed under any physical conditions. Because the sage was the symbol of perfection in knowledge of the Law, he became its representative; it was to him that the people turned with the hope that he might assure them continuity with the past and security for the future. As such, his central role in Rabbinic society was guaranteed.

Whereas Rabbinic teachings assured the spiritual survival of the Jewish people following the physical destruction of the Temple,

---

1 Judah Goldin, *The Fathers According to Rabbi Nathan* (New Haven: Yale University Press, 1955), p. 32.
2 *Ibid.*, p. 250. פרקי אבות VI:7.

Stoic philosophy, to a great extent, reacted to the seemingly unproductive opulence of the Roman aristocracy and its utter devotion to pleasure. "Mankind seemed to be driven hither and thither in a sea of contrary desires; one impulse overrode and frustrated another... blind Desire was the propelling force, and action was spasmodic, furious, vain—a misery of craving forever disappointed and forever renewed."[3] As a reaction to this confusion and frustration, Stoicism attempted to provide a desperately needed reevaluation of the ends of human life, a wisdom which could guarantee meaning to the life of the individual, despite the rapid crumbling of the traditional values of Greek civilization. Ultimately, the Stoics produced a depressing philosophy, for they could neither overcome nor circumscribe their belief in the purposelessness of human existence and the consequent futility of personal involvement in social reformation. They attempted to establish a moral author of the Universe, but the undeniable existence of evil precluded such a finding, and the failure produced a "deepening sense of vanity and distress." Instead of finding a moral force behind their universe, they concluded that the world was an unceasing process, forever changing, but never progressing. Earthly pursuit and human ambition were therefore futile. The sage involved himself in his study with an attitude of pessimistic resignation, in order to escape the growing sense of frustration and find the solace within that he could not find without. Seneca concluded that all dogma is mutable, except the belief in the final destruction of the world.[4] But "If you retire to your studies, you will escape all disgust with life and will not wish night to come on because you are weary of the daylight."[5] And reaching the height of pessimism, Marcus Aurelius, the greatest of the Stoic wise men, focused his whole personal philosophy on a study of death, "...a deliberate quenching of the will to live... by dwelling with remorseless analysis on the sordid details of life and trying to borrow from such consideration disgust for the whole weary business."[6] For Marcus Aurelius, life was purposeless, an endless process culminating only

---

3 Edwyn Bevan, *Stoics and Sceptics* (Oxford: Clarendon Press, 1913), p. 28.
4 F. W. Bussell, *Marcus Aurelius and The Later Stoics* (New York: Charles Schibner's Sons, 1910), pp. 27-28.
5 *Essential Works of Stoicism,* ed. Moses Hadas (New York: Bantam Books, 1965), p. 62.
6 Bussell, p. 242.

in death. "Man is born but to die; he wins self-consciousness only to discover its torture; the use of will only to feel its negative value."[7]

The Rabbis regrouped themselves about the House of Learning which became their new source of spiritual unity. They measured the success and devotion of its wise men by their ability and willingness to involve themselves in the religious development of the uninstructed.

> Rabbi Zadok said: Do not keep aloof from the community;
> do not [as a judge] play the part of a counselor; do not
> make of the Torah a crown wherewith to magnify yourself,
> nor a spade wherewith to dig.[8]

Rabbinic Judaism was a communal religion with a communal rather than individualist morality. As such, the responsibility of its sages, its avant-grade, was a collective one, and included every member of the religious community.

Stoic philosophy, however, represented an attempt to transcend the human condition; the wise man, by partaking of universal Reason, was established as an exemplary ideal, but one detached from active participation in the affairs of the uninstructed. Thus Aurelius identifies his real self with an attenuated spiritual and divine principle which has nothing in common with ordinary human interests.[9] The ideal is not he who works and creates for the sake of great purpose, he who is willing to make great sacrifices for the sake of his community, but he who knows how to free himself from the external world and finds his happiness in himself alone.[10] Stoicism attempted to create a refuge for the sensitive and discouraged personality, and therefore made the overcoming of the world the prerequisite to happiness.

> For nowhere either with more quiet or freedom from
> trouble does a man retire than into his own soul, particu-

---

[7] *Ibid.*

[8] Philip Birnbaum, *Daily Prayer Book* (New York: Hebrew Publishing Co., 1949), p. 506. פרקי אבות IV:7

[9] Bussell, p. 198.

[10] W. Windelband, *A History of Philosophy*, trans. James H. Tufts (New York: Macmillan and Co., 1896), p. 275.

larly when he has within him such thoughts that by looking
into them he is immediately in perfect tranquility...[11]

Implicit in this attempt at transcendence was the emphasis upon
the wise man's need of freedom—freedom from dependence upon
others as well as from his own emotions. The Stoics believed that
man is the cause of his actions in the sense that he is to be made
responsible for them in the form of an ethical judgment pronounced
upon their quality, quite independent of whether their cause was
within or beyond his control.[12] As such, the wise man had to free
himself from any influence, internal or external, which might adversely affect the quality of his deeds. Dependency on others was
equated with slavery. "Whoever then wishes to be free, let him
neither wish for anything nor avoid anything which depends on
others. If he does not observe this rule, he must be a slave."[13] But
more important was the Stoic wise man's freedom from his emotional
self, and from fear of the judgment of others. Since he has no
power over the external world, he must overcome it within himself
by overcoming the emotions and passions inherent in his nature.
The maintenance of control over the emotions is to a great extent
the essence of Stoic wisdom; the wise man must deny them with
the power of his reason.

In doing this, however, the Stoic was cutting himself off from
the fears and desires which subordinated man to the external
world, and was thereby suppressing the ordinary determinates of
his action. By exorcizing from his personality these commonly accepted motives for action, the Stoic was bound to seek other means
of direction, a none too easy task. But whatever the burden, it could
not overcome his conviction that it is only the inner dispositions over
which a man has full control, and that the external world, subjected
to the rule of emotion with all its method and order, has no correspondence to the will and purpose of the wise man. It is only the
inner dispositions over which a man has full control, and therefore
the independent rational will is the only thing which the wise man
can move with absolute security.

---

[11] Hadas, p. 122.
[12] Windelband, p. 193.
[13] Hadas, p. 88.

... the ruling faculty is invincible, when self-collected it is satisfied with itself, if is does nothing which it does not choose to do ... therefore the mind which is free from passions is a citadel, for man has nothing more secure to which he can fly for refuge and for the future be inexpugnable.[14]

This being the case, the goal of the wise man became the achievement of inner direction, the creation of an "inner Ruling Principle" to which the desires and impulses of an emotion-ruled external world have no access.

The problems of emotion, freedom, and will, are also dealt with in פרקי אבות and אבות דרבי נתן. Insofar as actual freedom is concerned, no attempt is made to resolve the contradiction between the principle of determinism and that of free will, the premise being that one does not preclude the other. "Everything is foreseen [by God], yet free will is granted [to man]; the world is ruled with divine goodness, yet all is according to the amount of man's work."[15] God's foreknowledge is undeniable, but it does not predetermine the ethical quality of man's actions, for he has the ability to choose between alternative possibilities of action. The Rabbis, like the Stoics, were held ethically responsible for their actions, regardless of whether they were the ultimate cause of them. Otherwise the whole institution of *Halakha* is valueless as a discipline, for it rests upon the fundamental convictions of *halakhic* scholars that man is responsible for his actions. Responsibility is inseparable from the principle of personal freedom, since the person who is not free cannot be held responsible for his actions. For this reason, the Rabbis concluded unequivocally that regardless how difficult it is for man to be free, freedom lies within his reach.

For both Stoic and Pharisee, freedom was not a state of being, a question of rights or liberty, but a state of mind wherein the individual has transcended the temptation of passion because of an awareness of his potential as a human being created in the image of God. Man was created, not in freedom, but with the potential

14 *Ibid.*, p. 168.
15 Birnbaum, p. 499. פרקי אבות III:19.

of achieving it. And the means of its realization is not merely reason, a non-moral instrument of inquiry. Rather, it is recognition of higher ideals and, more important, the consciousness that these ideals are within the individual's grasp, if he will only choose the right alternatives and detach his will from its bondage to the ideals of his non-spiritual personality.

Stoic and Pharisee here met face to face, for according to both, man can master his emotions. He can integrate them into his total personality if they contribute to his welfare and well-being, and can disown them if they are unworthy. But at the same time, this is an achievement which can be realized only with effort, and is not an automatic consequence of being a man. "The evil impulse is like iron which one holds in a flame. So long as it is in the flame one can make of it any implement he pleases. So too, the evil impulse: its only remedy is in the words of the Torah, for they are like fire."[16]

At this point, however, the Rabbis parted with the Stoics. The Pharisaic sage, unlike his Stoic counterpart, was relatively unconcerned with the influence of passion as the decisive motive for action. Conscious detachment is not considered necessary, for it is a natural result of study and consequent understanding and appreciation of the right reason embodied in the Law. "And the tables [of the Commandments] were the work of God, and the writing was the writing of God graven upon the tables... read not graven [harut] but freedom [herut], for whosoever studies Torah is a free man."[17] Elsewhere, this idea is stated even more explicitly.

He who takes to heart the words of the Torah is relieved of many preoccupations—with hunger, foolish preoccupations, unchasted preoccupations, preoccupations with the evil impulse...and preoccupations with the yolk of flesh and blood. For thus is it written in the Book of Psalms by David, King of Israel: 'The precepts of the Lord are right, rejoicing the heart; the commandment of the Lord is pure enlightening the eye.'[18]

16 Goldin, p. 85.
17 *Ibid.*, p. 20.
18 *Ibid.*, p. 94. תהלים XIX:19.

These preoccupations are the very ones which Epictetus and Aurelius both seek to deprecate and pessimistically meditate about. This idea is not found in פרקי אבות or in אבות דרבי נתן for the very reason that their deprecation is a natural, if unconscious, result of diligent occupation with the study of the Law and submission to its disciplines. The wise man who accepts completely, and with absolute preciseness, the discipline demanded by the law, is nonetheless the freest of men, the least available to the deleterious influences of emotion or external needs, precisely because he is so completely involved in the study of and devoted to the fulfillment of the Law. Thus, freedom, for the Stoics, was attainable only through a conscious and burdensome struggle resulting in total detachment; for the Rabbis, it was the natural concomitant to their wisdom.

If anything molded the differing attitudes and motivations of the Stoic and Pharisaic wise man, it was the character of the wisdom to which each was attached. Rabbinic wisdom is hardly speculative in nature. Rather, it is a practical wisdom which at times looks askance at philosophy and addresses itself instead to the daily and even most insignificant needs of the devout Jew. "The laws of bird offerings and interpretations of the laws of the menstruant—these are the essentials of the Halakha. Calculations of equinoxes and gematria are the deserts of wisdom."[19] Rabbinic Judaism required such practical wisdom because it demanded a very precise discipline from the committed individual.

Stoic wisdom, however, was highly speculative. It consisted in knowing how to distinguish between what is our own and what is not.[20] Though equally concerned with moral ideas, and moral consistency, the Stoics cared little for logical consistency and the limits to speculation which it engendered. This unwillingness to adhere to a logical system reflected the sage's fear that such discipline would restrict his liberty of choice, and was completely in keeping with the utilitarian nature of his wisdom. Stoicism was the philosophy of the "disappointed man of action," the wise man who, having failed to find contentment in meaningful social activity, now sought

---

19 *Ibid.*, p. 114.
20 Bevan, p. 210.

it in abstract or psychological studies. These studies defined the limits of his powers and freedom, justifying his disappointment and his consequent movement toward detachment. Logic, particularly that used in the Rabbinic legal code and philosophy, might have precluded such a subjective conclusion.

For the Rabbis, however, philosophical speculation was of secondary importance. Logical consistency was the objective of their study and the basis of their wisdom. I repeat this point for herein lies the explanation of the optimism and collectivism expressed in פרקי אבות and אבות דרבי נתן, and the disillusionment and fatigue expressed in the works of the Stoics. The Rabbis accepted one text, the Torah, as the ultimate in philosophical speculation. They found within it the answers to the fundamental questions raised by the Stoics, and were thereby secured from the philosophical and religious doubts which plagued them. The Rabbis' wisdom, admittedly in a sense less creative than that of the Stoics, did not consist in reposing questions to which Divine, therefore irredoubtable, answers had already been given. Rather, it was synonymous with their understanding and appreciation of the Torah, the text of the given answers. Their obligation was that of applying the philosophy and basic tenets embodied in the Torah to the more concrete and circumstantial problems of the day. Stoic wisdom was purely subjective, and its sages were therefore free to speculate in any direction and to any extreme that they wished. The Rabbinic obligation, however, was to interpret in accordance with a prescribed text; deviation from these limits was not permitted. In fact, פרקי אבות stresses the crucial importance of proper interpretation, and equates *halakhic* discussion not in accordance with the Torah with purposeful violation of its most fundamental commandments.

> The sword comes upon the world for the delay of justice,
> for the perversion of justice, and because of those that
> teach the Torah not in accordance with the *Halakha*.[21]

For the Pharisaic wise man, it was the very fact that he had a permanent source of guidance, a God-given Torah, that made it incumbent upon him to study. It was the Torah as concrete evidence

---

[21] Goldin, p. 245. אבות דרבי נתן V:8.

of God's existence and omnipotence which made study a religious
obligation. But of even greater significance is the belief that fulfillment of the obligation of study is more than a consequence of
personal responsibility, or a means of securing a place in the world
to come. It is an opportunity given to man by God to enhance his
own merit and thereby fulfill the purpose of his existence.

> The Holy One, blessed is He, was minded to grant merit
> to Israel; therefore hath He multiplied for them the Law
> and commandments, as it is written: 'It pleased the Lord
> for His righteousness sake to magnify the Law and make it
> honorable' (Isaiah XLII:21).[22]

For this reason R. Johanan Ben Zakkai warns his colleagues
that study should not be in fulfillment of selfish motives, but rather
in fulfillment of the responsibilities inherent in being a man and
a Jew.

> If thou hast wrought much in thy study of Torah, take no
> credit for thyself, for to this wast thou created: for men
> were created only on condition that they study Torah.[23]

Thus the Pharisaic wise man, in fulfilling the ideal of his position
and commitment, was fulfilling the purpose of his personal existence,
and perhaps even that of the entire community.

The Stoic wise man had no Torah, no permanent source of
guidance in which he might place personal faith. He could not
escape the doubts rendered so potent by the prevalence of evil in a
world supposedly ruled by an all-powerful and all-just Providence.
Before he could formulate a practical wisdom, he had to fortify his
faith in a Providence in order to find meaning for his existence.
Hellinism had proven insufficient to sustain individual morality and
a prescribed conduct of life. The Stoic, therefore, began with an insistence upon belief in a Providence and attempted to explain away
the existence of evil. This interpretation could be reached only by
admitting that the Stoic deity had no ongoing purpose and was

---

22 *Ibid.*, p. 252. אבות דרבי נתן VI:11.
23 *Ibid.*, p. 74.

incapable of maintaining a correspondence between deed and re-compense.[24] The Stoic, however, absolutely refused to let his belief be disillusioned. Thus Marcus Aurelius vindicates the "Divine goodness" at all cost. "Whatever my experience or discovery in life may be, it shall not interfere with this belief of mine..."[25]

How did the Stoic vindicate his belief and at the same time admit the absence of recompense? By defining evil as a qualtiy of judgment, rather than a characteristic of an object or event, both of which are neutral, he attempted to eliminate the contradiction. If evil is a product of judgment, which is within our control, then we need only circumscribe our judgment and thereby eliminate the challenge to Providence. In themselves things have no character; they are "blind and dumb, colorless and immovable."

> They become evil only when we attach negative judgments to them. Things themselves do not touch the soul, not in the least degree... but the soul turns and moves itself alone, and whatever judgments it may think proper to make, such it makes for itself the things which present themselves to it.[26]

If the only criterion of evil is individual judgment, how then did the individual maintain his morality, or was Stoicism a completely amorphous philosophy to which anyone could subscribe, regardless of his concrete moral beliefs? Here the Stoic sages illustrated outstanding optimism. They believed that the only obstacle to living a moral life was the power of passion to deter the soul from rational decisions. Indeed, the Stoics considered vice to be the control of reason by the passions, for all other things were regarded indifferent in themselves.

> ... as to living the best way, this power is in the soul, if it be indifferent to things which are indifferent. And it will be indifferent, if it looks on each of these things separately and all together, and if it remembers that not one of them

---

24 Bussell, p. 88.
25 Ibid., p. 215.
26 Hadas, p. 138.

produces in us an opinion . . . and it is we ourselves who
who produce the judgments.[27]

It is not until the sage makes judgments upon events that he
becomes dependent upon their value or harm. True, man cannot
hinder fate from preparing for him honor and dishonor, pleasure
and pain, but he can prevent their affliction or blessing from
threatening his inner tranquility.

The Stoic philosophers recognized that conformity, even if it
conflicted with liberty of choice, was still essential to morality. But
rather than insisting on conformity, with its coercive implications,
they identified man's morality with subordination to and harmony
with the Law of Nature. The Law of Nature was identical to both
the nature of man, defined as his reason, as well as the World-
reason, defined as deity. Accordingly, subordination of one's conduct
to the Law of Nature, the essence of moral conduct and the goal of
the wise man, was nothing more than achieving harmony with one's
reason, one's ideal self. Furthermore, because Nature was simultaneously identified with Providence, by submitting to one's reason, the
wise man was at the same time expressing his faith in a deity, and
submitting his will to a higher purpose, even if both deity and
purpose were his own creation.

This recognition of a higher order was a necessary source of
identity which Greek philosophy otherwise sorely lacked, and which
gave "to Stoic doctrine and life, backbone and marrow." Pre-
Socratic philosophy, as seen in the writings of Heraclitus and
Pythagoras, had already identified cosmic order with universal reason.
But the Stoics went further. They believed that the cosmic reason
could be identified with a universal moral reason, and that this
identification could be reflected by the wise man. Furthermore,
because the ability to reflect this identification was based purely on
harmony with one's ideal self, it involved no communal or religious
intermediary or approval. Its attainment was therefore dependent
completely upon the amount of discipline and control over sensuous
impulse which the wise man commanded, regardless of the attitudes

---

[27] *Ibid.*, p. 193.

and opinions advanced by his environment. "Reverence the faculty which produces opinion. On this faculty it entirely depends whether there shall exist in your ruling part any opinion inconsistent with nature and the constitution of the rational animal."[28] Indeed, for the Stoic sage, the mark of moral worth was not expertise, but recognition of the neutrality of all things and acceptance of total personal responsibility for the course and outcome of one's life.

> The condition and characteristic of an uninstructed person is this: He never expects profit nor harm from himself, but from externals. The condition and characteristic of a philosopher is this: He expects all advantage and all harm from himself.[29]

Whereas the Stoic conception of morality was natural and subjective, the Rabbinic conception was revealed and therefore beyond interpretation. Stoic morality established a circular system in that the conception was completely dependent upon the individual mind which was the mediator between the cosmic reason and the human being. Because it was sanctioned by individual experience rather than by a higher authority, it was impregnable to challenges by other individuals who were equally incapable of bringing forth a higher authority to give greater validity to their particular theory of morality. Indeed, this concept of a natural morality served to strengthen the exalted position of the sage in society. Because Nature is synonymous with the sage's reason, as well as Providence, the capacity to achieve a state of independent critical awareness was a sign that the sage possessed within his soul a spark of the divine. As such, the wise man took for himself an unlimited amount of freedom in determining the nature of virtue, for any purely rational decision was by definition the will of Providence. "Look within. Within is the fountain of good, and it will ever bubble up, if you will ever dig."[30]

But this spiritual kinship between the soul and its maker could not be sustained in light of the material law which governed the

---

28 *Ibid.*, p. 120.
29 *Ibid.*, p. 99.
30 *Ibid.*, p. 158.

real world. Any attempt at synthesis of the two realms was destined to failure, for the world was irretrievably two-fold. The moment the practical realm was approached, the harmony disappeared, for the work of the deity, reality, with its abundance of evil, contradicted his postulated perfection. While the philosophy of the Stoic sage pronounced itself to be a reasonable following of Nature and insisted on the possibility of harmony between the spiritual and material realms, it ended in isolating the sage from the latter, hence from his community, and afflicted him with a sense of dualism[31] which could be overcome only by indifference and retreat from an alien world. Thus Epictetus says, "Seek not that the things which happen should happen as you wish; but wish the things which happen to be as they are, and you will have a tranquil flow of life."[32]

Unlike the Stoics, the Rabbis insisted upon a revealed ethic which, notwithstanding the fact that it coincided with the natural morality experienced by man, derived its authority not from the soul through subjective awareness, but from the great community to which God had addressed himself at Sinai. This morality was to be achieved only through perception of the absolute goodness of communal authority, הצדק המחלט, and constant study of and involvement with the Torah. Again, the Torah is not only a source of ideals; it also provides the individual with the particular means of achieving moral conduct.

> If there is no study of the Law, there is no seemly behavior;
> if there is no seemly behavior, there is no study of the
> Law . . . if there is no knowledge, there is no discernment,
> if there is no discernment, there is no knowledge.[33]

The Pharisaic sage was also challenged by the harsh realities of the material world which failed to produce the rewards supposedly accruing to the wise man because of his involvement with Torah. But unlike the Stoics, he was able to resort to a higher authority to explain the realities, without weakening the cause of his revealed morality. In אבות דרבי נתן, the life of the poor man whose poverty

---

[31] Bussell, pp. 31-32.
[32] Hadas, p. 87.
[33] Goldin, p. 239. אבות דרבי נתן II:18.

is a result of his learning is explained by saying that when one studies Torah, his reward is set aside by God.

> When one sits by himself studying Torah, his reward is stored up on high, as it is said, 'Though he sit alone and keep silence, surely he hath laid up [reward] for him.'[34]

This promise is accompanied by a warning that he who forsakes study for the sake of worldly matters will in the end be punished for his distortion of priorities.

> He who makes the words of the Torah primary and worldly matters secondary will be made primary in the world to come; [but he who makes] worldly matters primary and words of the Torah secondary will be made secondary in the world to come.[35]

Unlike the Stoics, for whom retreat from the material world was a prerequisite to living an ethical life, the Pharisaic wise man was warned that full knowledge and appreciation of the Law could best be achieved within the material world, and under the harsh circumstances which it could impose.

> This is the way to get thee knowledge of the Law. Thou shalt eat bread with salt and thou shalt drink water by measure (Ezekiel 4:11) and on the ground shalt thou sleep and shalt live a life of trouble while thou toilest in the Law.[36]

Implicit in this statement is the conviction that understanding of the Torah is best acquired through sacrifice, even through hardship, for then the appreciation of its worth as a timely text, as a body of applicable laws, is most keen. Herein lies another important distinction between Stoic and Rabbinic wisdom. The duty of the Stoic wise man resides in contemplation, not in action; the question of whether acquisition of understanding and the power to contemplate

---

[34] *Ibid.*, p. 51. איכה III:28.
[35] *Ibid.*, p. 118.
[36] *Ibid.*, p. 249. אבות דרבי נתן VI:4.

must be accompanied by resignation is irrelevant. But the obligations of the Pharisaic wise man are not fulfilled with mere contemplation, for their essence is positive fulfillment within the context of daily life.

The conditions of the wise man's acquisition of his wisdom are relevant, and must not allow him to retreat or elevate himself above his community. Indeed, unlike the Stoic sage, who allowed himself to be revered, the Rabbis insisted upon humility as a prerequisite to the proper fulfillment of the role of the wise man. They forever recalled the Biblical description of the ideal of all wise men, "Now the man Moses was very meek, more so than all men upon the face of the earth."[37]

The Stoic wise man manifested a marked awareness of his own centrality within society. These characteristics, however, should not be mistaken for arrogance, for they were in fact the product of a profound anguish and sense of purposelessness. Unlike the Rabbis, the Stoics could not justify the hostility of an alien world to their wisdom and virtue by asserting that their reward was reserved for the future. The world in which he resided was a hostile one, for the Classical Roman spirit was averse to individualism, was stubbornly opposed to the introduction of philosophy and regarded the transcendent promises of the sage as a potential threat to the compact uniting governors and governed.[38] Nevertheless, the Stoics just as stubbornly held to their virtue and to their beliefs, and refused to compromise. Under these circumstances, resignation was inevitable for it was the only humanly possible way the sage could accept his professed inability to alter his destiny. If it was resignation, it was out of a mood of defiance, a refusal to let the world's course destroy the inward calm of the sage, his sole remaining uncontaminated possession. Thus Marcus Aurelius says, "Beneath the bludgeonings of Chance my head is bloody but unbowed."[39]

The anguish of the Stoic sage about his ineffectiveness was reinforced by a bewildering feeling of insignificance, an inability to

---

[37] *Ibid.*, p. 56. במדבר XII:37.
[38] Bussell, pp. 26-27.
[39] *Ibid.*, p. 168.

understand the finite duration of his life an its culmination in death. He attempted to explain death as simply one of the processes of Nature, and as such not to be feared.

> ... what death is, and the fact that if a man looks at it by itself ... he will then consider it to be nothing else than an operation of nature; and if anyone is afraid of nature, he is a child.[40]

If death could be identified as synonymous with an operation of Nature, it could be understood and accepted by the wise reflecting man, whose highest goal was harmony with its laws. Unable to defy it, he can only rise above it, by making the most out of the only part of his life of which he is certain, the present. Thus Seneca says,

> He who fears death will never do anything worthy of a living man; but he who realizes that this was settled for him as soon as he was conceived, will live according to the plan, and also by the same strength of mind will rise above this condition, lest any of these things which happen come upon him unexpectedly.[41]

But despite this valiant attempt to rise above the human condition without resort to belief in an afterlife, the Stoic sage could not cope with his frailty and was overwhelmed with insignificance and uncertainty. Dismayed by a Universe whose forces he could not control or even understand, he concluded that all endeavor is futile, all achievement is ephemeral, and drew back within himself to observe with disillusionment and self-imposed tranquility the ultimately meaningless world-process.

> How quickly all things disappear, in the universe the bodies themselves, but in time the remembrance of them; what is the nature of all sensible things, and particularly those which attract the bait of pleasure or terrify by pain ... how worthless ... and perishable and dead they

---

[40] Hadas, p. 114.
[41] *Ibid.*, p. 72.

are—all this it is the part of the intellectual faculty to observe.[42]

Like the Stoics, the Rabbis recognized the inescapability from death and considered it a great evil, but they made no attempt to reduce the horror by merely stamping it with God's approval. On the contrary, they saw death in all its naked brutality and shamelessness, and believed that in dying, man is defeated in his struggle for success. And yet, their fear did not adversely influence their optimistic approach to life, and did not negate their joy of living. Their faith in the immortality of the soul, the final resurrection of the body, and the collective destiny of the Jewish people was too strong to allow such a negative result.

> All Israel have a share in the world to come, as it is said: 'Your people shall all be righteous; they shall possess the land forever; they are a plant of my own, the work of my hands wherein I may glory'.[43]

The Rabbis were convinced that because the *Masorah* would be continued forever, the individual, by strengthening his commitment to his community, the guarantor of the *Masorah,* could achieve a sense of victory over death and the threat of extinction. They, however, began at the other extreme, by emphasizing the frailty of the individual, as proven by his finite existence.

> Akavyah ben Mahalalel said: Reflect on three things and you will not come into the grip of sin: know whence you came, whither you are going, and before whom you are destined to give a strict account. Whence you came—from a malodorous drop; whither you are going—to a place of dust, worms, and moths; and before whom you are destined to give a strict account—before the supreme King of kings, the Holy One, blessed is He.[44]

The purpose of this emphasis was to convince man that as an

---

42 *Ibid.,* p. 114.
43 Birnbaum, p. 484. פרקי אבות.
44 *Ibid.,* p. 492. פרקי אבות III:1.

independent entity he is weak, and subject to the threat of extinction.
The only way to overcome this loneliness and consequent weakness
was through the revitalization of one's religious commitment. This
strengthening was to be achieved through constant involvement in
the study of the Torah, for only the wisdom thereby acquired could
strengthen man and arm him for death, the final confrontation between
man and God.

> Furthermore, when a man dies, neither silver nor gold,
> nor precious stones, nor pearls accompany him, but Torah
> and good deeds alone, as it is said: 'When you walk, it
> shall guide you; when you lie down, it shall watch over
> you; and when you awake, it shall talk with you
> [Proverbs 6:22].' When you walk, it shall guide you in
> this world; when you lie down, it shall watch over you in
> the grave; and when you awake, it shall talk with you in
> the world to come.[45]

Whereas for the Stoic wise man, resignation and detachment were
the unavoidable concomitants to his wisdom, for the Rabbis, Torah
could be had by anyone who was willing to make the proper
sacrifice. In contrast to Stoic wisdom, which was the possession of
an intellectual aristocracy and was characterized by esotericism, there
was room for everybody in the scholarly class of the Jews. This idea
is expressed in a beautiful recollection of a miracle in אבות דרבי נתן.
"The greatest miracle of all was this; Even if a hundred men bowed
down at one time, the minister of the synagogue did not need to
call out and say: 'Make room for your brethren'."[46] Elsewhere in the
commentary, a dispute is described between the House of Hillel and
the House of Shammai concerning whether it is the responsibility
of the wise man to instruct everyone, or only those who are capable
of rising to great levels of wisdom.

> And raise many disciples . . . Shammai says: One ought to
> teach only him who is talented and meek and of distin-
> guished ancestry and rich . . . Hillel says: One ought to

---

45 *Ibid.*, p. 532. פרקי אבות VI:9.
46 Goldin, p. 146..

teach every man, for there were many sinners in Israel who were drawn to the study of Torah, and from them descended righteous, pious, and worthy folk.[47]

If one recalls that in these disputes Hillel was considered to be more representative of the traditional Rabbinic philosophy, then it seems clear that instruction of the masses, no matter how undeserving and unproductive in a religious or moral sense they may be, is a primary responsibility of the wise man.

Stoicism, on the other hand, having lost faith in a communal religion, substituted an emphasis on individual morality and suggested separation of those who subscribed to it from those who, through ignorance or unwillingness, did not. Unlike the Rabbis, who exuded confidence in their ability to draw men to the Torah, "the way Abraham our father used to bend men to and lead them under the Shekinah", the Stoics feared that active participation in the world process would lead to destruction of the wise man's inner tranquility and would ignite the passion and evil impulses character-istic of the uninstructed.

> We must retire more within ourselves, for intercourse with those of different disposition throws into disorder that which is well arranged, awakens low ignoble passions, and causes that to ulcerate which is still weak in the mind and not yet entirely healed.[48]

Because the condition of the wise man's power of reason, his inner Ruling Principle, was by far his primary concern, his service to the uninstructed man could not involve concern or sympathy. The Stoics knew that once love and pity entered the mind, the sage had admitted something whose influence he could not control, "and might just as well give up the idea of inner tranquility at once".[49]

Thus the key to the difference in the extent of social activity of the Stoic and Rabbinic wise men was their differing sense of com-

---

47 *Ibid.*, p. 26.
48 Hadas, p. 79.
49 Bevan, p. 70.

munal responsibility, but there were other differences as well. The Rabbis had an ambivalent view of man, and rejected a rigid interpretation of human nature. This view, as seen in the words of Hillel, precluded the practicality of a prior screening by the community of the moral potential of its members. Stoicism, however, in the traditional vein of Greek philosophy, feared contradiction, and never operated with diametrically opposed premises. Therefore, it did not adopt a dichotomous approach to man.

But the most important reason for the differing views of collective responsibility revolved about the Stoic and Rabbinic beliefs in the possibility of repentance. The Stoics did not know of this phenomenon, and rejected the possibility of change on the part of the uninstructed masses. Though not a determinist philosophy in the sense of predetermination by God, it believed that for the uninstructed, repentance, as an attempt to impose one's will upon the causal factors within the personality, is futile from the beginning.

The Rabbis, however, maintained an insurmountable faith in the possibility, even inevitability of תשובה. Indeed, righteousness achieved through repentance was more deserving than virtue which did not have to overcome the challenge of evil temptation.

> One hour spent in repentance and good deeds in this world
> is better [more exhilarating] than the whole life of the
> world to come; yet one hour of satisfaction in the world to
> come is better than a whole life of this world.[50]

The source of this optimistic belief lay in the confidence of the Rabbis that exposure to the environment of the Torah would lead to regret for past behavior and eradication of evil impulses, for the study of Torah is a redemptive process purging man. When its spirituality, its holiness, pervades the personality, the individual will feel contrition over his waywardness, and will gather the strength to destroy the evil inclinations within him.

I would like to conclude with a discussion of the differing Stoic and Pharisaic conceptions of work and of good deeds. The Stoics degraded work because they lived in a slave society. Because the

---

[50] Birnbaum, p. 510. פרקי אבות IV:22.

Greek deities had nothing else to do, work being beneath their dignity, they engaged in jealous conspiracies. The Bible, on the other hand, proclaimed the dignity of work at the very beginning. God created the world through work, and on the seventh day He discontinued and rested. In אבות דרבי נתן a balance is established between study of Torah and work. Both Torah and work are described as religious obligations deriving from Sinai.

> Love work: What is that? This teaches that a man should love work, and that no man should hate work. For even as the Torah was given as a covenant, so was work given as a covenant.[51]

In פרקי אבות an even stronger statement is made to the effect that study not combined with worldly occupation is insufficient to occupy the mind and purge it from any evil inclinations.

> Rabban Gamaliel, the son of R. Judah the Patriarch said: Excellent is study of the Law together with worldly occupation, for toil in them both puts sin out of mind. But all study of the Law without [worldly] labor comes to naught at the last and brings sin in its train.[52]

This positive attitude of the Rabbis toward exertion was particularly strong when it involved the performance of good deeds. Good deeds were conceived of as an integral part of the proper life, for its every duty was related to God's commandments. Unlike the Stoics, their ideal was one of action rather than a mere expansion of the understanding. The fulfillment of the obligation to achieve this ideal possessed the same ethical importance as did fulfillment of the obligation to study Torah, for both involved fulfillment of ones responsibilities to God. The individual Jew's obligation to his fellow man was not confined to the sphere of good will, affection, or even love; it was prerequisite to participating in the established relationship with God, which is common and equal to all, and therefore makes the performance of good deeds incumbent upon all, sage and simpleton alike. Rabbinic Judaism, unlike Stoicism could not accept a self-centered faith which demanded only knowledge of one's self and concern only with the salvation of one's own soul.

---

51 Goldin, p. 60. .
52 *Ibid.*, p. 233. אבות דרבי נתן II:2.

On the contrary, there could be no replacement for service to one's fellow man, not even immersion in the study of Torah. A hermitic existence was far from the ideal of the wise man. In fact, אבות דרבי נתן states that study of Torah which does not lead to practical application of the acquired wisdom would cause, instead, the same dualism which afflicted the Stoic sages.

> One in whom there are good works, who has studied much Torah, may be likened to a horse that has a bridle. But one in whom there are no good works, though he has studied much Torah, is like a horse that has no bridle: when one mounts it, it throws him off headlong.[53]

Good deeds are necessary to sustain wisdom, for it is only through its practical utilization that wisdom endures.

The Stoics were the victims of an endless retreat within because of the impracticality of their non-involvement philosophy which could not be adapted to a pragmatic Roman society. The Rabbis developed a wisdom which related to every aspect of life. A wisdom which does not call for the total involvement of the intellect as well as the mechanistic aspects of human existence, is bound to separate these two parts and will not be sufficiently strong to control human activity. For this reason, the Rabbis equated work and wisdom as covenantal obligations and insisted that knowledge be utilitarian and practically applicable. The Rabbinic outlook implies that man is a social being, maintaining his active citizenship in the natural and social commonwealth and performing the work of the world. Any attempt to raise his morality by taking from him his social aim and responsibilities will not positively influence mankind. The Rabbis recognized that the highest goal of man is the development of his moral sense within a social framework, for man is a social being created in the image of God. "He in whom the spirit of mankind finds pleasure, in him the spirit of God finds pleasure; but he in whom the spirit of mankind finds no pleasure, in him the spirit of God finds no pleasure."[54]

---

[53] *Ibid.*, p. 103.
[54] *Ibid.*, p. 238. אבות דרבי נתן III:11.

RABBIS AND COMMUNITY IN THIRD CENTURY BABYLONIA

BY

JACOB NEUSNER
Brown University

I

The Babylonian rabbis played no special role in the life of the synagogue. They exercised no sacerdotal functions. While some of them, notably Rav and Samuel, composed prayers, we have no way of knowing how widely, if at all, rabbinic liturgies were accepted in synagogues during their lifetimes. Many of these, for instance blessings to be said before eating various kinds of food, and the Grace after Meals, probably were initially recited in the school house alone, even there posing some complex difficulties for the students, as we shall see. In any event, the rabbis did not normally recite the services, read from the Torah, bless the people, or assume any other sacerdotal duties which set them apart from, and above, the people in the synagogue. While they quite naturally praised synagogue prayer, they held that *their* studies were more important. R. Ḥisda (late 3rd century), for example, explained (Ps. 87.2), "The Lord loveth the gates of Zion [ẓiyyon]" to mean that the Lord loves the gates distinguished [meẓuyan-im] through law [halakhah] *more* than synagogues and houses of study, and similarly we have the following sayings:

> Abaye said, "At first I used to study in my house and pray in the synagogue. Since I heard the saying of R. Ḥiyya b. 'Ammi in the name of 'Ulla, 'Since the day that the Temple was destroyed, the Holy One, blessed be He, has nothing in his world but the four cubits of the law alone,' I pray only in the place where I study..." Rav Sheshet used to turn his face to another side and study [during the public reading of the Torah], saying, "We with our [business], and they with theirs."
>
> (Bab. Talmud Berakhot 8a)

A contemporary of Rav Sheshet, R. Naḥman, said that he found it too much trouble to gather ten people in his home to permit him to engage in public prayer even there.[1] The rabbis' attitude was based

---

[1] Bab. Talmud, Berakhot 7b.

in part upon the theological presupposition, expressed many times from the first century A.D. onwards, that study of the Torah was the highest religious action, exceeding in sanctity the sacrifice of the Temple priests. Since Temple sacrifice had been replaced for the present age by synagogue worship, it was quite natural for the rabbis to regard their studies, particularly of law, as more important than synagogue prayer.

At the same time, it is quite likely that the rabbis in this period disapproved of aspects of synagogue affairs, but, possessing no power to change things to suit themselves, merely tolerated the status quo. We have a number of stories which indicate rabbinical objection to synagogue practices, not merely concerning which prayers were said at a given time, or whether the Torah was to be blessed before it was read, but more significantly, involving the presence in the synagogue of mosaics and statues. The chief sources are as follows:

> Was there not the synagogue which 'moved and settled' in Nehardea and in it was a statue [*andarta*[1])], and Rav and Samuel and Samuel's father used to go in there to pray...
>
> (Bab. Talmud Rosh Hashanah 24b)

> Rav happened to be in Babylonia on a public fast. The whole congregation fell on their faces, but Rav did not fall on his face. Why did Rav not fall on his face? There was a stone pavement there, and it has been taught, 'Neither shall you place any figured stone in your land to bow down upon it' (Lev. 26.1). Upon it you may *not* bow down in your land, but you may prostrate yourselves on the stones in the Temple. ...If that is the case, why is only Rav mentioned? All the rest should equally have abstained? ...
>
> (Bab. Talmud Megillah 22b[2])

> Rav once came to Babylonia, and noticed that they recited the Hallel on the New Moon festival. At first he thought of stopping them, but when he saw that they omitted parts of it, he remarked, 'It is clear that it is an old ancestral custom with them.'
>
> (Bab. Talmud Ta'anit 28b)

---

[1]) See Bab. Talmud 'Avodah Zarah 40b and Shabbat 72b (Sanhedrin 62b). In the latter discussion, bowing down to an *andarta* (carved image of a man) is not regarded as idolatry if the man did not regard it as a god. In the former, Samuel interprets the Tanna, R. Meir's prohibition of "all images" to include, quite explicitly, a royal statue. In any event, whether the rabbis permitted the placement of such a statue or not, it was clearly *not* they who instigated it, and the tenor of the Talmudic discussions leaves no doubt on that score.

[2]) Note that in the same source, it is reported Rav refrained from following the congregational practice in blessing the Torah. The geonic traditions *ad loc.*, say that later on, the synagogue floor-mosaics were covered up with dirt.

But we do not know what would have happened had Rav attempted to change their liturgy. In any event, it is possible that Rav did not approve of the mosaic, and quite clear that he would not prostrate himself upon it, but did not have the power to remove it. Despite the presence of a statue, Rav, Samuel, and Samuel's father prayed in a famous old synagogue in Nehardea, the town in which Samuel's father and, after him, Samuel himself were the rabbinical authorities. None of the three rabbis apparently had power over the synagogue's affairs. It stands to reason, therefore, that the synagogues in Sura and Nehardea were not subject to rabbinical control. And it was in these very cities that the rabbis lived, taught, and judged.

The situation in Palestine differed not at all. Sukenik long ago pointed out[1] that pictorial representations of animals and human beings occurred with extraordinary frequency in Galilean synagogues and elsewhere:

> A theory was evolved that the synagogues found were the work of sections of Galilean Jewry which took a more liberal view of the matter than the orthodox authorities. It was realized, however, that so widespread a lack of discipline as is indicated by the number of such synagogues was rather extraordinary in Galilee, the centre of Jewish national and religious life in those times.[2]

Sukenik held that there were those who held a more lenient view of Exodus 20:4 and Deuteronomy 5:8; in such a view these verses prohibit the worshipping of images only, and the latitudinarian tendency prevailed in normal times, while in crisis, "particularistic and rigoristic views prevailed." Thus Sukenik held that "pictorial art had its ups and downs... a period of greater laxity being followed by a reaction..."[3] Goodenough argued, however, that while the rabbis of a given period may have *permitted* one or another kind of ornament, the groups that *created* the art could not have been rabbis at all:

> Where are we to find the moving cause in the taking over of images, and with what objective were they taken over?...[4]
> Even if some rabbis tolerated such an image, the implication is that they were far from taking the initiative in introducing anything of this kind.[5]

---

[1] E. L. Sukenik, *Ancient Synagogues in Palestine and Greece*, (London, 1934) being the Schweich Lectures of the British Academy for 1930, 61-67.

[2] *ibid.*, 62.

[3] *ibid.*, 63-4.

[4] *Jewish Symbols in the Greco-Roman Period* (N.Y. 1953) IV, 10.

[5] *ibid.*, 15.

The rabbis did not *prohibit* paintings on walls,[1]) and they did not *hinder* their contemporaries from making designs in mosaic.[2]) They were not however, the people who directed the design of murals for walls and mosaics for floors, as Goodenough said, "the decorations... express a mood and a religious attitude which rabbinic Judaism...at best only grudgingly tolerated, [but] never itself championed or advocated."[3])

The limited evidence cited above, all of which Goodenough knew, should suggest, however, that Babylonia was not so different from Palestine as he conceived.[4]) He thought that the Jews in Babylonia were dominated by the rabbis, and in some ways, as we shall see, they were. But it is quite clear that all the evidence we have, slight though it is, and tentative though is our reading of it, points in one direction: the 3rd century Babylonian rabbis controlled synagogue affairs, including their decoration, no more effectively than did Palestinian rabbis. Goodenough understood Dura to have been a representation of Judaism before the "halakhic reforms" of Rav and his colleagues. Yet these reforms took place well before the second paintings at Dura were completed in 246; Rav died, according to the Ge'onic chronology, in 247.

In fact Goodenough assumed, before he wrote volume XII of *Jewish Symbols*, a thorough-going dichotomy between Hellenistic and rabbinic Judaism. With this assumption in mind, he had to accept available descriptions of Babylonian Judaism as wholly rabbinic in the narrowest sense. Being unable to find a rabbinic center in the Greco-Roman world, he simply assumed it was, as the works he consulted said, on the other side of the Euphrates. His survey of rabbinic views of iconography[5]) should have suggested the contrary, and I think had he lived he may have revised his view of Babylonian Judaism, just as in vol. XII he modified his idea of the relationships between rabbinic and Hellenistic Judaism. He would, I think, have subscribed to the view of Professor Judah Goldin:

> This need not necessarily suggest that the Judaism reflected by mid-rashic-talmudic sources is unrepresentative of Judaism of the time, nor that the artifacts demonstrate the existence of a different kind of

---

[1]) Yer. Talmud 'Avodah Zarah 3.3.
[2]) Cit. by J. H. Epstein, *Tarbiz* 3, 1931, 20.
[3]) Goodenough, *Symbols*, IV, 24.
[4]) *ibid.*, I 13f.
[5]) *ibid.*, IV, 1, Ch. 2.

Judaism; but perhaps current interpretations of rabbinic sources are still too narrowly, too partially formed. Even the literary texts may reveal hitherto only partially understood details when the realities this art reflects are taken into account.[1])

An example of such a revision of the interpretation of literary texts in the light of archaeological realities will be found in Professor Morton Smith's *Image of God*.[2]) If one accepts the interpretation of the literary texts provided in *Image of God*, he must admit that the people who produced these texts might well have 'instigated' the sort of decoration found in the synagogues. Goodenough's assertion to the contrary is not completely convincing in the light of Smith's study. The texts he discusses show a very vivid verbal symbolism. Similarly, Goodenough never confronted the question of how the rabbis and their followers faced the existential issues of salvation and immortality, which the groups who made use of pictorial symbolism confronted in a mystical manner. Given the stress upon acquiring the world to come which one finds in Talmudic sayings, I find it difficult to distinguish the fundamental concerns of these groups. One cannot overstress, therefore, the importance of Goldin's statement.

Even if the texts cited above prove that the rabbis opposed synagogue decorations, as it seems to me they may indicate, they *still* have not been subjected to a form-critical study. These are, after all, sixth century collections of material about third-century rabbis. One needs to ask which traditions were preserved for what purposes, and which were purposefully, or accidentally, suppressed, lost, or revised. The notion that third-century rabbis must have disapproved of synagogue frescoes or incantation bowls is not, therefore, proven. I offer it as a working hypothesis, subject to considerable revision. I do not know how we shall achieve a history of the traditions without first composing, however tentatively, a history of the Babylonian Jews and the tendencies, issues, and ideas characteristic of each period in that history. Upon such a basis, one can isolate later tendencies which may have caused earlier traditions to be revised. A provisional history must be subjected to continual revisions, but it must, nonetheless, be attempted, if a history of the traditions is to emerge at all. So I have argued in "In Quest of the Historical Rabban Yoḥanan ben Zakkai" [*Harvard Theological Review*, Oct., 1966], and the same argument applies here.

---

[1]) Charles J. Adams, ed., *A Reader's Guide to the Great Religions* (N.Y. 1965) 209-210.

[2]) *Bulletin of the John Rylands Library* 40, 2, 1958, 473-512.

II

If the Babylonian rabbis did not play a special role in the life of the synagogue, being unable even to effect their wishes in the ornamentation of synagogue buildings, as is quite possible in Dura, Nehardea, and Sura, then what was the basis of their authority? Were they *ever* able to effect their policies? The question is not whether there was a widespread lack of discipline or not, but rather, In *which* areas of life were the Jews of Babylonia subjected to rabbinical discipline at all? And how can we know?[1])

Our only extensive source is the Babylonian Talmud, mostly a legal document, the Babylonian part of which consists mainly of discussions of the Mishnah. These discussions provide explication of Mishnaic and external traditions on given point in law, inquiry into the authorities for given laws, and, in part, comparison of the legal views of two or more authorities. None of this material can, on the face of it, be used as evidence concerning the sociology of Babylonian Jewry. Even legal questions asked in the academies do not necessarily reflect the social conditions of the time, for we have no way of knowing which questions were devised for, or emerged from, theoretical discussion, and which were actually the result of the circumstances of day-to-day life. One kind of evidence, however, is of inestimable value, the reports of cases decided in rabbinical courts, or of questions brought to the rabbis by ordinary people. Laymen cannot be supposed to have devised such inquiries for purposes of logical or rhetorical exercise, but rather asked them because they needed the answers for practical reasons. If we have no way of knowing how much of Mishnaic law, and the legal doctrines arising from it, actually influenced the life of the people, we have at least the corpus of cases and popular inquiries.

We are not helped by the language of the Talmud. I think it most likely that the rabbis used Hebrew to preserve and transmit fixed legal dicta, while Aramaic (apart from a few fixed, rhetorical forms) was most likely used for more practical matters; e.g. most of the case reports are in Aramaic. (My research, however, does not as yet justify the assertion as a fixed rule that Aramaic usage invariably connotes a practical decision.) Further, the language of the rabbis' discourse does not vary, whether the subject is theoretical or wholly practical. For example, late-third-century Babylonian rabbis held that heathens are to be

---

[1]) See my *History of the Jews in Babylon*, II. *The Early Sasanian Period* (Leiden, 1966) ch. 8, pp. 251–287.

executed for violating the seven Noachide laws;[1]) they discussed what
is to be done to the layman who sacrificed the Red Heifer, a rite not
carried out, quite obviously, after 70, and only a few times before then;
and numerous other very serious discussions on sacrifical laws and
Temple procedures took place. Further theoretical questions were
considered, for instance, "How do we know that when one offers a
sacrifice without proper intention, it is invalid?"[2]) Other laws, such as
the following, could not have been enforced even by a vast, totalitarian
government.

> Rav said, "A man who wilfully causes an erection is to be placed under
> the ban."
>
> (Bab. Talmud Niddah 13a)
>
> Samuel said, "The domestic and wild goose are forbidden copulation."
>
> (Bab. Talmud Bekhorot 8a)
>
> Rav said, "It is forbidden to sleep by day more than a horse's sleep."
>
> (Bab. Talmud Sukkah 20b)

The legal sources cannot, therefore, be used indiscriminately to
provide testimony about the conditions of daily life.

The rabbis and the exilarch whom they served (see below) did not
have at their disposal means of physical coercion, except in very clearly
specified areas of law. The Sasanians were not at all willing for the Jews
to govern themselves without imperial supervision. On the contrary,
at the very outset of their rule, they made it clear that the Jewish courts
would be closely watched, expected to explain their actions to the
government, and required to conform to Sasanian law. Moreover,
Jews could easily leave the Jewish community, and some did when
confronted with rabbinic excommunication for Sabbath breaking.[3])
None of this proves that the rabbis had no authority whatever. It
should indicate, however, that Goodenough's critique of the view
that the Palestinian patriarchal apostles governed the whole Roman
diaspora applies with equal force to the Babylonian rabbis' relationships to their community. Without armies or police, merely tolerated
by the new regime, the third-century Babylonian rabbis depended, in
the end, upon the actual willingness of Jews to obey the law, because it
had been revealed by God to Moses on Mount Sinai and was authori-

---

[1]) Bab. Talmud Sanhedrin 57a.
[2]) Bab. Talmud Zevahim 46b.
[3]) See my *History of the Jews in Babylonia, I. The Parthian Period,* (Leiden 1965)
147-8.

tatively exposited and applied by them; upon the inertial force of accepted authority; and upon the willingness of the Persian government to allow them to govern some specific areas of life. The issue of rabbinic authority is therefore considerably more complicated than has been recognized.

The matter is made more difficult still by the one-sidedness of our evidence. Rabbinic sources mostly suppress or report only by indirection actions contrary to rabbinic dicta, and where such reports occur, it is only because the rabbis tell how they punished a law-violator. The two great bodies of independent archaeological evidence from Mesopotamia, the Dura synagogue and the incantation bowls, provide striking evidence that the masses of people were not living entirely in conformity to rabbinic law, but engaged in religious and magical activities which the rabbis might at best have tolerated, but which they would never in the first place have approved. When we review their sermons, moreover, we find considerable evidence that people displeased the rabbis. That, of course, is nothing new, nor can we discount the preacher's love for hyperbole. But when the rabbis preach against those who defer payment of a worker's wages, withhold wages entirely, cheat on communal taxes, behave arrogantly, and so forth, it is difficult to believe that they had the power to do more than curse the sinner and encourage penitence. Living in Babylonia were Jews who did not put on phylacteries, who did not meet the rabbis' standards for ethical economic and moral behavior, and who did not even respect the rabbis. Rav said that the blessings of the world to come are denied—a fearful threat—to anyone who insulted a scholar.[1]) We rarely, if ever, hear what those insults were, or why the rabbis were so exasperated about them. If, as we are told, an inhabitant of Naresh kisses you, count your teeth; if a Pumbeditan accompanies you, change your lodging; if thieves in Pumbedita open many casks of wine, the wine is not prohibited as it would be if it had been touched by an idolator, because the majority of thieves there are Jews.[2]) Such people as these are obviously not described by Mishnaic laws or academic discussions. And we do not know about the masses, who were neither learned academicians nor criminals.

It is hardly reasonable, moreover, to talk of the 'halakhic reforms' of Rav as if these greatly changed, in a very few years, the ancient patterns of Babylonian Jewish life. The rabbis were few in number.

---

[1]) Bab. Talmud Sanhedrin 99b.
[2]) Bab. Talmud Ḥullin 127a, 'Avodah Zarah 70a.

They were concentrated in central Babylonia itself. Elam produced students, but no teachers. Mesene was in such a state that the rabbis prohibited intermarriage between Jews from the south and those in Babylonia. Few rabbis, if any, came from Adiabene (which may by then have been Christian) and Armenia. The very instruments for the propagation and application of rabbinic laws were probably unavailable in the outlying districts. I estimate that there were from 600,000 to one million Jews in Babylonia in this period. We know the names of a handful of rabbis; certainly there were many others, but students and teachers together could not have amounted to over a thousand. Later on, the influence of the rabbis spread, as the academies grew in strength, and as large numbers of people attended their semi-annual adult-study sessions. But for the third century I have found very little evidence that the great masses of Babylonian Jewry always or even mostly conformed to Mishnaic law as expounded by the rabbis.

How then can we know which halakhic sayings affected the life of the people? As I said, minimal, but highly significant, evidence is to be derived from case reports and popular questions addressed to the rabbis. There are numerous such reports, and these are by no means scattered at random in the legal literature. Naturally, none at all exist on the laws pertaining to the Temple cult. But some of the laws did yield court cases, and while none can argue that *only* that law was enforced which produced judicial records, I think it clear that *at the very least*, here are areas of the common life which the rabbis did supervise.

Some of the laws were obeyed because the people believed that they were commanded by God. I did not expect that among these would be the laws about separating priestly gifts, and it is probable that whatever tithes were set aside, tithing ended after 260.[1]) But we have the story that Rav Ḥisda held in his possession the tithe of cattle,[2]) which suggests that some people even later gave priests their due. Samuel, moreover, fined a man for disobeying the laws on mixed seeds[3]) and Levi received a question, on 'mixed seeds' in a vineyard, asked by the citizens of Bashkar. The agricultural taboos would have been obeyed where they were explicit and well known, and held by the masses, contrary to Mishnah Qiddushin 1:9, to be valid even outside of Palestine. Hence a close study of such laws, as exposited by the rabbis, would be sociologically significant.

---

[1]) Evidence is cited in my *History*, II, chapter II.
[2]) Bab. Talmud Shabbat 10b.
[3]) Yer. Talmud 'Orlah 3.7.

Those laws which were actually enforced by the rabbis mainly concerned property matters. As a general rule, one can say that wherever exchange of property was involved, as in trade, real estate dealings, torts and damages, marriage and divorce, there the rabbis exerted full and unchallenged authority. It is, moreover, quite natural to suppose that this should be the case. What the farmers did on their farms would not normally come under the supervision of the rabbis, nor what the women did in their kitchens, nor what husbands and wives did in their beds (though, as we shall see, the menstrual taboos were widely observed). Transfers of property, in *any* form, were quite another matter. They had to be regulated by public authorities; documents had to be properly written and registered, and the rabbis and their scribes were the official registrars of such documents. Transfer of property required public authorization, recognition, and confirmation. It was the rabbis, acting for the exilarchate, who supervised property transfers. When the people came to them, the rabbis had a splendid opportunity to act as they thought proper. As judges, they had no difficulty in enforcing the law. Still they did not have an entirely free hand. Practices which the people accepted, such as the writing of a *prosbul*, could not be easily changed. (Samuel said that if he could, he would abolish it.[1]) He never did.) Where transfer of property was concerned, there people could find absolutely no way to avoid the rabbinical courts.

Transfers of inheritance and the execution of wills posed numerous knotty problems. Questions were addressed from outlying parts on the matter,[2]) and many cases came to the courts.[3]) There is no reason to doubt that the great corpus of civil law, in the tractates Bava' Qama', Bava' Meẓi'a, and Bava' Batra', mostly contains practical, not merely theoretical, law. Moreover, the rabbis' decisions on proper acquisition of property sometimes overrode ancient custom:

> A certain lady had usufruct of a date-tree...A man came and hoed underneath it a little, and claimed ownership. He asked Levi, who confirmed title to the land. The woman complained bitterly. He said, "What can I do for you, for you did not establish your title properly?"
> (Bab. Talmud Bava' Batra' 54a)

In this case, the woman had assumed she owned the tree for thirteen years, and until someone, probably better informed than she, challenged

---

[1]) Bab. Talmud Gittin 36b.
[2]) Bab. Talmud Bava' Batra' 127b and 152b, to Samuel, for example.
[3]) Bab. Talmud Bava' Batra' 143a.

her, no one assumed to the contrary. Hence it stands to reason that the
average person identified usufruct with possession. The rabbis, (at
least superficially) for exegetical reasons disagreed, and when they
came to apply Mishnaic law, they were able by *force majeure* to sustain
their decisions. For their part, they made great efforts to publicize
the law, encouraging people to avoid purchasing lands under disputed
title, publicly teaching how to acquire cattle, fields, trees, and so forth.
Nonetheless, cases came before them daily,[1] dealing with land, claims
for loss and damages,[2] and the like.

We have a number of instances, moreover, where a firm legal dictum
was stated in the name of one or another of the rabbis, and challenged
in dialectical argument, whereupon it was admitted that Rav or Samuel
never made such a statement, but rather the disciples deduced what
they *thought* was the rabbi's legal dictum on the basis of observation of
an action. These cases invariably occur in matters involving transfer of
property, mainly in civil and commercial law, rather than in liturgical,
ritual, cultic or agricultural law. The legal sayings of the rabbis on
dormant matters, such as the cult, or on theoretical issues, did not give
rise to any such speculation upon the basis of an observed action. It was
only where the law actually applied to daily affairs that the rabbis'
actions could be subjected to close scrutiny. And these cases, for Rav
and Samuel, all concerned civil law.

By contrast to the substantial number of civil suits reported by the
Talmud to have been adjudicated by the rabbis, I know of not a single
criminal, and certainly no capital, action reported as a precedent, described as a case at trial, or otherwise mentioned in a historically credible
setting in the time of Rav and Samuel. There are two cases in which
criminal action seems to be implied. In the first, a 'man wanted to
show another's straw' to the government for taxation; in the second,
a man had intercourse with a gentile woman. But these two cases
provide no striking exceptions, for they actually involved political,
and not judicial, policy, and prove (in the second case) that the Jews
could not in fact freely inflict the death penalty once the Sasanians took
power, although they could and did in Parthian times. (The former case
entailed at best civil damages, but political circumstance transformed it
into a more serious matter. This matter is fully discussed in my *History*,
II. Ch. 2. i, pp. 27–35). We have many sayings on criminal law and procedure, but no cases showing that the rabbis' courts ever judged such

[1] Bab. Talmud Bava' Batra' 110b.
[2] Bab. Talmud Bava' Qama' 11a, Bava' Meẓi'a' 13b, etc.

cases. Since criminal cases must have arisen, we can best assume that the Sasanians' courts tried them for the most part.

Laws of personal status were enforced in the rabbinical courts, and I think the reason is the same as that given above: the legality of a marriage and the legitimacy (for purposes of inheritance, for instance) of offspring involved not merely private acquiescence but also public recognition, because the drawing up of documents and, frequently, property-transfers were involved. On the other hand, the rabbis' *obiter dicta* could not have meant much. For example, Rav preached that a barren marriage must be annulled after two and one-half years, but we have no case in which such a law was enforced.[1]) The rabbis did use their power to flog to enforce good public morals; they discouraged betrothal by cohabitation, or in the open street, or without previous negotation. Since they were believed to have accurate physiological and medical information, their judgments on the legitimacy of children were respected. Divorce procedures, in which property always was an issue, yielded many cases, though even here[2]) the peoples' pattern of behavior took precedence over rabbinic opinion in some matters. The rabbis' power, however, depended not upon popular acquiescence, though it was considerable, but upon the coercive capabilities of their courts, and upon the practical consequences of the decrees these might issue.

It was the Bible which shaped the religious life of the masses. The rabbis did not need to urge the people to keep biblical laws. Popular practice may have required rabbinical supervision over the ways the commandments were carried out. Where biblical laws and rabbinical interpretations were clear, well-known, and widely accepted, there the rabbis merely guided the affairs of the people, who brought them their queries. Where rabbinical injunctions were not widely accepted, there the rabbis relied upon coercion when they could, or upon public instruction in their view of the biblical requirements. The construction of *'eruvin*, for example, was in the hands of the rabbis, and the laws pertaining to Sabbath-limits were therefore enforced by them.

This is not to suggest that the greater part of the people was so meticulously observant as the rabbis would have liked. Tension between a class of religious virtuosi and the masses of their followers is certainly a common phenomenon in the history of religions. But because they knew the Bible, the Jewish masses proved amenable to

[1]) Bab. Talmud Yevamot 64b.
[2]) Bab. Talmud Yevamot 102a.

the guidance of the rabbis, especially when the rabbis could base their decisions upon convincing Scriptural exegesis. Three kinds of ritual law were rigorously obeyed, those dealing with slaughter of animals, menstrual separation, and the Sabbath. In all three, the rabbis were frequently consulted. The menstrual taboos were probably universally observed because the Bible is explicit about them, and the rabbis were frequently consulted about how to keep them. The Sabbath was either publicly observed, or publicly profaned, and the rabbis did not have to wait to be consulted. They aggressively punished Sabbath breaking, and the people doubtless expected them to do so, because of the well-known biblical precedents. We do not know how the Sabbath laws were kept in areas not under rabbinical influence. We have, however, numerous inquiries from distant places, and from students who would have carried the rabbis' influence far beyond the academies. By contrast, since the rabbis had no special function in synagogue affairs, and no authority over them, they had to tolerate popular practice, which was based upon very ancient, tenacious, and widely accepted traditions.

Insight into the level of popular knowledge may be derived from the questions referred to above, of the citizens of Bashkar to Levi: "What about setting a canopy on the Sabbath, what about cuscuta in a vineyard, what about a dead man on a festival?" The first was prohibited, the second permitted, and the third elicited the reply that the burial of the corpse had to be held over to a weekday. These are fairly basic matters, and the simple inquiry would suggest that the people would have been unaware of other such laws.[1]) Unless they sent an inquiry or received a pastoral visit, the rabbis could not censure them. For the rest, as we have seen, the rabbis were relatively powerless:

> Rav saw a man sowing flax on Purim, and he cursed him, so the flax would not grow.
>
> (Bab. Talmud Megillah 5b)

Doubtless the rabbis' prestige far outweighed their powers of coercion, for people believed in the rabbis' curses.

On the other hand, the rabbinical viewpoint was quite easily enforced among their own students. Such laws included mourning and burial practice, blessings before and after meals, and the like. In these,

---

[1]) Yet I am not entirely persuaded that the "men of Bashkar" were not simply the local group of rabbinical disciples, rather than the leaders of the whole community.

we have questions addressed to the rabbis *only* by students, and the single case of enforcement of burial rites involved an academician. A student of Samuel had intercourse during a period of mourning; Samuel heard and was angry, and the student died. It is likely that many would prefer to obey a rabbi than to risk his curse or some worse results.

No legal system could depend for enforcement upon the success of curses, barren flax-seeds, and the like. The many stories in which a rabbi's curse was sufficient to bring down punishment upon the head of a recalcitrant Jew—invariably cases *not* involving property-transfers —reveal that in these matters, only the curse, and *not* court action, was available for enforcing the laws. The laws the breaking of which was punished by rabbinical curses were probably, therefore, those which rabbinical courts could not otherwise have adjudicated; or which were not subject to popular inquiries addressed to the rabbis about proper observance.

Reference has been made to liturgical dicta. Within their academies the rabbinical authority was unlimited. Hence we have numerous cases, all taking place in the school house or among disciples, in which a disciple made a mistake in saying grace, in which the proper posture during a given prayer was discussed and demonstrated, or in which some detail was elucidated for a questioning disciple. But we have only one liturgical case in which a non-academician was involved:

> Benjamin the shepherd made a sandwich and said, 'Blessed be the master of this bread,' and Rav said that he had performed his oligation.
> (Bab. Talmud Berakhot 40b)

Rav's judgment was very lenient, for he did not require the normal formula of the blessing. Since the rabbis' disciples found great difficulty in understanding and carrying out the laws of saying grace (Rav's students after his funeral lamented that they still had problems with them), it stands to reason that the common people would have found it quite impossible, without the elaborate education by precept and example provided in the academies, to do precisely the right thing. If this were so in the everyday act of blessing food, one may reasonably suppose that more difficult or unusual matters were quite remote from public comprehension, let alone observance.

As the students were trained and went to their homes, and as judges were sent out from the academies to various villages and towns, the legal doctrines of the rabbis radiated into the common life. This was not a process completed in one generation, nor was the transformation of the people's life effected by a few men alone. It took many centuries before Babylonian Jewry in the mass came to approximate rabbinical ideas of how religious, social, and personal affairs should be conducted. For my part, I do not knew precisely when it was the case that rabbinical law accurately described popular conduct. But it was not in the third century. One cannot conceive that before the foundation of Babylonian rabbinical academies, in consequence of the Bar Kokhba war, Babylonian Jewry possessed neither laws nor authoritative doctrines. During the six preceding centuries, indigenous traditions of law, exegesis, and probably doctrine, were surely cultivated. It could not have been otherwise. Babylonian Jews married, bore children and educated them, divided their estates and litigated their affairs, celebrated the festivals and Sabbath, and pursued the many matters which required legal adjudication, producing a rich corpus of precedents, long before the first rabbi appeared in their midst. What is remarkable therefore is that in the third century anything changed at all, for the inertia of earlier centuries must have made the process of social and legal change painful indeed. The available cases suggest that it was mainly where the rabbis were able to apply very specific judicial-administrative pressures that matters were influenced by them.

III

If so, then one must ask, What was the basis of the rabbis' power? The later, acute tension between the rabbis and the exilarch has obscured the obvious fact that in this period, most of the rabbis were agents of the exilarch, acting under his authority, and fully respectful of his person, his office, and his prerogatives. It is true that when Rav returned to Babylonia, he got into trouble with the exilarch for refusing to enforce his decree regulating market-prices; but Rav was the *agoranomos*, or market supervisor, by virtue of exilarchic appointment, and was forced, by imprisonment, to do just as the exilarch said. Samuel, for his part, recognized the superior status of the court of Mar'Uqba, exilarch of his time,[1] as well as its superior authority.[2] Samuel apparently regarded his chief function, however, as instructional, while Mar'Uqba's was judicial:

---

[1] Bab. Talmud Shabbat 55a; See my *History*, II, chapter III, pp. 92-125 and III, pp. 41-94.
[2] Bab. Talmud Qiddushin 44b.

When they were sitting together [at the school house] Mar'Ubqa sat before him at a distance of four cubits, and when they sat together at a judicial session, Samuel sat before him at a distance of four cubits, and a place was dug out for Mar'Uqba where he sat on a matting so that he should be heard. Every day Mar'Uqba accompanied Samuel to his house. One day he was engrossed in a law-suit, and Samuel walked behind him. When he had reached his house, Samuel said to him, 'Have you not been rather a long time at it? Now take up my case!' He realized that Samuel was angry, and submitted himself to 'reproof' for one day.

> (Bab. Talmud Mo'ed Qatan 16b)

Mar'Uqba cited Samuel's teachings on medicine, on judicial procedure, on the preparation of the *'eruv*, and other matters, while Samuel was guardian for the children of Mar 'Uqba after his death. The two men got on well together. Samuel taught law to the exilarch, who could not have had so extensive a legal training as the rabbi, while the exilarch honored him and submitted to his pedagogical authority. Mar 'Uqba had a good name for his generosity toward the poor, his learning, and his meticulous honesty. Rav and Samuel both explicitly stated that if a person wished to decide monetary cases without liability in case of judicial error, he *had* to obtain the sanction of the exilarch.[1]) For his part, the exilarch employed Qarna, Levi, Rav, and Samuel in his administration. Apart from the difference with Rav, based upon the latter's adherence to Palestinian traditions (and, one supposes, his ordination there), there is no evidence of tension between the exilarch and rabbis, and certainly *not* with the rabbis as a group. The exilarch was not an ignorant figurehead, but a powerful, learned man. As chief judge, the exilarch was, by analogy to the *Erpatan Erpat* of the Mazdean church, certainly head of the Jewish community.

To suppose, moreover, that the sages' rulings were based not upon the authority of the exilarch, but upon their own, requires an absurd postulate. One would have to conjecture that there were two separate systems of Jewish government in the troubled times of early Sasanian Babylonia, one run by the rabbis, the other by the exilarch. There was no question in the Sasanians' mind that minority groups, including the Jews, should continue to govern their òwn affairs. But their supervision of the Jewish courts suggests that they would surely intervene if matters developed contrary to their will. If they approved the continuing rule of the exilarch under specified conditions, it is hardly

---

[1]) Bab. Talmud Sanhedrin 5a.

likely that they would have also permitted the development of a second competing administration. Their politics required hierarchical centralization, in their own chancery, of all power, and the careful parcelling out of authority where necessary to specified bureaus and officials. It is inconceivable that they would have allowed the Jews to be subjected to competing authorities, and not to a single, hierarchical regime like their own. And, as we have seen, the actions of the rabbinical courts depended upon the willingness of the imperial regime to back up their decisions in exclusively practical cases. If the rabbi's decisions on the transfer of property were to be enforced, they must have been made with the consent of the Persian regime. If they were free of the danger of having to make restitution, it was certainly with Persian *and* exilarchic approval. The contrary would have been impossible, for the aggrieved party could simply repair to the imperial court, which, if the action was unauthorized or illegal, would doubtless reverse the decision, and probably also punish the 'judge' who made it. Moreover, the Persians collected taxes not from individuals but by millets or communities. The exilarch was responsible for collecttion of these taxes, as was the Christian *catholicus*. The sages had to collect the poll-tax in their own towns, and they must have done so as agents of the exilarch. The only Jewish judges in Babylonia whose decision could have stood, therefore, were exilarchic appointees, as Rav and Samuel explicitly stated.[1]

At the same time, the rabbis acted far more than merely as agents of the exilarch. They clearly possessed a law-code regarded by them as bearing divine sanction, and they knew how to study and exposit

---

[1]) But their language is noteworthy. "If a man wishes to be free of liability for judicial error, *he should acquire permission* from the exilarch." They do not say, he should *seek appointment* (ordination). Part of the reason, of course, is that the exilarch, unlike the patriarch, did not bestow such appointment in this period, so far as we know. But it may well be that I am presenting too neat and simple a view of affairs. It is possible that in some places, a local learned man would be recognized as aibiter among the people, with or without exilarchic knowledge and permission. Such a man could issue judgments, and popular support, combined with the absence of a competing authority, would have rendered them effective. The language of the rabbis suggests that if a man does not care about possible liability for judicial error, he might as well go ahead and judge cases. Their words may well mean that such was the case. The very limitations upon the police power of the Jewish government would have made it quite feasible for local authorities to operate entirely beyond its control. The case cited below, in which a man is dissatisfied with the exilarchic court's decision, and therefore repairs elsewhere for judgment, would suggest that even in so central a settlement as Nehardea it was possible for a respected person to ignore the exilarch. But I cannot, in any case, envision the development, in this period, of a completely separate system of

the numerous traditions relating to it. Rav and Samuel were prepared to insure that the Mishnah would be the law of the Jewish courts, as in the following case:

> Once a man drowned in the swamp of Samki, and R. Shila' permitted his wife to marry again. Said Rav to Samuel, 'Come, let us place him under a ban [for he has acted against the law of the Mishnah]'. 'Let us first,' Samuel replied, 'ask for an explanation.' On sending to him their inquiry, 'If a man has fallen into limitless waters, is his wife forbidden or permitted (to remarry),' he replied, 'Forbidden.' They asked, 'Is the swamp of Samki regarded as water that has a limit or not?' 'It is regarded as water that has no limit.' 'Why then did the master act in such a manner?' 'I was really mistaken,' he replied, 'for I was of the opinion that as the water was gathered and stationary, it was to be regarded as water which has a limit, but the law is in fact not so, for owing to the prevailing waves, it might well be assumed that the waves carried the body away...'
>
> (Bab. Talmud Yevamot 121a)

This story indicates that Rav and Samuel were prepared to enforce conformity to Mishnaic law by means of the ban of excommunication. I doubt that the needs of the exilarchate impelled them to do so. If, moreover, they were acting as the exilarch's agents, they could well have used force, as did the exilarch against Rav himself. The issue was therefore, *Which* body of laws and precedents would be enforced in the Jewish courts? Rav, who had come from Palestine and was deeply committed to the enforcement of R. Judah's Mishnah, here appeared eager to demonstrate the authority of that law, even before the case was adequately clarified, but Samuel was no less anxious to enforce the same principle. Their failure to resort to an appeal to the exilarch is noteworthy. It would suggest that the latter would not have supported the rabbis' position against a judge who differed. He would rather have preferred, where the matter was not immediately relevant to his political or administrative purposes, to allow the judges themselves to decide what the law should be. In a case of family law, the exilarch was apparently prepared to stand aside, while by contrast, in a case involving economic policy, he was not. Enjoying great prestige, Rav and Samuel could denounce a dissident judge, who

---

rabbinical courts, outside of exilarchic control. The Sasanians would never have permitted it, and they *did* know what was going on in Babylonia. And the sources suggest, quite to the contrary, that Rav, Samuel, Shila', Qarna, and others were working quite closely with the exilarchate, and were officials of that institution. Given the political pressures upon the Jews exerted by the early Sasanians, who owed them nothing and regarded them with great suspicion, the Jewish leaders could not have acted prudently had they ignored or competed with one another.

seemed to them inclined to inforce the law as he saw fit. They thus apparently possessed a measure of freedom of action in some areas of law, but not in others, with moral and religious, but not political, sanctions to enforce their views about laws which the exilarch neglected.

We may, in fact, discern three kinds of law in which the exilarchate and his rabbinical judges involved themselves. The first was law which strictly concerned the Jewish religion and the inner life of the Jewish community, as in the case cited here. Here the rabbis from the very beginning probably had a completely free hand, for the exilarch, using them as judges and agents for other purposes, and respecting their learning, would have been quite content to rely upon their traditional knowledge to decide cases with no practical bearing upon public order. The second involved the economic, social, and political welfare of the community. In this area, the exilarch proved to be quite willing to intervene as he saw fit, and to impose his judgment, based upon practical necessities of his relationship to the Persians, rather than upon traditional precedents. Such a case is represented by the imprisonment of Rav for refusing to supervise the pricing of goods in the market, a refusal based upon ample precedent in Palestine. One may conjecture that the Persians would not have respected the efficiency of an administration unable to control such important matters. The third concerned the relationship between the Jews and the government, as in the collection of taxes, the regulation of land ownership, and the like. Here both the rabbis and the exilarch had to submit to Persian hegemony, but with a major difference. The exilarch was held directly responsible by the Sasanian government, and the rabbis were not, but could foster their opinions among the people without regard to, or in outright opposition against, both the needs of the exilarchate and the will of the imperial power. Therein lay the germs of their later disenchantment with one another. Samuel, for example, regretted that riparian wharfage rights were governed by Persian law, but he enforced that law.[1]) In the next generation, we find the following case:

> A certain person cut down a date tree belonging to his neighbor. When he appeared before the exilarch, the latter said to him, 'I myself saw the place. Three date trees stood close together and they were worth a hundred zuz. Go, pay thirty-three and one-third zuz.' Said the defendant, 'What have I to do with an exilarch who judges in accord with

---

[1]) Bab. Talmud Bava' Meẓi'a' 108a.

Persian law?' He therefore appeared before R. Naḥman [student and heir of Samuel] who said that the valuation should be made in conjunction with sixty.

(Bab. Talmud Bava' Qama' 58b)

When Samuel decreed that the government's law is law, he did not mean to say that it must therefore take precedence in Jewish courts. After his death, the exilarchate may have gone much further than the rabbis approved in bringing into Jewish justice the precedents of Persian law, something the earliest *entente* may not have included. Hence the rabbis would have found themselves progressively more estranged from the less learned, ever more narrowly political, Jewish authority. In future research, I shall explain how it was that R. Naḥman, who was related by marriage to the exilarch, was able to act as a kind of appellate authority, if that is what the above case implies, and to ignore the exilarch's decision.[1]

IV

The bearing of these data on interpretation of the Dura synagogue art is quite obvious. The rabbis were not synagogue officials, but rather carried out wholly different political and social functions. They were teachers, judges, doctors of the law. (They were much else, but that does not concern us here.[2]) But the archisynagogus of Dura, like that of other synagogues, was not a rabbi, nor was the figure whom Goodenough called "the philosopher" of the synagogue. There was no reason why these men *should* have been rabbis. In any event, the rabbis, as we have seen, recognized a tension between their enterprise and that of the synagogue. "We with ours, they with theirs" said Rav Sheshet in explaining why he studied his traditions while the Torah was read in the synagogue. Abaye refrained from leaving his school house to attend synagogue services. Rav Naḥman did not even bother to assemble a quorum. In the earlier generation, Rav and Samuel tolerated the existence, in the synagogues of Dura and Nehardea, respectively, of a mosaic floor and a statue, though neither approved of such iconography. However much the rabbis may have wished it otherwise, they had no great role in third-century synagogue life, and

---

[1]) Compare vol. III, pp. 61-75.

[2]) Except for the sacerdotal function, they provided Jewish equivalents for the social-religious leadership of the Iranian Magi. See my *History*, II, chapter IV, pp. 126-150, and my "Rabbi and magus", *History of Religions*, 6, 2, 1966, 169-178.

the interpretation of synagogue art at Dura must take that fact into account.

If, moreover, the rabbis had wanted to assert their authority over synagogue decoration, what means of enforcement were available to them? The exilarch would surely have found their attempt troublesome, since large numbers of Jews would have been disturbed by rabbinical interference with what they doubtless believed to be ancient and honorable customs and practices. One can hardly suppose that the exilarch would have brought his influence to bear in support of his agents' interference with such delicate matters. He had no reason to do so. Indeed, if, as has been asserted, the *andarta* was a statue of the monarch, then it would surely have been contrary to the exilarchic interest to have tried to remove it from the synagogue building. For their part, the rabbis could have made use of the ban of excommunication, as they did in Parthian times against the inhabitants of a village who violated the Sabbath, and in this time as well. What could have been the result? The effectiveness of the ban depended upon popular acceptance including the virtual ostracism of the excommunicated party. But to excommunicate the Jews of a whole town would scarcely be practicable, (as R. 'Aḥai b. R. Josiah found out earlier), since they could doubtless survive by continuing their regular intercourse with one another and ignoring the rabbis' decree altogether. Its practical effectiveness would thereby have been vitiated. When it was contrary to popular desires, the ban bore no weight at all. It was precisely this fact which would have prevented rabbinical interference. Indeed, the subsequent discussions of Rav's behavior in the Sura synagogue suppose that he had a good, legal reason for refraining from issuing a decree of excommunication, but it seems more reasonable to suppose that his best "reason" was the ineffectiveness of such a decree in a synagogue-setting. During the years when Dura was in Roman hands, from ca. 165 to 256, moreover, the Babylonian rabbis could not have made use of exilarchic support even if it had been available. His power depended upon the Iranians' support. The Romans would not in any event permit its exercise within their borders, any more than the Persians would allow the Palestinian patriarch to govern their Jewish community.

As we have seen, however, it is not correct to phrase the problem in terms of communal discipline. The issue is not whether or not the rabbis had any authority over the Jews. The issue is what *kind* of authority they had and executed, and upon what basis. As I have said, their practical authority was based upon the support of the exilarchate, upon the prestige accruing to their learning, upon their power to issue decrees of excommunication, and upon the acquiesence of the people themselves. In the final analysis, it was the people who decided what they wanted to put on the walls of their synagogues, and, as Goodenough rightly pointed out, one will look in vain in rabbinical literature for proof texts upon which to hang interpretations of the Dura murals. The reason is not that we cannot find significant, relevant material, for we can. It is rather that whatever material we *do* find cannot tell us, standing by itself, which motifs and ideas were meaningful, indeed, which were even available to Dura Judaism. Goodenough has the merit of forcing us to reconsider our conceptions of Judaism in late antiquity, and especially, our view of what was normative and what was sectarian, indeed, of whether these categories even have bearing upon the social, cultural, and religious realities of Jewry and Judaism when viewed as historians must view them.[1])

---

[1]) My thanks are due to the following, who offered critical comments on earlier drafts of this paper: Professors Jonathan Z. Smith, Charles Liebman, and Robin Scroggs. I am especially indebted to Professor Morton Smith for extensive criticism.

ABBA, FATHER.

TITLE OF SPIRITUAL LEADER AND SAINT.

K. KOHLER

IN his well-known rebuke of Pharisean ostentatiousness and love of public recognition (Matt. xxiii. 1–10) Jesus says to his disciples: "They love to be called of men Rabbi. But be ye not called Rabbi; for one is your teacher, and all ye are brethren. And call no man your father on the earth; for one is your father, which is in heaven. Neither be ye called masters, for one is your master, even the Christ." Lightfoot already observed that reference is here made to the three titles by which the leaders of the school were addressed in Talmudical times: Rabbi, Abba, and Moreh (see *Maccoth*, 24 a). Still, a careful glance at the New Testament passage reveals the fact that the text has been tampered with, since Jesus cannot well have spoken of himself in this manner.

Let us then consider the three titles and the judgment passed on them: (1) the title most in use certainly was *Rabbi*, my master, or master, and gradually this became a standing title for every recognized teacher. The title *Rab*, master, which in its fuller form *Ribbon*, Great Master, was often applied to God in prayer, implies submission and awe. "Let fear of thy master be like the fear of God (heaven)" is the rule of the early fathers (*Pirke Aboth*, IV, 7), and *Shimmush hakamim*, "servile attendance of the wise," is one of the conditions of acquiring knowledge of the Torah. If the disciple, therefore, happen to be at the side of the teacher when he goes to the bath-house, he is bound to carry his clothes for him. Against such claims of superiority Jesus remonstrated, laying down the

150

principle of perfect equality. Instead of bidding his disciples to wash his feet before reclining at the supper table, as he might have done, he humbly washed the feet of each of them, as the Gospel of John relates. Accordingly he did not claim the rank of master for himself. He wanted, on the contrary, to reserve the name of *Rab*, master, for him who is the Master of the world, *Ribbono shel Olam*, and therefore they were to drop the name of Rabbi altogether: "One is your Master, and that is God." The Greek word *Didascalos*, teacher, is incorrect. Likewise is the sentence, "And all ye are brethren," misplaced; it belongs to the following verse which refers to *Abba*.

(2) The second title in use was *Abba*, "father." With reference to this Jesus says: "Call none of you on earth *Abba*, father, for one is your Father, he who is in heaven, and all ye are brethren." Who it was that the people addressed by this name, we shall see immediately. Let us first dispose of the third title.

(3) Next to Rabbi we find the title of *Moreh* (Aram. *Malfono*), teacher or guide, for which the Greek equivalent *Katechetes* was quite common in the philosophical schools. Of it Jesus says: "Neither let yourselves be addressed as teachers (or guides), for there is but one Guide, and that is . . . . . ." Obviously the name of Christ has been substituted here by the compilers for another word, and that is, in all probability, *the Holy Spirit* (compare Isa. xxx. 20, where the word *Moreh* is twice translated in the Targum by *Shekhina*). "God through his interpreter, the Holy Spirit, is your only Guide."

Coming now to our main object, the explanation of the title *Abba*, we can dismiss all that has been thus far written on the subject as decidedly unsatisfactory. Frankel's note to Abba Saul in his *Hodegetica in Mishnam*, p. 176, which says: "It is a title of honour, but less than rabbi," referring to Rashi, *Br'achoth*, 16 b, has been repeated by Jastrow and others without further inquiry. The head slave was called *Abba*, also, but that has no bearing upon our question. Dr. Buechler, in *Die Priester und der Cultus*, pp. 31–33, referring to a number of passages containing traditions concerning the temple and its mode of worship preserved by Tannaites bearing the title of *Abba*, comes to the conclusion that the title originated in priestly circles who had their chief seat—presumably after the destruction of the temple—in the South. But this does not explain the origin in the least.

Beginning with the Bible, we find the title of *Ab*, father, given not only to the originator, as in Gen. iv. 20, 21 (where the Targum translates *rab*), but also to an adviser (Gen. xlv. 8; Judges xvii. 10, where Targum has also *Ab*). Thus do also the young prophets call their master *Ab*, father (1 Sam. x. 12; 2 Kings ii. 12; vi. 21). In like manner are Hillel and Shammai called the "fathers of the world" (*Eduyoth*, I, 4), and also their schools (*Yerush. Haggiga*, II, p. 77 d); also R. Jishmael and R. Akiba (*Yerush. Shkalim*, III, 47 b); and, like Moses, R. Tarfon is called "father of entire Israel" (*Yer. Yoma*, I, 38 d).

"The fathers" became, therefore, the standing name for the ancient masters of the law, as is not only shown by the name of the treatise *Pirke Aboth*, "The Sayings of the Fathers," but the very word for tradition preserved both in the Talmud and by Josephus (*Ant.*, XIII, 10, 6) is Masoreth *Aboth*, Tradition of the Fathers (see Hoffmann, *Die erste Mishnah*, p. 6; 267).

There is little doubt that the Church, in according to their heads the name of *fathers*, simply followed in the footsteps of the Synagogue[1].

But the question is, whether particular individual teachers of the Law received the title of *Abba*, "father," and who?

Let us then take up the list of the men called *Abba* in the Talmudical literature, one after the other, and inquire into their peculiar merit.

---

[1] The *Falashas* also call their leaders *Abba*, and they represent a branch of the Hasideans of the old school.

Before doing so, however, we must take notice of one
spoken of as "father of the Jews" in the second book of the
Maccabees (xiv. 37-46). The passage has not received the
attention it deserves, because the name of the saint whose
tragic end is there related, *Razis*, is, owing to the hand of a
copyist, no longer to be recognized. Only Frankel, in his
Monatschrift, 1852, p. 106, has noted the identification.
He is described as one of the elders of Jerusalem, a lover
of his fellow citizens, and a man of very great renown,
and on account of his extreme piety called "a father of
the Jews." He "encouraged the separation of Judaism
from the Gentiles, and imperilled body and soul by his
steadfastness to Judaism." In other words, then, he was
the actual leader of the Hasideans, and, while he escaped
when the other sixty were slain by Bacchides and Alkimos
(1 Macc. vii. 16), he was now made the object of an
especial attack by Nicanor, the friend of Alkimos, who
sent five hundred men to capture him. He, however, preferred a cruel death by his own hands. Whatever legend
may have added to the facts, there can be little doubt that
the personality of the martyr is historical, and, if so, it
can be no other than Jose ben *Joezer* of Sereda, the uncle
of Alkimos, whose martyrdom is related in *Bereshith
Rabba*, § 65. He was the spiritual head of the Pharisees,
and remained their highest authority (see *Sota*, 47 a). The
people called him by the endearing name of "father."
But we may go a step further. According to the Rabbinical tradition he and Jose ben Johanan were the chiefs
of the Sanhedrin. This tradition, however, which speaks
of two Pharisean chiefs, does not stand the test of historical
scrutiny, as was shown by Kuenen and others. The real
chief, or *Nasi*, was the high priest, the head of the nation,
while, on the other hand, it seems quite natural that the
Pharisean, or Hasidean party, furnished the highest court
of justice with a spiritual head, one distinguished (Mufla)
by learning and saintliness. He, by his authority, was
to decide the difficult cases in place of the high priest,

153

since the oracle of the *Urim we-Tumim* had ceased to voice the will of God. He had the rank and title of *Ab Beth Din*, "father of the court of Justice," and Josephus, whose remark on this point has been strangely overlooked by the historians, speaks of him as "the prophet" alongside of the high priest (*Ant.*, IV, 8, 4). We find the title "father" and "prophet," for the head of religious bodies, frequently on inscriptions of the time (see Schuerer, *Gesch. d. jüdischen Volkes*, III, 3, 50). It is quite likely that a combination of the two powers represented by the high priest and the leader of the Hasideans was brought about in this form of a double régime (זוג Zeugos) under Judas Maccabee. Cp. Rappoport, *Erck Millin*, and Loewy, *Talmudisches Lexicon*, s. v. Ab Beth Din.

(2) The first man of distinction known to us as Abba is *Abba Hilkia*, the grandson of Onias the Saint, the story of whose martyrdom Josephus relates, while the memory of his miraculous power of intercession for rain in a time of great dearth is preserved alike by Josephus and the Mishna (see *Ant.*, XIV, 31, and *Taanith*, 19 a). Like Onias, who, according to Midrash Tanhuma (*Vaera*, ed. Buber, II, 37), traced his pedigree back to Moses, Hilkia also succeeded in bringing down rain in a time of drought by the prayer he and his pious wife offered, but he humbly refused to acknowledge that it was due to his merit that the rain came (see *Taanith*, 23 a, b). Singularly enough, it escaped the notice of the historians that this Abba Hilkia is none other than "Helkias the Great," of whom Josephus tells that he and Aristobulus, the brother of King Agrippa, went at the head of a deputation of Jews to Petronius, the Governor of Syria, to ask him to interfere in favour of the people with the Emperor Caligula that he should withdraw his edict concerning the erection of his statue in the temple, and when he showed his kind disposition to them, a miracle happened which greatly impressed the governor. It had not rained for a whole year, and in the midst of the great drought, behold, there

P p 2

came out of a clear sky great showers of rain, which
convinced the heathen governor of God's special favour
and providential care for his people (*Ant.*, XVIII, 8, 4–6).
Evidently the Talmudical legend and Josephus point to
the same fact and to the same personality.

(3) There is a similar story related in the Talmud of
another grandson of Onias, which throws light on the title
of Abba : There was another great drought in the land,
and the rabbis sent the little children to Hanan the
Hidden One, to ask him to pray for rain, as he would not
leave his hiding-place and join them. And when these
little ones came to him, and said: "Abba, Abba, Father!
Father! give us rain!" the saint knelt down in prayer,
and cried: "O Master of the world! For the sake of these
innocent ones, who know not how to discriminate between
the Father who giveth rain and the father who cannot
give, but only ask for rain, hear our prayer!" and, behold,
rain came.

Concerning the name "the Hidden One," it should be
observed that of his grandfather Onias, too, Josephus tells
us that he kept himself hidden, and the reason given there
(*Ant.*, XIV, 21) is a political one. It is much more likely,
however, that it was the common practice of these Essene
saints to keep themselves concealed and excluded from
the world, exactly as John the Baptist did long before
his life was imperilled. Elsewhere (Tosefta, *Rosh Hashana*,
IV, 11) our Hanan is mentioned as Honi (Onias) the Little,
or younger one. Our story, however, shows that the
people called him Abba, father, in view of his saintly life.

(4) Another Abba who lived before the destruction of
the temple exhibits traits which stamp him as Hasid,
or Essene, viz. *Abba Saul, the son of Bathnith.* He was
extremely scrupulous, giving full measure to such as
bought the wine he produced, and when he died, he held
his right hand up, saying, "See whether this hand was
not clean and righteous!" He denounced in the following
scathing terms the corruption and greed of the ruling

155

houses of the priesthood of his time: "Woe cometh unto me from the house of Boethus; woe from their club! Woe cometh unto me from the house of Kantharos; woe from their pen! Woe cometh unto me from the house of Ishmael ben Phabi; woe from their fist (grasp), for they fill the offices of high priests, and their sons are treasurers, their sons-in-law inspectors, while their servants go about beating us with their rods" (see Tosefta, *Menahot*, XIII, 21; *Babli Pesachim*, 57 a; and the remarks of Bacher, *Agada der Tannaiten*, I, 50, 377, note).

Two other *Abbas* are mentioned there also in that connexion.

(5) *Abba ben Hanin*, who either joined Abba Saul of Bathnith in denouncing the priesthood in the above words, or spoke in his name. He has preserved traditions concerning the temple (*Middoth*, II, 6; *Derech Eretz Zutta*, IX; *Sifra*, 9 a).

(6) *Abba Saul* also denounced the ruling priesthood as "the men of violence who appropriated other people's property" (Tosefta, *Menahoth eodem*), and his traditions concerning temple and priesthood were regarded as of especial value and weight. His ethical teachings have an Essene character: "As God is merciful, so be thou merciful" (*Sabbath*, 133 b). He also enjoins on the business man scrupulous care in selling goods, lest the buyer be misled (*Baba Metzia*, IV, 12). Regarding also the various trades and their influence on character, Abba Saul expresses an opinion which characterizes him as Essene. See *Jerushalmi Kiddushim*, IV, at the close (where the correct reading of Mishna is preserved). *Abba Gorion* of Sidon says in the name of *Abba Saul*: "A man should not train his son to be a driver of ass or camel, a potter, a barber, or a mariner, a herdsman, or a merchant, because each of these trades easily leads to some sort of dishonesty." It is superfluous to say that this is exactly *Essene* teaching. His warning against the use of the Tetragrammaton (Mishn., *Sanhedrin*, X, 1), and his rigid

view of the Levirate (*Tosefta Yebamoth*, VI, 11), betray also his Essene leanings.

(7) Another *Abba* famous for his *Hasidean* virtue was *Abba Jose ten Kitunta*, "the humble one." Of him they said: "When Abba Jose the Humble One departed, Hasidean virtue departed." (See Tosefta, *Sota*, XV, 5; Bacher, *Agada d. Tanaim*, II, 371).

(8) Of *Abba Hosaya of Tirayah* we are told that, when he died, the people saw his bier carried through the air heavenward, and they said: "No one was beloved by God like him" (Midrash Rabba, *Leviticus Emor*, 30). He was to his age sun and shield (*Kohelet Rabba*, Ve sarah hashemesh). He is also especially lauded for his scrupulous care in dealing with other people's property (Tosefta, *Baba Kama*, XI, 14; *Jerushalmi* B. K. 7 c and *Baba Metziah*, II, 4; Midrash Thillim, XII: he is called "a Hasid").

(9) Another *Abba*, whose name has been greatly disfigured, and undeservedly cast into obscurity, is *Abba Halifa ben Karuyah*. Of him we read that Rabban Gamaliel the Younger went to him, saying: "Pray for me!" whereupon he replied in the words of the Psalmist: "May the Lord give thee according to thy heart!" (Midrash Thillim, Ps. xx). That he must have been known for his piety and saintliness is evidenced by this very fact. In Mass. *Derech Eretz*, I, the same Abba Halifa gives in the name of *Abba Higra* the following *Hasidean* precepts: "Be not rash in making vows, lest thou violate an oath; nor be the guest of an ignorant priest, lest thou eat things holy to God; nor indulge in speaking with woman, lest thou mayest come to lust after her." In Tosefta, *Maaser Sheni*, IV, 5, and *Machshirin*, III, 3, he furnishes Hasidean rules regarding the tithes and Levitical purity. Tosefta, *Baba Kama*, IX, 31, it is Abba Halifa (not Rabbi Hilfai ben Agra, as the copyists have it) of whom the strange utterance is preserved by R. Johanan ben Nuri: "He who tears his hair or his garments, his furniture or other valuables in his anger, is like one who serves an idol, for he

obeys the spirit of evil." See also the dialogue between God and the angels at the destruction of the temple given by R. [Abba] Halifa Midrash Thillim, Ps. cxxxvii (ed. Buber, p. 176, note 33), and *Pesiktha Rabbathi*, 28 (ed. Friedman, 135 b); also Abba Halifa b. Karuyah in *Tos. Maaser Sheni*, IV, 5, *Tos. Makshirin*, III, 3.

(10) *Abba Jose ben Dosai* (often quoted in Tosefta and Midrash as Rabbi Jose ben Dosai of Tzaitor), for both Hagadic and Halachic utterances, had communion with the spirits, and the following story is told of him (*Tanhuma*, and Midrash, *Rabba Kedoshim*, and Midrash Thillim, Ps. xx): A *Hasid*, Abba Jose ben Dosai of Tzaitor, passed a spring, when the spirit of the well came to him, saying: "For many years I have dwelt here without doing harm to any creature, and now another spirit wants to drive me off and inflict harm upon the people. For their sake aid me in killing my opponent." "How can I do so?" asked Abba Jose. "Go thou and tell all thy disciples (townsmen) to come hither with iron spits or hammers and beat upon the surface of the water, crying forth, 'Ours is the victory; Ours is the victory!' and when you notice the following morning at daybreak a drop of blood in the water, be sure that the evil spirit is dead." Abba Jose did as he was told, and·they saw the blood in the water. The evil spirit was dead. Here also the title of *Abba* had something to do with the powers attributed to him as saint by the people. Cp. for Halakic utterances by Abba Jose ben Dosai Zuckerman's *Tosefta Index*.

(11) Of *Abba Tahna* (or Tehinna) the Pious (Hasida) the following story is told in Midrash, *Koheleth Rabba*, IX, 7: He came back to town with his heavy bundle upon his shoulder, on a Friday afternoon, shortly before the beginning of the Sabbath, when he met a disease-stricken man unable to move, who asked him to have pity on him and bring him into town where he could be attended to. He pondered for a while whether he could afford to lay down his bundle, containing the provisions for his house-

hold for the Sabbath and attend to the sick man, thereby
leaving his people without food, or whether he should
provide for his household and leave the unfortunate man
in his perilous condition. He decided to aid the sick man,
and after he had brought him to a safe place, he went back
to get his bundle. Meanwhile it had grown dark. The
Sabbath had approached, and people who saw him
carrying his bundle on his shoulder, wondered, saying:
" Is this father Tahna the pious ? " He felt conscience-
stricken at having violated the sanctity of the Sabbath,
when a miracle happened. The sun came forth shining
again, and a voice was heard saying : " Go, eat thy bread
in joy, and drink thy wine with gladness of heart, for God
has accepted favourably thy work." Here again the title
Abba was a tribute given by the people to the saint.

(12) Another popular saint distinguished by his great
philanthropy was *Abba Yudan*. R. Eliezer, R. Joshua,
and R. Akiba—so we are told in Midrash, *Vayikra Rabba*, 5,
and *Yerush. Horioth*, III, 7, p. 48 a—on a tour collecting
money for charity, came to the district of Antioch, where
Abba Yudan lived. Abba Yudan had then by reverses
in business lost wellnigh his whole fortune, and he was
much distressed at the thought of his inability to give
his full share as usual, but his wife, who was even more
generous-hearted than he, advised him to sell the acre
of land he still possessed and give half of the proceeds
to the great teachers. He did so, and they blessed him,
saying: " May God compensate your loss ! " After a while
they came again on the same errand and inquired after
Abba Yudan. The townspeople said: " Abba Yudan, the
owner of slaves, of cattle, goats and camels ; Abba Yudan,
the master of an immense fortune, he is inaccessible to
the people ! " Yet, no sooner did he learn of their arrival
than he went to see them, and said: " My prosperity is
all due to your blessing, your prayer was heard"; and
he gave them in full measure. To which they answered :
" Even when you gave no more than others the last time,

we placed you with your gift at the head of all. Your heart was large when you gave." Here, too, the name "father" was a popular recognition of the man's merit.

(13) *Abba Jose the Builder* (Banai) was famous for his intimacy with the mysteries of Creation—an especial privilege of the Essenes. The following is related of him in *Shmoth Rabba*, 13: Oenomaos of Gadara, the pagan philosopher, asked the rabbis: "How was the earth created at the beginning?" They answered: "None among us is familiar with these things except Abba Jose the Builder. Go and ask him." He went and found him working on the scaffold of a building. He addressed him, saying: "May I ask you a question?" "I am hired for a day's work and cannot leave here," he replied, "but you may ask while I remain up here." The philosopher repeated his question, and received the answer: "God took dust from beneath the throne of his glory and cast it into the primeval waters, and it thickened into earth, and the clods grew into hills and mountains" (according to Job xxxviii. 38).

(14) Another Abba shows his *Essene* views in a different way: *Abba Benjamin*, in a *Baraitha Berakot*, 5 b, gives his opinion concerning the position of the bed and the phylacteries [1] to be suspended over the same, concerning demons and the right time and place for prayer in order to be received favourably.

(15) Of one Abba we have a remarkable utterance of decidedly Essene character. *Abba Hanin*, pupil of R. Eliezer the great Shammaite saint, in whose name he preserved many traditions concerning the temple, says, not without reference to the priests of the last temple period: "Nadab and Abihu, the sons of Aaron, sinned by their false family pride, as no house seemed good enough for them to marry a daughter thereof, and so they remained single" (*Tanhuma Ahare Moth*, ed. Buber, III, 63; cf.

[1] Not prayer. Compare Schechter's *Aboth S. R. Nathan*, 165, and *Berachoth*, 24 a.

Pesikta R. Cahana, 172 b, and Midrash Thillim, Ps. lxxviii. 18).

(16) *Abba Jose the Hauranite* (*Tos. Mikvaoth,* III, 14), perhaps identical with R. Jose ha Horem, *Sifra Emor,* III a.

(17) *Abba Jose of Mahoz* (see Tosefta, *Mikvaoth,* III, 14; Mechiltha to Exod. xiv. 15; and Bruell in Frankel's *Monatsschr.,* 375, 1868).

(18) *Abba Elazar* (*Sifra,* II, 2). Cp. Abba Elazar of Bene B'rak, *Shir Nashirim Sutta,* ed. Buber, p. 40.

(19) *Abba Pnemon* (*Jerush. Terumma,* III, p. 42 b) is only mentioned as giving traditions concerning temple practice, and views concerning Moses' great powers, and concerning the evil spirit, &c.

(20) While all these, with the exception of Abba Hoshaya, belong to the age of the Tannaim, we see a new class of Abbas rise in the second century, viz. Meturgemans or preachers who receive the title of Abba, father. R. Juda ha Nasi had a preacher or Meturgeman by the name of *Abba Yudan* (*Bereshith Rabba,* 10), whose name was also contracted into Abdan (*Jerushalmi Berachot,* VII a; *Babli Jebamoth,* 105 b). To this class of preachers entitled "father" belonged, probably in a preceding age,—

(21) *Abba Gorion* the preacher (cp. Abba Yudan of Gorion, *Shir Nashirim Sutta,* ed. Buber, p. 38), and towards the close of the age of the Amoraim,—

(22) Abba Hoshaya, mentioned above (see Zunz, *G.,* V, 2, 185, and also about Abba, preacher, see Zunz, *G.,* V, 2, pp. 333 and 351). Abba Doresh and Abba bar Zutra, referred to by Zunz, do not belong here, as *Abba* is here a proper noun and not a title. So Abba the Barber in *Taanit.* 21 b.

It will be noticed that *Abba* as title was known only in Palestine, where the ancient Hasidean life continued long after the destruction of the temple. In Babylonia the name Abba occurs only as a proper name, not as a title.

Two more Abbas require explanation :—

(23) *Abba Sikra,* "Father (of) the Sicarian" head of

the zealots (*Gittin*, 56 a), identified by Rappoport (Erech, *Millin*, I, p. 257), Midrash, *Echa Rabbati*, ed. Buber, p. 66, n. 254, with Ben Batiah as nephew of Johanan ben Zakkai (Midrash, *Echa*, I, 5), "the Melon-like" man of robust form. Rappoport compares Athronges, the *Ethrog* or citron-like leader of a sedition soon after the death of King Herod (Josephus, *Ant.*, XVII, 107), but goes too far in identifying him with the same.

(24) Of *Abba Colon* we have a strange legend in *Shir Hashirim Rabba*, I, 6, according to which he was the founder of the island on which Rome was built. He brought earth from the river Euphrates and threw it into the Sea, and so the island was formed. He is therefore called the *Father Colonus*, "founder of the Colony." (Compare the story of Rome built on a piece of land formed by the angel Gabriel, *Sabbath*, 56 a, and the remark of Abba Banai on the formation of the earth above.) The name given to the Essenes by Strabo and Josephus is *Ktistes* or *Polistes*, "founders of townships," that is pioneers, Banaim, and this practice of an older generation of Essenes may have given rise to our odd legend.

Let us now see whether we cannot find some reason for the fact that *Abba*, father, was a favourite title among the Essenes or Hasideans.

Dr. Jastrow in his Dictionary, s. v. אבא, explains the expression "father Elijah" in *Sanhedrin*, 113 b, to be meant "sarcastically." But note that R. Jose was in constant communion with Elijah the prophet. He addressed him when he met him: "My master and teacher," *Rabbi u Mori* (*Brachoth*, 3 a). One day he spoke to his disciples of his impetuousness in his treatment of King Ahab, and he said: "Father Elijah was quick tempered." What happened? For three days Elijah did not appear to him. On the fourth day he again appeared to him, and R. Jose did not hesitate to take this very absence as due to the remark he had made and as corroboration of his statement. Thus far the Talmudical narrative. What sarcasm is there in the title Abba, father? "Väterchen Elias" translates Bacher (*Agada d. Tannaim*, II, 163) similarly, also mistaking the meaning of the word. Neither Bacher nor Jastrow noticed that, just because Elijah often appeared to the initiated in the garb of a venerable saint (as, in fact, he is often called in the Talmud, *hahu Saba*, yonder aged; see *Tosafoth Chollin*, 6 a), he is quoted, like any other teacher, as "father Elijah." Thus we read (Mas., *Calla*, III): "Abba Elijah, may he be remembered for good! said, 'The Torah is explained only to him who is not quick tempered.'" Likewise we read in *Tana de be Elijahu Zuta*, XV : "Abba Elijahu, may he be remembered for good and for blessing! said,' &c. Throughout the whole book *Tana de be Eliahu*, we find Elijah introduced like any other teacher, exactly as the prophet Jeremiah appeared to Philo while the latter was in a state of ecstasy, as a living "teacher and hierophant" (Philo, *Mang.*, I, 147).

Throughout the Bible, especially in the Wisdom literature, the instructor is the father, and the disciples, those that sit at the feet of the wise, his children. This fatherly relation of the teacher to his pupils was maintained also in the early days of the Scribes. Upon it rested the Essene mode of life. Both Josephus (*Wars*, II, 8, 2) and Philo ("The Virtuous being also free," XII) tell us that the young were regarded as children, and the pupils looked up to their teachers as to fathers. This patriarchal system was continued in the ecclesiastical and monastic institutions of the Christian community. As these relations, however, changed in the schools, and the head was invested with the dignity of the master, the title *Abba* became a survival of the ancient practice, an occasional token of honour bestowed upon some popular saint or preacher. This was little understood by later generations, and therefore the title was often dropped or replaced by the name "Rabbi."

163

IS THE TITLE "RABBI" ANACHRONISTIC
IN THE GOSPELS?

Hershel Shanks

THE TITLE 'RABBI' is used frequently in the Gospels, especially as a form of address for Jesus. Writing in *The Jewish Quarterly Review* (October, 1961), Professor Solomon Zeitlin reiterates his frequently stated [1] view that the use of the title "rabbi" in the Gospels is an "anachronism" (p. 122). He flatly states:

...[T]he term rabbi came into vogue after the destruction of the Second Temple. The title rabbi was not used by the Judaeans at the time of Jesus. (p. 122)

Neither this position, nor the reasoning on which it is based is original with Professor Zeitlin. On the contrary, it has become somewhat standard, having eminently respectable progenitors as well as descendants (e.g. Graetz, *Geschichte der Juden*, Vol. 3.2, p. 759; Vol. 4, p. 398-400 (1897 ed.); [2] *Jewish Encyclopedia*, "Rabbi"; *Encyclopedia Britannica* (14th ed.), "Rabbi"). Whether the position is sound is the subject of this discussion.

The best-known history of the title "rabbi" is contained in a letter to the community of Kairwan written by Sherira Gaon in the tenth century. [3][4] Sherira, of course, was not writing with reference to the

[1] Zeitlin, "Beginnings of Cyristianity and Judaism", *JQR*, Vol. 27, pp. 392-394 (1937);

Zeitlin, "The Pharisees and the Gospels" in *Essays and Studies in Memory of Linda R. Miller* (Davidson, ed.) (N.Y. 1938), pp. 269-272, 280;

Zeitlin, "Rashi and the Rabbinate", *JQR*, Vol. 31, pp. 11-12, 28-29 (1940);

Zeitlin, "The Crucifixion of Jesus Re-Examined", *JQR*, Vol. 33, p. 351 (1941);

Zeitlin, *Who Crucified Jesus?*, (2d ed.) (N.Y. 1942), pp. 221-222;

Zeitlin, "The Pharisees", *JQR*, Vol. 52, pp. 221 (1961).

[2] The English translation does not contain the notes which appear in the German edition.

[3] Sherira was Gaon of the academy at Pumbedita and is known chiefly for a letter to the community of Kairwan which forms one of the major sources for the history of talmudic, post-talmudic and gaonic times. The letter which gives the history of the title "rabbi", although written to the same community of Kairwan, is not the famous one referred to above.

[4] Graetz, the *Jewish Encyclopedia* and the *Encyclopedia Britannica* acknowledge their reliance on Sherira for the facts on which their

use of the term in the New Testament; rather, he was considering its history as a formal Jewish title of honor and authority. As we shall see, this fact has considerable bearing on our problem. The pertinent parts of Sherira's letter are short enough to quote almost in full:

> The title "rabbi" is borne by the sages of Palestine, who were ordained by the Sanhedrin in accordance with the custom handed down by the elders and were denominated "Rabbi", and received authority to judge in penal cases; while "Rab" is the title of the Babylonian sages, who received their ordination in their colleges. The more ancient generations, however, which were far superior, had no such titles as "Rabban", "Rabbi", or "Rab" for either the Babylonian or Palestinian sages. This is evident from the fact that Hillel I, who came from Babylon, had not the title "Rabban" prefixed to his name. Of the prophets, also, who were very eminent, it is simply said, "Haggai the prophet", etc. "Ezra did not come up from Babylon", etc., the title "Rabban" not being used. Indeed, this title is not met with earlier than the time of the patriarchate. It was first used of Rabban Gamaliel the Elder, Rabban Simon his son and Rabban Johanan ben Zakkai, all of whom were patriarchs or presidents of the Sanhedrin. The title "Rabbi" too came into vogue among those who received the laying on of the hands at this period, as, for instance, Rabbi Zadok, Rabbi Eliezer ben Jacob, and others, and dates from the time of the disciples of Rabban Jochanan ben Zakkai downward. Now the order of these titles is as follows: "Rabbi" is greater than "Rab"; "Rabban" again is greater than "Rabbi"; while the simple name is greater than "Rabban". [5]

The facts in this passage contain the only significant basis for concluding that "rabbi" was not used at the time of Jesus.

The important items from this passage which have led Zeitlin and others to the conclusion that "rabbi" is anachronistic in the Gospels are these: (1) The great Hillel, roughly a contemporary of Jesus, [6] did not have the title. (For this reason, "the simple name [without title] is greater than "Rabban' ".) (2) The first person to bear the title "Rabban" was Gamaliel the Elder (traditionally a son or grandson of Hillel), who was active in the last decades before and shortly after

---

argument is based. Zeitlin does not appear to. However, the facts on which he relies are the same. See n. 9.

[5] The translation is taken from the Jewish Encyclopedia's article on "Rabbi". The full text may be found in the *Aruk* under the title אביי, (Kohut, ed.), Vol. I, p. 6, Vienna, 1926).

[6] It is of course impossible to date lives such as Hillel with accuracy. A reasonable estimate is that his important activity occurred during the period 30 B.C.—10 C.E.

the destruction of the Seond Temple. [7] Apparently the title "Rabban" was given to him shortly after the Destruction when he alone stood as head of the Sanhedrin. [8] (3) Those scholars under Gamaliel who, after the destruction, were authorized by the Sanhedrin to decide the law were denominated "Rabbi". [9]

Largely, on this basis, it has been concluded that the term "rabbi" was not used at all among the Jews before the destruction of the Second Temple. [10] How sound is this conclusion?

The most serious defect in this reasoning lies in the fact that Sherira, as well as the tannaitic sources, [11] consider the term "rabbi" only as an official title of honor and authority. Sherira was explaining why various tannaim and amoraim bore different titles; his answer, of course, lay in history. But is it permissible to use this "official" history as evidence that the term was not used earlier as an unofficial form of address for a spiritual leader and teacher, which, as we shall note, is the manner in which the title is used in the Gospels.

Indeed, to rely on the facts in Sherira's letter to prove that the title

[7] As with Hillel (see n. 5), so with Gamaliel: It is difficult to establish with precision when he lived. "Gamaliel, a doctor of the law" (Acts 5: 34) is twice mentioned in the New Testament, once as Paul's teacher (Acts 22: 3). We cannot, of course, be certain that the Gamaliel referred to in Acts is Rabban Gamaliel. However, if Gamaliel was a contemporary of Jesus, as many believe he was (see e.g., Abernach, "The Change From a Standing to Sitting Posture By Students After the Death of Rabban Gamaliel", *JQR*, Vol. 52, p. 172 (1961), it can hardly be argued that the title 'rabbi' is anachronistic in the Gospels. Despite this weak reed on which Zeitlin's contention rests, we shall assume that Gamaliel did not take the title until after the Destruction.

[8] Zeitlin explains how this came about:
Up to the time of Gamaliel, two men stood at the head of the Sanhedrin, one a Nasi and the other an Ab bet din; while in the time of Gamaliel the position of Ab bet din was abolished and entire authority was invested in Gamaliel alone. Hence the title was given him "Rabban" "Master". The word "rabban" is derived from "rab" meaning "elder", "master". [Zeitlin, "The Pharisees and the Gospels", supra, n. 1, p. 270. See also Zeitlin, "Beginnings of Christianity and Judaism", supra, n. 1, p. 392 (1937)].

[9] These are the facts with which Zeitlin supports his position, although he does not cite Sherira. See "The Pharisees and the Gospels", supra, n. 1, 5; "Beginnings of Christianity and Judaism", supra, n. 1, 5; these facts are also incorporated by reference in the other citations listed in n. 1.

[10] Zeitlin, "The Crucifixion of Jesus Re-Examined", supra, n. 1, p. 351.

[11] E.g., Sab. 15a.

"rabbi" was not used at the time of Jesus really proves too much. It could as easily prove that the title was not used *in the sense it is used in the New Testament as an unofficial vocative* even after the Destruction. Jesus would at no time have met the requirements for this title as those requirements are laid down in Sherita's letter.

When the title rabban was officially bestowed on Gamaliel, the word was not coined for that purpose. It was not taken out of thin air. The etymology of the word traces back to the biblical רב. It must have had some development between biblical times and the Destruction. It is worth pointing out that, with the exception of the Dead Sea Scrolls, there is no original extant Hebrew or Aramaic literature between c. 167 B.C. and c. 130 C.E.: [12] Accordingly, we have no way of knowing with certainty just how the term developed and was used during any particular, relatively short period of time. [13]

It would seem not only possible, but indeed likely, that prior to its use as an official title (which is all that Sherira is concerned with), the term "rabbi" was used as an unofficial mode of address. [14] As a kind of unofficial title, it may well have been used in Jesus' time in much the same way that the unofficial title "preacher" is employed in certain strata of American society today.[15] It would seem that the adoption of the term "rabbi" as an official title would require a linguistic development which would include the use of the title apart from its subsequently adopted formal requirements; so that far from disproving the use of the term "rabbi" during Jesus' lifetime, the facts

[12] I am indebted to W. F. Albright for this fact.

[13] Bonsirvan has pointed out (*Le Judaïsme palestinien au temps de Jésus Christ*, (Paris, 1934), Vol. I, p. 274):
Les documents, desquels nous tirons nos renseignements sur les rabbins, sont tous postérieurs au temps de Jésus-Christ et décrivent la vie d'un organisme pleinement, développé et fonctionnant en des conditions sociales, religieuses et politiques spéciales: il est impossible de déterminer les transpositions et les réductions qu'il faut pratiquer dans ces renseignements, pour avoir une image du rabbinisme au début de notre ère.
W. F. Albright agrees. Commenting on this situation, Albright has stated: "How can he [Zeitlin] be so sure about what may have been true, about what may or may not have existed, in such a vacuum." [Letter to the author, dated September 10, 1962].

[14] Zeitlin insists the Gospel use of the word "rabbi" is as a "technical name", "The Pharisees and the Gospels", supra, n. 1, pp. 269, 280. It is not readily apparent what he means by "technical" or why he regards the Gospel use of the title as a "technical" use.

[15] Cf. Klausner, *Jesus of Nazareth*, (N.Y. 1925), p. 43, n. 92; p. 256, n. 16.

outlined in Sherira's letter concerning its adoption as an official title serve only to confirm its earlier unofficial use. That the term was used as an honorific, but unofficial vocative in Jesus' lifetime is not simply consistent with the history of the term as an official title; it is supported by this history.

Zeitlin's answer to the theory that "rabbi" may well have been in use as an unofficial title during Jesus' lifetime is only that "the name 'rabbi' or 'rabbanim' does not occur in the entire tannaitic literature before the destruction of the Second Temple." [16] From this "negative evidence," he argues that "in the time of Jesus, the title 'rabbi' was still *unknown* among the Jews." [17] [18]

How strong is this "negative evidence"? Is it really surprising that the early tannaitic halakah and haggadah make no reference to an unofficial vocative used by the man in the street to address a spiritual leader and teacher? I submit that it is not surprising at all.

Whatever persuasive force this "negative evidence" has, however, must give way to the "positive evidence" in the Gospels themselves. The term ραββει (transliteration: "rabbi") [19] appears at least fourteen times in three of the four Gospels, Matthew, [20] Mark, [21] and John. [22] In addition, the even more reverent [23] ραββουνυ (transliteration and translation: "rabboni"(appears both in the earliest Gospel, Mark, [24] and in the latest, John. [25] "Rabbi" is used to address John the Baptist, [26] as well as Jesus, [27] and is used in a passage denouncing the Pharisees and suggesting that the title is one which those alleged hypocrites crave. [28]

---

[16] Zeitlin, "Beginnings of Christianity and Judaism", supra, n. 1, p. 392.

[17] Zeitlin, "Rashi and the Rabbinate", supra, n. 1, p. 29, fn. 96, (emphasis supplied); and *Ibid*.

[18] Even the sources for this "negative evidence" are questionable. See n. 13.

[19] In order to be precise, we must use the original Greek, for, despite the fact that the transliteration is "rabbi", the word is not always translated as "rabbi" in English.

[20] Matthew 23: 7, 8; 26: 25, 49.

[21] Mark 9: 5; 11: 21; 14: 45.

[22] John 1: 38, 49; 3: 2; 3: 26; 4: 31; 9: 2; 11: 8.

[23] See Harper's Bible Dictionary, "Rabbi".

[24] Mark 10: 51.

[25] John 20: 16.

[26] John 3: 26.

[27] Matthew 26: 25, 49; Mark 9: 5; 11: 21; 14: 45; John 1: 38, 49; 3: 2; 4: 31; 9: 2; 11: 8.

[28] Matthew 32: 7-8.

Surely this frequent appearance of the term in the Gospels is more persuasive evidence that the title was in fact used at the time of Jesus than the absence of the term in pre-Destruction tannaitic literature is evidence that it was not used.

Thus, one of the obvious difficulties with Professor Zeitlin's position is that it requires an explanation of the frequent use of "rabbi" in the New Testament. Professor Zeitlin has recognized the problem; [29] he has not, however, come to grips with it, except to suggest that in each instance the term was inserted later. [30] But why? What motive lay behind such frequent tampering with fact or text?

It can perhaps be argued that the use of "rabbi" in Matthew 23: 6-8 [31] was a clumsy attempt to give the ring of authenticity to a spurious passage. [32]. However, this explains only two appearances of the word in the Gospels. Its other appearances, as terms of address for Jesus and John, are not so eaily explained. Why would the Gospel writers or later editors insert a Jewish title for Jesus when at the time they wrote the principal missionary activities of the new religion were already directed to Gentiles?

If they tampered with the facts or the texts, surely they would not do so in a manner to make their cause less attractive to the new religion's primary source of converts. That Jesus had been addressed as "rabbi" certainly did not make the religion founded in his name more palatable to the heathen. On two occasions John even felt it necessary to explain parenthetically, after using the title "rabbi", that it meant "teacher". [33] Why, if it were not part of the authentic Jesus tradition at the time John wrote, would he insert the title falsely when it was apparently so unfamiliar to his readers that its meaning must be explained. Thus, it would seem that the frequent appearance of the title in the Gospels is not so easily disposed of.

Finally, there is archaeological evidence which, if it does not disprove Professor Zeitlin's contention, at least casts doubt upon it. Or so argues the dean of biblical archaologists, Professor W. F.

[29] "We must admit that the name "rabbi" in the Gospels presents a problem". Zeitlin, "Beginnings of Christianity and Judaism, supra, n. 1, p. 393; see also, "The Pharisees and the Gospels", supra, n. 1, p. 280.

[30] Ibid.

[31] "...[A]nd they [the Pharisees] love the place of honor at feasts and the best seats in the synagogues, and salutations in the market place, and being called rabbi by men. But you are not to be called rabbi, for you have one teacher, and you are all brethren." ,

[32] Zeitlin makes this suggestion in "The Pharisees", supra, n. 1, pp. 121-122.

[33] The Greek word is "didaskalos", see pp. 140.

Albright in his *Archaeology of Palestine*. [34] If this reference has come to Professor Zeitlin's attention, he has not commented on it.

Albright questions what we have here been calling Zeitlin's position on the basis of an ossuary found by the late Professor E. L. Sukenik of Hebrew University. Sukenik reported his find in the Hebrew periodical *Tarbiz* in 1930 [35] and commented on it briefly the following year in a lecture to the Berlin Archaeological Society (printed separately in German in 1931). [36] Because Professor Albright's short reference to it in *The Archaeology of Palestine* is the only English mention of Sukenik's find, it deserves more detailed mention here, especially since Albright does not cite his original sources (although he does give Sukenik full credit).

In 1929, Hebrew University assumed responsibility for digging a Jewish cemetrey on the Mount of Olives. Among these pre-Destruction (and perhaps Hasmonean) graves, [37] Sukenik found an ossuary on one

---

[34] Harmondsworth, Middlesex, 1949; (Rev. ed., Baltimore, 1954).

[35] "A Jewish Tomb on the Mount of Olives (B)", *Tarbiz*, Vol. I, pp. 140-141 (in Hebrew).

[36] "Jüdische Gräber Jerusalems um Christi Geburt."

[37] The basis on which Sukenik dated the graves is described in the German pamphlet (pp. 12-14):

Verschiedene Gräber enthielten auch Beigaben, wie Keramik, Glas und ab und zu auch Schmucksachen aus Silber und Bronze. Letzthin wurde in einem Grabe eine Münze gefunden. Diese Beigaben sind von grosser Wichtigkeit für die Datierung der Ossuarien. Die Keramik gehört der spät-hellenistischen und der früh-römischen Zeit an. Sehr oft findet man Reste von gerippten Gefässen, die typisch für die herodianische Zeit sind. Auch die anderen Beigaben stimmen damit überein und die erwähnten Münze wird dem Hasmonäerkönig Alexander Jannaeus zugeschrieben. Die grosse Zahl dieser Gräber in Jerusalem zeigt an und für sich schon, dass sie in die Zeit vor der Zerstörung des Tempels gehören, als Jerusalem noch vollständig von Juden bevölkert war. Leider ist es sehr schwierig, auf Grund des Schriftcharakters der gefundenen hebräischen und aramäischen Inschriften etwas Genaueres über die Datierung zu sagen. Aber die ab und zu vorkommenden griechischen Inschriften weisen hauptsächlich auf das erste Jahrhundert nach Christo hin. Das wurde mir auch letzthin von Prof. Schubart, dem Leiter der Papyrus-Sammlung der Staatlichen Museen in Berlin, bestätigt. Auf keinen Fall sind die Jerusalemer Ossuarien später als der Barkochba-Aufstand zu datieren, wobei in Erwägung zu ziehen ist, dass diese Osteotheken nicht etwa ausschliesslich für Jerusalemer Bürger verwendet wurden, sondern, dass es leicht möglich ist, dass manche ausserhalb der Heiligen Stadt wohnenden Juden auch nach der Zerstörung des Tempels in Jerusalem begraben werden wollten. Einen solchen Fall kennen

of the long sides on which is carved the name חתדיטן =Theodotion in Hebrew characters and on the other long side the title ΔΙΔΑCΚΑΛΟΥ =Didaskalos in Greek characters. "Didaskalos" is the Greek word for teacher, and on two occasions is used by John to define both "rabbi" (ραββει) [38] and "rabboni" (ραββουνι) [39]. These terms he explains by the parenthetical phrase "which means didaskalos (teacher)." Moreover, on several occasions Jesus is addressed as "didaskalos", instead of "rabbi", further suggesting that the terms were very nearly interchangeable. [40]

Professor Sukenik was fully aware of the significance of his find for New Testament study and even traced the use of the title "didaskalos" through later periods:

The title διδάσααλος (didaskalos) which means teacher and corresponds with the title "rabbi" is found frequently in the Gospels as a title for Jesus. Martha designates Jesus as διδσααλος (didaskalos) in speaking about him with her sister Mary (John 11: 28). The title ραββουνι (rabbouni) or ραββονι (rabboni) with which the blind man in Jericho addresses Jesus (Mark 10: 51) is explained by John as meaning διδαρκαλος (didaskalos) when he relates the vision of Mary Magdalene after the crucifixion. On one of the tombstones of the Jewish catacombs in Monteverde [in Rome] the title διδασκαλορ νοποπαθηρ is used. This title was later identical with the title of the head of the synagogue (Archisynagogus). The head of the Jews of the West or in Italy was called Annatus didaskalos, in whose name some of the laws of the Codex Theodosianus were edited.

This title [didaskalos] appears for the first time in the inscriptions on the ossuary and this is also its earliest appearance in Jewish epigraphy in general. [41]

After calling our attention to the fact that many rabbinic scholars have insisted that the title "rabbi" is anachronistic in the Gospels, Professor Albright concludes that as a result of Sukenik's find:

wir bezuglich der Familie des jüdischen Patriarchen aud Jabne, von der im Talmud erzählt wird, dass sie in Jabne ein "geliehenes" Grab hatte, in dem sie zuerst ihre Toten bestattete, um sie später nach Jerusalem überzuführen. Jedoch müssen die Jerusalemer Ossurarien im grossen und ganzen ungefähr den letzten zwei Jahrhunderten vor der Zerstörung des Tempels zugeschrieben werden.

[38] John 1: 38.
[39] John 20: 16.
[40] Jesus is addressed or referred to as "disadkalos" in: Matthew 8: 19, 12: 38 (The Pharisees address Jesus with this vocative); Mark 4: 38; 5: 35; 9: 17; 38; Luke 18: 18; John 11: 28.
[41] p. 140.

...It cannot safely be alleged that the Gospel of John [and presumably Matthew and Mark as well] is anachronistic in this particular respect. [43]

Of course, the Sukenik ossuary is far from conclusive evidence that the title "rabbi" was used at the time of Jesus. We cannot be sure that if the title "didaskalos" was used, "rabbi" was used also. But the archaeological materials are certainly suggestive. They point to the more general conclusion of this article.:

We are working in a period of which our knowledge is lamentably thin. Our conclusion as to whether the title "rabbi" was used at the time of Jesus must depend on a series of inferences, each of which must be beset with doubts. Surely, the *ex cathedra* conviction of Zeitlin is not warranted at this late date. On the whole, the weight of the evidence would seem to lead to the conclusion that it is more likely than not that the term "rabbi" *was* used in the time of Jesus and that therefore its use in the Gospels is *not* anachronistic.

A REPLY

S. Zeitlin

MR. SHANKS TAKES ISSUE with my view that the title "rabbi" came into vogue after the destruction of the Second Temple and hence could not have been used by the Judaeans at the time of Jesus. He presents no conclusive evidence to the contrary. He makes the following statements: "We cannot be sure that if the title 'didaskalos' was used, "rabbi" was used also. But the archaeological materials are certainly suggestive. They point to the more general conclusion of this article... On the whole, the weight of the evidence would seem to lead to the conclusion that it is more likely than not that the term 'rabbi' *was* used at the time of Jesus and that therefore its use in the Gospels is *not* anachronistic." He further maintains that my contention that the title "rabbi" was not used before the destruction of the Second Temple is not original but that it is based on the Epistle of Sherira Gaon.

My contention could not have been based on the Epistle of Sherira Gaon since I hold that no medieval document written in the tenth century can be employed and used as a source for the history of the Second Jewish Commonwealth. My thesis was based on the internal evidence in tannaitic literature.

Mr. Shanks writes, "When the title rabban was officially bestowed on Gamaliel, the word was not coined for that purpose. It was not taken out of thin air. The etymology of the word traces back to the biblical רב." The title rabban does not trace back to the Bible רב. The word

[42] *The Archaeology of Palestine* (Rev. ed.), p. 244.

רב in the Bible has the connotation of elder, much, greater. The word *adonai* is rendered by רבונא in the Targum. The word *nasi* in the book of Ezekiel is rendered by רבא in the Targum. The *nasi* of the Sanhedrin was called *rabba* in Aramaic. Gamaliel, who became the sole leader of the Sanhedrin, had the title rabbon "our nasi". [1] Thus the title Rabban Gamaliel was not taken from a vacuum and is not derived from the biblical word רב. The title rabbi was never appended to any sage before the destruction of the Temple. After the destruction of the Second Temple those sages who attained ordination had the title rabbi preceding their names.

The author quotes passages from the Gospels wherein the term rabbi occurs: Mark 9. 5, where it is stated "And Peter said to Jesus Rabbi." In Matthew 17.4 the word κύριε. Lord is given instead of Rabbi. Apparently the original Hebrew had אדני. Matthew rendered it κύριε while Mark rendered it ραββί in Aramaic form. In Mark 11.21 the word rabbi occurs, while in the same connection in Matthew 21.20 the word rabbi is not found. In Mark 10.51 the word *rabboni* occurs, which is a real translation from the Hebrew *adonai*, my lord. In Mark 14.45 the word rabbi again occurs. In Matthew 23.7 and 8 the word rabbi occurs, "And greetings in the markets, and to be called of men rabbi but be not ye called rabbi for one is your διδάσκαλος teacher, even Christ and all ye are brethren." Some manuscripts have καθη-γητης, guide, master, instead of διδάσκαλος teacher. From internal evidence we have the right to assume that the correct reading was καθηγάτης since Jesus says "Ye are brethren. And call no man your father upon the earth: for one is your Father which is in heaven. Neither be ye called masters καθηγηται for one is your master καθηγητής even Christ." It is probable that the entire passage is a later interpolation or that the Greek translator did not fully comprehend the original text. In this section Matthew states that Jesus accused the Pharisees of being hypocrites, "They make broad their phylacteries." At the time of Jesus *tephilin* were not phylacteries. *Tephilin* were not used as a talisman, a charm, for protection against evil spirits. [2]

In his account of the betrayal of Jesus by Judas Matthew states, "Then Judas, which betrayed him, answered and said rabbi, is it I?" Further, when Jesus was seized, Judas gave the Roman cohort the sign of identification as to who Jesus was. "He (Judas) came to Jesus and said Peace, rabbi and kissed him." Mark, in describing the betrayal of Jesus, mentions the word rabbi only once when Judas kissed Jesus

[1] Cf. S. Zeitlin, "The Titles High Priest and the Nasi of the Sanhedrin", *JQR*, July 1957.

[2] Idem, "The Pharisees", *JQR*, October, 1961, pp. 131-122.

to identify him. Luke does not use the word rabbi in his account of the betrayal. We must note that the term rabbi never occurs in the Gospel according to Luke. In the Gospel according to John the term rabbi occurs a number of times. However in his narrative of the betrayal the term rabbi is not employed.

Mr. Shanks makes reference to the term rabbi employed in the Gospel according to John where it is used with the explanation *didaskalos* teacher, In Chapter 1.38 the disciples who followed Jesus "Said unto him rabbi which means teacher", In Ch. 3.2 John wrote that Nicodemus said to Jesus, "Rabbi, we know that you are a teacher come from God." The same evangelist employed the term rabbi to John the Baptist.

It is a historical fact, and we shall substantiate it, that the Gospel, according to John, was composed not earlier than the middle of the Second Century C.E. and it was written for gentile Christians. At the time of its composition the term rabbi was already in usage among the Jews. It is still a question as to whether even at that period this term had the connotation of teacher. It is possible that John in writing for the pagans, who were unaquainted with the term rabbi, interpreted it as meaning teacher.

I have pointed out elsewhere that the festival now known as Passover was called the Festival of Unleavened Bread during the period of the Second Commonwealth as it is so called in the Bible. The term Passover referred to the paschal lamb. After the destruction of the Second Temple this festival was renamed the Festival of Passover. The Synoptic Gospels adopt the name used by the Jews during the Second Commonwealth—the Festival of Unleavened Bread. In Mark 14.1 we have "It was now two days before the Passover and the Feast of Unleavened Bread." In Matthew 26.17, we have "Now in the first day of Unleavened Bread the disciples came to Jesus saying, 'Where will you have us prepare for you to eat the Passover ?' " In Luke 22.1, "Now the Feast of Unleavened Bread drew near which is Passover." In the same chapter 7, "Then came the day of Unleavened Bread, when the pascha was slaughtered." There is a clear distinction in the Synoptic Gospels between the Festival of Unleavened Bread and the slaughtering of the paschal lamb. The Festival of Unleavened Bread never occurs in the Gospel according to John but term Festival of Passover is employed which was the usage among the Jews after the destruction of the Second Temple. In John 2.23 "Now when he was in Jerusalem at the Passover Feast; 6.4 Now the Passover, the Feast of the Jews was at hand; 13.1 Now before the Feast of the Passover. That John employed the term Festival of Passover instead of Festival of Unleavened Bread shows that the Fourth Gospel was a late composition. Thus it is not surprising that term *rabbi* is employed in it.

Mr. Shanks refers to the late Professor Sukenik's findings and the ossuary on which the term *didaskolas* was carved in Greek letters and it is his opinion that the word *didaskolas* is the translation of the term rabbi. This term was used by the Jews during the Hellenistic and Roman periods for the word מורה teacher. Mr. Shanks says farther, "There is archaeological evidence which, if it does not disprove Professor Zeitlin's contention, at least casts doubt upon it." The archaeologists have not discovered any document of the period of the Second Commonwealth wherein the term rabbi occurs.

Mr. Shanks' lack of knowledge of rabbinic literature and the Jewish history of the Second Commonwealth, is shown from several examples. Here is one, "The first person to bear the title 'Rabban' was Gamaliel the Elder (traditionally a grandson of Hillel) who was active in the last decades before and shortly after the destruction of the Second Temple." Rabban Gamaliel the Elder died before the destruction of the Temple, and his son Simon was a member of the provisional government which had been established in the year 65 C.E. [3] after the Judaean victory over the Roman general, Cestius. Simon, the son of Gamaliel, was probably assassinated by the Zealots' or other fanatics before the destruction of the Second Temple. Mr. Shanks is in total confusion. There were two Gamaliels with the title of Rabban. One was Gamaliel the Elder who lived before the destruction of the Temple (according to Acts Paul sat at his feet), [4] and the other was his grandson, Gamaliel, who lived after the destruction of the Temple and who was the head of the Academy of Jabneh.

In another paragraph Mr. Shanks made the following assertion, "It is worth pointing out that, with the exception of the Dead Sea Scrolls, there is no original extant Hebrew of Aramaic literature between c. 167 B.C. and c. 130 C.E." While it is true that the Mishne was composed by Judah the Prince in the early part of the third Century C.E. there are however many sections in it which go back to great antiquity, some to the Hasmonean period and before. Even in the Talmud there are passages which date back to the time of the Hasmoneans. To cite one example: In the passage where the story of the struggle between the Pharisees and John Hyrcanus I, the conservive *waw* (that is a verb in the future tense whose meaning is converted to the past tense by prefixing the letter *waw*) was used. [5] This usage is employed frequently in the Bible. This passage goes back to the time of John Hyrcanus I c. 110-109 B.C.E. To assert, "There is no original extant Hebrew or Aramaic literature between c. 167 B.C. and c. 130 C.E." displays an

[3] Cf. Josephus, *Jewish War*, 4.3.9. (159); *Vita*, 190.
[4] 22. 3.   [5] Kid. 66a.

utter lack of knowledge. As to the Dead Sea Scrolls, it has *not* been established that they were written during the period of the Second Commonwealth. My contention that the Dead Sea Scrolls were written long after the destruction of the Second Temple has never been refuted. My appeals to the archaeologists and theologians that they reply to my arguments against the antiquity of the Scrolls were unanswered for the simple reason that they had no proofs to refute my arguments. To them the Scrolls became an article of faith. An article of faith is not in the category of argument.

Elsewhere I wrote that the Talmud may be compared to a primeval dense forest in which a person will lose his way without a skillful guide. Not having a guide, Mr. Shanks lost his way.

ORIGINS OF THE TITLE "RABBI"

Hershel Shanks

In 1963 I wrote an article which attempted to collect in English materials bearing on the question whether the frequent use of the title *Rabbi* in the Gospels was anachronistic, and to give some assessment of the available evidence.[1] I concluded that, contrary to considerable earlier opinion, the use of *Rabbi* in the Gospels was probably not anachronistic and that the title *Rabbi* was probably in use at the time of Jesus' ministry, a conclusion in which, now after five years, I feel somewhat more confirmed.

Professor Solomon Zeitlin promptly published a blistering reply to my article and its conclusions.[2] More recently Father Raymond E. Brown in his Anchor edition of *John* discusses the question.[3]

At this juncture, some minor elaboration and clarification appear worthwhile. This brief exposition will assume familiarity with my earlier article on the subject.

The first point I would like to make concerns the etymological history of the word. Although briefly treated in my earlier article, it deserves some elaboration.[4]

Between 60 and 70 Semitic dialects have been identified as having been spoken in the Near East during the 4000 years beginning approximately 3000 B. C.[5] Naturally, the extant materials in each varies from a few sherds to a veritable literature. Even on the available evidence, however, it is fair to say that some form of the word *Rab* (possessive, *Rabbi*) was used in most of these languages from the earliest to the latest. Moreover, this widespread use was not confined to the adjectival root-meaning, great or distinguished. In a large number of Semitic languages or dialects, from Akkadian to Hebrew

---

[1] "Is the Title 'Rabbi' Anachronistic in the Gospels?", *JQR*, Vol. 53, p. 337 (1963).

[2] *JQR*, Vol. 53, p. 345 (1963).

[3] *The Gospel According to John* (i-xii) (Anchor Ed.) (Raymond E. Brown, S. S., ed.) (New York, 1966), p. 74.

[4] In my article I traced the word back to the biblical רב, as does Dr. Broydé in his article on "Rabbi" in *The Jewish Encyclopedia* and Father Bonsirven in *Le Judaïsme palestinien au temps de Jésus Christ* (Paris, 1934), Vol. II, pp. 272-4. Professor Zeitlin flatly states I am wrong, although he gives no explanation.

[5] C. Rabin, "The Origins of the Subdivisions of Semitic" in *Hebrew and Semitic Studies Presented to G. R. Driver* (Oxford, 1963), p. 104.

and Aramaic, we have examples of some form of *Rab* being used as a title or as part of a title.

What follows should be considered illustrative, not exhaustive. Other examples could easily be found.

In Akkadian, *Rab* forms the first part of a great many titles, including chief astrologer, chief physician, chief herder, chief cupbearer and chief overseer of the vineyards.[6]

In 14th Century Ugaritic, we find *Rab* used not only as part of a number of secular titles, such as corporal (chief of ten), captain (chief of a hundred), chief of the town, chief of the craftsmen, chief of the grooms, but also as part of *religious titles*, like chief of the priests (*rb kknm*) and high priest (*rb ntbtš*).[7]

In early Aramaic, *Rab* was a part of the title for the commander of the army.[8]

Other titles containing a form of *Rab* are also reported from Assyria, Babylonia and Phonecia.[9] Nor did the development of this word cease with the Roman destruction of the Temple. Examples are numerous from Jewish, as well as other Semitic, languages. In Syriac, we have not only chief butler, chief baker, master architect, and chief justice, but also chief pastor, high priest, leader of the faithful, and ruler of the synagogue.[10] The name Barrabas is really a contraction of Bar-rabba (son of the great one, and not, as so commonly supposed, son of the father).[11] Still later, we find the Babylonian amora who headed the academy of Mahoza (Sura) bearing the title רבא; a senior teacher, רבה; and the chief of the academy at Pumbeditha, רבן.[12]

[6] W. Muss-Arnolt, *A Concise Dictionary of The Assyrian Language* (Berlin, 1905), p. 946.

[7] Cyrus H. Gordon, *Ugaritic Textbook* (*Analecta Orientalia* 38) (Rome—Pontificium Institutum Biblicum, 1965), p. 482; see also W. F. Albright, *From the Stone Age to Christianity* (Doubleday Anchor, 2d ed., 1957), p. 282.

[8] E. G. Kraeling (ed.), *The Brooklyn Museum Aramaic Papyri* (*New Documents of the Fifth Century B.C. From the Jewish Colony at Elephantine*) (Yale, 1953), pp. 226-27, 317.

[9] Francis Brown, S. R. Driver, Charles A. Briggs, *A Hebrew and English Lexicon of the Old Testament* (Oxford, 1962), pp. 912-13.

[10] J. Payne Smith (Mrs. Margoliouth) ed., *A Compendious Syriac Dictionary Founded upon the Thesaurus Syriacus of R. Payne Smith* (Oxford, 1957), p. 525.

[11] W. F. Albright, *From the Stone Age to Christianity* (Doubleday-Anchor, 2d ed., 1957), p. 246.

[12] Marcus Jastrow, "*A Dictionary of the Targumim, Talmud Babli and Yerushalmi, and the Midrashic Literature.* (Pardes Publishing House, Inc., N.Y., 1950), Vol. II, p. 1438.

Special attention should of course be given to the use of the title *Rab* in the Bible. It appears frequently in relatively early books as well as late books:

2 Kings 18: 17, 19, 27, 28, 37; 2 Kings 19: 4, 8; Isaiah 36: 2, 4, 11, 12, 13, 22; Isaiah 37: 4, 8	Chief or head of the officers ("the Rabshakeh" —RSV)	רב־שקה
2 Kings 18:17	Chief eunuch, a high military or diplomatic official [13] ("the Rab-saris"—RSV)	רב־סריס
2 Kings 25 and parallel passages in Jeremiah 30	Chief or head of the guard	רב־טבחים
Jeremiah 39:13	Chief soothsayer ("the Rabmag"—RSV)	רב־מג,
Jeremiah 39:13 Jeremiah 41:1	Chief officers of the King Chief officers of the King	רבי מלך בבל רבי המלך
Jonah 1:6	Chief of the sailors or shipmaster	רב החבל
Esther 1:8	Officers of the house	רב ביתו
Daniel 1:3	Chief officier	רב־סריסו

The point of this too lengthy demonstration is this: Forms of *Rab* as titles were used throughout the ancient Near East, both early and late, from Mesopotamia to Egypt, in Jewish as well as non-Jewish languages, in secular titles and in religious titles. In the New Testament we find the possessive form *Rabbi* in use as a title for an itinerant preacher. In light of the broad and varied use of *Rab* which we have described, it is understandable that the Gospel use of the title might well be authentic, even though its use as a title for ordained

[13] *Cf.* Francis Brown, S. R. Driver, Charles A. Briggs, *A Hebrew and English Lexicon of the Old Testament* (Oxford, 1962), p. 913 *with Jeremiah* (Anchor ed.) (John Bright, ed.) (New York, 1965), p. 243.

scholars does not appear in Jewish sources until after 70 C.E.[14, 15]

Let me emphasize, so as to avoid any possibility of being misunderstood, I do not suggest that these earlier uses of *Rab* prove that the Gospel use of the title *Rabbi* is authentic. My point is a narrow one: These earlier uses of *Rab* simply make to easier to understand that the use of *Rabbi* as a title for an itinerant preacher could easily have pre-dated the use of *Rabbi* as a title for an ordained scholar, just as many of these other *Rab*-forms pre-dated the use of *Rabbi* as a title for ordained scholars.

This etymological history is a picture of the forest rather than the trees. It gives a 4000 year picture rather than a 40 year picture. It suggests the overall presence of this root in the ancient Middle East. And it demonstrates the shaky foundations of the argument that the frequent Gospel use of *Rabbi* as a title for an itinerant preacher is anachronistic simply because our currently available materials do not show a use of the term as a title for ordained scholars prior to the Roman destruction of the Temple.[16]

The argument of the "anachronists" is even weaker·if we can show that the closely related Jewish title *Rabban* was in use prior to the Destruction, and this leads me to my second point, a point of clarification rather than elaboration.

The first person to bear the title *Rabban* was Gamaliel the Elder. My earlier article is unclear as to when Gamaliel took this title—before

[14] *Cf.* George Foot Moore, *Judaism in the First Centuries of the Christian Era* (Harvard, 1930), Vol. 3, p. 15.

[15] Moreover, there may well be a Jewish reference to the use of *Rabbi* before the Destruction. See A. N. Orenstein, אנציקלופדיה לתארי־כבוד בישראל (Tel-Aviv 1963) Vol. 4, pl 2272, n. 4. Rabbi Orenstein has suggested that a Tosefta at the end of עדיות may refer to a Jewish usage of *Rabbi* antedating Rabbon Yochanan ben Zakkai. The Tosefta reads as follows:

> He who has disciples and whose disciples again have disciples is called *Rabbi*. When his disciples are forgotten [i.e. because they taught so long ago] [or perhaps "are ordained"], he is called *Rabban*; and when the disciples of his disciples are also forgotten [or "ordained"], he is called simply by his own name.

Professor Saul Lieberman of the Jewish Theological Seminary, the unrivaled authority on the Tosefta in modern times, advises me that in his opinion this Tosefta is an unquestionably authentic reference to the use of *Rabbi* in pre-Destruction times.

[16] It should be noted that *Rabbi* is not used in the Gospels in the same sense as it was applied to ordained scholars who could rule on matters of law. Jesus would never have qualified for the title in this latter sense.

or after the Destruction—, and, as we shall see, Father Brown's discussion is in error on this point.

The confusion may be easily clarified: What little evidence we have suggests that Rabban Gamaliel the Elder lived his active life before the Destruction. Beyond this, however, it is difficult to say much.

According to Tannaitic tradition recorded in Shab. 15a, Gamaliel the Elder and his son Simeon were the last two heads of the Sanhedrin before the destruction of the Temple,[17] although some scholars have disputed the reliability of this tradition.[18] According to a recent study by Hugo Mantel, Gamaliel the Elder became head of the Bet Din ha-Gadol between 10 and 30 C.E.[19] Graetz dates Gamaliel's position as Nasi (head of the Sanhedrin) during the period *circa* 30-50 C.E.[20] It has been suggested that Gamaliel took, or was given, the title *Rabban* when the office of the Ab Bet Din (head of the court) was abolished and Gamaliel became, as Nasi, the sole head of the Sanhedrin.[21] Given the extremely uncertain history of the Sanhedrin and the lack of any scholarly consensus,[22] perhaps all that may safely be said is that Gamaliel the Elder occupied a leading position in the highest Jewish council in Jerusalem during the early and mid parts of the First Century and that he was the first to bear the title *Rabban*.[23]

The confusion as to whether Gamaliel lived before or after the Destruction was initially created by a passage in my 1963 article which assumed for the sake of argument that Gamaliel took the title *Rabban* after the Destruction. The reason I made this assumption, *arguendo*, may be explained in a footnote.[24] The passage has unfortunately been

[17] *The Babylonian Talmud, Seder Mo'ed* (Soncino edition), vol. I, p. 63. During the 100 years preceding the Destruction there were, according to the Talmud, four successive heads of the Patriarchate: Hillel, Simeon, Gamaliel and Simeon.

[18] See W. Bacher, "Gamaliel I" in *The Jewish Encyclopedia*, Vol. 5, p. 559.

[19] Mantel, *Studies in the History of the Sanhedrin* (Harvard, 1961), p. 22.

[20] *Geschichte der Jüden* (1908 Ed.), Vol. 4, p. 445.

[21] Zeitlin, "Beginnings of Christianity and Judaism", *JQR*, Vol. 27, p. 293.

[22] See Mantel, *op. cit., passim.*

[23] There is of course the possibility that Gamaliel survived the Destruction and perhaps even took the title *Rabban* after the Destruction. No known facts make this impossible. However, this is mere speculation. All the evidence points in the other direction.

[24] I was using as a point of departure Professor Zeitlin's articles on the "rabbi question". From these it was not clear that Professor Zeitlin conceded that the title *Rabban* had been applied to Gamaliel

read as stating as a fact that Gamaliel the Elder took the title after the Destruction.

Father Brown has now added significantly, if inadvertently, to the confusion: After reciting a paragraph of materials from my article, Father Brown cites it "with a caution that this article is sometimes inaccurate".[25] He has since advised me that the only inaccuracy he had in mind was what he thought was my error in dating Gamaliel the Elder after the Destruction.[26] Ironically enough, however, Father Brown himself erroneously, if inadvertently, dates Rabban Gamaliel after the Destruction,[27] as he has very graciously conceded in a letter to the author.

"...[Y]ou very rightly make [the point] that my own statement (the first person to bear the title Rabban was Gamaliel (end of the 1st century)) is wrong. How I ever made that incorrect dating after pointing out what I thought was your own confusion, I'll never know. It should of course be 'Gamaliel the Elder (mid-1st century)'.[28]

The point is an important one. For, aside from the Gospels themselves, the use of the philological sibling *Rabban* among Jews at the time of Jesus' ministry is the most significant datum available suggesting that the title *Rabbi* was also in use.[29]

before the Destruction. If it had, presumably Professor Zeitlin would have dealt with this piece of evidence which argued against his position that the Gospel use of *Rabbi* was anachronistic. Since he nowhere dealt with this datum, I stated I would "assume", *arguendo*, (footnote 7) that Gamaliel did not take the title until after the Destruction in order to show that even if this were Professor Zeitlin's position and even if on this question he were correct, the Gospel use of *Rabbi* was nevertheless probably not anachronistic. I also pointed out that if the assumption I was making in order to present Zeitlin's case in its strongest light was wrong (and I pointed out that many people believed that Gamaliel not only lived before the Destruction but was even a contemporary of Jesus), then Zeitlin's position rested on a "very weak reed" indeed (footnote 7), i.e., the distinction between *Rabbi* (not used pre-Destruction) and *Rabban* (used pre-Destruction).

[25] *Op. cit.*, p. 74.
[26] Letter to the author, July 24, 1967.
[27] *Op. cit.*, p. 74.
[28] Letter to the author. July 24. 1967.
[29] Since this article was submitted for publication, Father Brown has corrected his error in further printings of his edition of *John*.

10

THE TITLE RABBI IN THE GOSPELS
IS ANACHRONISTIC

S. Zeitlin

Mr. Shanks is of the opinion that the title Rabbi in the Gospels is not anachronistic, that means that at the time of Jesus the title Rabbi was in vogue among the Judaeans and was prefixed to the name of the sages. He presents an array of quotations from the Bible where the word rab occurs. He says that "It is fair to say that some form of the word Rab (possessive, Rabbi) was used in most of these languages from the earlies to the latest."

Mr. Shanks could have quoted other passages from the Bible where the word rab occurs. However one fact remains that during the Second Commonwealth the term Rabbi was not used. The sages were quoted by their names without the prefix of Rabbi, as Jose ben Joezer, Simon ben Shetah, Shmmai, Hillel, Shammai, Nahum and many others. We have substantial literature of that period—the writings of Josephus, the Apochryphal literature, Philo, the early tannaitic literature before the destruction of the Temple. In none of this literature does the word Rabbi occur. Josephus mentions sophists, teachers, Ben Sira refers to *grammateis, soferim.*

In the Gospels the title Rabbi, referring to Jesus, occurs frequently in John and also in Matthew chs, 23 and 26. However it does not occur in Luke. In the Gospel of Mark, ch. 9. 5, the term Rabbi occurs. Και ἀποκριθείς ὁ Πέτρος λέγει τῷ 'Ιησοῦ ῥαββί καλόν ἐστιν ἡμᾶς ὧδε εἶναι καὶ ποιήσωμεν τρεῖς σκηνάς... And Peter answered and said to Jesus, "Rabbi, it is good for us to be here; and let us make three tabernacles; one for thee, and one for Moses, and one for Elias. However in the parallel passage in Matthew 17.4 the word Rabbi does not occur but instead the word Κύριε, my master, is given. Neither in Luke 9.33, where the same story is given, does the word Rabbi occur, instead the word 'Επιστάτα is found; some manuscripts have διδάσκαλε, teacher.

In Mark 10.51 the word ῥαββουνί occurs. However in some manuscripts the reading is Κύριε, my master. The word *rabbouni* is the Aramaic rendering of the word *kurie*, my master. The Gospel, of John, according to most New Testament scholars, was compiled after the destruction of the Second Temple. This view is substantiated by internal evidence. Chapter 23 in Matthew is an interpolation of a later period. This is also substantiated by internal evidence. The word γέεννα *gehenna*, place of fiery torment for the dead, came into usage after the

183

destruction of the Second Temple. In the apocryphal literature before the destruction of the Temple the word *sheol* was used.

To sum up; During the Second Commonwealth the title Rabbi was not used among the Judaeans. It came into vogue after the destruction of the Second Temple. The conclusion is that the title Rabbi in John and Matthew is anachronistic. The title Rabbi prefixed to a name is not possessive, it is a noun. This is evident to any one who knows the Talmud in the original, not through translation. To give an example: Rabbi Judah the Prince said of Samuel, he "shall be called Hakkan but not Rabbi." It is clear that Rabbi Judah did not mean to say that Samuel, his disciple should not be his rabbi. He meant to say that Samuel should not have the title Rabbi.

Four sages had the title Rabban: Gamaliel the Elder, Jochanan ben Zakkai, Simon the son of Gamaliel and his son Gamaliel. The reason that these four sages had the title Raban being that they were the head of the *Bet Din*. The office of *Ab Bet Din* was abolished.

The word Rabban is the Aramaic rendering of the word our *nasi*. The Targum renders the word *nasi, rabba*. Gamaliel the Elder and his son Simon lived before the destruction of the Temple. To maintain that Gamaliel lived after the destruction of the Temple betrays ignorance of the Talmud.

Mr. Shanks, in order to substantiate his erroneous conjecture that the title rabbi was in vogue among the Judaeans before the destruction of the Second Temple, quotes a Tosefta Eduyoth and authoritties. The Tosefta reads as follows:

ומה משה (רנינ ו) שהוא רבו של אליהו לא רצה לגלות הממזרים עד שנתגלו
מעצמן אליהו. תלמידו של משה על אחת כמה וכמה שלא יגלה את הממזרים
עד שיתגלו מעצמן, מי שיש לו תלמידים (ותלמידיו) קוראין אותו רבי נשתכחו
תלמידיו קוראין אותו רבן נשתכחו אילו ואילו קוראין אותו בשמו•

In the article "The Tosefta", JQR, April 1957, I pointed out that we find many halakot which date from an early period of the Second Jewish Commonwealth and yet are not recorded in the Mishne. On the other hand we find some halakot and statements in the Tosefta which date from a late period, after the time of R. Judah. The fact that we find many statements in the Tosefta of a later period led I. H. Weiss to state that the compiler of the Tosefta was a Palestinian by birth, who lived in Babylonia in the latter part of the fifth century and that he drew his material from different sources, making use of the discussions in both Talmuds.[1]

To utilize the Tosefta for the history of the development of the

[1] 2. דור דור ודורשיו

halaka and for the establishment of historical facts referred to, one must critically scrutinize the readings and establish the text in its proper historical prespective.

The *Aruch*, in quoting this Tosefta, has a reading which reads as follows:

ואעפ׳ שמפורש בסוף מסכתא עדיות תוספתא בלשון הזה מי שיש לו תלמידים
ותלמידיו תלמידים קורין אותו (רבן) נשתבהו תלמידיו קורין אותו נשתבהו
אלו ואלו קורין אותו בשמו אעפ״כ לא מצאנו רבן אלא נשיאים•

In the text of the Tosefta quoted in the *Aruch* the word rabbi is not found. The word נשתכחו has no meaning; The *Aruch* amended it to נשתבהו. The *Aruch* after quoting the Tosefta said correctly אעפ״כ לא מצאנו רבן אלא נשיאים "nevertheless the author of the *Aruch* said that we do not find the title of Rabban except in connection with the Nasi".[2] As a matter of fact only the four נשיאים carried the title Rabban. Before their period the sages had no title. The *Aruch* quoted a well known saying: גדול מרב רבי, גדול מרבי רבן, גדול מרבן שמו•

Even if we should assume that this Tosefta Eduyoth had the term rabbi in the text it must be disregarded. It is a historical fact that the title rabbi prefixed to the name of a sage is not found in the tannaitic literature before the time of the destruction of the Temple. Due to the clear historical perspective of the spiritual life of the Judaeans during the Second Commonwealth the text of the Tosefta cannot be used as a historical document.

We may venture to say that the last two lines of this Tosefta is a later interpolation to explain the previous lines where it is said that Moses was the rabbi of Elijah and that Elijah was the disciple of Moses. In this text the title of rabbi or rabban was not prefixed to the name Moses (in a later period Moses was called our master משה רבינו) Neither were the title rabbi or rabban prefixed to the name Elijah. To explain, the interpolator added מי שיש לו תלמידים • • • נשתכחו (נשתבהו) אילו ואילו קוראין אותו בשמו

With regard to authorities, may I state that scholarship is not theology. Scholarship does not recognize authorities. Scholarship is based on diligent research of sources which are the sole authorities. The sources must be critically scrutinized in order to establish the correct text.

---

[2] Cf. *Aruch, ibid.* והדורות הראשונים שהיו גדולים מאד לא היו צריכים
לרברבם לא ברבן ולא ברבי ולא ברב שהרי הלל לא נאמרה רבנות בשמו
• • • ואין מרברבין אותן עם הזכרת שמותיהן • • • כי התחילה זו אלא בנשיאים
מרבן גמליאל הזקן•

Section Three—

TEACHER AND STUDENT

THE TEACHER IN TALMUD AND MIDRASH

By Max Arzt

It is the purpose of this study to ascertain the status of the elementary school teacher as reflected in Talmud and Midrash. Despite the paucity of available material one can delineate a fairly definite picture of the role of the teacher, his economic and social status and the educational imperatives and methods to which he was committed.

BIBLE AND "MISHNA" TEACHERS

There seems to have been a clear distinction between the elementary school or Scripture teacher and the teacher of the Mishna. The former was variously called חזן, probably because of his duties as sexton of the synagogue,[1] ספר, סופר or ספרא[2]— the teacher of "the book" i. e. the Scriptures, מקרי דרדקי or מקרי ינוקי[3] which are the Aramaic equivalents of the term מלמד תינוקות found already in older Tanaitic sources.[5] Some teachers had their calling attached to their name with the title ספרא or קרא.[6]

The "Mishna" teachers are known in Hebrew as משנה[7] and in

---

[1] M. Shab. 1:3, Lekah Tov on Num. 14:25, Jer. Sheb. 36d, Jer. Yeb. 13a. Frankel, מבוא הירושלמי, p. 118b, ventures the opinion that the חזן taught prayers to beginners. For a discussion of the term חזן see Krauss, *Synagogale Alterthümer*, p. 126.

[2] M. Giṭ. 3:1, Jer. Giṭ. 44c interpret סופרים as מלמדי תינוקות, teachers dictating to the children an excercise in writing. M. Ḳid. 4:13, Jer. Dem. 26b, Sotah 49a, Lev. Rab. 30:2, Ekhah Rab. to 3:7, Tanh. Tezave 13.

[3] B. B. 21b, Ket. 111b, Mak. 16b, Giṭ. 36a.

[4] B. B. 21b.

[5] *Ibid.*, cf. Pes. 49b, B. B. 8b.

[6] Among teachers so designated are: ר' חנינא קרא, Ta'an. 27b, Ber. 30b, Yeb. 40a, Ket. 56a (see ח"ב *ad loc.*) Jer. Ket. 29d, cf. ר' חייא קרא in Ekhah Rab. 4:4. ירמיה קרא, Jer. Ber. 7c, Jer. Ta'an. 67c, Jer. Meg. 74b, בר שלמיה ספרא, Jer. Ber. 7c, בר אבונא ספרא, Jer. Meg. 74b, אלעזר ספרא, Ḥul. 55b, נקיי ספרא, Jer. B. B. 15c, Koh. Rab. 7:7. See לוין: אוצר הגאונים קידושין, p. 85, where we are told of the transmission of accurate Biblical texts through generations of Bible scholars beginning with נקיי, the teacher of R. Hamnuna. Jer. Ma'as. Sheni 56a, cf. Ekha Rab. to 3:7, Pesikta Beshalah (Buber) p. 91.

[7] Found in singular form of משנה in Jer. Ma'as. 50d there in contradistinction to ספר, otherwise in plural form משנים: Jer. Peah 21a, Lev. Rab. 30:1, Lev. Rab. 27:2, Shir Hash. Rab. on 1:9.

Amoraic as מתני or מתניין.[8] While the functions of the סופר and משנה were distinct, the same person often occupied both positions, especially in small communities, even as he fulfilled other communal functions. Thus Levi b. Sisi was appointed to perform the functions of preacher, judge, supervisor of the synagogue, elementary teacher (ספר) and also that of a Mishna (oral law) teacher, among other communal responsibilities.[10] R. Simeon b. Lakish was asked by the community of Bozra to provide them with a person who could be preacher, judge, teacher, beadle (חזן) and attend to all other communal needs.[11]

POPULAR KNOWLEDGE OF THE BIBLE

The universality of education among Jews was so striking, that Josephus in his polemics against the enemies of the Jews, finds occasion to boast of the widespread literacy among Jewish children. "Among us, every child must know how to read. We rarely find a Jewish boy who would not be able to read the Bible and Jewish fathers deny themselves necessities to give their children an education."[12] Jerome in the fourth century C. E. makes the observation that the Palestinian Jews of his day were able to recite the Pentateuch and Prophets by heart.[13] Teachers must have been effective in giving youngsters between the ages of five and ten — the years of Bible study,[14] a thorough knowledge of the Scriptures. In the third century in a Babylonian Jewish community, a letter in the scroll during the reading of the Torah was found to be blurred. Whereupon the sage R. Zeira[15] ruled that *any* average child that is "neither brilliant nor dull" be called upon to read the blurred word (at sight) and that upon the accuracy of the child's reading of the text, the eligibility of the scroll for purposes of public reading at the synagogue service was to be determined.[16]

---

[8] Ket. 8b (מתני בריה דר'ל). Jer. Yeb. 13a (מתניין). The plural form is מתניינין: Jer. Ḥag. 76c.

[9] On the wider meaning of the term משנה, see Bacher ערכי מדרש, p. 84.

[10] Jer. Yeb. 13a. The clear distinction between a Bible teacher and a "Mishna" teacher is evident from the two traditions concerning חייא בר אבא 'ר, the teacher of the son of Resh Lakish, Ket. 8b.

[11] Jer. Sheb. 36d, cf. מדרש דברים רבה, ed. Lieberman, p. 60, where מתניין is mentioned among his professional occupations.

[12] Contra Apion II, 25.

[13] See Lieberman, *Hellenism in Jewish Palestine*, p. 52, and note 50 *ad loc.*

[14] M. Ab. 5:21, cf. Ket. 50a.

[15] See Hyman, תולדות תנאים ואמוראים, p. 1104, where the reading זעירי is suggested.

[16] Men. 29b.

When in the second century R. Joshua ben Hananya visited Rome he heard of a Jewish child incarcerated in a prison. He stood at the entrance to the cell and tested his knowledge of the Bible by quoting the first part of a verse in Isaiah and the child readily completed the verse. While the child in later years became the sage R. Ishmael b. Elisha, the question was by no means intended as more than a normal test applied to an average child.[17]

In the well known story of R. Meir and Elisha ben Abuyah, the former took the latter to thirteen synagogues (= schools) and in each instance asked young pupils to quote their Bible verse (פסוק לי פסוקיך). Without hesitation, children quoted verses from Isaiah, Jeremiah and Psalms (only some of the verses are mentioned) — evidencing the wide range of Bible books mastered in the elementary schools.[18] Remarkable Bible knowledge and self-confidence were displayed by the child of Simeon b. Lakish' in answer to questions addressed to him by R. Johanan (fourth century C. E.).[19] But such versatility was by no means the exclusive prerogative of the sons of the great. R. Aha suggested to R. Ashi that one of the ways of calling a person who happened to be in the synagogue without incurring the irreverence of entering the synagogue for a personal, mundane purpose, was to ask one of the children of the synagogue's school to quote the Bible verse he was then studying.[20] A later Midrash envisions Mordecai as beholding good omens in Bible verses quoted by children coming from school. This legend indicates that school children normally expected their elders to test their mastery of the Bible.[21] We even have an instance where an ignorant man (עם הארץ) suggested to the sage R. Hoshaia a novel interpretation of a verse in the book of Psalms and R. Hoshaia promised to repeat this interpretation in a public lecture in the name of the "unlearned" author thereof.[22]

A similar tale of popular knowledge of the Bible is told of a cattle-driver who, when he received permission of R. Jonathan to answer a Samaritan's (כותי) comment on the Biblical flood story, displayed his Bible acumen when he proved that comment to be in contradiction

[17] Tos. Hor. 2:5–6, Jer. Hor. 48b, Giṭ. 58a, Ekha Rab. 4:4.

[18] Ḥag. 15a, cf. Koh. Zuta (Buber) 7:8. For use of Bible verses as omens, see Lieberman, *Hellenism in Jewish Palestine*, p. 195, note 20. The child cited the last verse studied during a particular day. This is evident from Esth. Rab. to 3:9 where the second child says: ובזה הפסוק עמדתי מבית הספר, see Bacher, ערכי מדרש, p. 259.

[19] Ta'an. 9a.

[20] Meg. 28b.

[21] Esth. Rab. to 3:9 ed. Romm. 13a.

[22] Gen. Rab. 78:12.

to the plain text of the Bible, causing the refuted Samaritan to slip away. The story goes on to say that R. Jonathan was so grateful to the cattle-driver and so respectful toward him, that he descended from his mule and allowing him to ride thereon, followed him on foot for a distance of four miles.[23]

A COMMUNAL SYSTEM OF EDUCATION

An old tradition attributes the introduction of public primary education to Joshua ben Gamala. He is said to have organized a school system in Jerusalem — thus having the community share with the father of the child the responsibility for the education of his son. We are told that the first to benefit from this enactment were youths of 16 and 17, youths who had no parents or whose parents had neglected to teach them. Joshua ben Gamala then further established the age of 6 and 7 as the age when mandatory school education would begin.[24]

The Aggadah records that in the first century no less than 480 such schools with Bible and Oral Law divisions (בית ספר ובית תלמוד) existed in Jerusalem[25] and 500 such schools in Bethar.[26] The figures are no doubt highly exaggerated, but they reflect the widespread nature of the public education system initiated by Joshua ben Gamala. A more realistic figure is suggested in the implication that there were thirteen schools in Tiberias in the days of R. Meir.[27] At the instance of the Nasi Judah III emissaries were sent to establish community schools where they were lacking.[28] A Halakha of Tanaitic origin registers the mandatory nature of the community's responsibility in stating that it is forbidden to reside in a community which lacked a school[29] and in the emphatic statement to the effect that a community without a school deserved to be excommunicated![30] Indeed in Rabba's days (Babylonia third century C. E.) the parent could demand the appointment of a teacher for his community and could not be compelled to send his child to a neighboring city, though he would be

[23] Lieberman, Deut. R., p. 79.
[24] B. B. 21a.
[25] Jer. Meg. 73d, Jer. Ket. 35c, Pesikta d' R. Kahana, ed. Buber, p. 121, Ekha R. Petiḥta 12, Ekha R. to Ekha 2:2.
[26] Lam. R. to 2:2, cf. Giṭ. 58a.
[27] Ḥag. 15b.
[28] Jer. Ḥag. 76c.
[29] Sanh. 17b.
[30] Shab. 119b.

expected to transfer his child to another school in his own community, when the school in his own neighborhood was bereft of its
teacher.[31]

Popular esteem for schools and for teachers was distilled in terse
sayings scattered through Talmud and Midrash. God Himself is
envisioned as a teacher of children.[32] School children are "the an-
nointed ones of God."[33] Not even the rebuilding of the Temple would
justify the suspension of children's study of the Torah.[34] Teachers
were "they that turn many to righteousness, as the everlasting stars."[35]
To teachers who taught their pupils faithfully was applied the verse
"Thy cheeks are comely with rows of jewels" and to their pupils,
the second half of the verse "and thy neck with chains of gold."[36]
While neglectful teachers were severely condemned,[37] the average
teacher was sincere and was "like the gardens by the side of the
river."[38] They who teach their pupils with sincerity are destined to
stand at the right hand of God.[39] "Teachers rather than the police
are the true guardians of a city," a delegation of school inspectors
advised the residents of a Palestinian community which had provided
no teachers for their children.[40]

ECONOMIC SITUATION OF TEACHERS

To assure the economic welfare of teachers, direct Biblical warrant
was deduced for the payment of tuition fees for "Bible Teachers."
Teachers of the Oral Law were by law forbidden to accept compensation but since they were paid, their practice was rationalized by the
theory that they were paid for being idle from other gainful occupations (שכר יושב בטל).[41] While the amount of tuition seemed to vary

[31] B. B. 21a.
[32] 'Ab. Zarah 3b, Ex. Rab. 28:5 (להיות סופר ומלמד תינוקות).
[33] Shab. 119b.
[34] Ibid.
[35] B. B. 8b (Dan. 12:3).
[36] Cant. Rabba to Canticles 1:10.
[37] B. B. 21b.
[38] Yalkut Shimoni to Numb., section 771.
[39] Lev. Rab. 30:2, R. Samuel b. Shilat was an example of a highly sincere
teacher who did not attend his garden for 13 years because he was so devoted to his
pupils (B. B. 8b).
[40] Jer. Ḥag. 76c.
[41] Jer. Ned. 38c, cf. Lev. Rab. 30:1. From the discussion in Ned. 37a it appears
that in Babylonia even the acceptance of tuition fee for Bible teaching had to be
rationalized as being שכר שימור or שכר פיסוק טעמים.

according to the parents' economic circumstances, assurance was given that the request for generous tuition fee charges did not constitute excessive communal exaction and parents were commended for augmenting the amount they were expected to send with the child in payment for tuition.[42] Unmarried men were morally required to help maintain the school teachers.[43] In Palestine all families resident in a community for twelve months were subject to taxes for support of schools[44] and monetary matters relating to a child's education could be determined even on the Sabbath.[45] From a Mishnaic source it appears that in Palestine there were communities which supplied a house for the teacher. This house was used as his private residence as well as for school purposes.[46] All available evidence leads to the conclusion that efforts were made to protect teachers against dire poverty. We even have instances of well circumstanced teachers. Thus, the income of Samuel ben Shelat, the exemplary teacher of Sura, supplied his basic food needs and enabled him to live comfortably in his own home. The governmental authorities made no levies against him because it would never occur to them that a teacher could have a taxable income.[47] The teaching profession attracted to it some who seemed to have independent means and who loved their vocation. Thus, a saintly teacher, a contemporary of Samuel ben Shelat, taught rich and poor alike, refusing to accept tuition fees from the poor and even luring children to his school by offering them fish from his fisheries.[48] An Aggadah tells us about a rather affluent teacher in the period of the second Temple, who because of his great learning, was offered fifty gold pieces to settle in Jerusalem, but he preferred to remain in his own locality because he owned vineyards which were extremely productive.[49] To perform his duties, a teacher was expected to be cheerful and in good health. When the Palestinian sage R. Johanan (4th century) visited a town, he met a teacher who looked

[42] Lev. Rab. 30:1.
[43] Lev. Rab. 27:2. Community funds were used to supplement tuition fees paid by parents and to provide for payment of assistant teachers (B. B. 21a).
[44] Jer. Peah 21a.
[45] Ket. 5a.
[46] בית ספר ובית תלמוד, Jer. Ma'as. 50d, טובלין לספר ולמשנה.
[47] Ket. 62a. See Rashi on ולא חליף פריסתקא דמלכא.
[48] Ta'an. 24a, cf. Story of R. Hiya who provided orphaned pupils with food and clothing in addition to organizing a unique tutorial system for the education of all children, Ket. 103b, B. M. 85b.
[49] Tanḥ. Tezave 13. That it was not unusual for a scholar to be offered monetary inducements to settle in a community can be seen from the story of Jose b. Kisma in Ab. 6:9.

dejected. He seemed to have been surprised and demanded the reason
for his despondent condition. When the teacher admitted that he
was fasting (for reasons of piety) he chided him for this, since his
weak state adversely affected his sacred vocation.[50]

Some teachers who attained affluence evinced undesirable traits
of character. A late Midrash speaks of ignorant, wealthy and extravagant teachers. One such teacher whose economic prosperity was
attested to by the expensive coat which he wore, admitted to R. Jose
his complete ignorance of the Oral Law. Upon being asked for the
source of his prosperity he declared that he was a teacher of little
children.[51]

The above cited Midrash brings into bold relief an aspect of an
adverse attitude toward school teachers already found in earlier
sources. The learned scholars in the Palestinian academies accentu-
ated the study of the Oral Law. They viewed with suspicion and even
disparagement school teachers whose knowledge was limited to the
Bible. A סופר was of a lower hierarchy of learning than the (חכם)
scholar of Talmudic lore. "From the days when the Temple was
destroyed," says R. Elazar, "the knowledge of the sages (חכמיא) has
deteriorated to that of school teachers (ספריא), the knowledge of the
latter deteriorated to that of the sexton (חזנייא) of the synagogue and
the latter in turn has become as ignorant as the ''am haaretz.''[52]

One Baraita implies that the סופר is just above the ignoramus
(עם הארץ) who cannot recite a simple benediction and the grace after
meals.[53] A similar shade of meaning of the word סופר as a person of
just elementary knowledge is implied in R. Zeira's contrast between
familes of סופרים — people with an elementary knowledge (i. e., who
are only familiar with the Bible and prayers) and בני תורה (i. e., people
who are scholars in the realm of the Oral Law).[54]

The derogation of the intellectual status of the teacher is evidenced
in the following passage: לעולם ימכר אדם כל מה שיש לו וישא בת תלמיד
חכם לא מצא בת תלמיד חכם ישא בת גדולי הדור לא מצא בת גדולי הדור ישא בת
ראשי כנסיות לא מצא בת ראשי כנסיות ישא בת גבאי צדקה לא מצא בת גבאי צדקה

[50] Jer. Demai 26b.
[51] Lieberman, מדרשי תימן, p. 28, cf. שרפשטיין, החדר בחיי עמנו, p. 18. The economic
situation of the teacher among Jews compared favorably with that of the Greeks.
See Marrou, *Histoire de l'Education dans l'Antiquité*, pp. 204–205.
[52] Sota 49a.
[53] Ber. 45b. Ḥul. 106a. It is quite possible that the word סופר here means one
who has had an elementary education, cf. Meg. 28b, where the word קרא seems to
have a similar meaning. Cf. Tosefot on לא ילמד רווק סופרים, Ḳid. 82a.
[54] Eccl. Rab. to 4:9.

יּשא בת מלמדי תינוקות ולא יּשא בת עמי הארץ.⁵⁵ Here again the status of the
teacher is just above that of the עם הארץ. A further instance of disparagement is mentioned both in the Babylonian as well as in the
Jerusalem Talmud, but both passages are of Palestinian origin. The
Mishnaic law states: "If a sage comes from the east let my erub be to
the east, if from the west let my erub be to the west etc."⁵⁶ The
Babylonian Talmud, quoting a Palestinian sage, interprets this as
referring to a learned scholar for it is him whom a person might want
to hear on the Sabbath rather than a mere teacher of children⁵⁷
(מקרי שמע). Likewise the Jerusalem Talmud comments that only for
a חכם would a person establish an erub but not for an ordinary teacher
(רניל).⁵⁸ It is in the light of this attitude that we can understand the
rebuke given by the Palestinian Amora R. Jannai to the teacher
R. Hanina on occasions when the latter ventured to speak author-
itatively on matters of Halakha. In each instance he said to him
"go outside and read your Bible" as if to say: "Do not venture opinions
on matters beyond the scope of a mere teacher."⁵⁹ Since the ספרא
was thoroughly familiar with the text of the Bible, one of his functions
was to read the Torah scroll at the synagogue. R. Simeon the teacher
of the Galilean city Terbenth⁶⁰ was requested by the members of the
congregation to read the Torah verses with pauses (קטע בדבורייא) so
that their children might repeat the phrases. He went to Sepphoris
to inquire of R. Hanina ben Hama. The latter emphatically prohibited him from assenting to the suggestion whereupon the teacher
was removed from his post. R. Zeira, a later sage, spoke commendingly
about the teacher's refusal to accede to his congregants' request and
said "Had that teacher lived in my day, I would have appointed him
as a חכם (i. e. an authority in the law.)"⁶¹ The special interest of school
teachers in laws relating to Torah reading, prompted scholars of the
Oral Law to speak caustically about this field of learning. Thus when
Bar Shelemya, the teacher, asked R. Mana concerning the number of
people called to the Torah on Sabbath Hanukkah when it falls on
Rosh Hodesh, the sage curtly answered "only a school teacher would

⁵⁵ Pes. 49b.
⁵⁶ M. 'Er. 3:5.
⁵⁷ 'Er. 36b.
⁵⁸ Jer. 'Er. 21b.
⁵⁹ Ket. 56a, Ta'an. 27b, Yeb. 40a, Jer. Kilaim 32d, cf. Giṭ. 11b.
⁶⁰ See L. Wiesner, *Die Jugendlehrer der Talmudischen Zeit*, p. 27, note 1.
⁶¹ Jer. Meg. 75b. Reading of Bible verses in sections was permitted only in
actual teaching situations, see Ta'an. 27b, cf. Meg. 22a, 27a. On the accurate
knowledge of the text of the Torah displayed by the teacher R. Huna, see Jer. Shab.
12a (top).

ask such a question!"[62] All these instances of the derogation of teachers of the Bible reveal a special prejudice in favor of the Oral Law, a subject which was not taught by the school teacher and of which he was often ignorant. Centuries later the gap between the Bible-centered teachers and the scholars who championed the Oral Law widened considerably. School teachers were considered to be unwitting accomplices of the Karaites though they were in their personal life and attitudes loyal Rabbinites.[63]

SUBJECT MATTER OF INSTRUCTION

Preliminary to learning the Bible, children were given instruction in the reading of certain simple prayers. Even before the child entered the school, the father taught him to recite by heart the verses שמע ישראל and תורה צוה לנו משה וגו'.[64] Such verses were also recited daily in the school.[65] Certain other simple prayers such as קדוש קדוש קדוש and a short grace after meals were mastered even by those who did not go to school.[66] The teacher wrote the letters of the alphabet on a tablet and the child memorized the names and sounds of the letters.[67] Various pedagogic devices were used to fix the names and sounds of the letters in the minds of the children.[68] The three basic prayers taught in the school were the שמע, the שמונה עשרה and the ברכת המזון.[69] The Hallel was also a special subject of study. Both the שמע and the הלל were written on tablets though there were some Halakhic objections to this practice.[70] Certain sections of the Torah were written on a roll (מגילה) and in the preliminary stages of Bible teaching, these rolls were the "text-books" used. In some schools, Bible teaching began with the opening chapters of the Book of Genesis. The "text-

---

[62] Jer. Ber. 7c, cf. Jer. Ta'an. 67c, Jer. Meg. 74b, Giṭ. 11b, cf. Ginzberg, פירושים וחידושים בירושלמי, vol. III, p. 141.

[63] See Lieberman, מדרשי תימן, pp. 29–31.

[64] Sukka 42a.

[65] Lev. Rab. 9:3 (ושכעית קולהון דמניקיא וכו').

[66] Ibid., סב בריך, cf. Num. Rab. 4:21. Here is an instance of an untutored person who knew only the simple response קדוש קדוש וכו'. In Caesarea people were so ignorant of the Hebrew prayers that even the Shema was read in Greek, Jer. Sota 21b. This was evidently an exceptional instance, hence the visiting scholar, R. Levi, was shocked.

[67] Ab. R. N. 6:2, אחז רבי עקיבא בראש הלוח כתב לו א'ב ולמדה.

[68] Shab. 104a.

[69] P. R. E. 1, סימיך לא למדת לא ק'ש ולא תפלה ולא ב'ה.

[70] Tos. Yad. 2:11 (אע'פ שאינו רשאי לעשות), cf. Tos. Sota 6:2, cf. Lieberman, Hellenism in Jewish Palestine, p. 206.

book" roll contained the section from creation till the section about Noah.[71] In others, children began with the Book of Leviticus. Perhaps this was an atavism of Temple days when children of priests were given such functional instruction.[72] The opening section of Leviticus transcribed on the "text-book" roll ended at the verse ויהי ביום השמיני.[73] Thereafter instruction was given in Torah scrolls (בספר), covering first the Pentateuch, then the Prophets and finally the Hagiographa.[74]

The Bible was taught together with its Aramaic translation and even sections never translated in public could be taught with translation, if the teacher so desired.[75] Children were also taught to write. The teacher dictated to them sentences with mundane content which they transcribed on tablets. This is evidenced by the Mishnaic instance of a passerby who heard a teacher dictating to his pupils: איש פלוני מגרש את אשתו פלונית ממקום פלוני (The specific names were included in the dictated sentence).[76] Numerous other Talmudic and Midrashic passages imply that a passerby could hear clearly the subject matter of instruction. There was a good deal of loud group reading[77] which was a source of disturbance to neighbors living in the vicinity of the school. An Amoraic decision nullified the right of a neighbor to object to a school being set up in a house located in his courtyard.[78] School houses were located in synagogues (בי כנישתא)[79] and in the home of the teacher (בית הסופר) where perhaps very young children were taught.[80]

The children sat in a semi-circular row.[81] They were brought to school by their mothers. The latter are highly praised for this meri-

---

[71] Giṭ. 60a.

[72] A Midrashic interpretation of this practice is suggested in Lev. Rab. 7:3. See Finkelstein, מבוא למס' אבות ואבות דר'נ, p. 108.

[73] Giṭ. 60a, see Freedman, Mekilta d' R. Ishmael, Introduction, p. 35.

[74] Deut. Rab. 8:3, תחלה קורא במגלה ואח'כ בספר ואח'כ בנביאים.

[75] The phrase ברכת כהן is omitted in other manuscripts. The priestly benediction was to be given only in Hebrew (see Sifri Nasso 39, Num. Rab. 11:10).

[76] M. Giṭ. 3:1, cf. Jer. Giṭ. 44c: מהו מקרין.

[77] Gen. Rab. 65:16 (תינוקות מצפצפין בקולן), cf. M. Teh., ed. Buber 416, ושמעית קלהון דטליא בנו כנישתא.

[78] B. B. 21a, cf. Tos. B. B. 1:4, where an earlier law is cited establishing the right of neighbors to object to a school being set up in a house of a joint courtyard because it increases human traffic through the courtyard: שמרבין עליהם את הדרך, cf. Jer. B. B. 13b.

[79] Jer. Meg. 73d, Jer. Ket. 35c, B. B. 21a, מקול התינוקות . . . אינו יכול לישון, Meg. 28b.

[80] Tos. Sota 6:2. As indicated above, it appears from the passage in Jer. Ma'as. 50d that the home of the teacher, used as a school house, was community property. Other instances where children were taught in the home of the teacher are mentioned in Ḥag. 5b, Sanh. 111b and Ḥag. 13a, cf. Yalkut Amos 542 (end).

[81] Cant. Rab. to 7:13.

torious deed.[82] An unmarried man was forbidden to teach, since he would have frequent contact with the mothers who brought their children to school.[83] But fathers did not abdicate their interest in the education of their children. We have instances of fathers who hurried every morning to bring their children to school. An instance is given of a father who reviewed with his child the Bible verses of the previous day and taught him part of the new lesson.[84]

It was the practice of R. Joshua b. Levi to review the weekly portion with his grandson every Friday. Once he forgot that he had a weekly self-imposed assignment with his grandson and he went to the Tiberias baths. Suddenly he reminded himself of his grandson, and though he had already anointed himself and (according to another report) taken off his clothes, he quickly dressed and rushed home to meet his grandson.[85]

It was customary for parents to teach their children on the Sabbath. According to an old Tanaitic source new lessons were not to be taught to a child on the Sabbath, since such would be an undue strain on both parent (who would examine the child) and child, but rather to review verses which the child had studied at least once.[86]

The normal number of pupils for a teacher was set at 25. For forty pupils an assistant (ריש דוכנא) was appointed and community funds were made available to the teacher toward the compensation of the assistant.[87] Among the ancient Greeks there were assistant teachers (proscholus) in the elementary schools. The assistant sat near a curtain which divided the school room into two. In an article describing the typical Greek school, Doctor Schwabe indicates that a similar arrangement seemed to obtain in the Jewish schools of Babylonia and Palestine.[88] We find mention of an instance of a unique tutorial system, where pupil-teachers were prepared to specialize in teaching respective books of the Pentateuch and respective orders of the Mishna.[89] As in all ancient school systems teachers did not desist from using corporal punishment. We find Rab admonishing R. Samuel b. Shelat to use a mild form of punishment for pupils and to secure the attention of the indolent pupil by placing him next to a diligent

[82] Ber. 17a, cf. Jer. Ḥalla 57b.
[83] Kid. 82a.
[84] Kid. 30a.
[85] Jer. Shab. 3a.
[86] Ned. 37a–b.
[87] B. B. 21a.
[88] תרביץ, שנה כ'א, ספר ב'.
[89] B. M. 85b, Ket. 103b.

one.[90] High praise is given to a teacher who, among other saintly qualities, did not punish inattentive pupils but rather "bribed" them by offering them fish from his fishpond.[91] An instance is mentioned of a teacher who was dismissed because of his addiction to severe corporal punishment of his pupils. He was however restored to his position because no other teacher could be found so efficient and accurate in his teaching.[92]

A maid passing a school house "saw" a teacher administering excessive physical punishment to a pupil. When she declared that that person should be placed under a ban (נדוי), the teacher inquired of Rabbi Aha who warned him that excessive corporal punishment was a misdeed for which a person might be put under a ban.[93] A teacher in Caesarea (3rd century C. E.) was so severe that he kept the children long after the regular school period. R. Abbahu would deliberately cross the courtyard of the synagogue (though it was considered improper to use the courtyard as a short-cut), so that the strict teacher who knew that R. Abbahu was averse to his methods of severe discipline, would upon seeing R. Abbahu then dismiss the fatigued children.[94]

Supervision of teachers was exacting. They were expected to cover ground and to teach accurately the text of the Bible. Rabba preferred the teacher who covered ground though he might be teaching with less accuracy while R. Dimi of Nehardea expressed the opinion that accuracy was an indispensable prerequisite for a teacher.[95] We do not have sufficient information about the hours of instruction. From the story of the saintly Abba Hilkiah who gave his younger child a double portion of food for supper "because he goes to school,"[96] it appears that school hours lasted from morning till dusk. The hours of instruction must have begun very early, for during the three weeks between the 17th day of Tamuz and the Ninth of Ab when the weather was very hot, children were dismissed at 10 A. M.[97] Perhaps their daily schedule provided for the reading and study of prayer till 10 A. M. with the Bible instruction following immediately thereafter. This seems to be implied in R. Aha's statement that at that hour "God

[90] B. B. 21a.
[91] Ta'an. 24a.
[92] Giṭ. 36a, Mak. 16b.
[93] Jer. M. Ḳ. 81d.
[94] Jer. Meg. 74a (bottom).
[95] B. B. 21a.
[96] Ta'an. 23b.
[97] Num. Rab. 12:3.

teaches the Torah to school children (who died in childhood)."[98] It was during these three weeks that all corporal punishment was prohibited.[99]

Whether girls were given instruction is a moot question.[100] There is no indication that they were part of the community school system. They must have been taught by the father. From one reading in the Mishna it seems to be taken for granted that girls were given instruction in Bible.[101] Nor is the famous statement of R. Eleazar's to the effect that כל המלמד בתו תורה כאילו מלמדה תיפלות conclusive. It rather implies that such teaching was not an infrequent occurrence. Rabbi Joshua's statement: רוצה אשה בקב תיפלות מט' קבין פרישות seems to be a facetious observation that if for women Torah study is תפלות, they have a strong desire for it.[102]

[98] 'Ab. Zarah 3b, see Rashi ad loc.

[99] M. Teh. Buber, p. 398.

[100] On education of girls, see טשארנא, לתולדות החנוך בישראל, p. 11.

[101] M. Ned. 4:3.

[102] For a thorough discussion of the passage, see אפשטיין, מבוא המשנה, p. 670.

The Relations Between Master and Disciple in the Talmudic Age

by M. ABERBACH

Since very early times, Jewish teachers and their students maintained a relationship, which was in many respects indistinguishable from that of father and son.[1] Scholars would not only address their pupils as sons,[2] but would often love them all like their own children.[3] Indeed, in terms of the respect and honour due to them, the master enjoyed precedence over the father.[4] It was the disciple's duty to return first a lost article of his master's and only afterwards his father's; to relieve first his master and then his father, if both were carrying a burden; and to ransom first his master and then his father, if they were both imprisoned.[5] The reason for the preferential treatment to be accorded to the teacher was that 'his father brought him (only) into this world, but his teacher who taught him wisdom brings him into the world to come'.[6]

The disciple was expected to behave towards his master with deep respect and selfless devotion. R. Akiba went so far as to interpret Deut. x, 20 – 'Thou shalt fear the Lord thy God' – to include scholars;[7] and his disciple, R. Eleazar ben Shammua actually demanded that 'the fear (or reverence) of your teacher be as the fear of Heaven'.[8]

To a considerable extent this attitude of respect and veneration was to be extended to any one from whom one had gained knowledge, however limited in scope: 'He that learns from his fellow a single

[1] Cf. Sifré ואתחנן, para. 34, ed. Friedman, p. 74a. לבניך אלו תלמידיך.
[2] Cf. e.g. Ab. R.N., ed. Schechter, Version I, ch. 6, p. 15b; y. Ber. II, 1, 4b; b. Ber. 34b; 'Er. 13a; b. Bezah 15b; Yeb. 121a; b. Sanh. 14a.   [3] Cf. y. Ber. I, 8, 5b; cf. also Maimonides, Hilchoth Talm. Tor. V, 12.   [4] Cf. Kid. 32a. For a similar attitude in the New Testament, cf. Matt. VIII, 21 f.; x, 37.   [5] Cf. Mishnah B.M. II, 11; T. ibid., II, 29; T. Hor. II, 5; Hor. 13a. Whether such precedence was due to any master or only to one's teacher par excellence was a matter of dispute; cf. Tos. B.M. II, 30; T. Hor. II, 5; y. B.M. II, 13, 8d; B.M. 33a.   [6] Mishnah B.M. II, 11.   [7] Cf. Pes. 22b; Kid. 57a.   [8] M. Ab. IV, 12.

I—I.B.C.R.

chapter or a single *halachah* or a single verse or a single expression or even a single letter is in duty bound to pay him honour.'[9] Even a person from whom one had learnt nothing, but who was superior in some sphere of knowledge, had to be treated with deference.[10]

Since the teacher was elevated in status above the father, it followed that the obligations incumbent upon the son were equally – and indeed more so – to be shouldered by the disciple. As a son had to render services to his parents, so the student was expected to minister unto his master. In fact, the first duty imposed on the disciple during his student days was attendance upon one or, preferably, several masters.[11] This custom – known as שימוש תלמידי חכמים or, more briefly, שימוש חכמים – probably dates back to the times of the Hebrew prophets. Thus, when Elisha was called upon by the prophet Elijah to join him, he chose to abandon his agricultural pursuits, kiss his parents goodbye – a remarkable example of the preference given even then to the master over the parents – and to remain with the prophet to the end.[12]

That this close association involved the rendering of services by the student-prophet to the master is clearly implied in II Kings iii, 11: 'Elisha the son of Shaphat is here, who poured water on the hands of Elijah.' This was indeed, the conclusion drawn in the second century c.e. by R. Simeon b. Yoḥai, who inferred from this verse that attendance upon scholars was more important than study itself.[13]

There was a general concensus of opinion on the vital function of *Shimmush Talmidé Ḥakamim* in educational life – so much so that the verb שמש was often used as a synonym for למד in the sense of studying under a master.[14] For all practical purposes attendance upon a teacher was a *sine qua non* for any student who aspired to scholastic distinction. *Shimmush Ḥakamim* was among the forty-eight qualifications re-

---

[9] *Ibid.*, VI, 3.   [10] Cf. *Pes.* 113b.   [11] Cf. *A.Z.* 19a; but cf. *Ab. R.N.* ed. Schechter, Version I, ch. 8, p. 18b for a different opinion: הלומד תורה מרב אחד האדם ההוא מלא טובה וברכה . . . Krauss, *Talm. Arch.* III, 220, attempts to reconcile this divergence of views by assuming that, while for specialization many teachers were required, one master was preferable for general studies; for at this stage multiplicity of opinions might have a confusing effect. Bacher, *Agada der Tannaiten* II, 20, explains similarly that one should not acquire different sections of study from various masters; but once basic studies had been completed, it was considered proper to consult many teachers.   [12] Cf. I Kings, xix, 19–21; II Kings ii, 1–12.   [13] Cf. *Ber.* 7b.   [14] Cf., e.g. *M. Demai* II, 3; *Mishnah B.B.* X, 8; y. *Nazir* VII, 1, 56b; y. *Ḥag.* III, 1, 78d; y. *Shab.* X 5, 12c; *Ḥul.* 54a; '*Er.* 13a.

203

quired for the acquisition of the Torah.[15] According to one opinion, moreover, 'even if one has studied the Bible and the Mishnah, but has failed to wait upon scholars, he is considered an 'Am ha-Arez' (uncultured peasant, a boor, an ignoramus).[16] Other derogatory designations of this type of student were 'a cunning rogue',[17] 'a brutish person', 'a Samaritan', and 'a magician'.[18]

While such exaggerated statements were probably not meant to be taken too literally, there is no doubt that both in Palestine and in Babylonia attendance upon scholars was regarded as an inescapable obligation, which no serious student could afford to shirk. Hillel's dictum[19] – later repeated by R. Akiba[20] – that refusal to wait upon scholars (which could lead to grave misjudgments) was an offence deserving of the extreme penalty was not disputed by anybody, despite the obvious severity of such a view. On the contrary, the example of a priest whose failure to attend upon scholars had caused him to be ignorant of some elementary rules of levitical purity,[21] was regarded as sufficient reason to justify an extreme attitude on the subject. Similarly, the acrimonious disputations between the schools of Shammai and Hillel were attributed to the disciples' neglect to wait upon scholars.[22] Failure in this respect was thus deemed dangerous to the religious life of the people, and everything possible, therefore, had to be done to ensure compliance with this custom.

Not only was it the disciple's obligation to attend upon his teacher, but the teacher, too, was in duty bound to accept his pupil's services, even if he did not need them: 'Whosoever deprives his disciple of (the privilege of) ministering unto him, acts as if he had deprived him of (an act of) kindness.'[23] According to another opinion, 'he causes him to cast off the fear of heaven'.[24]

There were several reasons for this custom. As already explained, the teacher-student relationship was virtually the same as that existing between father and son. The services normally rendered by a son to his

[15] Cf. *Aboth* VI, 5.　[16] Cf. *Ber.* 47b; b. *Soṭ.* 22a.　[17] Cf. *Soṭ.* 21b–22a. [18] Cf. *Soṭ.* 22a. In the post-Talmudic era, neglect in attendance upon scholars was said to be the cause of ignorance of the deeper secrets of the Torah, cf. *Lev. r.* III, 7, ed. M. Margulies, vol. I, p. 74, and *Seder Eliyahu rabba*, ch. VI.　[19] Cf. *Ab. R.N.*, ed. Schechter, Version I, ch. 12, p. 28a.　[20] Cf. *y. Nazir* VII, 1, 56b; *Der. Er. z.*, ch. VIII (end).　[21] Cf. *Ab. R.N. ad loc.*, ed. Schechter, p. 28b. [22] Cf. *T. Sanh.* VII, 1; *Sanh.* 88b; *Soṭ.* 47b.　[23] Cf. *Ket.* 96a.　[24] *Ibid.* Note that reverence for the teacher was compared to the fear of Heaven, cf. *M. Aboth* IV, 12; see above, p. 1.

father were, therefore, equally to be rendered by a disciple to his master. Furthermore, many students were wandering scholars,[25] who were attracted from afar by the fame of a rabbi or a college. For such students, the master or the head of the college would take entirely the place of the father, and he would treat them like his own children.[26]

To this must be added the fact that instruction was generally free of charge,[27] thus involving no financial burdens for advanced disciples other than the inevitable neglect of their trade or business affairs. It was therefore, only fair to expect students to repay a small part of the debt they owed their teachers by rendering them certain services. Since, moreover, many students were impecunious[28] and had to dine at their master's table[29] or subsist on his charity or on an allowance provided by him[30] – or else depend on contributions collected by the master for them[31] – it was but natural for the beneficiaries to demonstrate their gratitude in a practical manner.

[25] Cf. e.g. M. Aboth IV, 14; Ber. 63b; 'Er. 54b; b.B.B. 8a; Ket. 62b for a number of cases of itinerant students; cf. also Shab. 127a.   [26] See above, p. 1, notes 2 and 3; cf. also Ned. 40a; Men. 18a.   [27] Cf. Ned. 37a; y. ibid., IV, 3, 38c; Bekoroth 29a; Sifre, Deut. עקב 48, ed. Friedmann, p. 84a; Der. Er.z, ch. IV. The rabbis strongly objected to making the Torah 'a spade wherewith to dig' (M. Aboth IV, 5; cf. ibid., I, 13). Nevertheless, because of unavoidable circumstances, Bible and Mishnah teachers – for whom teaching was a full-time occupation – were paid for their work, cf. y. Ned. IV, 3, 38c; Ned. 37a; M. Ned. IV, 2–3; y. Pe'ah VIII, 7, 21a; y. Ḥag. I, 7, 66c; Lev. r. XXX, 1, ed. Margulies, vol. IV, p. 688. Cf. also Krauss, Talm. Arch. III, 212; E. Ebner, Elementary Education in Ancient Israel, pp. 56 f. On the other hand college teachers and masters who taught advanced students were not given any remuneration. Hillel's entrance fee at the Beth Hamidrash of Shemayah and Abtalyon (cf. Yoma 35b) was altogether exceptional, and was probably payment for the janitor's services (cf. ibid. לשומר בית המדרש rather than a fee for instruction).   [28] Cf. Ned. 81a.   [29] For examples of disciples dining with their master, cf. T. Yom-ṭob II, 14; Ber. 39a; 43a; 46b; Sanh. 38a; Der. Er. r. VII; Lev. r. XXXIII, 1, ed. M. Margulies, IV, 758. According to A. Ornstein הנשיאות בישראל p. 197, distinguished students would be invited to dine with the Patriarch. It is noteworthy that occasionally a master might also provide food for his disciples outside his home; cf. 'Er. 73a; Pes. 51a–b.   [30] Cf. 'Er. 73a: של רבי . . . אנו סומכין על שלחנו של ר'חייא; cf. ibid., Rashi, s.v. תלמיד אצל; רבו: דר עמו בחצר ומקבל פרס הימנו; cf. also y. Soṭ. III, 4,19a; y.B.M. II, 3, 8c; Ḳid. 32a; B.B. 8a; Ruth r. V, 7.   [31] For examples of appeals and donations for the benefit of students and scholars, cf. y. Pes. VII, 1, 34a; y. M.Ḳ. III, 1, 81d; y. Hor. III, 7, 48a; Pes. 53b; Ket. 105b; Lev. r. V, 4, ed. M. Margulies I, 110 f.; Esther r. II, 3; Eccl. r. XI, 1, 1; Pesiḳ. R.K., ed. Buber XI, 99b; Tanḥuma ראה 17, ed. Buber 14a.

Above all, however, there were sound educational reasons for the custom of *Shimmush Talmidei Hakamim*. Disciples were expected not only to study the Law in all its ramifications, but also to acquaint themselves with a specific way of life, which could be done only through constant attendance upon a master. The student would have to take note of the teacher's ordinary daily conversation – which itself required study[32] – and he had to observe his master's habits,[33] including at times his most intimate activities.[34] Personal attendance on scholars enabled the student to learn far more of the deeper spirit of Judaism than conventional study at the *Yeshibah* or *Beth Hamidrash*. Since the rabbis taught as much by example as by precept, *Shimmush Talmidei Hakamim* constituted an indispensable means of attaining a higher standard of morals and ethics. It was, as has been said, 'in itself a good education in righteous conduct and fear of the Almighty'.[35]

The duties involved in attendance upon a master were sometimes easy, but often menial and burdensome. There was, indeed, hardly any service which the disciple was not required to perform for his teacher. 'All manner of service that a slave must render to his master, the pupil must render to his teacher – except that of taking off his shoe'[36] (because in that case he might be mistaken for a non-Jewish slave).

A regular task of the disciple was in all probability associated with monitorial duties at the *Yeshibah* or *Beth Hamidrash*, where he might have to arrange the benches morning and evening or place mats on the floor for the use of junior students who had not yet been promoted to bench seats. It was perhaps to encourage such services that a late Midrash attributes Joshua's success in gaining the leadership of Israel, to his assiduity in performing such tasks on behalf of Moses.[37]

Another common duty – usually performed by senior students – was

[32] Cf. *Suk.* 21b; *A.Z.* 19b.   [33] Cf., e.g. *y. Ber.* I, 8, 3d; *ibid.*, III, 5, 6d; cf. also *Ber.* 24a–b; *Shab.* 12b and 41a.   [34] Cf. *Ber.* 62a, where several instances are cited; cf. also *Ber.* 24a, where we are told that Raba deliberately instructed a student of his to fetch his (Raba's) phylacteries from his bed, thereby exposing a matter concerning his marital relations – all for the sake of indicating a halachic ruling in a practical manner; cf. also *ibid.*, 23a (end) and *y. Ber.* I, 1, 2d.   [35] *Soncino Talmud, Kethuboth* 96a, p. 611, n. 5.   [36] *Ket.* 96a. Even this exception was so qualified by leading Babylonian Amoraim as to render it virtually inoperative; cf. *ad loc.*; also Krauss, *Talm. Arch.* II, 102.   [37] Cf. *Num. r.* XXI, 14. Similar conditions are likely to have prevailed during the Talmudic Age.

to accompany the master wherever he went, so as to enable him to lean for support on one or two of his disciples[38] – not necessarily because of the infirmities of age,[39] but because this was a privilege which the teacher enjoyed by virtue of his position. If the master was sick, his pupils would try to nurse him back to health.[40] We even hear of a case where a saintly disciple was asked by his teacher to pray for his (the teacher's) sick son.[41]

Other services known to have been rendered by disciples to their teachers included shopping,[42] preparation and cooking of food[43] and waiting at table.[44] The latter duty was frequently performed even by eminent rabbis, and to justify this practice it was pointed out that Abraham, Moses and even the Almighty himself had performed similar services.[45] On Sabbaths students would often take turns ministering to their teacher and fellow students.[45a]

A highly characteristic service was attendance by the student at the bath-house whenever his master went there. The duties included carrying the master's garments,[46] washing and oiling the floor, warming oil for anointing, and various other services; yet, significantly, even at the bath-house the disciples found a good deal to learn, both in respect of rules of conduct and of halachic principles.[47] Although a student was not supposed to bathe together with his master, an exception was made if the master required his services.[48] So widespread was this type of service that it became a proverbial expression to say of a person of exceptional scholarship, 'I shall bring his clothes after him to the bath-house'[49] – in other words, 'I shall become his disciple'.

The duties of the students were not confined to the home or college of the master. Disciples would often follow their teacher wherever he

---

[38] Cf. *y. Ber.* II, 1, 4b; *y. Demai* III, 2, 23b; *y. Ḥallah* III, 6, 59b; *y. Shab.* I, 1, 3a, *y. Sheḳ.* II, 7, 47a; *y. M.Ḳ.* III, 7, 83c; *Yeb.* 42b; *Ket.* 62a; *B.B.* 111a; *Exod. r.* XLVII, 5; *Lev. r.* XXX, 1; *Pesiḳ. R.K.* 28, ed. Buber 178b. [39] Cf. *Ket.* 62a. [40] Cf. *y. Ber.* I, 2, 3a; *y. Shab.* 14, 3, 14c; *B.M.* 85b. [41] Cf. *Ber.* 34b. [42] Cf. *y. Sheb.* IX, 9, 39a. [43] Cf. *Lam. r.* III, 17, 6. [44] Cf. *y. Ber.* VIII, 5, 12b; *T. Ber.* VI (V), 4–5; cf. *b. Ber.* 52b. According to the school of Hillel, a waiter who was not a *Talmid Ḥakam* was not to be employed at all because he might carelessly destroy bread-crumbs, cf. *Ber.* 52b. [45] Cf. *Mekilta*, יתרו, ed. Friedmann 59a; *Ḳid.* 32b. Cf. also *Shab.* 74a: שבתא דרב ביבי הואי and Rashi *ad loc.* [45a] Cf. *Shab. ad loc.*; *T. Nega'im* VIII, 2. [46] See below, notes 48 and 49. [47] Cf. *y. Ber.* II, 3, 4c; *y. Shab.* VII, 2, 10a; *Shab.* 40b; 41a. [48] Cf. *Pes.* 51a. [49] Cf. *'Er.* 27b; *Sanh.* 62b; cf. Krauss, *Talm. Arch.* I, 231.

went.[50] They would even accompany him if he went abroad.[51] A rabbi who had incurred the penalty of exile would take his students with him, and it was, in fact, a halachic norm that, if a master had inadvertently committed manslaughter, thus being obliged to seek the shelter of a city of refuge, his *Yeshibah*, i.e. his disciples, would be exiled with him.[52]

Since students might be exposed to heretical or Hellenistic influences while abroad, Abtalyon – a leading Pharisee who flourished in the first century B.C.E. – aware of the existence of spies and informers[53] who reported to the Herodian or Roman authorities anything of political import that might be discussed at the 'meeting place of the Wise',[54] advised sages to "give heed to your words lest ye incur the penalty of exile and ye be exiled to a place of evil waters, and the disciples that come after you drink of them and die (spiritually), and the name of Heaven be profaned'.[55]

Not all the sages heeded this counsel, and there were some whose religio-national enthusiasm exceeded their discretion. Thus in 4 B.C.E., two zealot-minded Pharisees instigated their students to remove the golden eagle which Herod had set up over the Temple gate; some forty of them were caught in the act and were burnt alive together with their teachers.[56]

Although following the destruction of the Second Temple the rabbis took great care not to endanger the lives of their pupils,[57] the duties imposed on students continued to be heavy and exacting. There were probably some who were not too anxious to shoulder the burden of *Shimmush Talmidei Hakamim*. The emphasis so frequently set on this indicates a certain laxity on the part of some individuals. There were apparently students who for this very reason preferred to study alone, without the aid of a teacher. It was to counteract such tendencies that

---

[50] There are numerous references to students 'walking behind', i.e. following their teacher, during walks or journeys; cf., e.g. *Ber.* 23a; 23b; 24a; 44a; 60a; *Shab.* 12b; 108b; 112a; *'Er.* 30a; *R.H.* 34b; *y. Ber.* I, 5, 3a; *y. Hag.* II, 1, 77a; *B.M.* II, 3, 8c. (For N.T. references of a similar character, cf. Matt. iv, 18–22; viii, 19–23; ix, 9; Mark i, 16–20; Luke v, 11, 28; vii, 11; John i, 37–43; ii, 12; iii, 22.)   [51] Cf. e.g. *y. Ber.* III, 1, 6a; *y. Nazir* VII, 1, 56a.   [52] Cf. *Mak.* 10a.   [53] Cf. Josephus, *Ant.* XV, 8, 4 (285); 10, 4 (366–7); cf. *B. B.* 4a.   [54] For an actual example of such a case, which occurred about the middle of the second century C.E., cf. *Shab.* 33b.   [55] *M. Ab.* I, 11.   [56] Cf. Josephus, *Ant.* XVII, 6, 2–4 (149–167); *Bell.* I, 33, 2–4 (648–55).   [57] Cf. e.g. *Pes.* 112a; *Sanh.* 14a.

the inadequacy of private study and the advantages of collegiate study
under the guidance of a recognized teacher, and in close association
with fellow students, were stressed time and again.[58]

Pupils were also required to show their respect for their teachers in a
variety of other ways. During study sessions a mood of reverence and
awe was the rule, and no frivolous lightheartedness was allowed,[59]
unless the teacher himself chose to enliven the proceedings by means of
jests or stories.[60] Thus, the Babylonian Amora, Rabbah, used to com-
mence his lectures with humorous tales and anecdotes in order to
amuse and arouse the interest of his pupils before beginning the serious
work of halachic discourses, during which he would sit in awe, both as
a mark of respect for the Torah and as an example to his students.[61]
Particularly strict in this respect was R. Judah the Patriarch whose love
for his students did not prevent him from adopting a severe attitude
even towards his star pupils,[62] and to advise his son Gamaliel to 'cast
bile among the disciples'[63] or, in other words, to enforce discipline at
his college.

Outwardly, the obligatory attitude of deep respect and awe was
expressed by sitting bent over reverentially during the master's discourses, and even senior rabbis did not consider it beneath their dignity
to assume this humble posture.[64] Any act of disrespect, even if quite
unintentional, was frowned upon. Thus, to cough and spit in the
presence of the master was condemned as an act of irreverence deserving the harshest penalty.[65]

According to one opinion, the disciple was not to sit before his
master on a couch or a bench, but on the ground, and he was to absorb
every word spoken by the teacher 'with awe, fear, dread and
trembling'.[66] R. Abbahu, a leading third-century rabbi, contested this
view to some extent, maintaining that a master must not sit on a couch

[58] Cf. e.g. M. Aboth I, 6; VI, 5; Ab. R.N. ed. Schechter, Version I, ch. 14,
p. 30a; Ber. 63b; Shab. 63a; 147b; Ta'an. 7a; Keth. 111a; Mak. 10a; Gen. r.
LXIX, 2, ed. Theodor II, 791; Eccl. r. VII, 7, 2.   [59] Cf. Shab. 30b; Pes. 117a;
cf. also Tanḥ. בהעלותך 11.   [60] Cf. Gen. r. LVIII, 3, ed. Theodor I, 621;
Cant. r. I, 15, 3.   [61] Cf. Shab. 30b; Pes. 117a.   [62] Cf. y. Kil. IX, 4, 32b;
y. Ta'an. IV, 2, 68a; y. M.Ḳ. III, 1, 81c; M.Ḳ. 16a–b; Sanh. 11a; Gen. r.
XXXIII, 3, ed. Theodor I, 306.   [63] Keth. 103b.   [64] Cf. Shab. 17a; 51a; Sanh.
24a.   [65] Cf. 'Er. 99a.   [66] Ab. R.N. ed. Schechter, Version I, ch. 6, p. 14a;
cf. also Der. Er. Z., ch. I (beg.); ישב ומשנה ומטנף כסותו לפני תלמידי חכמים
'Soiling one's garment' would presumably be caused by sitting on the
ground.

while his pupil was seated on the ground. They were either to sit both on the ground or both on a couch.[67] He evidently saw the psychological advantages of maintaining, within limits, a certain measure of equality between master and disciple.[68] This does not, however, appear to have been a widely accepted view, and in practice it was probably not often adhered to. Students, especially juniors, were frequently seated on the bare floor[69] or on mats,[70] while the master sat on a stone,[71] a jug,[72] a basket[73] or on cushions,[74] and, it may be assumed, also on stools or benches, which were sometimes also available for students.[75]

Pupils were not supposed to ask questions irrelevant to the subject under discussion lest the teacher be put to shame.[76] It was the mark of a wise disciple to confine himself to relevant questions, while the uncultured *Golem* would do precisely the opposite.[77] On the other hand, students were not only permitted but encouraged to ask the master to explain whatever they had failed to grasp during the discourse. It was a well-known principle that 'a shamefaced person cannot learn',[78] and it was further said that 'he who abases himself (i.e. exposes his ignorance by asking questions) for the (sake of learning the) words of the Torah will eventually be exalted, but he who muzzles himself (i.e. refrains from asking questions) will have to put his hand to his mouth' (viz., when he, in turn, will be asked to answer questions).[79]

Students could also argue freely with their teachers during discussions, which formed the essence of instruction at all higher educational institutions; but they were expected to do so not in a contentious spirit but reverently and with due restraint.[80] Nevertheless, halachic discussions and arguments were often keen-edged to the point where students could be described as being 'enemies' of the master. Such 'hostility', born out of the vehemence of the arguments in the

---

[67] Cf. *Meg.* 21a and Rashi *ad loc.*   [68] It is, nevertheless, significant that two of R. Abbahu's senior disciples would not speak up when they visited him 'because of their reverence for him'; cf. *y. Sanh.* VI, 10, 23d.   [69] Cf. *M. Ab.* I, 4; *B.Ḳ.* 117a; *B.M.* 84b; *Sanh.* 17b; 36b (see Rashi *ad loc.* in reference to *M. Sanh.* IV, 4). Cf. also Krauss, *Talm. Arch.* III, 206.   [70] Cf. *Ber.* 25a; *Num. r.* XXI, 14.   [71] Cf. e.g. *Cant. r.* I, 3, 1.   [72] Cf. *Ned.* 49b.   [73] *Ibid.*   [74] Cf. *M.Ḳ.* 16b; *B.Ḳ.* 117a.   [75] Cf. *y. Ber.* IV, 1, 7d; *y. Beẓ.* I, 6, 60c; *y. Ta'an.* IV, 1, 67d; *Ber.* 28a; *B.M.* 84b.   [76] Cf. *Shab.* 3b.   [77] Cf. *M. Ab.* V, 7; *Der. Er. Z.* I (beg.).   [78] *M. Ab.* II, 5.   [79] *Ber.* 63b.   [80] Cf. e.g. *Tanḥ.* בהעלותך 11. Note the polite language used by R. Akiba whenever he opposed his masters; cf. *T. Yom-ṭob* II, 12; *Ber.* 37a; *R.H.* 25a; *A.Z.* 16b.

'war of the Torah', was usually short-lived: 'They do not move from there until they come to love each other.'[81]

To leave a lesson or a lecture prior to its conclusion, permission had to be obtained from the teacher.[82] This practice, known as נטילת רשות was particularly frequent when a student wished to emigrate.[83] Such permission was not always granted, especially when a disciple wanted to leave the Land of Israel for economic reasons.[84] Even to leave Babylonia for Ereẓ Israel was not always approved of, and students sometimes had to resort to devious means to attain their goal.[85]

On no account was a student permitted to render a legal or religious decision, and if he did so, his decision had no legal validity.[86] To render a decision in the presence of one's master was regarded as an offence of such serious import that the culprit morally incurred the penalty of death.[87] According to one opinion, he deserved to die even if his master was not present during his presumptuous act.[88]

Severe imprecations were hurled at the rash and over-confident disciple – irrespective of his merits and qualifications – who displayed lack of respect towards his master by rendering a legal or religious decision in his presence. He deserved to be bitten by a snake; he was to be called a sinner; to be deprived of whatever greatness he possessed; and he was doomed to 'go down to *Sheol* childless.'[89] The case of a student who had committed this offence and died in consequence was cited as a warning,[90] and ancient historical precedents were quoted to lend strength to this severe rule.[91]

A disciple who disregarded all these warnings was likened to the 'strange woman' who 'hath cast down many wounded' (Prov. vii, 26) – interpreted as a reference to the legal errors arising out of irre-

---

[81] *Ḳid.* 30b.   [82] Cf. *A.Z.* 19a. Cf. also the case of R. Eliezer's students who dared not leave the *Beth Hamidrash* during their master's long-drawn-out festival discourse, although everyone else had already left, cf. *Beẓ.* 15b.   [83] Cf. e.g. *y. Ber.* II, 8, 5c; III, 1, 6a. The practice of נטילת רשות was customary even when departing from one's teacher in the street; cf. *Der. Er. r.* IV (end); *ibid.* V (beg.); see below p. 15, n. 144.   [84] Cf. *y. M.Ḳ.* III, 1, 81c; *Exod. r.* LII, 3.   [85] Cf. *Ber.* 24b; *Shab.* 41a; *Ket.* 110b; *y. Ber.* II, 8, 5c.   [86] Cf. *Sifra*, שמיני, ed. Weiss. 45b; *y. Shebi'ith* VI, 1, 36c; *y. Giṭ.* I, 2, 43c; cf. also Maimonides, *Hilchoth Talm. Tor.* V, 2–4.   [87] Cf. *Ber.* 31b; *'Er.* 63a; *y. Shebi'ith ad loc.*; *y. Giṭ. ad loc.*, *Lev. r.* XX, 6, ed. Margulies II, 459; *Pesiḳ. R.K.* אחרי מות, ed. Buber 172a.   [88] Cf. *'Er.* 63a.   [89] *Ibid.*   [90] *Ibid.*, Sifra, *ad loc.*; *y. Shebi'ith ad loc.*; *y. Giṭ. ad loc.*; *Lev. r., ad loc.*; *Pesiḳ. R.K., ad loc.*   [91] See note 87 (on Nadab and Abihu); cf. also *Ber.* 31b (on Samuel).

sponsible decisions rendered by unqualified persons.[92] A student of this type was contemptuously referred to as 'a minor whose months (viz., of gestation) are not completed'[93] and he was included in a list of people who 'bring destruction upon the world'.[94]

It was inadmissible even to speak in the presence of a person greater or wiser than oneself,[95] and one who indulged in this practice was an uncultured *Golem*.[96] The Rabbis were, however, by no means concerned only with questions of etiquette and good manners. Their extreme reluctance to permit students, however learned, to render halachic decisions – even when the matter at issue was perfectly straightforward and did not admit of any doubt[97] – can be traced back to the early Tannaitic period.[98] The ultra-conservative attitude of R. Eliezer ben Hyrcanus may have had a decisive influence in this direction.[99] But since R. Eliezer's views were rarely accepted as halachic norms, it is highly probable that the attitude of later rabbis was shaped by an incident during the Patriarchate of R. Judah ha-Nasi, who discovered that a disciple, in rendering a halachic decision, had failed to make his meaning clear, thus causing widespread transgression of the laws of purity.[100] To a considerable extent these restrictions applied also to fully qualified rabbis, who often refrained from rendering halachic decisions during their master's life-time.[101] Legally, however, even a qualified disciple who had become the intellectual equal of his teacher – thereby attaining the status of a תלמיד חבר – was permitted to decide legal-religious questions not only after the master's death, but also during his life-time, and even in areas under the latter's jurisdiction.[102] According to another opinion, however, a qualified disciple was not authorized to render halachic decisions within twelve Roman miles – according to another view, within three Persian miles – of his master's residence.[103] On the other hand, where a master or any greater authority was not available, a scholar-disciple who possessed the necessary qualifications was not only entitled but in duty bound to decide halachic questions, and if he

[92] Cf. *Soṭ.* 22a; *A.Z.* 19b.   [93] *Soṭ.* 22a.   [94] *Ibid.*   [95] Cf. *Der. Er. Z.,* ch. II (beg.).   [96] Cf. *M. Ab.* V, 7.   [97] Cf. *'Er.* 62b.   [98] Of special interest in this connection is Judah b. Tabbai's resolve – due to an erroneous verdict in a capital case – to render no decision without Simeon ben Sheṭaḥ's consent; cf. *T. Sanh.* VI, 6; *Ḥag.* 16b; *Mak.* 5b.   [99] Cf. *Suk.* 27b–28a; see above, n. 90.   [100] Cf. *y. Shebi'ith* VI, 1, 36 b–c; *y. Giṭ.* I, 2, 43c; *Sanh.* 5b.   [101] Cf. *'Er.* 62b–63a.   [102] *Ibid.*   [103] Cf. *y. Shebi'ith, ad loc.; y. Giṭ. ad loc.; Sanh.* 5b; *Lev. r.* XX, 6, ed. Margulies II, 459; *Pesiḳ. R.K.* אחרי מות, ed. Buber 172a.

refused to do so he was denounced in strong terms.[104] Likewise, when a court of law was making an erroneous decision a student enjoyed the privilege of expressing his dissent, and was, indeed, in duty-bound to do so.[105] In capital cases, a disciple was silenced if he attempted to speak against the accused, but encouraged and promoted if he offered to speak in his favour.[106]

The same attitude of respect expected of students during lectures and studies was also obligatory during prayer-time. Unless a disciple had attained the status of *TALMID ḤABER*, he was not supposed to stand either next to his teacher or immediately behind him.[107] According to R. Eliezer ben Hyrcanus, who was rather strict with his disciples,[108] a student who stood behind his master during services was causing the divine presence to depart from Israel.[109] It is likely that disciples regarded it as a matter of status and prestige to be close to the master while praying. This was presumably regarded not only as unworthy but also as distracting from one's devotion.

Whenever students dined with their master, their table manners were under strict scrutiny. They were considered important enough to be included among the rules of behaviour and etiquette enumerated in the tractate *Derek Erez*.[110] Although applicable generally, they were no doubt more strictly enforced in the company of the teacher. R. Akiba used the opportunity afforded by a banquet he had provided for his students to give them lessons in table manners.[111] The disciple had to make sure his hands were clean or else he was liable to be rebuked by his master. Thus, at a dinner given by R. Judah ha-Nasi, Rab was told by the Patriarch to wash his hands. The guest began to tremble because he thought he had committed an offence against table etiquette. It turned out, however, that R. Judah ha-Nasi merely wanted Rab to prepare to say grace.[112]

Generally, the privilege of reciting grace was reserved for the leading scholar in the company; but he could honour a disciple by conferring this privilege on him.[113] The person who would break the bread was usually the first to take his food; but if he wished to give

---

[104] Cf. *Soṭ.* 22a; *A.Z.* 19b.   [105] Cf. *Sanh.* 7b; *Hor.* 3b.   [106] Cf. *M. Sanh.* V, 4; *T. ibid.*, IX, 3.   [107] Cf. *Ber.* 27a–b.   [108] Cf. *ibid.*, 16b; *y. ibid.* II, 8, 5b; *Sanh.* 68a; *Ab. R.N.* ed. Schechter, Version I, ch. 25, p. 40b. See also above, n. 90.   [109] Cf. *Ber.* 27b.   [110] Cf. *Der. Er. Z.* V; cf. also *Ber.* 46b–47a; *T. ibid.* V, 5–10.   [111] Cf. *Der. Er. r.* VII.   [112] Cf. *Ber.* 43a; 46b.   [113] Cf. *ibid.*, 47a.

precedence to his master or to one who surpassed him in knowledge, he could do so.[114] The same rule applied to the mixing of the wine-cup after the meal.[115]

The master might also call on one of his students to recite the blessing before the meal; but the latter had to be on his guard that he picked the most important course for the blessing, not necessarily the one he liked best. Two of Bar Ḳappara's disciples, it was said, had died because they had failed to show proper respect to their master when one of them was called upon to recite the blessing before one of the courses.[116]

A student was never to refer to his master by name[117] or greet him in a familiar light-hearted manner without the appellation 'Rabbi'.[118] The disciple was expected to bow down to his teacher and salute him respectfully.[119] According to R. Eliezer, one who greeted his master was causing the Divine Presence to depart from Israel[120] or, according to another version, deserved to die.[121] The reason is discussed below.

Ben Azzai went still further, stating that even one who returned his teacher's greeting deserved to die.[122] According to both Rashi and Tosafoth on Berakoth 27b., it was only a greeting without the appellation 'Rabbi' which was forbidden, but otherwise there was nothing wrong with saluting one's master in the proper manner. In support of this interpretation, one may cite the fact that permission was granted to students to greet their teacher during the reading of the *Shema‘*[123] – from which it was deduced that 'a man must salute one who is greater than himself in (the knowledge of) the Torah'.[124] Additional evidence pointing in the same direction is indicated in the fact that the length of the greetings exchanged between master and disciple served as a halachic time-measure.[125]

Nevertheless, the possibility that R. Eliezer and Ben Azzai regarded any sort of greeting addressed by a disciple to his teacher as presumptuous – evidently because it implied a certain degree of equality –

---

[114] Cf. *T. ibid.*, V, 8. [115] Cf. *ibid.*, V, 7. [116] Cf. *ibid.*, 39a. [117] Cf. *Ḳid.* 31b; *Sanh.* 109b. Cf. also Maimonides, *Hilchoth Talm. Tor.* V. 5. [118] Occasionally, the word ומורי 'and my teacher' was added; cf. e.g. *b. Ber.* 3a; *B.Ḳ.* 73b. Cf. also Maimonides *ad loc.* [119] Cf. *Ḳid.* 32b–33a; *Tanḥ.* בהעלותך 11 (beg.). [120] Cf. *Ber.* 27b. [121] Cf. *Kallah* (end); but in *Kallah r.* ch. II (end), the author of this statement is given as R. Eliezer ben Jacob. [122] Cf. *Kallah ibid.* [123] Cf. *y. Ber.* II, 1, 4a; *Ber.* 14a. [124] *y. Ber.*, *ad loc.* [125] *Ibid.*; cf. also *y. M.Ḳ.* III, 7, 83c; *B.Ḳ.* 73b.

cannot be entirely excluded;[126] for we are expressly informed that the Babylonian students would altogether refrain from saluting their teachers at any time,[127] so as not to bother the master to reply or because they felt that this would detract from the respect due to a teacher.[128] R. Eleazar ben Pedath, a Babylonian by birth,[129] actually went so far as to hide himself on one occasion in order to avoid having to salute R. Joḥanan bar Nappaḥa,[130] who was both his master and his colleague.[131]

Some rabbis deemed it sufficient for a disciple to salute his master once or twice a day.[132] This was not meant to be an alleviation of a burden, but rather a restriction of undue familiarity on the part of disciples in their daily contact with their teachers.

As a rule, a student was not allowed to walk by his teacher's side[133] unless, of course, the master required his assistance. The numerous references to disciples walking behind their teacher[134] prove conclusively that reverence for the teacher required that the student keep a certain distance between himself and the master when walking on the way. Hence one was also not supposed to walk directly behind the teacher, which was regarded as arrogant.[135]

[126] L. Ginzberg, פירושים וחדושים בירושלמי I, 243, dismisses this possibility on the ground that it was only in Babylonia that students refrained from saluting their masters (see below, n. 127). One should not, however, ignore the time-factor. What was exclusively a Babylonian custom in the third century C.E. may well have been a Palestinian custom in the first and early second centuries. It may have been transplanted to Babylonia and subsequently discarded in Palestine.   [127] Cf. y. Ber. II, 1, 4a; y. Sheḳ. II, 6, 47a; y. M.Ḳ. III, 7, 83c; cf. also Job xxix, 8, which was cited in support of this custom.   [128] Cf. P'né Mosheh to y. Ber. II, 1, 4a, and Ḳorban ha-'Edah to y. M.Ḳ. III, 7, 83c.   [129] On the question of R. Eleazar's country of origin, cf. Bacher, אגדת אמוראי ארץ ישראל Vol. II, Part 1, p. 3, n. 2; L. Ginzberg, פירושים וחדושים בירושלמי I, 242.   [130] See above, n. 127.   [131] Ibid., cf. Keth. 111b (where R. Eleazar addresses R. Joḥanan as 'Rabbi'); B.B. 135b; 154b; Tem. 25b; y. Sanh. I, 1, 18b (where R. Eleazar is described as R. Joḥanan's חבר ותלמיד). Bacher, op. cit. p. 7 and Vol. I, Part 2, p. 10, considers that the relations between R. Joḥanan and R. Eleazar were unfriendly and that for a time at least there was friction between them because R. Eleazar did not consider himself to be R. Joḥanan's disciple (cf. y. Ber. II, 1, 4b; y. Sheḳ. II, 7, 47a; y. M.Ḳ. III, 7, 83c.). Against that, however, one must set R. Eleazar's attitude of reverence towards R. Joḥanan (cf. Yoma 53a), which would indicate that R. Eleazar did recognize R. Joḥanan as his master.   [132] Cf. y. Bik. III, 1, 65c.   [133] Cf. Yoma 37a.   [134] See above, n. 50.   [135] Cf. Yoma 37a; cf. Krauss, Talm. Arch. III, 6.

On entering a house, the disciple would wait for his master to enter first.[136] If the teacher and his student happened to be riding, the usual rules of etiquette were not, it seems, too strictly followed, though Abaye, a fourth-century Babylonian Amora, was annoyed about such negligence in regard to the respect due to a master.[137] It goes without saying that one was not permitted to walk in front of one's teacher, and R. Zera, or, according to another version, R. Ada bar Ahaba, claimed that he·had never walked in front of anyone who was superior in learning.[138]

Senior disciples, especially those who had risen to the rank of *Talmid Ḥaber*, were allowed to walk by the master's side,[139] and when two senior students accompanied the teacher, the greater of them would walk on his right, while the less important would be on the master's left.[140] The same rule would apply if the teacher was riding and senior disciples or, possibly, junior teachers would walk by his side.[141]

When taking leave of one's teacher, anything resembling abrupt departure was deemed to be in exceedingly bad taste.[142] If the disciple had already taken leave of his teacher but remained overnight in the same town, he was expected to take leave once again next morning.[143] Departure from one's master became almost a hallowed ceremony. The student had to get first permission from his master to go away.[144] He was not to turn his back on his teacher, but he was to turn his face sideways as he was leaving his master's presence.[145] Of R. Eleazar ben Pedath it was related that whenever R. Joḥanan[146] went away from him, he (R. Eleazar) would stand with lowered head until R. Joḥanan was out of sight;[147] and if R. Eleazar wished to leave first, he would walk backwards, with his face towards R. Joḥanan until he was out of sight.[147]

---

[136] Cf. *Ber.* 47a.   [137] *Ibid.*   [138] Cf. *Ta'an.* 20b; *Meg.* 28a.   [139] Probably, they were expected to walk not exactly next to the master, but slightly behind him, so as to avoid covering him entirely from sight, which was regarded as unseemly; cf. *Yoma* 37a.   [140] Cf. '*Er.* 54b; *Yoma* 37a; *Der. Er. r.* ch. IV. Note the somewhat similar arrangement according to status prevailing at the Temple service on Yom Kippur, cf. *M. Yoma* III, 3. The three angels who visited Abraham were likewise depicted as having been placed in accordance with their importance; cf. *Yoma* 37a. Seating arrangements at the 'academy' of Moses were said to have been on similar lines; cf. '*Er.* 54b.   [141] Cf. *Pes.* 53b.   [142] Cf. *Yoma* 53b.   [143] Cf. *M.Ḳ.* 9a.   [144] Cf. *Der. Er. r.* ch. IV (end); ch. V (beg.).   [145] Cf. *Yoma* 53a.   [146] R. Joḥanan was R. Eleazar's master and colleague, see above, p. 14, no. 131.   [147] Cf. *Yoma* 53a.

The same custom also prevailed in Babylonia where, we are told, Raba, when taking leave of Rab Joseph, would walk backwards – with the result that on one occasion at least his feet were bruised, and the threshold of Rab Joseph's house was stained with blood.[148]

Perhaps the most common form of reverence, which both students and the general public were required to display toward scholars, was to rise at their approach.[149] Only craftsmen engaged in their tasks were exempt from this provision.[150] According to R. Eleazar's opinion, a student preoccupied with the study of Torah must not stand up before his teacher. This was, however, strongly opposed by Abaye,[151] who was himself extremely meticulous in such matters – so much so that it was hyperbolically said that he would rise as soon as he saw the ear of the ass on which his teacher, Rab Joseph, was riding.[152]

As a general rule, Abaye insisted that, while it was sufficient to rise for an ordinary scholar when he approached within four cubits, in the case of one's principal teacher one must rise as soon as he came into sight.[153] On one occasion, when Abaye was riding an ass along the bank of a river, he became annoyed with some of his students who were on the other bank of the river, and had failed to rise before him.[154] Abaye's colleague, Raba, was likewise offended when senior students did not stand up before him.[155] A century earlier, R. Simeon, son of R. Judah the Patriarch, repeatedly complained to his father because fellow scholars whom he had taught a little, had not risen before him.[156] R. Simeon's older contemporary, R. Ishmael ben R. Jose, made a similar complaint against R. Ḥiyya, whom he had in fact never taught.[157] R. Ḥanina even went to the length of scourging anyone who refused to rise before him, claiming that failure to stand up before a scholar constituted a flagrant disregard of the Torah.[158]

Some students apparently tried to escape the burden of constantly rising at the approach of a rabbi by closing their eyes and pretending not to see him. Such practices were, however, sharply condemned.[159]

---

[148] Cf. *Yoma* 53a. [149] Cf. *Ḳid.* 32b; מפני שיבה תקום... ואין זקן אלא חכם.
[150] Cf. *Ḳid.* 33a; Ḥul. 54b; *y. Bik.* III, 3, 65c.   [151] Cf. *Ḳid.* 33b.   [152]*Ibid.*, 33a.
[153] *Ibid.*   [154] *Ibid.*   [155] *Ibid.*, 32b.   [156] *Ibid.*   [157] Cf. *y. Kil.* IX, 3, 32b.
[158] Cf. *y. Bik.* III, 3, 65c. R. Ḥanina's strictness whenever disrespect towards him seemed to be indicated is well illustrated in his refusal to forgive Rab an unintended slight despite the latter's numerous entreaties; cf. *Yoma* 87a-b.
[159] Cf. *Ḳid.* 32b; 33a.

A particularly serious view was taken of a disciple who refused to rise before his own master. Even R. Eleazar, who was more lenient than other rabbis in this respect,[160] stated that such a student was deemed wicked and would suffer dire punishment.[161]

The importance of standing up in honour of scholars was underlined by a daring Aggadic interpretation of Leviticus xix, 32, according to which the Almighty Himself had been the first to rise before scholars.[162] Because of the importance attached to this practice, some students and even some rabbis would deliberately look for opportunities to fulfil this *Miẓwah*.[162a] There was even an opinion that a rabbi should purposely pass in front of people to make them respectfully get up before him, thus 'bringing them to the fear of Heaven'.[163] This must have been rather burdensome, especially in view of the constant coming and going of scholars at the *Yeshibah* and *Beth Hamidrash*.[164] The prevailing opinion was, therefore, that scholars ought not to molest people unduly by walking past them and making them rise at all times.[165] An attempt was made to limit the times of rising before one's master to mornings and evenings on the ground that no more honour should be paid to a teacher than to God.[166] According to R. Eleazar ben Pedath, even once a day was sufficient.[167] There were also rabbis who went out of their way to avoid being honoured in this manner.[168] Whether a master had the right to forgo the reverence due to him was a disputed point,[169] but by and large the matter was, it seems, left to individual discretion.

In spite of the extraordinary reverence in which rabbis were held by their students, the relations between them were usually very close and far from formal. It was, as already pointed out, essentially a paternal-filial relationship transcended and surpassed by the intense love master and disciple bore to each other. As an example, one may cite the case of R. Ḥiyya bar Abba who burst into tears when told by his teacher, R. Joḥanan, that, in his anxiety to secure the means to devote himself to the study of the Torah, he had sold all his property. 'I am weeping',

---

[160] Cf. *ibid.* 33a; 33b. See above, pp. 15 f., and below, n. 167.   [161] *Ibid.* 33b.
[162] Cf. *y. Bik.* III, 3, 65c.   [162a] *Ibid.*; cf. *Ber.* 28a; *'Er.* 28b.   [163] *Tanḥ.* בהעלותך 11.   [164] Cf. *Meg.* 18a.   [165] Cf. *Ḳid.* 32b; 33a; 33b; *y. Bik.* III, 3, 65c.   [166] Cf. *b. Ḳid.* 33b.   [167] *Ibid.*, 33a. Note R. Eleazar's objection to standing up before a teacher during studies; cf. *ibid.*, 33b. See above, pp. 15 f. [168] *Ibid.*, 33a; 33b; *Ḥul.* 54b; *y. Bik.* III, 3, 65c, *Tanḥ.* בהעלותך 11.   [169] Cf. *Ḳid.* 32a.

2—I.B.C.R.

said the faithful disciple, 'because you left yourself nothing for your
old age.'[170] Another of R. Joḥanan's disciples, R. Eleazar, was
reported to have wept when he observed his master's beauty,
which, he realized, would one day rot in the grave.[171] We
also hear of students bursting into tears on seeing their teacher in
pain.[172]

Disciples would sometimes counsel and assist their master in his
private affairs. Thus, R. Jose the Galilean was advised by his students to
divorce his wife from whom he was suffering a good deal, and when he
found himself unable to pay her *Kethubah*, they collected the requisite
amount among themselves and gave it to him. Subsequently, they
even found another wife for him.[173]

Students would, as a matter of course, visit their teacher whenever
he was sick[174] or in mourning, and try to comfort him.[175] Occasionally
they would even attempt to console their master for the loss of a slave,
although certain formal expressions of condolence on the death of a
slave were not always acceptable and might even draw forth a sharp
rebuke.[176]

After completing their course of studies, disciples were expected, as
far as possible, to follow and propagate their master's teaching. The
perfect scholar was one who, like Eliezer, Abraham's servant, had
'fully absorbed his master's teaching' and 'was drawing on it to spread
it abroad'.[177] Ideally, the ex-disciple was to undertake nothing of
importance without consulting his teacher first.[178] Of R. Joḥanan ben
Zakkai and R. Eliezer ben Hyrcanus it was related that they never laid
down any halachic rule which they had not heard from their

---

[170] Cf. *Cant. r.* VIII, 7.   [171] Cf. *Ber.* 5b.   [172] Cf. *Sanh.* 101a.   [173] Cf.
Gen. r. XVII, 3, ed. Theodor I, 152 f.; *Lev. r.* XXXV, 14, ed. Margulies, pp. 802–4.
According to the parallel account in *y. Keth.* XI, 3, 34b, it was R. Eleazar
ben 'Azariah – a colleague rather than a disciple – who counselled and financially
assisted R. Jose the Galilean to dissolve his unhappy marriage. But the fact that
the Midrash attributes this to R. Jose's students is nevertheless significant, since
it indicates an amazingly close relationship between teachers and disciples, so
that there was nothing incongruous in students assisting the master in his private
affairs.   [174] Cf. e.g. *Ber.* 28b; *Keth.* 103b; *Sanh.* 68a; 101a; *y. Ḥag.* II, 1. 77b
(end). Delay in visiting a sick teacher was considered a very serious offence;
cf. *Ab. R.N.* ed. Schechter, Version I, ch. 25, p. 40b; *Sanh.* 68a.   [175] Cf. e.g.
Ab. R.N. op. cit. ch. 14, p. 29b; *y. Sanh.* VI, 10, 23d–24a.   [176] Cf. *M. Ber.* II,
7; *y. Ber.* II, 8, 5b; *Ber.* 16b.   [177] *Yoma* 28b.   [178] Cf. *Ber.* 4a (in reference to
King David imagined in the role of Mephibosheth's disciple): כל מה שאני
עושה אני נמלך במפיבשת רבי. Cf. also *y. Shab.* I, 7, 4a; *y. Beẓ.* III, 2, 62a.

teachers.[179] A disciple's statement, however authoritative in itself, was sometimes dismissed – if unsupported by his master's authority – with the classic question, 'If Rabbi did not teach it, whence would R. Ḥiyya know it?'[180] While it would have been impossible to make any real progress with the development of the Halacha, if everybody had strictly adhered to the principle of never saying anything original, the trend to keep at least generally to the master's basic ideas and to his methods of interpretation was unmistakable.[181]

Great importance was attributed to naming the master whenever a statement of his was quoted: 'Whosoever says anything in the name of its author, brings deliverance into the world.'[182] Quotations had to be precise, not only in their general sense, but also in their wording.[183] Failure to live up to these rules was strongly disapproved, and even resented as an act of intellectual robbery.[184]

Accurate quotations and the naming of authors were regarded as acts of piety towards teachers whose highest ambition it was that their words should be cited in synagogues and houses of study.[185] This was particularly necessary in the case of scholars who had departed this world; for it was only thus that the names and teachings of the masters could be immortalized, 'making their lips to move in their graves'.[186]

A disciple was not supposed to contradict or dispute with his master, still less quarrel with him or express criticism or resentment – no matter how severe the master might be.[187] One was not even to oppose the master's *Yeshibah*.[188] In practice, a distinguished student (תלמיד ותיק) or a fully qualified *Talmid Ḥaber* would often pursue an

[179] *Suk.* 27b; 28a. R. Eliezer considered anyone who stated something he had not heard from his teacher to be guilty of an act of impiety which would cause the Divine Presence to depart from Israel; cf. *Ber.* 27b; *Kallah* (end). [180] *'Er.* 92a; *Yeb.* 43a; *Nid.* 62b. [181] This was particularly noticeable in local usage, where halachic rules laid down by a local rabbi were observed by his followers as well as visitors, even though these rules were not recognized elsewhere as binding; cf. e.g. *y. Ber.* VIII, 1, 12a; *Shab.* 37b; 46a; 60b; *Yeb.* 14a. [182] *Ab.* VI, 6; *Meg.* 15a; *Ḥul.* 104b; *Nid.* 19b. [183] Cf. *M. 'Ed.* I, 3; *Ber.* 47a; *Shab.* 15a; *Bekor.* 5a. To facilitate the recollection of the exact wording, scholars were advised to draw a mental picture of the author; cf. *y. Shek.* II, 7, 47a. [184] Cf. *y. Ber.* II, 1, 4b; III, 1, 6a; *y. Shek.* II, 7, 47a; *y. M.Ḳ.* III, 7, 83c; *y. Nazir* VII, 1, 56a; *Pes.* 53b; *Yeb.* 96b; *Keth.* 25b; *Mak.* 5b; *Men.* 93b; *Tanḥ.* ed. Buber, במדבר 27, p. 11b; cf. Ginzberg, פירושים וחדושים בירושלמי, II, 93. [185] Cf. *y. Ber.* II, 1, 4b; *y. Shek.* II, 7, 47a; *y. M.Ḳ.* III, 7, 83c; *Yeb.* 97a. [186] *Ibid.* [187] Cf. *Ber.* 63b; *Sanh.* 110a; *Tanḥ.* בהעלותך, 11. [188] Cf. *Ber.* 27b; *Kallah. r.* II (end).

independent line in his approach to halachic questions. Qualified students generally could and frequently did oppose their master's views on certain questions. Thus, R. Akiba often opposed his teachers, R. Eliezer and (to a lesser extent) R. Joshua.[189] All of Rab's disciples decided a certain problem in direct opposition to Rab's view on the matter.[190] R. Abbahu did not always follow the teachings of his master, R. Johanan,[191] and there are other instances that could be cited.

Students would not hesitate to question their teacher when his actions seemed to contradict his teachings[192] or when his behaviour appeared unseemly.[193] Halachic discussions between teacher and pupil were often keen-edged to the point where they could be depicted as 'enemies'. Such hostility, born out of the vehemence of the argument, was however, short-lived: 'They do not move from there until they come to love each other.'[194]

While during their student days disciples would often spend the Sabbath with their master,[195] after they had completed their course of studies they were expected to pay visits to their teacher at least during the pilgrim festivals.[196] If possible, a disciple was to live in the same town as his master, thereby preserving the teacher's restraining influence, as an antidote to any evil course the disciple might be inclined to pursue in later life.[197] In fine, as long as one's teacher was alive, one was to maintain contact with him, follow his precepts and examples, and satisfy him in every respect. Such, indeed, was the way to the life of the world-to-come,[198] where those who had faithfully attended upon and studied under their master in this world would continue to minister and learn the secrets of the Torah.[199]

There were disciples whose loyalty to their teacher survived even the severest test. One of the most beautiful and touching stories of the Talmud describes R. Meir's efforts to save his apostate teacher, Elisha

[189] Cf. e.g. *M. Ber.* IV, 3; *M. Shab.* XIX, 1; *M. Pes.* VI, 2; *M. Ker.* III, 9–10 *y. Pes.* VI, 3, 33b; *Bekor.* 20b. It is noteworthy that R. Eliezer did not take kindly to R. Akiba's halachic opposition despite its moderation in tone, cf. e.g. *Pes.* 69a; cf. Weiss, *Dor*, 6th ed. II, 75. [190] Cf. *Ber.* 42b. [191] Cf. e.g. *Ber.* 34b. Cf. also *y. Ber.* VIII, 1, 12a, where we are informed that R. Abbahu did not follow R. Johanan's ruling when he was not at Tiberias. [192] Cf. e.g. *M. Ber.* II, 6–7. [193] Cf. *y. Soṭ.* I, 4, 16d. [194] *Ḳid.* 30b. [195] Cf. *T. Negaʿim* VIII, 2; cf. N. Drazin, *History of Jewish Education*, p. 74. [196] Cf. *Suk.* 27b; *R.H.* 16b. [197] Cf. *Ber.* 8a. [198] Cf. *Shab.* 153a. [199] Cf. *Keth.* 103a; cf. *b. Ber.* 64a.

ben Abuyah, from his spiritual fall.[200] There were also disciples who stayed with their master, who had been condemned to death, during the execution.[201]

The death of a teacher was a major disaster for his students – both former and present – all of whom would observe many of the mourning customs associated with the death of a close relative. The grief of the disciples would sometimes take extreme forms such as rending all or most of one's garments, and beating one's flesh until the blood flowed.[202] The loss of a great teacher was, indeed, irreparable, and students would at times find themselves unable to solve halachic problems once their teacher had passed away.[203] It was a matter of course for disciples to attend their master's funeral or even to bury him themselves.[204]

Extensive as were the duties of students towards their teacher, his obligations towards his students were even greater.[205] In addition to providing unpaid tuition, the master would take a deep personal interest in his pupils' welfare. He would encourage and praise them for their achievements[206] – of which he would naturally be proud[207] – and occasionally he would even reward a star pupil with a kiss on the head or brow.[208] When students failed in their intellectual tasks or strayed from what he considered the right path, he would indeed chide and rebuke them[209] – so much so that a teacher's anger not only frightened

[200] Cf. *y. Ḥag.* II, 1, 77b–c; *Ḥag.* 15a–b.   [201] Cf. *Ber.* 61 b; *A.Z.* 18a. Note that a disciple would also visit his master in prison; cf. *b. Pes.* 112a; *b. 'Er.* 21b. [202] Cf. *Ab. R.N.* ed. Schechter, Version I, ch. 25, p. 41a; *y. Ber.* III, 1, 5d, 6a; *y. M.Ḳ.* III, 5, 83a; III, 7, 83b–c; III, 8, 83d; *y. B.M.* II, 13, 8d; *y. Sanh.* II, 1, 20a; *y. Hor.* III, 3, 47d; *Ber.* 42b–43a; *Shab.* 153a; *Ket.* 103b–104a; *Sanh.* 68a; *M.Ḳ.* 24a, 25b; 26a; *Semaḥoth* VIII; IX (beg.); *Eccl. r.* IX, 10, 3; cf. also Maimonides, *Hilchoth Talm. Tor.* V. 9.   [203] Cf. *Ab. R.N.*, *ad loc.*; *Ber.* 42b–43a; *Sanh.* 68a; *Tanḥ.* בהעלתך 15. Cf. especially *y. Ber.* II, 8, 5c, on the irreplaceability of a deceased scholar.   [204] Cf. *y. Ber.* III, 1, 5d; 6a; *y. M.Ḳ.* III, 5, 83a; *Ber.* 42b; *Sanh.* 68a; *Semaḥoth* XI (end). (For N.T. instances, cf. Matt. xiv, 12; xxvii, 57–60 and parallels.)   [205] Cf. Krauss, *Talm. Arch.* III, 224 f.   [206] Cf. *M. Nazir* VII, 4; *M. Ab.* II, 8–9; *y. R.H.* II, 5, 58a–b; *Gen. r.* ed. Theodor II, 1262. Note also Samuel's habit of referring to his disciple Rab Judah as שננא (keen scholar), cf. e.g. *Ber.* 36a; *Shab.* 55a; *'Er.* 54a.   [207] Cf. e.g. *y. B.M.* II, 13, 8d.   [208] Cf. *Ab. R.N.* ed. Schechter, Version I, ch. 6, p. 16a; *T. Ḥag.* II, 1; *y. Ber.* I. 8, 3d; *y. Ḥag.* II, 1, 77a; *y. Hor.* III, 5, 48c; *Ḥag.* 14b; *b. Hor.* 12b. Cf. also Ginzberg, *op. cit.* I, 300, who points out that it was never customary for a student to kiss his master. The famous 'Judas-kiss' (Matt. xxvi, 49; Mark xiv, 45; Luke xxii, 47) may have been a sectarian custom.   [209] Cf. e.g. *Ber.* 16b; *Pes.* 62b; *Meg.* 25b; *B.Ḳ.* 34b; *b. Sanh.* 62b; *y. Ber.* II, 8, 5b; III, 1, 6a; *y. Nazir* VII, 1, 56a.

222

his students,[210] but was believed to have potentially serious consequences.[211] Yet, of his love for his pupils there could be no doubt.
Thus, it was related of R. Johanan ben Zakkai that he was so devoted
to his students that no one ever opened for them the door of his home
but he himself.[212]

The master would recommend his disciple for a communal position;[213] visit and even nurse him during sickness;[214] comfort him
when he was in mourning;[215] try his utmost to save his life if he was
in danger;[216] and mourn for him as for a son if he died in his teacher's
lifetime.[217] He would display boundless patience and understanding
during lessons. Among the earliest rabbinic maxims we find the statement that 'the impatient man cannot teach',[218] and there are countless
maxims in the Talmud and Midrash criticizing outburts of temper and
excessive anger.[219] Many of these refer to Moses, the exemplar for the
Jewish scholar, and were, therefore, clearly designed to inculcate the
virtue of patience among rabbis. It was the master's duty to explain the
subject matter thoroughly, repeating each lesson at least four times or –
if that was not enough – more often.[220] Of one scholar it was related,
hyperbolically, that he would repeat each lesson four hundred times
to an extremely slow-witted student, while on one occasion he had to
do so eight hundred times before the pupil was able to grasp the subject.[221]

Occasionally, a rabbi would institute a special search for disciples,
especially for neglected or fallen sons of scholars, and it was also regarded as a highly meritorious act to teach the son of an ignoramus
('Am-ha-'Arez).[222] But while it was the cardinal aim of rabbinic Judaism
to 'raise many disciples'[223] there were many students who fell far
short of the ideal. However, Rabban Gamaliel II's attempt to keep
unworthy students out of his Beth Hamidrash was so unpalatable, that

[210] Cf. Ber. 43a; 46b; Bez. 15b.   [211] Cf. e.g. y. Hag. II, 1, 77a; Ber. 39a.
See also above, n. 90.   [212] Cf. Suk., 28a.   [213] Cf. y. Shebi'ith VI, 1, 36d;
y.M.K. III, 1, 81c; y. Hag. I, 8, 76d; y. Yeb. XII, 7, 13a; Sanh. 5b; Hor. 10a;
Gen. r. LXXXI, 2, ed. Theodor II, 969.   [214] Cf. Ber. 5b; Ned. 40a.   [215] Cf.
Ket. 8b.   [216] Cf. y. Terum. VIII, 9, 46b; Pes. 112a; Sanh. 14a. It is noteworthy that, theoretically at least, a master was expected to accompany his
disciple into exile; cf. b. Mak. 10a.   [217] Cf. y. Ber. I, 8, 5b–c; Eccl. r. V,
11, 3.   [218] M. Ab. II, 5.   [219] Cf. Sifra שמיני, ed. Weiss 47b; Ab. R.N. ed.
Schechter, Version I, ch. 1, pp. 1b–2a; Version II, ch. 1, p. 2a; y. Pes. VI, 1, 33a;
Shab. 30b–31a; Pes. 66b; Ned. 22a; 22b; Lev. r. XIII, 1, ed. Margulies II, 269 f.
[220] Cf. 'Er. 54b.   [221] Ibid.   [222] Cf. B.M. 85a.   [223] M. Ab. I, 1.

all restrictions were removed as soon as he was deposed from his position.[224] While the rabbis continued to express different views on the subject of teaching 'wicked' students,[225] the general tendency was to admit all those who thirsted for knowledge, even if their character was not all that might be desired. It was very rare for a rabbi to refuse to teach a student who genuinely wanted to learn, except in the case of specialized studies which were not part of the normal curriculum.[226]

Occasionally, there were scholars who preferred study to teaching, but rabbinical opinion was overwhelmingly opposed to ivory-tower scholarship. To study without imparting knowledge to others was compared to a myrtle in the wilderness whose fragrance was wasted.[227] Even for those who preferred to gather knowledge for themselves, teaching was the best method of attaining their object: 'I have learned much from my masters, more from my companions, but most of all from my disciples.'[228]

A more serious problem than scholars who were unwilling to teach, was that of masters who were religiously or morally unfit to teach. At a time when heretical sects and especially Christian missionary propaganda posed a major challenge to Judaism, most rabbis felt that 'if the master is like unto a messenger of the Lord of Hosts, they should seek Torah at his mouth; but if not, they should not do so'.[229] The proverbial exhortation, 'Adorn yourself first, and then adorn others'[230] was particularly applicable to scholars who had not only to teach but also to guide and set an example to the younger generation.

Nevertheless, even in this respect there were some exceptions. Thus, R. Meir continued to study under his master Elisha ben Abuya even when the latter had become an apostate,[231] and it was probably due to R. Meir's influence that maxims enunciated by Elisha ben Abuya were included in rabbinic literature.[232] In the Amoraic age, too, we meet

[224] Cf. *Ber.* 28a; *y. Ber.* IV, 1, 7d; *y. Ta'an.* IV, 1. 67d.   [225] Cf. e.g. *Tos. A.Z.* VI (VII), 18; *Ta'an.* 7a; *Soṭ.* 47a; *Sanh.* 107b; *Mak.* 10a; *Ḥul.* 133a. [226] Cf. *M. Ḥag.* II, 1; *y. ibid.*, II, 1, 77a; *Ḥag.*, 13a; 14b; *Pes.* 62b.   [227] *R.H.* 23a.   [228] *Ta'an.* 7a; *Mak.* 10a; cf. also *Ab.* VI, 5: והמחכים את רבו. For an actual example of a teacher learning from his disciple, cf. *y. Sanh.* III, 8, 21b; cf. also *Mek.* יתרו, ed. Friedmann 60b on the threat of punishment for a teacher who accepts a student's services, but refuses to teach him. Cf. also Maimonides, *Hilchoth Talm. Tor.* V, 13.   [229] *M.Ḳ.* 17a; *Ḥag.* 15b; cf. also *Yoma* 72b. [230] *B.M.* 107b; *B.B.* 60b; *Sanh.* 18a; 19a.   [231] Cf. *y. Ḥag.* II, 1, 77a–b; *Ḥag.* 15a–b.   [232] Cf. *M. Ab.* IV, 20; cf. also *Ab. R.N.* ed. Schechter, Version I, ch. 24; Version II, ch. 35, pp. 39a–b.

with the opinion that 'a scholar, though he may have sinned, his Torah is not contemned'.[233] Several stories of students who had reason to be suspicious of their teachers but adjudged them favourably[234] may have been designed not only as illustrations of the old Tannaitic maxim, 'Judge every man in the scale of merit',[235] but also as hints not to condemn a scholar or refuse to learn from him because his private conduct did not seem all that might be desired.

Perhaps the greatest privilege enjoyed by the student – apart from free tuition – was the respect and honour accorded to him by his master. R. Eleazar ben Shammua, who required divine reverence for the master, also demanded that the teacher uphold the honour of his disciple as much as his own.[236] Later it was decided that a disciple might be honoured even in the presence of his master.[237] Sometimes, a distinguished student would even be offered the hand of the master's daughter in marriage[238] – a practice which became very widespread in the Middle Ages.

There was thus much to compensate the disciple for the onerous burdens of studying under a recognized teacher. Such burdens, however, mattered little to the serious and conscientious pupil. All indications point to a relationship of mutual trust and respect between master and student[239] – indeed, of boundless love and devotion which, as we have seen, transcended and surpassed the natural bonds of love between father and son.

[233] Ḥag. 15b.   [234] Cf. Shab. 127b.   [235] M. Ab. I, 6.   [236] Ibid., IV, 12. [237] Cf. Yoma 69a; Soṭ. 40b; 41b; B.B. 119b; but cf. Maimonides' qualification of this ruling, Yad, Hilchoth Talm. Tor. V, 8.   [238] Cf. e.g. Ket. 63a; Ḳid. 71b; B.M. 84a; Hor. 12b.   [239] Cf. Drazin, History of Jewish Education, p. 74.

STUDENTS AND TEACHERS: A RABBINIC MODEL

Aaron Kirschenbaum

 HE STUDENT UNREST that shook Berkeley University a number of years ago inaugurated a new era in the history of American higher education. The student activism, militancy, and radicalism which transformed the campus into a fierce battleground of local, national, and international issues raised broad questions concerning the very bases upon which universities were built and according to which they have hitherto operated.

What is a university? Who does and who should rule an institution of higher learning? What is the nature of discipline in an academic community? What are the limits of academic freedom? What are the limits of dissent? Who is worthy of being a teacher and what is the nature of his authority? How does one qualify as a student?

Even though activism has subsided, its effects are apparent in the agonizing reappraisal of the substance, value, and direction of American higher education, and the widened gap between generations. The high percentage of Jewish students active in student revolutionary movements also placed the campus at the center of Jewish communal concern; the fact that ninety percent of Jewish youth of college age are to be found on the campus makes the broad implications of student disorders of the greatest moment to the American Jewish community.

American Jews have always placed great store upon advanced education. They have seen it as the key to economic success, social mobility and cultural advancement. Indeed, they have been nurtured by a deep faith in higher education, regarding it as the very foundation-stone of Western civilization. Moreover the Jew has always been deeply committed to advanced education, for his religious heritage puts a premium on learning and analysis, on the accumulation of knowledge and the deepening of wisdom.

It would appear, then, to be a most profitable project to examine this heritage of learning and to apply the major insights of such analysis to the problems that perplex the contemporary educational scene.

Rabbi Kirschenbaum, a graduate of The Jewish Theological Seminary of America, is Professor of Hebrew law at Tel Aviv University.

the talmudic academy and its curriculum

THE TALMUDIC ACADEMY, the institution most deeply at the heart of Jewish learning, existed not only during the talmudic period but throughout a major part of the Middle Ages. For close to two thousand years, it was the center of Jewish intellectual and spiritual life. On what principles of freedom and authority were student-teacher relationships in the academy based? What was the mode of dispute and dissent among the talmudic and post-talmudic academicians?

In the Jewish religious tradition, it is axiomatic that the very same intelligence which called the universe into existence, God the Creator, revealed His will to His chosen people at a specific point in history. The revealed will of the Creator is expressed partially in a written, but mainly in an oral, Torah which is essentially a manual of human conduct, a code of ritual and ethical, civil and criminal law. It follows then that man's duty on earth is to obey the revealed law of the Creator. Obedience, of course, implies knowledge and training; the tradition of the past must be studied and continuously subjected to perceptive intellectual analysis.

Anti-intellectualism is a cardinal sin in Judaism. "He who hates the sages and their disciples," declares an ancient author on human behavior, "has forfeited his share in the world to come."[1] To substitute "doing one's thing" for learning from the accumulated wisdom of generations is the heresy of a child. Indeed, even more than prayer, the study of Judaism's hallowed law and ancestral lore has traditionally been regarded as the chief means of communion with God.

In the eyes of the Talmud, the academy was to address itself to the basic problem of man: proper behavior. Of course, central to this approach was the firm belief that the proper norms of behavior either are known or can be made known. It was inconceivable to the deepest thinkers of Jewish history that God could be so cruel as to give man life and not to furnish him with the sources of knowledge as to how to live that life. These sources are two: God's revealed code (embodied in Sacred Scripture as interpreted by the Oral Tradition) and man's intellect.

These two sources, moreover, must be combined. Man must understand the revealed law, analyze and ponder its implications and, on the other hand, he must temper the conclusions of his finite reasoning in accordance with the limits set by the received traditions. It was the fervent belief of the architects of the Talmud, the creators of normative Judaism, that revelation and reason, combined, are sufficient to guide man—if he will only be humble enough to obey. In the great debate among the Rabbis

---

1 *Tosefta Derekh Eretz* 6:13, ed. M. Higger p. 313.

as to which is more important, theory or practice, the conclusion was, typically, "Theory, for it leads to practice."[2]

The interaction of revelation and reason carries with it extraordinary implications. Although theoretically the texts of the sacred law provide the religious Jew with an easily identifiable locus of authority, the meaning of these texts is subject to a rather wide array of interpretations. Thus, while the framework of the curriculum in the academies was dogmatic and authoritarian, the inner functioning of the educational process encouraged—indeed, thrived on—critical analysis. The intellectual prowess of the talmudic Rabbis and of their medieval successors subjected the sacred texts of Judaism to the deepest possible scrutiny and analysis. This study by first-rate minds inevitably resulted in a literature pervaded by debate and dispute, replete with controversy and disagreement. Differences of opinion among colleagues and between teacher and student in the Talmud, in the Commentaries, in the Codes and Responsa, are commonplace.

Talmudic theory visualizes the entire compass of human activity as subsumed under 613 categories of obligatory, meritorious or forbidden acts. In the class of obligatory acts, education is unique. It is the only activity which is always incumbent upon man. In Jewish tradition, the study of Torah, i.e. the examination of human behavior, is an endless task, yet it is considered the most worthwhile pursuit. Jewish preoccupation with the pursuit of excellence is reflected in the novel concept of an Academy on High. The talmudic "heaven" is nothing more than an academic community of angels and the souls of saintly scholars, headed by the Master Teacher, God Himself—all occupied in the study of Torah.[3]

The striking image of God as the Teacher of Israel is found in the Prayerbook which contains the following benediction from the Talmud to be recited every morning before one begins to study Torah:

> *Blessed art Thou . . . who hast sanctified us by Thy commandments and commanded us to study the Torah. Make pleasant, therefore, we beseech Thee, O Lord our God, the words of Thy people to the house of Israel, so that we with our offspring and the offspring of Thy people the house of Israel may all know Thy name and study Thy Torah.*

Note especially the formulaic conclusion: "Blessed art Thou, O Lord, who teaches Torah to Thy people Israel."[4]

---

2 B. *Kiddushin* 40b.
3 Cf. the talmudic dictionaries on *metivta derakia*.
4 B. *Berakhot* 11b; cf. *Daily Prayer Book* (ed. P. Birnbaum), p. 13.

faculty-student relationships

THE CENTRALITY OF TORAH and learning in Jewish traditional life leads inevitably to attitudes of the deepest reverence and the highest esteem for the teacher of Torah, as evident in the rabbinic term for teacher—*rav*, "master"*—whence arose the term *rabbi*, "my master," which developed into the title for the revered religious leaders of Israel. In fashioning the moral character of the student as well as in guiding him in the fulfillment of his destiny as a human being, the teacher in Judaism is viewed as the analogue to the parent. "Whoever teaches the son of his fellow-man is viewed as having begotten him."[5]

The status of the teacher in Israel as one's spiritual father is no mere literary fancy. It is taken literally. Thus, all that is included in the Fifth Commandment, "Thou shalt honor thy father and thy mother" is equally applicable to one's teacher.

> *Scripture (Leviticus 19:32) declares, "And thou shalt honor the sage," which teaches that the student may not stand in the place assigned to his master, he may not sit in his permanent seat, he may not contradict him. When he poses a question, it must be asked in reverence. When he answers his master, it must not be done in haste. He may not interrupt him. For whoever does not observe these marks of respect toward his teacher is termed a wicked man before the Omnipresent: his learning slips from his memory, his years are shortened, and finally he sinks into poverty.[6]*

In instances where the honor and service due to one's parents come in conflict with those due to one's teacher, the latter is given priority, "for his father brought him into this world, but his teacher who instructs him in wisdom brings him thereby into the world to come."[7]

There is no honor, declares Maimonides, higher than that which is due to the teacher; no more profound reverence than that which should be paid to him.[8] Whoever disputes and rejects the teachings of his master, by setting up a rival school, is considered to have disputed and rejected God Almighty Himself.[9] Nonetheless, as will be seen later, a disciple could

---

* Even a master craftsman who teaches an apprentice may be called *rav* (B. *Avodah Zarah* 17b).
5 B. *Sanhedrin* 19b.
6 *Bamidbar Rabbah* 15:17.
7 M. *Bava Metzia* 2:11. The Talmud then continues with pragmatic examples. Of course, in all these cases if the father is a scholar, even though he may not be of a calibre equal to that of the teacher, his son must give him priority, for it is taken for granted that he, too, is his son's teacher. In any event, conflicts between the interests of the father and those of the teacher were rare indeed,. for the father invariably deferred to his son's religious mentor.
8 *Knowledge—Talmud Torah* 5:1.
9 B. *Sanhedrin* 110a and B. *Berakhot* 27b.

24

disagree with his teacher out of loyalty to the truth which was supreme.

The reader at home in the educational mores of the twentieth century, examining the following rules governing student-teacher relationships,[10] vividly perceives the chasm between the then and the now.

— A disciple is forbidden to call his teacher by name.

— In his presence, the pupil must never mention his teacher's name, even if his intention is to call another person bearing the same name.

— A disciple may not greet his teacher or return his greeting in the same manner that others greet their friends. Rather, he should bow to his teacher and address him deferentially, "Peace be unto thee, my master."

— One may not remove his *tefillin* in his teacher's presence, nor recline in his presence, but he must sit respectfully as one sits before a king.

— He must not sit in his teacher's seat. He may not sit down in his teacher's presence until he is told to do so, nor may he stand up unless he has received permission to do so. When he leaves his master's presence, he must not turn his back, but should retire with his face to his master. He must not go with his teacher into the bath at the same time.

— When one's teacher and a colleague dispute with one another, the student must not, in his teacher's presence, interpose his opinion as to who is right. Nor may he contradict his teacher's statements.

— When the master is walking by, it is one's duty to rise before him from the moment one sees him and to remain standing till he disappears from view.

qualifications of a teacher

WHO IS THIS TEACHER to whom such profound reverence and such extravagant self-effacement are due? First, he is the teacher of God's law. Second, he is one's principal teacher (*rabbo muvhak*), the rabbi whom one could single out as the major source of one's knowledge of Torah.[11] Third, the teacher who is singled out for such distinction is one who embodies within himself the highest moral and religious qualifications: sterling character, ideal behavior, deep piety, and profound commitment to all that the Jewish religion stands for.

It is interesting to note how the talmudic sages found the suggestion

10 Based upon the classical codes of Jewish law: Maimonides, *Knowledge—Talmud Torah* 5:5–7; *Tur* and *Shulḥan Arukh Yoreh Dea* 242:15–16.
11 An instructor who has given one course in Bible, a teacher who has trained someone in one aspect of the religion, a rabbi who has enlightened us in a limited number of ethical and moral questions do not warrant the self-effacing awe that we have described. (*B. Kiddushin* 33a; *B. Bava Metzia* 33a; and commentaries.) Nevertheless, Jewish religious law legislates respect for any teacher. In an appendix to the *Ethics of the Fathers* it is taught: "He who learns from someone a single chapter of Scripture, a single rule of ethical-religious behavior, a single verse, a single expression—even a single letter—must treat his teacher with honor."

for this idea in a biblical verse. Malachi, the last prophet of Israel, states (2:7): "For the lips of the priestly teacher should keep knowledge, and instruction should be sought from him, for he is the messenger of the Lord of Hosts." The Rabbis, basing themselves on the fact that the Hebrew word for "messenger" is *malakh*, angel, insist: "If the teacher is like an angel of the Lord, accept Torah instruction from him; if he is not like an angel of the Lord, do not accept Torah instruction from him."[12] This was their way of saying that a man who has accumulated a string of degrees after his name but has not grown in personal stature, one who has gone through tomes of the wisdom of the ages but little of the wisdom of the ages has gone through him, is *not* the man contemplated by the Jewish code of law as the focal point of elaborate homage.

The implications are obvious. Jewish law prescribes for one's religious mentor the deep respect and marked obeisance that are reserved for God because as far as the disciple is concerned his master (*rabbo muvhak*) is indeed the true representative of God on earth.[13] Callousness to human plight, frivolity in personal behavior, indifference to the ethics of the spoken word, or lack of moral discipline in private life are opposed to the revealed will of the Creator as Judaism understands it.

Lest these talmudic standards strike one as totally unrealistic and engender skepticism as to their applicability to everyday life, the reader is encouraged to consult M. Güdemann, *Geschichte der Erziehungswesen und der Cultur der Abendländischen Juden.*[14] This classic on the education, manners and morals of the Jews in the Middle Ages reveals that although all rabbis were not saints nor were all disciples angels, Jewish students and teachers in medieval times almost invariably conducted themselves in accordance with the demands of traditional law.

Thus, writing about academic life in fifteenth century Germany, Güdemann relates:[15]

> *The rabbi comported himself among his disciples with great dignity, and they paid homage to him as though he were a sovereign. He, however, was always careful to show them affection and respect. The rabbi also insisted that students conduct themselves respectfully one to the other. The only ban of excommunication which Rabbi Jacob Molin[16] ever decreed in his lifetime was directed against*

---

12 *B. Moed Katan* 17a.
13 A disciple who detracts in any way from the honor due his master causes the Divine Presence to depart from the Jewish community (*B. Berakhot* 27b and Maimonides, *ibid.* 5:8).
14 Three volumes, (Vienna, 1180–88). Hebrew translation: *HaTorah VeHaHaim*, (Warsaw, 1896–99).
15 Hebrew edition, III, pp. 68–70. Translation my own; documentation omitted.
16 *Maharil*, the world-renowned authority on the Ashkenazic *minhag* of the fourteenth-fifteenth centuries.

the son of a sexton, for having reviled one of the young men of the Academy with the epithet Sau schelm *("pig corpse"). The excommunicated young man remained under the ban for two days. The intercession of friends and relatives secured the lifting of the ban only after "the rabbi went to the Academy accompanied by fifty students; and the sexton with his son begged pardon from the insulted student and from the entire student body. The son and the father doing so separately." . . .*

It is a mistake, however, to look upon the students as depressed or dejected, removed from living and closed in upon themselves. There were among them some bold fellows who were far from humility and forbearance. It happened once in the Rhineland that a student had the gall to call his teacher "fool." It also happened at a Friday night meal that some of the students sitting at the master's table became drunk, and uttered words of impudence against the faculty. . . .

The rarity of such lapses in the homage paid the rabbi-teacher, and the resulting scandals, assured their place in the annals of Jewish history; they simply could not be passed over with indifference.

salary scale

THE TALMUD MAKES IT ABUNDANTLY CLEAR that one may not accept payment for teaching God's Word,[17] for just as God taught Israel without fee, so is every (non-elementary) teacher duty-bound to teach without monetary compensation. Moses Maimonides was a most forceful exponent of this doctrine. An implacable foe of the commercialization of religion, he decried the practice of granting fellowships to students and paying salaries to rabbis.[18]

The reasoning behind this extreme position may be found in the *Guide of the Perplexed.*

The more a thing is necessary for a living being, the more often it may be found and the cheaper it is. On the other hand, the less necessary it is, the less often it is found and it is very expensive. Thus, for instance, that which is necessary for man is air, water, and food. But air is the most necessary, for nobody can be without it for a moment without perishing. As for water, one can remain without it for a day or two. Accordingly, air is indubitably easier to find and cheaper than water. Water is more necessary than food, for certain people may remain for four or five days without food if they drink. Accordingly in every city you find water more frequently and at a cheaper price than food.[19]

Maimonides' strong opposition to monetary compensation for the teaching of religion would seem to be based upon the analogy that the Torah is the

---

7   B. Bekhorot 29a; cf. *Torah Temimah* on Deuteronomy 4:5, and *P. Nedarim* 4:3.
8   Maimonides, *Commentary to Avot* 4:7, and *Knowledge-Talmud Torah* 3:10–12.
9   *Guide* 3:12, ed. S. Pines pp. 446–447.

spiritual air; he cannot survive without it.[20] How incumbent then must it be upon the teacher of Torah to make God's Word available as freely as the air that is breathed!

The Talmud recognizes, however, that there may be situations in which one cannot find someone to teach him without payment. Indeed, Rabbi Joseph Caro, second only to Maimonides in his profound influence upon the legal development of post-talmudic Judaism, openly disagrees with the latter and permits (non-elementary) teachers of Torah to accept a salary.

He held that any scholar who had no other source of income was permitted to accept a salary, either from his students or the community. Although Rabbi Caro did not challenge the correctness of Maimonides' interpretation of the traditional sources, he suggested that perhaps the scholars of Israel had decided to change the law because the times had changed. For if support for teachers and scholars were unavailable, they could not devote themselves to Torah study, and the Torah would be forgotten, Heaven forbid.[21]

Despite the dispensation of Rabbi Joseph Caro and of others[22] the strictures of Maimonides pricked the Jewish conscience. And so for many generations the remuneration of scholars who served as teachers, preachers and judges was never referred to as "wages" or "salary," but as *sekhar batallah*, the honorarium one receives as a compensation for having taken time off from a profit-making or salary-producing activity in order to attend to an economically non-productive matter.

ethical dimensions of education

IT MUST BE EMPHASIZED that the term "teaching" and the title "teacher" have always carried with them a moral and religious connotation.[23] Judaism has always insisted that education bereft of its ethical dimension is a monstrosity. Our generation is all too aware that the insistence of medical practitioners that medicine is a value in and of itself reaped the furious whirlwind of Hitler's doctors. Since Hiroshima, too, nuclear physicists know fully well that they cannot hide from the moral implications of their scientific endeavors.

---

20 B. *Avodah Zarah* 3b: Rab Judah says in the name of Samuel: Why is it written, "And Thou makest man as the fishes of the sea" (Habakkuk 1:14)? As soon as the fishes of the sea come on to dry land they die; similarly, as soon as man abandons the Torah and its percepts, he incurs destruction. Cf. further Rabbi Akiba's parable of the fox (*B. Berakhot* 61b).
21 *Kesseph Mishneh, Knowledge–Talmud Torah* 3:10.
22 Cf. also Rabbi Shimeon ben Zemah Duran, *Magen Avot*, and Rabbi Jacob Emden, *Glosses to Avot, ad loc.*
23 Cf. *Pseudo-Rashi* and *Midrash Shmuel* on *Avot* 6:3.

The ethical requisite that Judaism establishes for the office of teacher, and the religious framework within which it locates the act of teaching, affects the status of the student as well. A student must prove himself worthy of "matriculation" by exemplary conduct[24] or, at the very least, may not be accused of moral turpitude.[25] However, "one who walks in a way that is not good," declares Maimonides, "should first be reformed, trained in the right way, tested as to his sincerity, and only then admitted into the *bet hamidrash* for instruction."

The Rabbis of the Talmud saw a special danger in teaching a student who did not possess the necessary moral and religious qualities. They said: "He who teaches a student who is not worthy is as one who throws stones at Mercury."[26] This was a form of worship peculiar to the cult of Mercury,[27] in which each stone thrown became sacred to the cult and enhanced the glory of the god. The simile chosen by the Rabbis reveals that they viewed the teaching of unworthy students not only as wasted effort, but as a positive source of ruination. By providing unscrupulous people with the wisdom of the Torah, the hand of evil in the world is strengthened and its success is furthered.[28]

It is of considerable significance to note that this moral requirement was the *only* requirement to be fulfilled by a student. This is no accident. It is the result of an ancient conflict that was waged in the talmudical academy.

At about the dawn of the Common Era, a controversy broke out among the Palestinian scholars regarding the proper interpretation of a mandate they had received from their predecessors: "Raise many disciples."[29]

> For the School of Shammai says: "One ought to teach only one who is talented and meek, of distinguished ancestry and rich." But the School of Hillel says: "One ought to teach every man, for there were many sinners in Israel who were drawn to the study of Torah, and from them descended righteous, pious, and worthy folk."[30]

Another version supports the opinion of the School of Hillel with the following parable: "To what may our opinion be compared? To a woman who places a hen on eggs: From many she succeeds in producing a few; from few she produces none."[31] Although later generations usually followed

---

24 B. *Taanit* 7a; cf. B. *Makkot* 10a.
25 Abraham de Boton, *Lehem Mishneh.*
26 B. *Hullin* 133a.
27 M. *Sanhedrin* 7:6.
28 Cf. *Maharsha, Hullin* 133a.
29 M. *Avot* 1:1.
30 *Avot d'Rabbi Natan* 3 beg.
31 *Ibid.,* version B. ed. Schechter pp. 14–15.

the opinion of the School of Hillel, the moral requirement of the School of Shammai was retained.

The Rabbis of the Talmud would not accept a student who debased or scorned his parents.[32] Sexual license was a prime cause for expulsion from their academic community.[33] Violence, the destruction of property, and the threat of personal assault[34] were unheard of in all the intellectual ferment among the various schools in Jewish history.

A student who possesses the required moral qualities and has been admitted to instruction in the talmudic academy must be treated with courtesy and friendliness by the master: "Let the honor of thy disciples be as dear to thee as thine own."[35] If the student fails to understand a point that has been made, the teacher may not be angry with him nor fall into a rage. He must repeat his lesson patiently.[36]

a higher law

THE RELIGIOUS QUALITY which informs the educational process of traditional Judaism mitigated against the absolute authority of the master and qualified the obedience due him. The Rabbis held that "Whenever the Divine Name is being profaned, the honor due to one's teacher must be disregarded."[37]

The talmudic sages laid great stress on law and order, civil obedience and respect for authority, for without these, man would retrogress into the jungle.[38] Nevertheless, human authority is never unlimited, and obedience to a higher law takes precedence over any command or over any law which may be unjust, unethical or immoral.[39] The determination of this "higher law," of course, is the crux of the problem.

Elementary psychology indicates that what one hears as "the still, small voice" may be one's own predilections. The Rabbis of old were perceptive, experienced men who knew how effective man's baser instincts were in manipulating his "conscience."[40] Thus, when Maimonides summar-

---

32   B. *Kiddushin* 31b, *Tosaphot* s.v. Rabbi Tarphon, citing the Palestinian Talmud, *Peah* 1:1.
33   Cf. the story of Jesus and Rabbi Joshua ben Perahiah; T. Herford, *Christianity in the Talmud and Midrash*, 51ff; and the Soncino edition of the Talmud, *Sanhedrin*, p. 736, n. 2.
34   "He who raises his fist against someone, even though he does not strike him, is already considered a *rasha* [a wicked man]," B. *Sanhedrin* 58b.
35   M. *Avot* 4:12.
36   M. *Avot* 2:5; B. *Eruvin* 54b.
37   B. *Sanhedrin* 82a.
38   M. *Avot* 3:2: "Rabbi Hanina, the deputy High Priest, said: 'Pray for the welfare of the government, since were it not for the fear of it, men would swallow each other alive.'"
39   B. *Sanhedrin* 9a.
40   Viz. their numerous tales about the *yetzer hara*.

izes Jewish insistence upon the subservience of all human authority to a higher law, he formulates it in the following significant terms:

> *A subject who neglects to perform a duty decreed by the king because he is fulfilling a commandment of the Torah may not be punished. For if the words of the Master [i.e. God] conflict with words of the disciples [i.e. the king], whose words must be obeyed? Obviously, those of the Master. Moreover, it goes without saying that a king who has issued a decree contrary to the [divine] commandments is not to be obeyed.*[41]

For the Jew, the higher law was no vague ethical creed, nor was it the sum of the dictates of the individual conscience. It was nothing less than the will of God as revealed to Moses at Sinai. And to Maimonides, as to *all* Jewish religious thinkers throughout the ages, the higher law was none other than the Rabbinic system of law, based upon that transcendental revelation, "interpreted and applied as best it may be by the leading authorities of each generation disciplined for the task by a lifetime of scholarship and saintliness, and informed by a deep sense of humility and responsibility."[42] The higher law could not be invoked by the individual alone, but had to be corroborated by men of serious scholarship, unimpeachable character, deep piety and profound wisdom. In the last analysis, this higher law reigns supreme over all other authorities: parental, educational, or governmental.

teacher fallibility

WHEN THE MASTER IS IN ERROR, a conflict in Jewish values takes place. Profound respect for the master is a divine imperative, but the seal of God is Truth.[43] A mistake committed by the master leaves the disciple no alternative: truth must prevail; the master must be corrected. But how? The requirement of respect demands that correction be made discreetly, politely, and indirectly.[44]

Must we then infer that the student-teacher relationship as dictated by the tenets of Jewish tradition stifled free discussion, intellectual integrity and honest disagreement? Nothing could be further from the truth. Almost any page of the Talmud will reveal a disciple subjecting a statement of his master to critical analysis. The academies looked favorably upon *talmid hamahkin et rabbo*, "a disciple who enriches his master"—by constructive suggestions, critical questioning and honest disagreement.

---

41 Maimonides, *Judges—Kings* 3:9.
42 A. Kirschenbaum, "Rabbi Moshe Feinstein's Responsa," *Judaism* 15 (1966), p. 364.
43 See *B. Kiddushin* 32a. The text is concerned with the son-father relationship, but Maimonides, *Knowledge-Talmud Torah* 5:9 applies equally to the student-teacher relationship.
44 *B. Yoma* 69b.

Controversy between student and teacher could be sharp, debate heated and exchange lively. Disagreements were welcomed by the Rabbis as indispensable for the growth of true religious intelligence,[45] provided they were conducted with pure motives, humble conviction and proper respect. The Rabbis believed that such disputes would invariably end in reconciliation and in a deepened affection between the disputants. "Said Rabbi Hiyya bar Abba: Even father and son, master and disciple, who study Torah at the same Academy or on the same subject become enemies of each other. Yet they do not stir from there until they come to love each other."[46]

"A man may be envious of any and everyone except his son and his disciple," observe the Rabbis.[47] If the true student was viewed as constituting continuity of the master's teachings, the lack of envy between the two is psychologically understandable.

The deep recognition that students eternalize the traditions of the master apparently was the force which impelled the greatest teacher of talmudic times to give his life for the propagation of Torah. When the Roman Emperor Hadrian forbade the practice and teaching of Torah, Rabbi Akiva ben Joseph (50-132C.E.) defied the edict. He was arrested, imprisoned, and finally martyred. The Talmud defines two main ideas which drove him to his defiant action: the indispensability of the religious heritage for the survival of the Jewish people, and the crucial role of students as the perpetuators of that tradition.[48] Rabbi Akiva had thousands of students; the greatest rabbinic leaders of the second century, Rabbis Meir, Judah b. Slai, Simeon b. Yoḥai, Jose b. Halaphta, Eleazar b. Shammua, and Neḥemiah, were products of his school.[49]

Indeed, in the opinion of Rabbi Akiva, the teacher needs the student more than the student needs the teacher. Or, as he himself put it, "More than the calf wishes to suck does the cow desire to suckle."[50]

then and now

WE HAVE ATTEMPTED TO PRESENT a picture of the community of higher education among the Jews of talmudic and post-talmudic times. It is a remarkable fact of history that throughout the centuries the Jew successfully

---

45   See A. Kirschenbaum, *The Talmud and You* (Hadassah, 1967), Unit II, pp. 24–41.
46   B. *Kiddushin* 30b. The analogy of father-son and teacher-student noted earlier, can be carried further. Just as a son perpetuates the father's genetic makeup, so the disciple guarantees the spiritual continuity of the master.
47   B. *Sanhedrin* 105b.
48   B. *Berakhot* 62b; Tanhuma, Haye Sarah 8 (ed. Buber, p. 122, n.65); cf. B. Z. Bacher, *Aggadot HaTannaim*, Vol. I, pt. 2, p. 48, n.4; B. *Nedarim* 40a.
49   *Genesis Rabbah* 61:3; B. *Yevamot* 62b; B. *Nedarim* 50a.
50   B. *Pesaḥim* 112a.

achieved the ideals of education, as taught by his religious tradition, to an extraordinary degree.

Viewed against the background of the talmudic academy, the modern university tends to give one the impression that it is not an institution of education at all. Departments intent upon the development of professional skills and expertise seem to be nothing more than glorified trade schools. Curricula in the humanities appear to contribute to the growth of student movements characterized by fuzziness of thinking and anti-intellectualism, and point to academic sterility and pedagogic bankruptcy. Social science faculties staffed by people who could not possibly serve as models of moral and ethical behavior are contradictions in terms. And the natural and biological sciences that recognize man's fragility yet fail to emphasize his concomitant need for compassion are, in the long-range view of Jewish tradition, enmeshed in trivia.

If these are the results of the educative process today, then, with caricature and exaggeration discounted, the need for reappraisal is long overdue. Perhaps the time has arrived for Jewish faith in "education" to be shaken by several "heretical" questions:

Is the university of today, where the unbridled questioning of all *values* has left many a student with none, truly educational?

Is the college dormitory, where freedom has degenerated into license, the place where a young Jew should be spending his formative years?

Should the generation gap be financed by the parents who are its main victims?

Indeed, does American education, from elementary school on, offer today's pupil the intellectual stimulation he should be receiving? Does it create the moral climate in which he should be growing?

In a word, the talmudic code of personal behavior, and the rabbinic standards of academic activity, constitute a challenge to modern educationists who would destroy education by depriving it of its moral roots.

Section Four—

THE TEACHING PROCESS

THE TRANSMISSION OF THE EARLY
RABBINIC TRADITIONS

LOUIS FINKÈLSTEIN

JEWISH THEOLOGICAL SEMINARY OF AMERICA

A S IS well known, the Rabbinic traditions were handed down orally for many centuries. It was thought a sacrilege to put them into writing, for that was considered an attempt to add to the Scriptures. Only when the mass of tradition grew to such proportions as to tax even the most prodigious memory, did the ancient Sages agree to commit the oral traditions to writing. Before that time the *Mishna*, the *Tosefta*, and the *Tannaitic Midrashim*, as well as the vaster Talmudic discussions, were studied by rote in the academies and quoted from memory. Nevertheless, they were preserved with precision and accuracy; evidence of the love bestowed on the Torah, as well as the mental prowess and diligence of the ancient students.

There is reason to think that as an aid to memory, students developed the habit of formulating certain phrases in each tradition, which served as pegs on which the unformulated portion depended. In later times these formulated phrases were reduced to writing and formed the shorthand notes, by which much of our *tannaitic* tradition was preserved during the centuries before it was completely edited and put into writing. Such notes were perhaps not used in the study of the *Mishna*, which was the basic text of the academies, and which everyone was supposed to know. The notes were employed for the *baraitot*, the traditions which had been compiled by the older scholars as parallel studies to the *Mishna*. And apparently the notes were used more frequently for informal *aggadic* study, than for that of the more formal *halaka*.

Elsewhere I have shown that the variant versions of the

aggadic texts, whcih have been preserved in the *tannaitic mid-rashim*, frequently have some written texts at their base.[1] This can be seen from the fact that errors which could only have arisen in written copies, are found in both versions. But at the same time the variant forms of the text show a certain fluidity which indicates that while part of the text — the catchwords — were written down, the major part was left to be reconstructed from memory by the person reciting the passage.

In certain instances, it will be shown, the catchwords were fixed, before they were reduced to writing. While the texts of the various versions of the *baraitot* differ from one another considerably, they all contain these fixed catchwords. Yet other evidence proves conclusively that in these instances, the fixed catchwords were transmitted orally rather than in writing.

Thus there emerge five forms in which traditions were handed down:

I. The anecdotal form. This is the primitive tradition, no part of which is formulated in fixed words or phrases. The tradition is determined only so far as the basic idea or story is concerned.

II. The semi-normative form. This is the stage in which the tradition has assumed fixed form in regard to certain catchwords, which appear in all its versions. It still remains an oral tradition, no parts have been committed to writing.

III. The fully formulated oral tradition or norm. In this stage, an editor or teacher has decided to transmit the older idea or story in a fixed form, his students actually memorize the words in which he expresses the idea or tells the story.

IV. The earliest written form. This derives not from III but from II. Instead of being submitted to final formulation, in a normative form, the tradition is handed down through the catchwords indicated under II; but to assist the memory further, these catchwords are committed to writing.

V. The written text. This may emerge either out of III or out of IV.

[1] *Proc. Amer. Acad. Jew. Research* VI (1935), pp. 206 ff.

An interesting example of the transmission of a tradition is to be found in the manner in which a sermon by Rabbi Eleazar of Modin, dealing with Psalm 29, has come down to us. In this address, Rabbi Eleazar of Modin explained the Psalm as referring to the revelation on Mt. Sinai. The verses 3–9, describing the power and majesty of the Voice of the Lord, naturally were taken to refer to the Voice which came to Moses. Verse 9a, was interpreted by Rabbi Eleazar as follows: "And in his palace, everyone says, Glory." This meant to him that each king, hearing the Divine Voice, trembled in his palace, and wondered what the significance of It might be. The kings, alarmed, rushed to Balaam for an explanation of the miracle. "Does God intend to bring another flood?" they asked. (Hence the verse, "The Lord sat enthroned at the flood.") When he reminded them that God had sworn never again to bring a flood on the world, they asked, "Whether that oath applied only to a flood of water, but did not apply to a flood of fire." (This is apparently derived from the verse, "The Lord sitteth as King forever," indicating that despite His promise never to bring a flood, God might still bring penalties on the world.) Thereupon Balaam replied, according to Rabbi Eleazar's interpretation of the Psalm, "The Lord is giving strength (i. e., the Torah) to His people," thus explaining the unusual disturbance of the elements. To which the various kings responded, with verse 11b, "(If that be so) May the Lord bless His people with peace."

The text of Rabbi Eleazar of Modin's remarks has come down in the following forms:

I. That preserved in (A) *Mekilta, Jethro, Amalek* chap. 1, H-R 188, Laut. II 162; (B) the corresponding passage in *Mekilta* of R. Simeon (18.1; p. 85); (C) *Zebahim* 116a; and (D) *Midrash Mishle* 21.22, ed. Buber 45b.

II. That preserved in (E) *Mekilta Bahodesh* chap. 5, H-R 220, Laut. II, 233; (F) the corresponding passage in *Mekilta* of R. Simeon (19.16, p. 99).

III. That preserved in (G) *Sifre* Deut. 343, Fr. 142b, Fi. 397; and (H) *Midrash Tannaim* 33.2, p. 209.

The texts are as follows:

B

מכילתא דרשב"י י"ח א'

ר' אלעזר המודעי אומר מתן תורה
שמע ובא שכן מצינו ביום שניתנה
תורה לישראל זעו כל מלכי תבל
בהיכליהם שנ' ובהיכלו כלו אומר
כבוד נתקבצו כל אומות העולם
אצל בלעם אמרו לו דומה שהמקום
מאבד את עולמו במים כדרך שאיברם
לאנשי דור המבול כענין שנ' ה'
למבול ישב, אמר להן שוטים כבר
נשבע שאינו מביא מבול לעולם שנ'
כי מי נח זאת לי אשר נשבעתי מעבור
מי נח עוד על הארץ אמרו לו בודאי
מבול של מים אינו מביא אבל מבול
של אש מביא אמר להן אינו מביא
לא מבול של מים ולא של אש תורה
נותן לעמו ושכר משלם ליראיו כיון
ששמעו ממנו הדבר הזה פנו כולם
איש איש למקומו.

A

מכילתא יתרו עמלק פ"א

ר' אלעזר המודעי אומר מתן תורה
שמע ובא שבשעה שנתנה תורה לישראל
זעו כל מלכי האדמה בהיכליהם
שנאמר ובהיכלו כלו אומר כבוד
(תהלים כ"ט ט') באותה שעה נתקבצו
כל מלכי אומות העולם אצל בלעם
הרשע אמרו לו בלעם שמא המקום
עושה לנו כמו שעשה לדור המבול
שנא' ה' למבול ישב וישב ה' מלך
לעולם. אמר להם שוטים שבעולם
כבר נשבע הקב"ה לנח שאינו מביא
מבול לעולם שנא' כי מי נח זאת לי
אשר נשבעתי מעבור מי נח עוד על
הארץ (ישע'-) נ"ד ט') אמרו לו שמא
מבול של מים אינו מביא מבול של
אש מביא. אמר להם אינו מביא לא
מבול של אש ולא מבול של מים אלא
תורה נותן הקב"ה לעמו ולידידיו
שנא' ה' עז לעמו יתן. כיון ששמעו
כולם מפיו הדבר הזה ענו כולם
ואמרו אחר כך ה' יברך את עמו
בשלום ופנו והלכו איש למקומו.

D

מדרש משלי כ"א כ"ב

ר' אליעזר המודעי אומר נתינת
תורה שמע ובא שבשעה שנתנה תורה
לישראל זעו כל מלכי אדמה
בהיכליהם שנאמר ובהיכלו כולו

C

זבחים קט"ז ע"א

ר' אליעזר המודעי אומר מתן תורה
שמע [ובא] שכשנתנה תורה לישראל
היה קולו הולך מסוף העולם ועד
סופו וכל [מלכי] א"ה אחזתן רעדה

D

מדרש משלי כ"א כ"ב

אומר כבוד באותה שעה נתקבצו
כל מלכי אומות העולם אצל בלעם
הרשע אמרו לו בלעם מה טיבו
של עולם כולו מתרעש שמא הקב"ה
מביא מבול של מים לעולם ומחריבו
אמר להם שוטים שבעולם כבר נשבע
הקב"ה שאינו מביא מבול של מים
לעולם שנאמר כי מי נח זאת לי וגו'
אמרו לו שמא מבול של מים אינו מביא
אבל מבול של אש מביא אמר להם
לא מבול של מים ולא מבול של אש
תורה הוא נותן לעמו שנאמר ה' עז
לעמו יתן וגו' כיון ששמעו כלם
מפיו הדבר הזה הלכו כל אחד
ואחד למקומו.

C

זבחים קט"ז ע"א

בהיכליהן ואמרו שירה שנאמר
ובהיכלו כולו אומר כבוד נתקבצו
כולם אצל בלעם הרשע ואמרו לו
מה קול ההמון אשר שמענו שמא
מבול בא לעולם אמר להם ה' למבול
ישב [ואמר להם] וישב ה' מלך לעולם
כבר נשבע הקב"ה שאינו מביא מבול
לעולם אמרו לו מבול של מים אינו
מביא אבל מבול של אש מביא שנא'
כי הנה באש ה' נשפט אמר להן כבר
נשבע שאינו משחית כל בשר ומה
קול ההמון הזה ששמענו אמר להם
חמדה טובה יש לו בבית גנזיו שהיתה
גנוזה אצלו תתקע"ד דורות קודם
שנברא העולם וביקש ליתנה לבניו
שנאמר ה' עז לעמו יתן [מיד] פתחו
כולם ואמרו ה' יברך את עמו בשלום.

F

מכילתא דרשב"י י"ט ט"ז

וכן הוא אומר (תהלים כ"ט נ') קול
ה' על המים אל הכבוד הרעים ה'
על מים רבים קול ה' בכח קול ה'
בהדר קול ה' שובר ארזים קול ה'
חוצב להבות אש קול ה' יחיל מדבר
קול ה' יחולל אילות ויחשוף יערות
ובהיכלו כלו אומר כבוד מגיד הכתוב
שביום מתן תורה היו רעמים וברקים
וירידת גשמים וכן הוא אומר (שופטים
ה' ד') ה' בצאתך משעיר בצעדך
משדה אדום ארץ רעשה גם שמים

E

מכילתא בחודש פ"ה

באותה שעה נתכנסו כל מלכי
אומות העולם אצל בלעם הרשע
ואמרו לו שמא מבול מביא לעולם
אמר להם כבר נשבע הקב"ה שאינו
מביא מבול לעולם שנאמר כי מי
נח זאת לי אשר נשבעתי אמר לו
שמא מבול של מים אינו מביא אבל
מביא מבול של אש אמר להם לא
מבול של מים ולא מבול של אש
הוא מביא אלא הב"ה רוצה ליתן
תורה לבניו שנא' ה' עז לעמו יתן

245

F	E
מכילתא דרשב"י י"ט ט"ז	מכילתא בחודש פ'ה

E — מכילתא בחודש פ'ה

וכיון ששמעו הדבר הזה פנו כולם
והלכו איש למקומו.

F — מכילתא דרשב"י י"ט ט"ז

נטפו גם עבים נטפו מים ואומר
(תהלים ע"ז מ"ט) קול רעמך בגלגל
האירו ברקים תבל וכמו קול שופר
נשמע באויר שנא' וקול שופר חזק
מאד עד שרעש כל העולם כולו
תתקבצו כל אומות העולם אצל
בלעם בן בעור אמרו לו דומה
שהמקום מאבד את עולמו במים
כענין שנא' (תהלים כ"ט י') ה' למבול
ישב אמר להן שוטים שבעולם כבר
נשבע שאינו מביא מבול לעולם כענין
שנאמר (ישעיה נ"ד ט') כי מי נח
זאת לי אשר נשבעתי מעבור מי נח
עוד על הארץ אמרו לו ודאי מבול
של מים אינו מביא אבל הוא מביא
מבול של אש אמר להם אינו מביא
לא מבול של מים ולא מבול של אש
אמרו לו והקול הזה למה אמר להם
תורה הוא נותן לעמו שנאמר ה' עז
לעמו יתן (תהלים כ"ט י"א) ואין עז
אלא תורה שנאמר עמו עז ותושיה
(איוב י"ב ט"ז) אמרו לו אם כן ה'
יברך את עמו בשלום.

H	G[2]
מדרש תנאים ל"ג ב'	ספרי דברים שמ"ג

G[2] — ספרי דברים שמ"ג

כשנגלה הקב"ה ליתן תורה לישראל
הרעיש את העולם כולו על יושביו
שנ' קול ה' על המים אל הכבוד
הרעים כיון ששמעו אומות העולם

H — מדרש תנאים ל"ג ב'

כשנגלה הקב"ה ליתן תורה לישראל
הרעיש כל העולם כולו על יושביו
שנ' קול ה' על המים קול ה' בכח
קול ה' בהדר קול ה' שובר ארזים

---

[a] For this passage I have followed the text of ed. Friedmann. Ed. Finkelstein was not available for this nart of *Sifre* Deuteronomy when the article
was written.

H	G
מדרש תנאים ל"ג ב'	ספרי דברים תמ"ג

H — מדרש תנאים ל"ג ב'

קול ה' חוצב קול ה' 'יחיל מדבר
קול ה' יחולל אילות באותה שעה
נתכנסו כל אומות·העולם אצל בלעם
בן בער אמ' לו תאמר שהקב"ה·
מביא מבול על עולמו ומחריבו כשם
שעשה לראשונים ה' למבול ישב
אמ' להן לאו היום הוא מולך בעולמו
היום הוא מישב את עולמו שג' וישב
ה' מלך לעולם תורה הוא נתן לעמו
שבח הוא נותן לבניו שכר טוב לידיאיו
שג' ה' עח לעמו יתן אמרו לו אם
כן ה' יברך את עמו בשלום.

G — ספרי דברים תמ"ג

את הקולות נתקבצו כולם אצל
בלעם אמרו לו כמדומים אנחנו
שהמקום מאבד את עולמו אמר
להם הלא כבר נאמר ולא יהיה
עוד המים למבול (בראשית ט' ט"ו)
אמרו לו הקול· הזה מהו אמר להם
ה' עח לעמו יתן ואין עח אלא תורה
שנאמר עמו עח ותושיה (איוב י"ב
ט"ז) אמרו לו אם כן ה' יברך את
עמו בשלום.

A comparison of these texts indicates the basis for the recognition of three major versions of the tradition. It is interesting to note, however, that while the different forms of II vary fundamentally from I, through the omission of the larger part, both I and II contain the following characteristic expressions:

א) שאינו מביא מבול לעולם שנא' כי מי נח זאת לי.

ב) אמרו לו שמא [מכילתא דרשב"י, בודאין] מבול של מים אינו מביא, של אש מביא.

ג) פנו כולם [ל' א] והלכו [ל' נ] איש למקומו.

We note also that III G, which differs radically in its form, from either I or II, contains the expression כמדומים אנחנו שהמקום מאבד את עולמו which is similar to that found in I B, דומה שהמקום מאבד את עולמו במים.

On the other hand though III H reads: באותה שעה נתכנסו כל and II C reads: באותה שעה נתכנסו כל מלכי אומות העולם אצל בלעם אומות העולם אצל בלעם הרשע.

Yet it is clear from the fact that both III G and III H begin with the expression כשנגלה הקב"ה ליתן תורה לישראל הרעיש כל [את] העולם כולו על יושביו and contain the ending (otherwise found only in *Zebahim* 116a) אמרו לו אם כן ה' יברך את עמו בשלום that III G and III H belong to a special group.

It is also clear that the parent text, from which all the extant versions are descended, apparently contained at the very beginning the words: שבשעה שנתנה תורה לישראל and was a description of the Revelation.

It is finally evident that the text was handed down with a number of formulated phrases, which do not occur in all the texts, but are found in texts belonging to widely different groups. This phenomenon can be explained most readily on the premise that originally the phrases occurred in the sources of the various versions, but were not retained by the later transmitters of the *baraitot*. The assumption is that the catchwords were memorized, but not written.

Further evidence that the catchwords were originally memorized, rather than committed to writing, can be found in the *baraita* telling the story of the discussion among the three Sages, Rabbi Eliezer, Rabbi Joshua, and Rabbi Zadok, at the wedding of the son of Rabbi Gamaliel II. The *baraita* has been transmitted in four forms, which represent two major versions. They may be arranged as follows:

Version I.
> Text A. *Sifre* Deut. 38, Fr. 77a, Fi. 74.
> Text B. *B. Kiddushin* 32b.

Version II.
> Text C. *Mekilta Jethro, Amalek* chap. 1.
> Text D. *Mekilta* of Rabbi Simeon 18.12, p. 88.

B	A
קדושין ל"ב ע"ב	ספרי דברים פ"י ל"ח
מעשה ברבי אלעזר ורבי יהושע ורבי צדוק שהיו מסובין בבית המשתה בנו של רבן גמליאל והיה רבן גמליאל עומד ומשקה עליהם נתן הכוס לר' אליעזר ולא נטלו נטלו לר' יהושע וקבלו אמר לו ר' אליעזר מה זה יהושע אנו יושבין ורבן גמליאל ברבי	וכבר היו רבי אליעזר ורבי יהושע ורבי צדוק מסובים בבית משתה בנו של רבן גמליאל מזג רבן גמליאל את הכוס לרבי אליעזר ולא רצה לטלו נטלו רבי יהושע אמר לו רבי אליעזר מה זה יהושע בדין שאנו מסובים וגמליאל ברבי עמד ומשמשנו

A

ספרי דברים פ"י ל"ח

אמר לו רבי יהושע הנח לו וישמש
אברהם   גדול   העולם
שמש מלאכי שרת וכסבור
שהם   ערביים   עובדי
עבודה זרה שנאמר וישא עיניו
וירא והנה שלשה אנשים והלא דברים
קל וחומר ומה אברהם גדול העולם
שמש מלאכי שרת וכסבור שהם
ערביים עובדי עבודה זרה גמליאל
ברבי לא ישמשנו אמר להם רבי
צדיק הנחתם כבוד מקום ואתם
עסוקים בכבוד בשר ודם אם מי
שאמר והיה העולם משיב רוחות
ומעלה ענים ומוריד גשמים ומגדל
צמחים ועורך שלחן לכל
אחד ואחד גמליאל ברבי
לא ישמשנו.

B

קדושין ל"ב ע"ב

עומד גמשקה עלינו אמר ליה מצינו
גדול ממנו ששמש אברהם גדול ממנו
ושמש אברהם גדול הדור
היה וכתוב בו והוא
עומד עליהם (בראשית י"ט
ח') ושמא תאמרו כמלאכי
השרת נדמו לו לא נדמו
לו אלא לערביים ואנו
לא יהא רבן גמליאל ברבי עומד
ומשקה עלינו אמר להם ר' צדוק
עד מתי אתם מניחים כבודו של
מקום ואתם עוסקים בכבוד הבריות
הקב"ה משיב רוחו ומעלה נשיאים
ומוריד מטר ומצמיח אדמה ועורך
שלחן לפני כל אחד
ואחד ואנו לא יהא רבן
גמליאל ברבי עומד ומשקה
עלינו.

C

מכילתא יתרו, עמלק, פ"א

אמרו הדבר הזה דרש ר' יצחק
ואמר כשעשה רבן גמליאל סעודה
לחכמים היו כל חכמי ישראל מסובים
אצלו עמד רבן גמליאל ושמשן אמרו
החכמים אין אנו כדי שישמשנו אמר
להן ר' יהושע הניחו לו שישמש שמצינו
שגדול מרבן גמליאל שמש את הבריות
אמרו לו אי זה זה אמר להם
אברהם   אבינו   גדול
העולם   ששימש   מלאכי
השרת והיו סבור בהן

D

מכילתא דרשב"י י"ח י"ב

דבר זה דרש ר' צדוק כשהיה רבן
גמליאל עומד ומשמש אמרו בדין
שאנו מסובין ונמליאל ביר' עומד
ומשמשנו אמר להן ר' יהושע מצאנו
גדול מרבן גמליאל שעמד ושמש
אמרו לו היה (איזה) [זה] אמר
להם אברהם שג' והוא עומד
עליהם (ברא' י"ט ח') ולא
בני אדם כשרים אלא
בני אדם שעובדין ע"ז
ומכעיסין לפני המקום על אחת

249

D
מכילתא דרשב"י י"ח י"ב

כמה וכמה לרבן גמליאל שעומד
ומשמש לפני בני אדם כשרים ועוסקין
בתורה. אמר להם ר' צדוק מצאנו
גדול מאברהב ומרבן גמליאל שעומד
ומשמש אמרו לו היזה אמר להם
אלוה השמים ברוך הוא
שנותן לכל אחד ואחד
צרכיו ולכל גויה וגויה
די מחסורה שנ' נותן
לחם לכל בשר ‹תה' קל"ו
כ"ה› ואומר נותן לבהמה
לחמה ‹שם קמ"ז ט'› ולא בני
אדם כשרים אלא בני אדם
עובדין ע"ז ומכעיסין לפניו
על אחת כמה וכמה לרבן
גמליאל שעומד ומשמש
לפני בני אדם כשרים
ועוסקים בתורה.

C
מכילתא יתרו, עמלק, פ"א

שהם בני אדם ערביים
עובדי עבודה זרה רבן
גמליאל שישמש חכמים לומדי תורה
על אחת כמה וכמה. אמר להן ר'
צדוק הניחו לו שישמש מצינו גדול
מרבן גמליאל ומאברהם ששימש את
הבריות אמרו לו אי זה זה. אמר
להם שכינה שבכל שעה
מספיק מזון לכל באי
העולם כדי צרכן ומשביע
לכל חי רצון ולא לבני
אדם הכשרים והצדיקים
בלבד אלא אף הרשעים
עובדי עבודה זרה רבן
גמליאל על אחת כמה
וכמה שישמש חכמים
ובני תורה.

It is obvious from even a cursory examination of these texts that neither A and B nor C and D are identical. But the differences in style between A and B, and between C and D, are slight in comparison with their similarities.

We may therefore draw the following diagram of the transmission of this *baraita*:

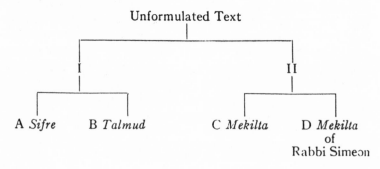

Unformulated Text

I   II

A *Sifre*   B *Talmud*   C *Mekilta*   D *Mekilta*
of
Rabbi Simeon

In view of the fact that A, B, and C belong to different versions, it is curious to find all three using the same words in describing Abraham: גדול העולם. (In D, these are replaced by גדול הדור.) Obviously these words were formulated as a fixed expression, before·the remainder of the *baraita* had been given such a formulation. The person repeating the *baraita* in the source used by *Mekilta Jethro* had no hesitation in changing the greater part of it, and expressing it in his own language. But he felt compelled to use the expression: גדול העולם.

Yet certainly it could not have been written down. If it had been written down, how could that particular expression have been altered in D (*Mekilta* of Rabbi Simeon)? What actually happened then is that the early transmitters of the *baraita* had put the expression גדול העולם into a fixed formula; which was repeated in every case when the *baraita* occurred, namely, the *Talmud*, the *Sifre*, and the source of *Mekilta*. When the compilers of our present *Mekilta* and *Mekilta* of Rabbi Simeon came to put the words into writing, they felt free to use their own style. The compiler of *Mekilta* retained the ancient expression; the compiler of *Mekilta* of Rabbi Simeon did not.

In the following example we are fortunately able to recognize the older version, and see how it became corrupted in its later form, while retaining some of the original expressions. The *aggadist* contrasts the attitude of Moses and David; the former desiring that his sin be told, the latter that his be concealed.[3] The principal places where the incident is cited are: *Sifre* Num. 137, Fr. 51b, Hor. 183; *Sifre* Deut. 26, Fr. 70b, Fi. 36; *B. Yoma* 86b; *Lev. R.* 31.4. Of these the older version (I) occurs in *Sifre* Numbers (A) and *Yoma* (B); the younger version (II) in *Sifre* Deut. (C) and *Lev. R.* (D). The texts are as follows:

A

ספרי במדבר פי' קל"ז

שני פרנסים עמדו לישראל אחד אמר אל יכתב סורחני ואחד אומר יכתב
סורחני. דוד אמר אל יכתב סורחני שנאמר לדוד משכיל אשרי נשוי פשע כסוי

---

[3] For the discussion of the contemporary references in this parable, see I. Ziegler, *Die Koenigsgleichnisse des Midrasch*, p. 121.

251

חטאה (תהלים ל"ב א'). משה אמר יכתב סורחני שנאמר על אשר מריתם פי במדבר
סין במריבת העדה להקדישני. משל למה הדבר דומה לשתי נשים שהיו לוקות
בבית דין אחת לוקה על שקלקלה ואחת לוקה על שגנבה פני שביעית זו שגנבה
פני שביעית אומרת בבקשה מכם הודיעו סורחני שלא יהיו העומדים סבורים לומר
כשם שזו קלקלה אף זו קלקלה. תלו לה הפנים בצוארה והיה הכרח מכריז לפניה
על הפנים זו לוקה.

B
יומא פ"ו ע"ב

שני פרנסים טובים עמדו להם לישראל משה ודוד משה אמר יכתב סורחני
שנאמר יען לא האמנתם בי להקדישני דוד אמר אל יכתב סורחני שנאמר אשרי
נשוי פשע כסוי חטאה משל דמשה ודוד למה הדבר דומה לשתי נשים שלקו בבית
דין אחת קלקלה ואחת אכלה פני שביעית אמרה להן אותה שאכלה פני שביעית
בבקשה מכם הודיעו על מה היא לוקה שלא יאמרו על מה שזו לוקה זו לוקה הביאו
פני שביעית ותלו בצוארה והיו מכריזין לפניה ואומרין על עסקי שביעית היא לוקה.

C
ספרי דברים פי' כ"ו

שני פרנסים טובים עמדו להם לישראל משה ודוד מלך ישראל, משה אמר
לפני הקדוש ברוך הוא, רבונו של עולם, עבירה שעברתי תכתב אחרי שלא יהו
הבריות אומרים דומה שזייף משה בתורה או שאמר דבר שלא נצטוה משל למלך
שמר ואמר כל מי שאוכל פני שביעית יהיו מחזרים אתו בקנפון הלכה אשה אחת
בת טובים לקטה ואכלה פני שביעית והיו מחזרים אותה בקנפון אמרה לו בבקשה
ממך אדוני המלך הודיע סרחוני שלא יהו בני המדינה אומרים דומה שנמצא בה
דבר נאוף או שנמצא בה דבר כשפים הם רואים פנים תלוים בצוארי ויודעים
שבשבילם אני מחזרת כך אמר משה לפני המקום עבירה שעברתי תכתב אחרי
אמר לו הקדוש ברוך הוא הריני כותבה שלא היתה אלא על המים שנאמר כאשר
מריתם פי וגו'.

D
ויקרא רבה ל"א ד'

ר' יהודה משלו משל למה"ד למלך שמר ואמר כל מי שילקוט ויאכל מפירות
שביעית יהו מחזירין אותו בקמפון הלכה אשה אחת בת טובים ולקטה ואכלה מפירות
שביעית התחילו מחזירין אותה בקמפון צווחת והיתה אומרת בבקשה ממך אדוני

המלך תלה את הפנין הללו בצוארי כדי שלא יהו הבריות אומרות דומה לנו שנמצא
בה דבר של ערוה או דבר של כשפים אלא מתוך שרואים את הפנין בצוארי הן
יודעין שבשבילן אני מחזרת כך אמר משה לפני הקב"ה רבון העולם כתוב בתורתך
מפני מה איני נכנס לארץ שלא יהו ישראל אומרים דומה לנו שזייף משה את התורה
או אמר דבר שלא נצטוה אמר לו הקב"ה חייך שאני כותב שלא היתה אלא על
המים הה"ד כאשר מריתם פי במדבר צין.

Version I is clearly the older, and comes from a time when
Jewish courts still retained the right of inflicting the punishment
of stripes. This would be inflicted on a woman who transgressed
the law of the sabbatical year, as well as one who violated the
laws of chastity. Version II apparently derives from a time when
the Jewish courts no longer could exercise such jurisdiction.
Accordingly, it transfers the scene from the Jewish court, to the
royal court, and substitutes the Roman custom of leading the
criminal through the arena for the Jewish punishment of stripes.
Nevertheless, the sin for which the lesser offender is punished
still remains "gathering the fruits of the sabbatical year," a sin
which the Romans would not recognize.[4]

Another example of this textual phenomenon may be found
in a *baraita* which is less typically *aggadic*. The following *baraita*
occurs in (A) *Tosefta Berakot* 1.4, p. 1; (B) *B. ibid.* 11a; (C) *Yer.
ibid.* 1.6, 3b; (D) *Sifre* Deut. 34, Fr. 74b, Fi. 62:

A

תוספתא ברכות א' ד'

מעשה בר' ישמעאל ור' אלעזר בן עזריה שהיו שרויין במקום אחד והיה ר'
ישמעאל מוטה ור' אלעזר בן עזריה זקוף והגיע זמן קרית שמע נזקף ר' ישמעאל
והיה ר' אלעזר בן עזריה מוטה אמר לו ר' ישמעאל מה זה אלעזר אמר לו ישמעאל
אחי אומרין לאחד למה זקנך מגודל אמר להם כנגד המשחיתים אני שהייתי זקוף

---

[4] Ziegler, (*loc. cit.* n. 121) presumes that the later version refers to some
prohibition of the export of figs during the year of a bad harvest. But obviously
such a prohibition is not what the text presupposes. The most natural explanation of the later text is that given, namely that it was formulated when
gathering figs of the Sabbatical year was punishable, but changes the form of
punishment to suit contemporary conditions.

היטיתי, אתה שהיית מוטה נזקפת. אמר לו אתה היטית לקיים כדברי בית שמאי
ואני נזקפתי לקיים כדברי בית הלל, דבר אחר שלא יראו התלמידים ויעשו קבע
כדבריך.

B

ב' ברכות י"א ע"א

ומעשה ברבי ישמעאל ור' אלעזר בן עזריה שהיו מסובין במקום אחד והיה
ר' ישמעאל מוטה ור' אלעזר בן עזריה זקוף כיון שהגיע זמן קריאת שמע הטה
רבי אלעזר זקף ר' ישמעאל אמר לו רבי אלעזר בן עזריה לר' ישמעאל ישמעאל
אחי אמשול לך משל למה הדבר דומה משל לאחד שאומרים לו זקנך מגודל אמר
להם יהיה כנגד המשחיתים אף כך אתה כל זמן שאני זקוף אתה מוטה עכשיו כשאני
הטתי אתה נזקפת אמר לו אני עשיתי כדברי ב"ה ואתה עשית כדברי ב"ש ולא עוד
אלא שמא יראו התלמידים ויקבעו הלכה לדורות.

C

ירו' ברכות א' ו'

תני מעשה בר' אלעזר בן עזרי' ור' ישמעאל שהיו שרויין במקו' אחד והיה
ר' אלעזר בן עזריה מוטה ורבי ישמעאל זקוף. הגיע זמן עונת קרית שמע נזקף ר'
אלעזר בן עזריה והטה רבי ישמעאל. א'ר אלעזר לר' ישמעאל אומר לאחד בשוק
מה לך זקנך מגודל והוא אומר יהיה כנגד המשחיתים. אני שהייתי מוטה נזקפתי
ואת' שהיית זקוף הטית. אמר לו אתה נזקפת כדברי בית שמאי. ואני היטיתי כדברי
ב"ה. ד'א שלא יראוני התלמידים ויעשו הלכה קבע כדברי בית שמאי.

D

ספרי דברים פי' ל"ד

וכבר היה רבי ישמעאל מוטה ודורש ורבי אלעזר בן עזריה זקוף, הגיע זמן
קריית שמע נזקף רבי ישמעאל והטה רבי אלעזר בן עזריה, אמר לו רבי ישמעאל,
מה זה אלעזר, אמר לו, ישמעאל אחי, אמרו לאחד, מפני מה זקנך מגודל, אמר
להם הוֹי כנגד המשחיתים, אמר לו, אתה הטיתה כדברי בית שמי ואני נזקפתי
כדברי בית הלל. דבר אחר שלא יקבע הדבר חובה שבית שמי אומרים בערב
כל אדם יטו ויקראו ובבוקר יעמדו.

The extant texts clearly disagree as to whether the incident
occurred with regard to the morning or evening recitation of
the *Shema*. Three texts, *Tosefta*, *Babli*, and *Sifre*, report that it

occurred in the evening; and that Rabbi Eleazar followed the
view of *Bet Shammai* by lying down to read the *Shema*. But
Yerushalmi maintains that it was the morning *Shema*, and that
Rabbi Eleazar *arose* to recite it. All texts agree that Rabbi
Ishmael did the opposite of what the Shammaites demand; and
that Rabbi Eleazar explained .that he acted according to *Bet
Shammai*, precisely because Rabbi Ishmael acted according to
Bet Hillel. The words which are identical in all texts are:

אומרין לאחד למה זקנך מגודל אומר להם כנגד המשחיתים
(תוספתא) אמרו לאחד מפני מה זקנך מגודל אמר להם יהי כנגד
המשחיתים (ספרי) שאומרים לו זקנך מגודל אמר להם יהיה
כנגד המשחיתים (בבלי) אמר לאחד בשוק מה לך זקנך מגודל
והוא אומר יהיה כנגד המשחיתים (ירושלמי).

This is apparently a fixed formula, about which the whole story
revolved. So fluid was the text that it was possible for one transmitter, (*Yerushalmi*) to change a number of details, with regard
to it. But even the oldest form had had the final phrase, reading
approximately, ד"א שלא יראו התלמידים ויעשו קבע כדבריך which
occurs in various forms in all texts.[5]

It is obvious from the examples cited, that in most instances
the catchwords which were transmitted either orally or in writing, were subsequently enlarged to form our present complete
baraitot. But that was not always done. Frequently only part of
the *baraita* was recalled by the transmitter from the catchword,
and the rest was forgotten. Thus even in the examples cited
above, the words of Rabbi Eleazar of Modin, as a comment on
Psalm 29, can be reconstructed fully, through the use of all the
texts of the *baraitot*. I have elsewhere[6] called attention to the
interesting passage in *Abot* of Rabbi Nathan (chap. 1, p. 3b)
which has been preserved in two different forms, which supplement each other. The texts follow:

[5] The expression ויעשו קבע כדבריך can only mean what is made more
explicit in the version of *Yer.* ויעשו הלכה קבע כדברי בית שמאי "they will fix a
legal formula."

[6] JBL LVII (1938), p. 40.

אדר"נ נו"א

ר' שמעון בן אלעזר אומר אמשול לך משל למה אדם הראשון דומה לאדם
אחד שנשא את הגיורת היה יושב מפקדה אמר לה אל בתי אל תאכלי פת בשעה שידיך
טמאות ואל תאכלי פירות שאינן מעושרין אל תחללי שבתות ואל תפרצי בנדרים
ואל תלכי עם איש אחר הא אם עברת על אחת מהן הרי את מתה. מה עשה האיש
ההוא עמד ואכל פת בפניה בשעה שידיו טמאות ואכל פירות שאינן מעושרין וחלל
שבתות ופרץ בנדרים והושיט לה בידיו מה אמרה גיורת ההיא בלבה כל הדברים
שפקדני בעלי מתחלה שקר הם מיד עמדה ועברה על כולם.

אדר"נ נו"ב

ר' ישמעאל [ור' שמעון] בן אלעזר אומר למה היתה חוה דומה באותה שעה
לאחד שנשא אשה גיורת ואמר לה אל תאכלי מן הפת עד שתטילי את ידך ולא
מן הפירות עד שתעשרי [אותם] הלכה ואכלה מן הפת ולא נטלה את ידיה ומן
הפירות ולא עשרה ומצא הפתח ליכנס בו.

Version I reads: "Rabbi Simeon ben Eleazar says, I will
explain the matter to you by a parable. To whom may Adam
be compared? To a man who married a proselyte, and was
admonishing her. He said to her, My daughter, do not eat
bread with hands that are levitically unclean; and do not eat
fruits which are not tithed; do not violate the Sabbath; and do
not break your vows; and do not go about with another man.
But if you transgress these rules, you shall die. What did that
man, however, do? He ate bread in her presence with hands
unwashed, and ate fruits which were not tithed, and violated
the Sabbath, and broke his vows, and offered some of the forbidden foods to his wife. What did that woman naturally think?
Everything which my husband commanded me is false, and immediately she arose and violated his other commands."

Version II reads: "Rabbi Simeon ben Eleazar says: To whom
may Eve be compared at that time? To a person who married a
proselyte. And he said to her, Do not eat bread before you wash
your hands; nor fruits before you tithe them; and she went and
ate bread without washing her hands, and fruits without tithing
them, and so found a door to enter through it (into graver sin)."

It is clear that the point which Rabbi Simeon ben Eleazar
really made was that Adam by forbidding Eve to touch the

Tree of Knowledge, and threatening her with death if she did, (whereas God had only forbidden eating its fruit) opened the way to her transgression. She violated Adam's command against touching the Tree without punishment, and was led to the further sin of eating the fruit. Version I indicates this by telling us that the unwise husband of the proselyte had warned her against eating untithed fruit with the same emphasis which he placed on her observance of her marriage vows and the sabbath. Nevertheless the point is not specifically stated. Version II, which is briefer, indicates the point less clearly. The husband did not err in warning his proselyte wife against eating untithed fruit or eating bread with unwashed hands. He erred in saying that such action would lead to her death. When she found that these sins did not, other sins of a graver nature, followed.

The fact that each of the versions contains only an abbreviated form of the story, suggests that the compilers of the present version relied on the imagination of the reader to supply the missing parts, or that part of the tradition had actually been lost in the process of transmission.

This phenomenon accounts for the curious fact that frequently parables occur in the *tannaitic midrashim* in syncopated, and therefore unintelligible form. Thus in *Sifre* Deut. 3, Fr. 66a, Fi. 11, we find the following interesting passage:

משל למלך שיצא הוא וחיילותיו למדבר אמרו לו חיילותיו תן לנו גלוסקאות חמות אמר להם אני נותן שוב אמרו לו חיילותיו תן לנו גלוסקאות חמות אמר להם הפרכוס שלו בשביל שהמלך כשר מאין לו ריחים מאין לו תנורים במדבר כך אמר משה אם מוכיח אני את ישראל תחלה עכשיו יאמרו עלי בשביל שאין בו כח להכניסנו לארץ ולהפיל סיחון ועוג לפנינו הוא מוכיחנו הוא לא עשה כן אלא לאחר שהכניסם לארץ והפיל סיחון ועוג לפניהם אחר כך הוכיחם.

"This is to be compared to a king, who went out, with his armies, into the wilderness. His armies said to him, Give us warm loaves. He said, I will provide them. Again they said, Give us warm loaves. Thereupon the hyparchos said to them, Because the king is worthy (you make demands on him); otherwise, whence shall he obtain a mill, whence shall he obtain ovens in the wilderness. So Moses said, If I reprove Israel first, they will say

257

about me, Because he lacks the power to take us into the Land, and to vanquish Sihon and Og before us, he reproves us. He did not do so; but after he had vanquished Sihon and Og before them, then did he reprove them.''

Now in the form in which the parable is given in the text, there is no similarity between it and the incident to which it is compared. The whole point, namely that the hyparchos reproved the army for asking the impossible, *after the king was victorious and was able to give them their wants*, is omitted from the text! This omission cannot be ascribed to an error of the copyist; the gap is fundamental. It is the result of the transmitter's or copyist's failure to supply the missing or implied part of the text.

In one interesting passage, the extant versions of the *Sifre* Deut. have preserved what are apparently the shorthand notes for an ancient *aggadic baraita*, without any expansion. The text, (*Sifre*, Deut. 304. Fr. 129a, Fi. 323) reads as follows:

ק ר א א ת י ה ו ש ע,‏ משיב משה לפני הקב״ה רבש״ע הואיל ואני נפטר בנסיס
גדול מן העולם הראיני אדם נאמן שיעמוד על ישראל שאצא ידיהם לשלום וכן הוא
אומר אשר יצא לפניהם ואשר יבא לפניהם ואומר ויאמר ה' אל משה קח לך את יהושע
בן נון ואומר אחות לנו קטנה ושדים אין לה ארבע מלכיות מושלות בהם בישראל
ואין בהם בישראל ואין בהם חכם ואין בהם נבון בימי אחאב מלך ישראל ובימי
יהושפט מלך יהודה היו ישראל נפוצים על ההרים כצאן אשר אין להם רועה
ויאמר ה' אל משה קח לך את יהושע בן נון קח לך גברתן שכמותך ..... ר'
נחמיה אומר אין לי רשות הא יש לי רשות אכניסם בצד אהלי רועים שיהו יושבים
בו.

The words are quite unintelligible as they stand. "Moses said before God, Since I am departing in the midst of deep anger from this world, show me a faithful person who will stand before Israel, who will satisfy them with peace. And thus Scripture says: 'Who may go out before them, and who may come in before them, . . . that the Congregation of the Lord may not be as sheep which have no shepherd (Num. 27.17).' And another verse reads, 'We have a little sister and she has no breasts; what shall we do for our sister, etc. (Cant. 8.8).' Four Kingdoms will rule over Israel; and there is none among them who has understanding, and none who has wisdom. And thus in the days of Ahab, King of Israel, and Jehoshaphat, King of Judah, Israel was scattered on the mountains, like sheep which have no shepherd. (I Kings 22.17). *And the Lord said unto Moses:* Take thee Joshua *the son of Nun*, a man as strong as thou ... R. Nehemiah says, 'I have no authority. But had I authority, I should bring them into the shepherds' tents.' "

Some light is thrown on the passage, by the parallel *baraita* cited in *Sifre* Numbers 139, Fr. 52a, Hor. 186: which reads:

ספרי במדבר פי' קל"ט ק"מ

ולא תהיה עדת ה' כצאן אשר אין להם רועה ועליו מפורש בקבלה הגידה
לי שאהבה נפשי איכה תרעה איכה תרביץ בצהרים שלמה אהיה כעוטיה (שה"ש
א' ז') כענין שנאמר ועטה את ארץ מצרים כאשר יעטה הרועה את בגדו (ירמיה
מ"ג י"ב). שלמה אהיה כעוטיה על עדרי חבריך על עדרי אברהם יצחק ויעקב.
צא וראה מה הקב"ה השיבו אם לא תדעי לך היפה בנשים מעולה שבנביאים צאי
לך בעקבי הצאן בעקבים אני עושה עמהם. ורעי את גדיותיך מנין אתה אומר
שהראהו המקום למשה כל הפרנסים העתידים לשמש את ישראל מים שיצאו מן
המדבר עד שיחיו המתים שנאמר צאי לך בעקבי הצאן. ויאמר ה' אל משה קח לך
את יהושע בן נון קח לך את שבלבך קח לך מה שבדרוק לך ועליו מפורש נצר
תאנה יאכל פריה <ושומר אדניו יכבד (משלי כ"ו י"ח)> איש אשר רוח בו שיכול
להלוך כנגד רוחו של כל אחד ואחד.

"*Who may go out before them, and who may come in before them ... that the Congregation of the Lord may not be as sheep which have no shepherd.* Regarding him it is explained in the Hagiographa, 'Tell me, O thou whom my soul loveth, where thou feedest, where thou makest thy flock to rest at noon; for, why should I be as one that veileth herself, beside the flock of thy companions (Cant. 1.8).' ... (This is to be interpreted as follows) 'Why should I be as one that veileth herself, beside the flock of Abraham, Isaac, and Jacob?' Go forth and see what the Holy One replied to him: 'If thou know not, O thou fairest among women,' (this means) 'thou fairest among the prophets,' 'Go thy way forth by the footsteps of the flock,' (this means) 'the final steps which I am preparing for them'; 'And feed thy kids (besides the shepherds' tents).' Whence do we know that God

259

showed Moses all the leaders who are destined to serve Israel from the day when they left the wilderness until the Resurrection? Because it is said, 'Go thy way forth by the footsteps of the flock (and feed thy kids besides the shepherds' tents).' ".. .

We notice at once that Rabbi Nehemiah's enigmatic statement in *Sifre* Deut. about the shepherds' tents, is simply a reference to the longer explanation preserved in *Sifre* Numbers. The shepherds' tents of Cant. 1.9, are interpreted to mean the day of final Judgment and Resurrection. Moses is made to say that he had no authority to do so; but had it depended on him he should have liked to lead Israel to that day. The remark that Moses saw all the future leaders of his people also explains the brief reference to the four kingdoms which will rule over Israel. These kingdoms are not, clearly, as Friedmann in his note maintains, the four divisions of the Hebrew tribes in the wilderness. The kingdoms refer to the four world empires, to which that expression usually refers, and are predicted in Dan. Chap. 3. According to the usual rabbinic interpretation, these empires are: Babylonia, Persia, Macedonia, and Rome. Interpreted in the light of these facts the passage on *Sifre* Deut. must be expanded as follows:

"Moses replied to God, 'Since I am departing from the world in the midst of great anger, show me a faithful person who will stand before Israel, so that he may satisfy them with peace.' And thus he says, 'who may go out before them, and who may come in before them, . . . that the Congregation of the Lord may not be as sheep that have no shepherd.' And in another verse this thought is explained more fully, (Moses saying to God), 'We have a little sister (i. e., Israel) and she has no breasts; what shall we do for our sister, etc. (Cant. 8.8).' (He said further) 'Four kingdoms are destined to rule over Israel, and (how can they survive) if they have neither man of understanding nor sage? (And he pointed) to the days of Ahab, King of Israel and Jehoshaphat, King of Judah, when (Scripture says) Israel was scattered on the mountains, like sheep which have no shepherd. Thereupon the Lord God said unto Moses, Take thee Joshua the son of Nun.''

This passage was doubtless intended to be followed by one

similar to that cited above, making Cant. 1.8 the subject of a conversation between God and Moses. The final reference to the "shepherds' tents" in that verse led to Rabbi Nehemiah's remark that Moses wished he had authority to take Israel into the shepherds' tents.

We have then in *Sifre* Deut. 304, the curious phenomenon of the preservation of ancient notes for a *Midrash*, instead of the text of the *Midrash* itself.

THE RŌBEH רוֹבֶה

OR

THE OFFICIAL MEMORIZER OF THE PALESTINIAN SCHOOLS

SOLOMON GANDZ

TO THE INSTITUTION OF THE PROFESSIONAL MEMORIZER IN GENERAL

In our times, when an author finishes some literary work, he relieves himself by committing it to writing and forgetting about it. In the olden bookless times, when writing was not yet invented or not yet in general use for literary purposes, the creative author had the same desire of relieving his mind from the burden of retaining in his memory all his spiritual products. But instead of committing his work to writing, he entrusted it to the well tested memory of some pupil or personal attendant of his. In the stage of oral literature there was, almost among all the nations, a class of such professional memorizers, whose task it was to learn by heart and to recite the works of the poet, prophet and religious teacher. Thus we find in India a whole class of priests whose duty it was to memorize the Vedas. In Arabia there were the Rāwīs, who, originally, were attached to the poets as their official memorizers, and, later on, in the time of Islam, were also known as ḥuffāẓ, "the holders" of the Koran and Ḥadīth in their memories. Similarly, the Greek Rhapsodists and, in mediaeval times, the European minstrels and bards preserved in their memories the oral literature of their respective countries. In short, the professional memorizer was a universal institution; he was the living book. And our books of today are the mechanical tools substituting the human organ and human labor.[1]

---

[1] More details about the professional memorizer in general will be found in the writer's book on *The Dawn of Literature* which is soon to appear in print.

5

II. THE TANNA AND THE RŌBEH.

The Hebrews, too, had their period of oral tradition, which, however, did not, as usually assumed, start with the Mishnah or the so-called Oral Law, and was not merely a commentary, interpreting and supplementing the Written Law. The fact is that the period of oral literature among the Hebrews extended from the Pre-Mosaic times till about 1000 C.E. An elaborate discussion of the problem will be found in the writer's paper "Oral Tradition in the Bible."[2] Here, a few details only may suffice. Joshua, the chief disciple of Moses, is also described as his official memorizer. Thus we read in Ex. 17:14: And the Lord said unto Moses: Write this for a memorial in the book and *put it in the ears of Joshua.* כתב זאת זכרון בספר ושים באזני יהושע. Hence in addition to the new written record, introduced by Moses, the old traditional method of oral transmission was retained, and this was to "put it in the ears of Joshua," to entrust it to the memory of the best disciple. Similarly in Dt. 31:19 it is said: "Write you this song for you and teach it the children of Israel; *put it in their mouth.*" In the times of the prophets there was a special class, probably of priests, who were known as "the holders of the Torah."[3]

The so-called Holy Scriptures, which were canonized and committed to writing, constituted only a very small portion of the Hebrew literature. The great bulk of this literature, especially rich in religious and legal lore, continued to live on by oral tradition and formed the Oral Law. This lore was cultivated in several higher schools of learning in Palestine and Babylonia, and was known as Mishnah, "repetition," because the whole system of instruction and preservation consisted in oral repetition and recitation. Each school had a number of professional memorizers, who served, so to say, as living text books. They were known by the name of Tanna, pl. Tannaim, i.e.: "Repeater, Reciter." Later on, the term was also used for the teachers of traditions mentioned in Mishnah and Baraita. We may assume that, as a

---

[2] See *Jewish Studies in Memory of George A. Kohut*, New York, 1935, pp. 248–269.

[3] See Jer. 2:8 הכהנים לא אמרו איה ה' ותפשי התורה לא ידעוני.

rule, the favorite student, distinguished through his memory and other good qualities, was first appointed as "memorizer" or assistant Professor, and later on advanced to become the ordinary Professor; but he retained his original title of Tanna. Similarly in Arabia we find that the erstwhile Rāwīs became later famous poets themselves. Originally, however, the title Tanna was employed for the young disciples who excelled only through their retentive memory, and were not recognized as the teachers and masters. They simply served as assistants to the teachers of the Academies and as a kind of living reference books. If somebody wanted to verify the reading of a text, he was referred to these Tannaim. This system of oral instruction, with the official and professional memorizers, was continued in the Palestinian and Babylonian Academies up to the end of the Gaonic time, which is, till about 1000 C.E. There were, of course, already some written copies of the Talmud, but officially only the Tannaim were employed and recognized as the "holders" of the text.[4]

That the term Tanna applies to the professional memorizer, is a well-known and established fact, as seen from the above quoted literature. In this paper the writer proposes to demonstrate that the title Rōbeh, often attached to the names of Palestinian teachers, and mostly occurring in the Palestinian Talmud, serves to designate the same function of the Official Memorizer. Usually, the term is explained to be identical with Rabbah רַבָּה and to mean "the Great" or "the Elder," as for instance in R. Hiyya Rōbeh ר' חייה רובה. The writer, however, understands it in the sense of "the young man" and then "the famulus, amanuensis, personal attendant." The Aramaic term Rōbeh corresponds to the Hebrew word na'ar נער, which also has the double meaning of "youth, adolescent, lad" and "servant, personal attendant." The young disciple attached to the teacher as his famulus served him also as his professional memorizer, and

---

[4] See Bacher, *Terminologie der juedischen Traditionsliteratur*, II, p. 238 ff.; I, p. 194; *idem, Tradition und Tradenten*, pp. 20 and 255 ff.; Strack, *Einleitung in den Talmud*, 5th ed., p. 2; and especially J. N. Epstein, *Der gaonaeische Kommentar zu Tohoroth*, p. 48–50, and in *Festschrift Adolf Schwarz*, p. 319 ff.

hence the latter was simply called the "young man, famulus."
The writer believes that the Hebrew term *na'ar* sometimes also
applies to the disciple who serves as the memorizer. Thus in
Ex. 33:11 ומשרתו יהושע בן נון נער Joshua is designated as the official
memorizer of Moses. The institution of the Rāwī is universal
in the East, says Professor D. B. Macdonald.[5] "The wandering
teacher is always attended by one or more pupils who are his
recorders and who preserve his weightier utterances." The old
Arabian poet usually addresses his two attendants to stop with
him at the deserted encampment of his mistress. The "two young
men of his" accompanying the poet Bileam on his way[6] may
probably also refer to his Rāwīs. Even of Abraham we are told
that he travelled with "his two young men."[7] Now Abraham is
never described as a poet, but the narrator certainly wants to
depict him as a distinguished gentleman. Hence he is in the habit
of taking along "his two young men," of whom most likely the
one was for manual service, while the other one would while
away the time by story-telling and poetical recitations. In like
wise the Hindu knight is accompanied by his priestly story-teller,
and the mediaeval minstrel and bard is usually to be found in the
retinue of the chief and prince. Even as we nowadays like to take
along a book on our journey, so would a gentleman in olden times
like to have with him his literary servant.

III. R. ISAAC RŌBEH, THE OFFICIAL MEMORIZER OF R. JUDAH.

There is an interesting passage in the Palestinian Talmud[8]
which reads as follows:

"Zuga once asked Rabbi (Judah ha Nasi, the final editor of the
Mishnah, *c*.200 C.E.): How does the Mishnah read? *Kerem*

---

[5] *The Hebrew Literary Genius*, p. 89.
[6] Num. 22:22 ושני נעריו עמו.
[7] Gen. 22:3 ויקח את שני נעריו אתו.
[8] *Ma'aser Sheni*, V, 51 (55d). זוגא שאל לרבי מה ניתני. כרם רבעי או נטע רבעי? אמר לון
פוקון שאלון לרבי יצחק רובא דבחנת ליה כל מתניתא. נפקון ושאלון ליה. אמר לון קדמיא כרם
רבעי ותיניינא נטע רבעי. רבי זעירא מקבל לסביא דהוון ביומוי דרבי יצחק רובא דלא בחנון כל
מתנייתא מיניה.

Reba'i, or *Neṭa' Reba'i?* He said to them, go out and ask R. Isaac Rōbeh to whom I entrusted the whole Mishnah. They went out and asked him. He answered them: the first Mishnah reads: *Kerem Reba'i*, and the second Mishnah reads: *Neṭa' Reba'i.* Rabbi Ze'irà found fault with the elders that were living in thẻ days of R. Isaac Rōbeh, because they did not learn from him all the Mishnahs." This passage clearly demonstrates the fact that the scholars, whenever in doubt about the reading of the Mishnah, had no written copy by which they could easily ascertain the text. Rabbi himself, the editor of the Mishnah, was unable to answer the question. He did not remember,[9] nor had he any written copy. When asked about the genuine text, he referred the students to R. Isaac Rōbeh, to whose *memory* he had entrusted the Mishnah. This R. Isaac Rōbeh was the man who usually transmitted traditions in the name of Rabbi. He is also known to have been the teacher of Rab to whom he handed down whole treatises or collections of Halakahs.[10] Later on, it was found very deplorable that the elders living in his time neglected to absorb all his traditions. The quoted passage not only decides (in the negative) the question as to the redaction of the Mishnah in writing, it also proves the existence of official memorizers, attached to the person of the great teachers and leaders of the Academies, whose task it was to absorb and preserve in their memory the whole body of legal tradition. It is evident that the term Rōbeh cannot be understood here in the sense of "the elder," in order to distinguish this R. Isaac from another one who lived in a later generation, as apparently R. Judah and his other contemporaries already refer to him by this title.[11]

It will be interesting to observe that the Prophet Muhammad once found himself in a somewhat similar situation, which, however, was much more embarrassing to him than to R. Judah. Sura 25 was recited in two different versions, the one was given by Omar, the later Caliph, and the other one by a certain Hishām

[9] About the weakening of his memory see *Nedarim*, 41a.
[10] Cf. B. B., 87a; *Ḥullin*, 110a; Frankel, *Mebō ha-Yerushalmi*, 106a; I. Halevy, *Dorot Harischonim*, IIa, 1901, pp. 88, 228, 500.
[11] This was already remarked by A. H. Weiss, *Dōr Dōr ve-Dōreshav*, III, p. 50, note 2.

b. Ḥākim. Both claimed to recite the Sura as they have heard it from the mouth of the Prophet. Omar became very indignant at the stubborn insistence of Hishām and brought the matter before the Prophet himself. Thereupon Muhammad listened to the recitation of both, Omar and Hishām, and had to admit that both had their text from his own mouth. He therefore explained it by saying: The Koran was revealed to me in seven different forms or versions; you may choose what seems more convenient to you.[12] It is clear that in his role of an inspired Prophet, Muhammad could not possibly admit his forgetfulness or error. Hence he resorted to the theory of the seven forms.

IV. THE OTHER ROBEHS.

R. Ḥiyya and his disciple R. Hoshaʻya, who are well known as the great collectors and editors of the Baraitot, are regularly mentioned with the title Rōbeh.[13] The reading Rabbah רַבָּה, is a corruption of Rōbeh. Similarly the reading ר' חייה הגדול[14] owes its origin to a mistake of the copyist, who understood רובה in the meaning of גדול.[15] The fame of R. Ḥiyya and R. Hoshaʻya as faithful memorizers of the Baraita was so well established that the rule was laid down:[16] "Any baraita which was not transmitted by the schools of R. Ḥiyya and R. Hoshaʻya is corrupt." In Nedarim 41a R. Ḥiyya is described as the memorizer of R. Judah ha Nasi. R. Hoshaʻya is referred to as "the father of the Mishnah."[17] The profession of the Rōbeh was continued by the two sons of R. Ḥiyya, Judah and Ḥizqiyah, who, as a

---

[12] See Sprenger, Das Leben des Mohammed, III, p. XXXVI-VII; Encyclopaedia Britannica, eleventh ed., XV, p. 899a.

[13] For R. Ḥiyya, see, f. i., Yer. Ber. II, 4 (5a); IV, 5 (8c); Kilayim, IX, 4 (32b); Ketubbot, XII, 3 (35a); Giṭṭin, VIII, 10 (49c); Niddah, III, 2 (50c). For R. Hoshaʻya, see Ber., II, 7 (5b); Meg., I, 6 (70d). Cf. also Frankel, loc. cit., f. 74, 81b; Weiss, loc. cit., p. 48–50.

[14] In Yer, Shabbat, III, 1 (5c); Peah, VII, in fine, (20c).

[15] See Shabbat 38b.

[16] Hullin 141a כל מתניתא דלא מתניא בי ר' חייא ובי ר' אושעיא משבשתא היא.

[17] See Yer. Qid. I, 3, in fine (60a); B. Q., IV, 7 (4c).

267

rule are known and quoted by this title only. Thus we read in
Ḥullin 20a א״ר ינאי יקבלו הרובין את תשובתן and in *Yer. Ḥagīgah*,
III, *in fine*, (79c), again א״ר ינאי הרובין היו אומרים. In Ḥallah, IV,
10, R. Joḥanan refers to them by this term א״ר יוחנן רבותינו שבגולה
היו מפרישין תרומה ומעשרות עד שבאו הרובין ובטלו אותן. מאן אינון הרובין?
תרגמניא. Hence the Rōbim were also active as interpreters,
which office was usually connected with that of the young scholar
who served as an assistant to his teacher. And we find indeed
that the two sons of R. Ḥiyya are referred to as "the two interpreters" תרין אמוראי and that Ḥizqiyah is cited as the תורגמינא.[18]
Resh Laqish once tells us[19] that the Torah had been forgotten
until R. Ḥiyya and his two sons ·came and restored her. This
praise is very fitting for scholars who specialized as conscientious
memorizers. The Babylonian Talmud once, in referring to the
sons of R. Ḥiyya, renders the term Rōbim by the synonym
דרדקי.[19] The young priests mentioned in Mishnah *Tamid*, I, 1,
as Rōbim[11] may perhaps have been the professional memorizers
of the sacerdotal traditions. One of the oldest Palestinian
Amoraim, a contemporary of R. Ḥiyya, was known as R. Aḥa
Rōbeh.[22] And a certain R. Huna (or Ḥuna) Rōbeh of Sepphoris
relates traditions in the name of R. Joḥanan.[23] A passage in
Yer. Yeb., IV, 11 (6b) seems to indicate that two different kinds
of Rōbeh were distinguished, a memorizer of Mishnah and
Baraita, and a memorizer of the traditions of the schoolhouse
אולפנא, and that R. Ḥiyya was known as the memorizer of the
Mishnah. The passage reads: ר' זעירא בעא קומי ר' מנא: הידינו רבה?[24]
רבה דמתניתא, רבה דאולפנא? לית מילתא, דר' לעזר אמרה: רבה דמתניתא.
כד שמע דתני לה ר' חייא בשם ר' מאיר, אמר: יאות סבא ידע פירקי גיטא.[25]

---

[18] See *B. B.*, 75a; *Gen. Rabbah*, chap. 65; Bacher, *Die Agadah der palaestinen-
sischen Amoraeer*, p. 48–49, note 5.
[19] *Sukkah*, 20a.
[20] *Sanh.* 38a.
[21] Cf. Ginzberg, Tamid, p. 197 f.
[22] See *Yer. Ber.*, II, 4, *in fine* (5a), and Frankel, *loc. cit.*, 62a.
[23] See *Yer. Ber.*, IV, *in fine* (8c), and Frankel, *loc. cit.* 73b–74a.
[24] Instead of רבה read throughout רובה.
[25] Cf. also Weiss, *op. cit.*, p. 49.

The same passage has also another reference to the Rōbeh. We
read there אמר ר' יוחנן: כל מקום ששנה סתם משניות, דרבנן, עד שיפרש
לו רובו. ר"ש בן לקיש אומר: כל סתם משניות דר"מ, עד שיפרש לו רובו The
commentaries explain רוֹבוֹ as identical with רַבּוֹ. However, it is
obvious that both, R. Johanan and Resh Laqish, refer not to
a teacher, but to a Rōbeh, who, like the Arabian Rāwī and the
other memorizers, had to preserve in his memory all the particulars connected with each Mishnah. Hence in the case of an
anonymous Mishnah, the Rōbeh had to know who the real
author was.

269

רטין מגושא

by JONAS C. GREENFIELD

The Talmud (BT Sötä 22a) sought an apt comparison for a student who came under the category of קרא ושנה ולא שימש ת"ח, one who had acquired the ability to recite the Bible and the Mishna but who had not mastered their interpretation by studying with recognized scholars. He was compared, among other things, to a *magus* רב אחא בר יעקב אומר הרי זה מגוש. This comparison was considered proper by Rabbi Nahman bar Yishaq who supported it by quoting the folk saying רטין מגושא ולא ידע מאי אמר תני תונא ולא ידע מאי אמר. I follow Professor Saul Lieberman in translating "the magian mumbles and understands not what he says. [Similarly] the *Tanna* recites and he understands not what he says." Professor Lieberman had adduced this text in his discussion of the oral publication of the Mishna, the *Tanna* in this case is the professional reciter of the Mishna.[1]

In this article I propose to show that the phrase רטין מגושא as used in the folk saying and applied by the rabbis had its roots in the linguistic usage of the day in the Sassanian empire. The root רטן as "to mumble, murmur" is known from various Aramaic dialects—Jewish Aramaic, Mandaic and Syriac.[2] In Jewish Aramaic it is found, beside the above quoted רטין מגושא only twice as the Targum of חובר

---

1. Cf. S. Lieberman, *Hellenism in Jewish Palestine* (N.Y., 1950), 88. As we shall see below the term in Syriac *retna demagushuta* has also been used in discussions of the oral transmission of the Avesta.

2. The root *rtn* is also found in Arabic. There it is used, on the whole, for indistinct speech or for a foreign language. Professor Joshua Blau has drawn my attention to J. Fück, *Arabiya* (French edition, Paris, 1955), p. 88, note 1 where different uses are noted and also to H. Schmidt-P. Kahle, *Volkserzaehlungen aus*

63

חבר/חברים (Deut. 18,11 Onqelos; Ps. 58,6). The use clearly shows that "murmured, mumbled spells" were meant.[3] In Mandaic the usage is similar. The verb *rtn* is used for muttering or for murmuring a spell *ritna ritnit d-harsaia* (*Ginza Yamina* 165:10).[4] In general it may be said that the meaning of this verb and also the noun *ritna* in Mandaic has negative overtones for it is used for speaking evil, for telling lies, for the speech of the simple and for secret languages.[5] In Syriac the use is slightly different for *retan* although translated *murmuravit* by the *lexica* has the added nuance of "to murmur in complaint, to complain." In the Peshitta to the Hebrew Bible it is widely used for forms of the verb און as "to complain" and the noun תלונה (Exod. 16, 2; Num. 14, 27; 17, 6, 19 etc.) and in the Peshitta New Testament it is even more widely used as the translation of Greek *gongúzo*, *diagongúzo* and the noun *gonguzmós* (Math. 20, 11; Mark 10, 41; John 6, 43; 61 Acts 6, 1, etc.).[6] The verb *rtn* and the noun *retna* are also frequently used in one of the classics of Syriac literature, the tale of Julian the Apostate: *'etmeliyw tenānā wamrattenin (h)wō bēnēhōn 'al Shabūr*, "they became angry and complained among themselves against Shapur" (182, 12); and *we 'ā'el ... retnehōn deḥērē qodam*

Palaestina II (Göttingen, 1930), Glossary, p. 216 where *ratan* is used in this Palestinian dialect for "Geheimsprache" and for speaking Turkish or the Gypsy dialect.

3. Both passages deal with murmurers of spells. It may be assumed that the usage in Targum Psalms is dependent on the usage in Onqelos. There is also an adjective רוטננית applied to a woman who complains too much. This use of *rtn* is very similar to that of Syriac.

4. For full context cf. M. Lidzbarski, *Ginza, Der Schatz*, etc., (Göttingen, 1925), p. 172.

5. Cf. Drower-Macuch, *A Mandaic Dictionary* (Oxford, 1963) *s.v. RTN* (p. 432), *ritna* (p. 433); for "Modern Mandaic" cf. *ratna* (Drower-Macuch, p. 420) "Spoken language, vernacular: modern designation of the spoken Mand. dialect" and *retan* "gossip" (R. Macuch, *Handbook of Classical and Modern Mandaic* [Berlin, 1965] 504b).

6. Cf. R. Payne-Smith, *Thesaurus Syriacus* II (Oxford, 1901), 3894-3896; C. Brockelmann, *Lex. Syr.*[2], p. 726. In these lexica the specific meaning of *retan/reten* for the "murmuring of the magians" is not listed. It is only in the *Compendious Syriac Dictionary* of J. P. Margoliouth (Oxford, 1903), p. 539 that one use is noted. In her *Supplement* (Oxford, 1923) to her father's *Thesaurus* J. P. Margoliouth lists some other examples. For N.T. see W. Jennings, *Lexicon to the Syriac New Testament* (Oxford, 1926), p. 207.

Shabur melak malkē, "and he . . . brought the complaint of the nobles before Shapur, King of Kings" (182, 18).[7]

There is, however, a specialized meaning of *retān* in Syriac which has not received sufficient attention. It is used for various cultic acts of the Magians (Zoroastrians) such as the reading of scripture, the recitation of prayers and the strange murmuring sound made before and during eating. It is the equivalent of Pehlevi *dranjishn* and Arabic *zamzama.*[8] These prayers were murmured in a way that was unintelligible to the hearers and in antiquity this was known as *Zoroastrei susurri* and *Magicum susurramen.*[9] Instances of the *retna* as the prayer being said over food can be found for example in the martyrology of Giwargis *qashishā* where we read than an early sign of Giwargis' turn to Christianity was his despising the *retna dēmāgūshūtā* which is described as a magus reciting a *wasqa* (blessing?) with him during the meal.[10] In the martyrology of Mar Aba we read that he forbade the

7. J. G. E. Hoffman, *Iulianos der Abtruennige, Syrische Erzaehlungen* (Leiden, 1880).

8. As Dr. Shaul Shaked, of the Hebrew University, has clarified for me that Pehlevi *dranjishn* means "recitation, saying" and was also used for the recitation of prayers. To the uninitiated this sounded like a murmur. I. Goldziher, *Muhammedanische Studien* II (Halle, 1889), p. 170, assembled the material known at that time about the usage of *zamzama* for the recitation of prayer and scripture among the Zoroastrian. Dr. Shaked has drawn my attention to M. Mo'in's *Mazdayasna ve adab-i-parsi* (Teheran, 1959), pp. 391-399 s.v. *zamzama* where the pertinent Arabic and Persian material is gathered and discussed. In the Christian dialect of Sogdian *zmzm* was used to translate Syriac *rtn* cf. O. Hansen, *Berliner Sogdische Texte* II (Berlin, 1954), p. 872, text c 2/6 (2) vs. 1.5. It is not amiss to note that the verb *zamzem* is found in Mishnaic Hebrew with the meaning "to gossip, tattle" as was noted by Professor S. Lieberman (*Tarbiz* 5, 99; *Tosefta ki-fshutah* VI [New York, 1967] 129, n. 20). Goldziher *l.c.* in dealing with *zamzama* mentioned Syr. *retan* and the passage in Sota 22a and Lieberman in the *hōsāfōt* to *Tosefta ki-fshutah* (VII, 588) has brought together Arab. *zamzama* with Sota 22a to clarify the latter text.

9. The material was assembled by Bidez and Cumont in their magistral *Les mages hellenisés* (Bruxelles 1933) II, 285 ff.

10. Cf. P. Bedjan, *Histoire de Mar-Jabalaha, de trois autres patriarches, etc.* (Paris, 1895), p. 440 11. 9-12. This text was translated by G. Hoffman, *Auszüge aus syrischen Akten persischer Märtyrer* (Leipzig, 1880), 96. Hoffman translated *wasqa* as "blessing" but this is doubtful. For *wasqa* cf. W. B. Henning, "The Middle-Persian word for 'beer'," *BSOAS* XVII, 1955, 603-04; *wasqa* would then mean ritual

eating of *besrā deretnā* to the Christians of Persia.[11] Bar Bahlul explained *retnā demāgōshē* as *damgashū bizban laḥma*, "They said magus-prayers during the meal."[12] It is to this practice that reference is made in the *Arukh* where in the name of Hai Gaon '*amgūshtā* is defined as "muttering ('*al-zamzama* in Arabic) which the magians do during their meal; they don't speak clearly but make a noise which has no clear sound."[13]

The other use of *rtn* is to describe the recitation of the Avesta (and other holy books) used during the prayers. The sound made during the prayers were strange to the Christian writers and they used the

food over which a prayer was said. Reference is made to the Mazdean custom of "intoning" during meals in the Mandaean *Ginza Yamina* where the word *wasqa* is also used, cf. Lidzbarski's translation (note 6, above) p. 225 and note 3. It is worth recounting that Giwargis, who was the scion of a good magian family and was a child prodigy of sorts had been called before the emperor at the age of seven to recite the Avesta *dantanne mennāh damgūshūtā* (p. 436, 1. 13). Note the use of the verb *tanne.*

11. Bedjan, *ibid.*, p. 229, 11. 3-4. The story of Mar Aba has been analyzed in a thorough going manner by the Belgian Bollandiste Paul Peeters, "Observations sur la vie syriaque de Mar Aba, Catholicos de l'église perse (540-552)" reprinted in *Recherches d'histoire et de philologie Orientales* II (Bruxelles, 1951) 117-163. The Mar Aba narrative is of particular interest for Talmudic studies and I hope to return to it at another occasion.

12. Bar Bahlul as quoted by Payne-Smith, *Thesaurus,* 2009-2010 *s.v. magōshā.* I have not been able to find this passage in Duval's edition. Bar Bahlul *s.v. retna* gives only the meaning "to murmur, complain" (cf. ed. R. Duval, p. 1897). The verb *megash* for a prayer said during the meal is also found in the tale of Mar Aba: "you shall also not forbid Christians from eating meat over which a Magian prayer has been said (*besrā damgīsh 'aloy*)," p. 238, 11. 10-11.

13. Cf. Arukh *s.v. magōshā* and '*Osar ha-Geonim Shabbat* (Jerusalem, 1930) *perushim* section, p. 34 to BT Shab. 75a where the tradition is quoted anonymously. Prof. Lieberman (see above n. 8) has explained Rabba Hai Gaon's concentration on the murmuring during the meal as being based on the fact that the *retna/zamzama* of the Zoroastrian scriptures had ceased by then. The one difficulty with this is that although the Avesta was surely committed to writing by this time Parsi priests until this day commit their scripture to memory and recite it from memory. A thorough study of prayer over food during meals may be found in Mary Boyce's "Zoroastrian BAJ and DRON," BSOAS XXXIV, 1971, 56-73; 298-313, which appeared after this article was in print.

term *retna* "murmuring" for it.[14] In the life of Mar Aba we have a description of the central school of Magism in Azerbaijan: "all the magians (*magōshē*) from all Persia gather there to learn the murmur (*retnā*) of Zaradusht son of Spitama. These people are opposed to all Truth, they walk about in groups and factions and walk behind their masters. They whisper the foolishness of their blasphemy, they mumble and talk indistinctly (*wamnahmin wamtamtemin*)."[15] It was to such a school that the renowned magus Mihrin sent his son to be educated as we learn in the narrative preserved at the beginning of the martyrdom of Pethion: "After a short while the boys grew up. He took the one called Yazdin and placed him in a house of the magians (*bēt magōshē*) so that he be given a magian education דנאלף ונתחכם ביולפנא דמגושותא and that he become skilled in the 'murmur of the magians' (דנחוא מחירא וחכימא ברטנא דמגושא)."[16] The boy later fled and in time became a Christian martyr.

What was the mode of study like among the magians? We have two sources that are very instructive. The first stems from the Zoroastrian tradition of the Sassanian period and describes the teaching role of the *herbad*. It was studied most recently by Mlle. M. L. Chaumont.[17] As Dr. Chaumont has shown, there is near accord among the sources that the essential function of the *herbad* was to impart *orally* the Avesta and its commentaries (the *zand*). The faculty chiefly used in

14. The sources for *retna* with this particular meaning have been gathered by F. Nau in two important articles "Etudes historiques sur la transmission de l'Avesta," *Revue de l'histoire des religions*, 1927, pp. 149-99 and "L'époque de la dernière redaction de nostre Avesta," *Journal Asiatique*, 1927, 150-168. Nau's purpose in gathering these and other sources was to emphasize the oral transmission of the Avesta.

15. P. Bedjan, *ibid.*, pp. 240-241. Note too the remark of Bar Bahlul, quoted by P. de Lagarde, *Gesammelte Abhandlungen* (Leipzig, 1866), p. 45: *Zardusht hu dashlem retna demagōshā* (brought to my attention by Dr. Shaked). The verb *tamtem* is defined by Brockelmann (*Lex. Syr.*[2] 727a) as "balbutivit," *tamtāmōnā* "indistincte loquens."

16. P. Bedjan, *Acta Martyrum et Sanctorum* II (Paris, 1891), p. 561.

17. M.-L. Chaumont, "Recherches sur le clergé zoroastrien," *Revue de l'histoire des religions*, CLVIII, 1960, 55-80, 161-179. Chaumont, as well as F. Nau, translated *retna* as "psalmodie" or "murmuration psalmodiée."

this mode of learning was memory and the means of memorization was repeated murmuring. The term used in Pehlevi books is, as noted above, *dranjenitan*. This verb means among other things to "recite in murmuring" and "learn by heart" and the noun *dranjishn* "murmuring" is found in the texts that deal with the *herbad* and his profession. The disciple, she points out, was to learn by heart and in their entirety the texts that the *herbad* taught him. The Hērpatistan, a text which is a guide for the *herbad*, informs us that the "student studies three years with a *herbad* but if during the second part of this period he omits something while murmuring he should go to another *herbad*, or to a third or a fourth. After this process he should know his material and should omit nothing while murmuring." He is to study until he knows the *staōta yesnya*—thirty-three chapters of the Yasna which contain the Gathas. The master and disciple both recited them without understanding their sense. To memorize them well with their proper intonation was not an easy task and took much study.[18]

From a very interesting Syriac source written about the year 630 C.E., the *Tash'itā da mari Yeshusabran*, dealing with the martyrdom of Yeshu-Sabran, we have a report from a convert to Christianity of his early experience and training in the *retna demagūshūtā*.[19]

Yesu-Sabran, who was originally named Mahanus, was a member of a distinguished Persian priestly family, his father having been a judge in the district of Arbela. After Yeshu-Sabran converted to Christianity he wandered about in a monk's habit reciting constantly the "Lord's Prayer" which was the only Christian prayer that he knew. He then asked the priest of his village to have the priest's son Yeshu-Zaka give him instruction. We read that Yeshu-Sabran, who was

---

18. Cf. in particular pp. 61-68 of Chaumont's article and cf. too the material discussed by S. Wikander, *Feuerpriester in Kleinasien und Iran* (Lund, 1946), 28-34.

19. This martyrdom was edited by J.-B. Chabot in *Nouvelles Archives des Missions scientifiques*, VII (Paris, 1897), 485-584. The story of the education of Yeshu-Sabran is on pp. 524-525. Another tale of education in the *retna demagūshūta* is that of Mihrikhoust related in the Yesu-Sabran narrative (p. 569). There, after Mihrikhoust denies Christ, he begins the study of the *retna*. Four *magōshē* are placed with him in order to properly instruct him.

learned in the *retna demagūshūtā*, asked his young teacher "what should
one learn first?" The young man answered him, "One learns at first the
letters, then to make words of them, then one recites the Psalms, then
little by 'little all the holy books, then when one is trained in the
reading of the holy books one begins to study their interpretation.
The martyr-to-be said to the young man: "Before I begin to learn the
letters, recite ten Psalms to me." He said that because he was accustomed to receive orally (*min pūmā*) the *retna de magūshūtā* because
"the horrid teaching of Zoroaster (Zaradusht) is not written down with
letters" and he asked the young man to teach him the verses orally.
When he had received a verse he repeated it with great force, shaking
his head strongly in the manner of the Magians. But the young man
restrained him saying "Do not do like the Magians do [דלא לם תעבד
איך דעבדין מגושא] but be still and recite with your mouth alone."
Thus in a short while he learned many verses. They both went out and
informed the priest of this. The priest advised Yeshu-Sabran to learn to
read the letters first so that he could then read any book. Yeshu-Sabran
followed the priest's advice and did so. The narrative informs us that
in a few days he learned the letters and in a short while he recited ten
Psalms. Jeshu-Sabran went on to greater things and was martyred
in 619.

It is clear then that the term *retna demagūshūtā* refers to a specific
type of oral instruction in which the accent was placed on memorization of a text without comprehension of the content. The *retna* itself
sounded like indistinct murmuring and mumbling to the outsider since
it was in all likelihood recited in an unaccentuated monotone. The sort
of *tannā* who could do no more than repeat the text since he came
under the category of קרא ושנה ולא שמש ת"ח was aptly compared
with the מגושא.[20]

----

20. The other references to the *magōshā* in Talmudic literature also bear reinvesti-
gation in the light of present day knowledge of Iranian religious and cultural history.

THE CHANGE FROM A STANDING TO A SITTING POSTURE BY STUDENTS AFTER THE DEATH OF RABBAN GAMALIEL

Baltimore Hebrew College

By M. Aberbach, Baltimore

In Megillah 21a, we read the following enigmatic passage: "Our Rabbis taught: 'From the days of Moses up to Rabban Gamaliel, the Torah was studied only standing. When Rabban Gamaliel died, illness came down upon the world, and they studied (viz., the Torah) sitting. That is why we have learnt (viz., in the Mishnah):[1] 'From the time when Rabban Gamaliel died, the glory of the Torah[2] ceased' ".[3]

Before proceeding to discuss the substance of the text, we have to determine to which Rabban Gamaliel this passage refers. Some[4] identifies him with Rabban Gamaliel II of Jabneh who flourished at the end of the first and the beginning of the second century C.E., [5] others, identified him with Rabban Gamaliel I Hazaken, the grandfather of Gamaliel II, who lived in the first half of the first century C.E.

The Talmudic tradition strongly supports the latter contention; for, although in the current editions of Meg. 21a the word הזקן is omitted after "Rabban Gamaliel", it is added in the Munich text. Moreover, the passage quoted from M. Sot. IX, 15[6] includes הזקן and it is also to be found in both the Talmud Babli and Talmud Yerushalmi editions of Sotah.[7] Further-

---

[1] M. Sot. IX, 15.
[2] Or: the honour paid to the Torah, viz., by standing while studying it.
[3] Meg. 21a: ת"ר: מימות משה ועד רבן גמליאל לא היו למדין תורה אלא מעומד. משמת ר"ג, ירד חולי לעולם והיו למדין מיושב, והיינו דתנן: משמת ר"ג, בטל כבוד (ה)תורה.
[4] Cf. Morris, *The Jewish School*, pp. 52 and 252, n. 15.
[5] *Elementary Education in Ancient Israel*, pp. 110, n. 15.
[6] See above, n. 3 end.
[7] B. Sot. 49a; y. ib. 23b.

more, the deceased scholars mentioned in M. Sot. IX, 15 are enumerated in reversed chronological order (with the exception of R. Judah the Patriarch, editor of the Mishnah, whose name was added after his death)[8], and Rabban Gamaliel is placed after R. Johanan ben Zakkai and before R. Ishmael ben Phabi, a High Priest appointed by Agrippa II.[9] It is, therefore, evident that the Rabban Gamaliel referred to must be the one who belonged to the generation preceding the destruction of the Temple in 70 C.E. Moreover, in the Yerushalmi text of the Mishnah (Sot. 23b), which differs considerably from the ordinary Mishnah editions, Rabban Gamaliel II is mentioned in addition to Rabban Gamaliel Hazaken, though it is likely that in this particular case some confusion has arisen between Rabban Gamaliel and Rabban Simeon ben Gamaliel, as is indicated by a comparison with M. Sot. IX, 15.

Even more decisive in favor of Ebner's identification is the fact that we are repeatedly informed that during Rabban Gamaliel II's Patriarchate, benches were used at his great academy at Jabneh.[10] The practice of standing or walking during halachic discussions must, therefore, go back to earlier times.

A more serious difficulty raised by this passage is the problem how it was ever possible to spend long hours of continuous study in a standing posture. To say the least, it must have been an extremely hard task, which could hardly have contributed to keeping the mind fresh and alert for the complicated discussions which were the essence of the study of the Oral Law. It is true that similar practices prevailed at the

---

[8] Cf. Obadiah of Bertinoro *ad loc*; Bacher, *Agada der Tannaiten* II, 222, n. 4.

[9] Cf. Josephus, *Ant.* XX, 8, 179.

[10] Cf. b. Ber. 28a: 'וכו הההוא יומא אתיסטו כמה ספסלי — On that day (when Rabban Gamaliel II was deposed) many benches were added, etc.; cf. y. Ber. IV, 1, 7d; y. Taan IV, 1, 67d: 'וכמה ספסלין היו שם וכו — And how many benches were there (vi t, at Rabban Gamaliel II's Academy)? etc.

Athenian schools of Plato and Aristotle.[11] Indeed, Aristotle's
famous school of "Peripatetics" was so called because students
would walk about while carrying on their discussions.[12]
Possibly, even in a place like "the vineyard of Jabneh"[13],
which may well have been a real vineyard,[14] the scholars who
met there walked about or stood in groups while discussing
the subtleties of the Oral Law.[15] It is also noteworthy that
long after this period there were scholars who preferred to
stand if they had something on which to lean rather than sit
on benches—or, for that matter, on the ground—with nothing
to lean on.[16] Even down to our own day, students of the
Talmud have often been in the habit of standing bent over a
lectern on which a tractate of the Talmud would be placed.

Yet, even when every allowance is made for all this, our
passage still presents some very real difficulties. In the first
place, there were often large numbers of scholars present
during halachic disputations which might continue for a
considerable period. During such major discussions it would
have been rather awkward, if not impossible, to walk about;
while prolonged standing would have been physically un-
endurable, especially for older scholars. Secondly, what illness
or weakness was it that suddenly brought about the end of an
old-established, time-honored practice, thus causing the
"glory" of the Torah to cease?

The answer to these questions is perhaps to be sought in
the extraordinary development of the educational system
during the last decades before the destruction of the Second

[11] Cf. Ebner, *Elementary Education in Ancient Israel*, p. 66.
[12] *Ib.*, p. 110, n. 16.
[13] כרם ביבנה , cf., *e.g.*, M. Ket. IV, 6; M. Eduy. II, 4; b.B.B. 131b;
y. Ber. IV, 1, 67d; y. Taan. IV, 1, 67d.
[14] Cf. Krauss in *Levy Festschrift*, pp. 22 ff.
[15] Cf. y. Ber., *ad loc.*; y. Taan., *ad loc.*: חוץ מן העומדין לאחרי הגדר—
Apart from those who were *standing* behind the fence (viz., at the
כרם ביבנה). This particular case, which falls after the time of Rabban
Gamaliel Hazaken, is, of course, inapplicable here.
[16] Cf. b. Ket. 111a-b: עמידה שאין בה סמיכה עמידה שיש בה סמיכה
נוחה הימנה.

Commonwealth. It was the time when Pharisaism, which was still a relatively restricted movement, developed into rabbinic Judaism with its wide popular appeal [17]; when the schools of Shammai and Hillel were at the height of their activities, shifting the main emphasis of their studies from the Written to the Oral Law; when Joshua ben Gamala made the first nation-wide attempt to establish a universal school-system for boys throughout the country.[18] In short, it was the time when education at all levels, which previously had depended on small-scale sporadic efforts, became centrally organised, with a view to the embracing within the educational network of all sections of the population. Such a transformation implied that some of the traditional methods of study had to be discontinued.

As long as the study of the Law was, for the most part, only a part-time occupation[19] for a restricted circle of enthusiastic seekers after knowledge; as long as the curriculum even in the higher institutes of learning centred in the main around the study and exposition of Scripture (which required the use of scrolls and accordingly presupposed a sitting posture during Biblical studies)[20]—it was possible to stand or walk about during the relatively brief halachic discussions. Indeed, the first major disputations on record—other than those between the Pharisees and Sadducees—emanated from the schools of Hillel and Shammai, and, according to the Talmudic tradition, even these would not have occured but for the fact that too many of the disciples of these schools had not adequately attended upon scholars (which would have enabled

[17] Cf. Rabin, *Qumran Studies*, pp. 60-61.

[18] B.B. 21a.

[19] Hillel and Shammai are themselves instructive examples of part-time scholars, cf. Yoma 35b; Shab. 31a (Shammai seems to have been a builder who, we are told, held a builder's cubit (אמת הבנין) in his hand even while he was being consulted by would-be proselytes).

[20] As there is no evidence of reading-desks or tables being available in schools or colleges (except, perhaps, for one reading-desk in a synagogue used for the public reading of the Law), the Scrolls could have been read only in a sitting position.

them to master the Law thoroughly), so that "the Torah became like two Laws"[21]. Evidently, this refers to the later period of these schools, roughly to the time following that of Rabban Gamaliel I when the Oral Law was no longer merely a useful supplement to Scriptural Studies, but became a major subject requiring intense concentration, often for many hours at a time. Study in general took up much more time than in the past, and fulltime students such as Rabbi Eliezer[22] and Rabbi Akiba[23] were becoming more frequent.

Thus, in depicting the contrast between the earlier and the later periods, we get approximately the following picture: in earlier times, say, up to the middle of the first century C.E., small groups of scholars and students would meet during their spare time and study scriptural texts while sitting on benches or on the floor. Having completed the reading of a given text, the scholars would rise from their seats and begin to discuss and expound the text in question, with a view to either Halachic or Aggadic interpretations.[24] These discussions conducted in small circles for relatively short periods at a time could quite comfortably be carried on in a standing posture or even while walking about, as we sometimes still do in the case of political discussions. Admittedly there must have been some exceptions to this rule, particularly where a man, following Jose ben Joezer's advice,[25] had made his home "a meeting place for the Wise".[26] In such cases, the scholars would presumably be seated on couches, chairs or benches, while the master of the house and members of his family

---

[21] Cf. Sot. 47b; Sanh. 88b: משרבו תלמידי שמאי והילל שלא שימשו כל צורכן, רבו מחלוקת בישראל ונעשית תורה. כשתי תורות.

[22] Cf. Ab.-R.N., Vers. I, ch. 6; Vers. II, ch. 13, ed. Schechter, 15b-16a.

[23] Cf. Ket. 62b-63a; Ned. 50a; y. Shab. VI, 1, 7d.

[24] The Tannaitic Midrashim such as Sifra, Sifri and Mekhiltha are instructive examples of this method of study.

[25] It may have been prompted by the religious persecution initiated by Antiochus IV in 168 B.C.E., which brought about the closing of the colleges, thus forcing scholars to meet in private homes; cf. Halevy, *Doroth Harishonim* I, 201.

[26] M. Ab. I, 4: יוסי בן יועזר אומר: יהי ביתך בית ועד לחכמים

would "sit amid the dust of their feet and drink in their words with thirst".[27] Generally, however, there is no reason to doubt the genuineness of the Talmudic tradition that in earlier times the study of the Law—i.e., the discussion and interpretation of Scriptural texts—was conducted in a standing (or walking) posture. It is most improbable that anybody would have invented this account, unless he meant to advocate a "return to the former" practice. Of that, however, there is not the slightest indication in our text, which is a purely factual account.

With the growth of the schools of Hillel and Shammai, and the development of highly involved and lengthy disputes on the Oral Law, the old methods of study were no longer practicable. Fulltime students could not spend the whole day standing during discussions, neither could major debates be carried on among large numbers of students while walking in the groves of the Academy or within the assembly halls. In this way, the practice of sitting during the study of the Oral as well as the Written Law became gradually established —indeed, so much so that Yeshiva (ישיבה)—literally, "sitting"—became synonymous with "college" or, generally, any institute of higher learning.[28]

It is unlikely that this process of change from standing to sitting was carried through with one stroke. It must have extended over a period of time until approximately the middle of the first century C.E.—i.e., the time of Rabban Gamaliel Hazaken's death[29],—when sitting during study became the

---

[27] The . והוי מתאבק בעפר רגליהם והוי שותה בצמא את דבריהם :.Ib whole passage clearly points to a private house to which scholars were invited with a view to acquiring some information from their conversation and discussions. This does not, however, provide us with any indication as to the prevailing practice in colleges and Houses of Study, which had not yet attained an advanced state of development.

[28] Cf. Ab. II, 7: מרבה ישיבה מרבה חכמה — The more schooling the more wisdom: cf. y. Ber. IV, 1, 7d; y. Taan. IV, 1, 67d: הלכו ומינו את ר׳אלעזר בן עזריה בישיבה — They appointed R. Eleazar ben Azariah (viz., President) in regular session; cf. Yoma 28b: זקן ויושב בישיבה — An elder sitting in the college council; cf. Ebner, ad loc., p. 110, n. 15.

[29] The change-over from a standing to a sitting position seems to

general practice. In later times, however, the real reason for
that change was no longer known. It was, therefore, naturally
assumed that it must have been due to reasons of health, and
since, following the disasters of 70 and 135 C.E., there was in
all cases a tendency to idealise the Temple times, to praise
the former generations and to magnify their spiritual and
physical capacities[30], it was taken for granted that the physical condition of scholars and students must have declined—
hence "a feebleness descended upon the world".

have begun already during Rabban Gamaliel Hazaken's lifetime,
cf. Acts XXII, 3.

[30] A considerable section of the Midrash Rabba on Lamentations
consists of variations on this theme; cf. also b. Shab. 112b; y. Dem.
I, 3, 21d; y. Shek. V, 1, 48c-d: אם ראשונים בני מלאכים, אנו בני אנשים,
ואם ראשונים בני אנשים, אנו כחמורים — If the earlier (scholars or generations) were sons of angels, we are sons of man; and if the earlies
(scholars or generations) were sons of men, we are like asses.

Section Five—

SCHOOLS AND ACADEMIES

THE JEWISH PRIMARY SCHOOL

Louis Ginzberg

The development of the intellect is the development of man, says Auguste Comte, one of the profoundest thinkers of modern times. He does not fail to recognize the momentous influence exerted by factors other than mind in the evolution of society, but he wished to emphasize this point, that whether a single nation is to be appraised or an epoch in the history of mankind as a whole, it is in every case intellectual attainment by which the degree of development must be gauged. In point of fact, it is, as Comte says, "the heart that propounds all questions; to solve them is the part of the intellect." An old Palestinian saying quoted in the Talmud[1] puts the same idea in empiric form: "He who has knowledge, has everything; he who lacks knowledge, lacks everything." And this proverb in turn is an epigrammatic summing up of the biblical notion of the Hakam, "the wise," "the knowing one," who is at the same time the good and pious man, the just. the God-fearing, the truthful, and the pure.

Because writers take too little account of this general historical principle set up by Comte and at the same time are blind to the peculiarity of Jewish history in particular, a misunderstanding has arisen regarding the nature of the transition from the Prophets to the Scribes, from biblical Judaism to rabbinical Judaism.

287

The intellectual endeavors of the Scribes are apt to be considered as a degeneration and decline from the idealism which pervades the conception of life laid down in the Scriptures. The truth is that the Scribes succeeded where the Prophets had failed. Through them the teachings proclaimed in the schools of the Prophets became the common property of the whole people.

The eradication of paganism, against which the prophets fought in vain, among the Jews, together with the immorality that accompanied it, is essentially the achievement of the first great Scribe, Ezra, and of his associates. And again, if three centuries after Ezra the defeat of degenerate Hellenism by the Maccabees was a possibility, it was only because the Scribes, by their constant devotion, had inspired a whole nation with the lofty ideals of the Torah and the Prophets.

In spite of the many vicissitudes to which the Jewish people has been subjected during nearly twenty centuries of dispersion, its intellectual development has suffered no interruption. Under the leadership of the Scribes, the masses of the people were ready to defend the prophetic ideals at every cost and hazard— the same people that had assumed an indifferent, if not a hostile, attitude toward the living words of the Prophets. It must be confessed that the victory of the intellect was not gained at a single blow. The 'Am ha-Arez² continued to be a common figure in Jewish life even at the time when the Talmudist stood at his zenith. Theoretically the 'Am ha-Arez submitted him-

288

self entirely to the teachings of the rabbis. But in the ordinary course of his life he was little influenced by them; sometimes he was even filled with deadly hatred for the exponents of Jewish learning. The deep veneration shown the scholar among the Jews of the Middle Ages and the extraordinary respect felt for the educated man were phenomena that co-existed and were bound up with a wider spread of knowledge among all classes and with a deepening of religious feeling throughout all the strata of the people. The last link in this long chain of Jewish intellectual development is the *Lamdan*[3] as the dominant figure in Jewish life, especially with the Ashkenazim, and among the Ashkenazim especially in Eastern Europe.

The historical process just described comes out well in the popular sayings of various epochs. To this day many a Jewish woman in Poland and Lithuania soothes her child with the lullaby[4]:

What is the best Sehorah?
My baby will learn Torah,
Seforim he will write for me,
And a pious Jew he'll always be.

In talmudic times words of an entirely different tenor were likely to fall upon the ear of a Jewish child. "O that I had a scholar in my power, how I'd bite him,"[5] were the words often uttered by the lower classes in the early days of the Rabbis. And if we go further back in history, to biblical times, we find the popular characterization of the spiritual leader expressed in such harsh words as "The prophet is a fool, the man that hath a spirit is mad." These extreme

289

epochs of Jewish development lie worlds apart. But even two adjoining periods, the modern and the mediaeval, display a striking contrast. It is a far cry from the time in which the Jewish scholar was a merchant or an artisan to the time in which the Jewish merchant or artisan was a scholar. In the Middle Ages there was no learned estate among the Jews, because the number of scholars was not large enough to constitute a separate class. In Poland and Lithuania later on, when they became the centers of Jewish culture, there was again no learned estate because the people itself was a nation of students. Every Jew was either a teacher or a pupil, or both at the same time. The Lamdan did not belong to a distinct class; he was the representative *par excellence* of the people as a whole.

The many centuries lying between the Prophet and the Lamdan are marked by two apparently incongruous phenomena. The suffering of the Jews was indescribable, yet their intellectual development proceeded apace without interruption. They are the enigma of history, contradicting by their existence the principle *mens sana in corpore sano*, true of nations as well as individuals. Their enslavement by the Persians, the tyrannous oppression of the Greek rulers, the cruelty of the Romans and, finally, the persecutions set afoot by Holy Mother Church, who was so concerned about the salvation of the soul of the Jew that she was ever ready to purchase it with his body—such conditions make one exclaim in wonderment, not at the survival of the Jew, but at his survival unstunted.

290

Our sages clothed the solution of the riddle in the form peculiar to them. Once upon a time, they say, the heathen philosopher, Oenomaos of Gadara, was asked, "How can we make away with this people?" His answer was: "Go about and observe their schools and academies. So long as the clear voices of children ring forth from them, you will not be able to touch a hair of their head. For thus have the Jews been promised by the father of their race: 'The voice is the voice of Jacob, but the hands are the hands of Esau.' While the voice of Jacob resounds in the schools and the academies, the hands of Esau have no power over him."[6]

We have here more than a suggestive interpretation of a Bible text. It is a subtle comment on an historic fact. The school is the most original institution created by post-biblical Judaism—a magnificent institution, a veritable fortress unshaken by the storms of the ages. To borrow a simile from the Midrash, the school was the heart that kept watch while the other organs slept. Ideals pass into great historical forces by embodying themselves into institutions, and the Jewish ideal of knowledge became a great historical force by embodying itself in the Jewish school.

Like the beginning of all genuine life, the beginning of the Jewish school is lost in the mist of ancient days. There can be no doubt, however, that the higher school for adults, the Bet ha-Midrash, or house of study, is of earlier origin than the Bet ha-Sefer, the elementary school. The Bet ha-Midrash was the sphere in which the *Soferim*, the Scribes, displayed their activity. They were the guardians of literature and culture, who made the *Midrash*, the interpretation of the Scripture, their special care and object, and hence their name, Soferim, "Men of the Book." For it must be borne in mind that the trend of the times was toward religion. Literary interest was determined by the sacred traditions. To the Soferim, however, was entrusted not only the higher education of young and old, but also the dispensation of justice and the leadership of the community—in short, the guidance of the entire spiritual and intellectual life of the people. Nothing perhaps better illustrates the position of the Scribe than the following lines of Ben Sira, who lived at the time when the Soferim had reached their zenith. Ben Sira's description of the Scribes reads:[7]

Not so he that applieth himself to the fear of God,
   And to set his mind upon the Law of the Most High;
Who searcheth out the wisdom of all the ancients,
   And is occupied with the prophets of old;
Who heedeth the discourses of men of renown,
   And entereth into the deep things of parables;
Searcheth out the hidden meaning of proverbs,
   And is conversant with the dark sayings of parables;
Who serveth among great men,
   And appeareth before princes;
Who travelleth through the lands of the peoples,
   Testeth good and evil among men;
Who is careful to seek unto his Maker,
   And before the Most High entreateth mercy;
Who openeth his mouth in prayer,
   And maketh supplication for his sins.
If it seem good to God Most High,
   He shall be filled with the spirit of understanding.

He himself poureth forth wise sayings in double measure,
  And giveth thanks unto the Lord in prayer.
He himself directeth counsel and knowledge,
  And setteth his mind on their secrets.
He himself declareth wise instruction,
  And glorieth in the law of the Lord.
His understanding many do praise,
  And never shall his name be blotted out:
His memory shall not cease,
  And his name shall live from generation to generation.
His wisdom doth the congregation tell forth,
  And his praise the assembly publisheth.
If he live long, he shall be accounted happy more than a thousand;
  And when he cometh to an end, his name sufficeth.

The wisdom of the Scribe is culture, and Jewish culture is primarily religious. The Scribe was not a hermit; "He serveth among great men and appeareth before princes," yet his "Mind was set upon the Law of the Most High." Though the exponent of culture, he "Openeth his mouth in prayer and maketh supplication for his sins."

By the side of the Soferim were the *Hakamim*, "the sages," in their *Yeshibot*, their conventicles. Their knowledge was based on experience and practical observation. It was secular rather than religious. The distinction between the two classes soon disappeared as they were merged into one, that of the scholars, who were now called the Hakamim. That happened when the study of the Torah was enlarged to include every department of human intellectual endeavor. By the time of the Hasmoneans, Hakamim had become the accepted designation of the masters in the knowledge of the Torah, the legitimate leaders of the people.[8]

It was characteristic of the time of the Men of the Great Assembly, a favored name for the leaders of the early Soferim in rabbinic sources, that they urged the duty of "raising up many disciples." Once this idea of higher education had taken root and the system of higher schools had spread as a network over the whole country, the next step could be taken, namely the consideration of the problem of elementary instruction. A well-authenticated talmudic tradition has this to say upon the subject: "In the ancient days every father taught his own son. The fatherless boy (and, it should be added, the child of an ignorant father) was given no instruction. Later, schools were erected in Jerusalem, where the boys were sent from all over the country. But these were inadequate. The fatherless were still left without teaching. Thereupon schools were opened in the largest town of every district, to which youths of sixteen or seventeen, who could do without the care of their parents, were sent. But it was soon apparent that school discipline had no effect upon young men who had come in as adolescents. Then, finally, schools were instituted in every city and town for children of six or seven."[9]

The large, bold strokes in this outline sketch of the history of Jewish education mark out the progress made during a period of two centuries, roughly speaking, from the time of the Soferim (about three hundred before the common era) to the time of the Pharisees (about one hundred before the common era). It is a highly significant fact that the man who deserves the title "Father of the Jewish School," was a great leader of the Pharisee party, Simeon ben Shatah (about seventy A. C. E.). Of the results achieved by the work inaugurated by Simeon, we can gain a good idea from Josephus, who proudly points them out to the Greeks one hundred and fifty years later. "Our principal care of all is this," he says, "to educate our children well," . . . "and if anybody do but ask any one of them (the Jews) about our laws, he will more readily tell them all than he will tell his own name, and this is in consequence of our having learned them immediately, as soon as ever we become sensible of any thing, and of our having them, as it were, engraven on our souls."[10]

It cannot be denied that the ratio of rhetoric to truth in Josephus' writings is sometimes very high. Yet, after his statements are stripped of exaggerations, there still remains a residuum of facts sufficient to certify to the important place assigned to elementary education in his day. However, we must not fail to take into account that Josephus was conversant chiefly with conditions as they existed among the dwellers in cities. The country folk, constituting perhaps the majority of the Jewish people at that time, were still debarred from the blessings of education.

The catastrophes that overwhelmed the Jewish nation in the year seventy and in the year one hundred and thirty-three, and reduced flourishing cities and populous villages to ruins, gave a set-back to the cause of primary education. Accordingly, in the third century of the common era, the leading intellects among the Jews were constrained to devote their attention to the rehabilitation of elementary schools and teaching.[11]

Political and economic conditions went on growing worse for the Jews in Palestine. In spite of all the efforts put forth to promote and develop educational work, the Holy Land ceased to be the spiritual center of Judaism. It was replaced by Babylonia. There the work had to be started anew, for the Jews of the Persian empire occupied a very low intellectual plane, and generations passed by until the Palestinian spirit began to take root and flourish on the banks of the Euphrates.[12] And yet, comparatively speaking, it cannot be said that a long time elapsed before a Jewish culture had established itself in Babylonia. The political and economic conditions of the Jews living there in the third century were very favorable. Under the Sassanids they formed an all but autonomous body. Influenced by great intellectual leaders, the exilarchs and the communal authorities fairly vied with each other in fostering and promoting Jewish studies and culture. Scholars were exempt from the poll tax, from communal tributes and similar imposts. They were permitted to settle wheresoever they would, a great advantage to them if they engaged in business or trades, which as a rule were subjected to restrictions protecting residents against a much-feared competition.[13] Education and knowledge in the course of time became actual marketable possessions, instead of being, as at first, ideal acquisitions—the best standard by which to measure the degree of idealism prevailing in a nation. Where education and intellectual attainments are considered a material asset, idealism must be the attribute of large classes of the people. The natural features of the Babylonian country were another propitious factor. The earth there yielded its products without demanding more than a minimum of human labor. The poorest were in a position to devote several hours of daily leisure to study, and without a great sacrificè they could forego the assistance of their minor children, who thus were permitted to enjoy a schooling of many years' duration.[14]

The wide spread of culture among the Babylonian Jews appears strikingly in the definition of the 'Am ha-Arez found in the Babylonian Talmud. They applied the harsh term to one who, though he had mastered the Bible and the Mishnah, had not penetrated more profoundly into Jewish lore. Contrast this with what the Palestinians called an ignoramus, and the vast progress made in two centuries, more or less, will be apparent. To the Palestinian, the man who could not recite the *Shema'* was an ignoramus; one who knew the Bible, let alone the Mishnah, was if not a scholar, surely an educated man.[15]

In spite of the important place occupied by the school in the intellectual life of Babylonian Jewry, the material dealing with educational work and facilities preserved in the Talmud is so sparse that there is little hope of our ever being able to reconstruct the educational edifice of the time with any degree of completeness. But there is more than enough to warrant the general impression that the school went on increasing in influence under the Babylonian Jews, and the later development of the Jewish educational system in all

297

the lands of the Dispersion is directly traceable to
these vigorous Babylonian beginnings.

Unfortunately, the talmudic time is not the only
period in Jewish educational history of which we are
ignorant. We are in no better position to attempt a
presentation of educational conditions among the Jews
in a time much nearer our own, namely the Middle
Ages which, to quote Zunz, extended for the Jews to
very recent times. At most we might venture to deal
with the higher institutions of learning. For the
primary schools our information is too meager by far.
Our reports do not become full and detailed enough to
justify an attempt at description until we reach the
elementary school of the so-called Polish Jews, the
word Polish being here used as a generic term for
Slavic countries and Lithuania. We must, therefore,
limit ourselves to an attempt at gaining some glimpses
of the intellectual and spiritual life nursed and developed in the elementary schools of the Polish Jews.

Jews had been living in Poland for centuries before
anything was heard of them, certainly before anything
was heard about their intellectual life.[16] The persecutions of the Jews in Germany that extended in unbroken sequence from the First Crusade to the Age of
the Reformation cast large numbers of them into
Poland, whither they carried their talmudic learning
and piety; for it must not be forgotten that there was
a time when the Jews of Germany excelled all others in
strength of faith and rigorous observance of the Torah.
In these times of the almost superhuman suffering of the
German Jew, we meet with his long-enduring march to

the East of Europe, especially to Poland, the country which, according to a well-known Latin saying[17], is "the heaven of the nobleman, the purgatory of the citizen, the hell of the peasant, and the paradise of the Jew"—such a paradise as the Christian love of those days was likely to concede to him. We may be sure that the narrow-minded town guilds and the fanatical clergy took care not to rob the Jew of his hope of a real Paradise. The economic conditions were far from brilliant even in the sixteenth century, when Polish Jewish prosperity was at its height. In the middle of that century, Rabbi Moses Isserles wrote to a friend in Germany: "Thou hadst been better off in Poland, if only on dry bread, but that at least without anxiety of mind[18]." Of rich Jews, like Simeon Günzburg[19] in Germany, for instance, there were none in Poland. But that is not altogether regrettable. The salvation of the Jews was never wrought by the rich among them. What gave Poland its pre-eminence was the circumstance that it offered means of subsistence, however wretched, to the middle class, by permitting the Jews to enter many branches of business, while in the rest of Europe they were confined to petty trading and money-lending.

Such economic conditions sufficed to give an impetus toward a new Jewish culture, and with an external impulse superadded it resulted in an irresistible movement. The outer force that came to aid the inner was the invention of printing, which made knowledge a common possession of the people. The first notable Jewish scholar in Poland of whom we hear, lived and

worked at the end of the fifteenth century[20]. Scarcely
a generation after the pioneers, the Jews of Poland had
leapt into the forefront of Jewish learning, a sovereign
position from which they have not yet been dislodged.
The significant fact is that the publication of the first
editions of the two Talmudim and of other classical
works of Jewish literature fell in the interval that
elapsed between the time when Poland had but one
scholar of eminence, Rabbi Jacob Pollak, and the time
when it produced Rabbi Solomon Loria, the most
eminent Talmudist of his day[21].

Hand in hand with the development of the higher
education went the education of the Jewish child,
which began at home before he was sent to school,
quite in agreement with the principle of one of the
greatest educators of modern times, who holds that
education is the concern of the family; from the family
it proceeds, and to the family for the most part it
returns. Of Jewish pedagogy the characteristic feature
was that the three chief ends of education were sub-
served as a unity at one and the same time.) The
earliest instruction kept in view at once the intellectual,
the moral, and the religious training of the child. As
soon as he was able to speak, he was taught Hebrew
words and sentences, bringing into play his memory
and his perceptive faculties, and the sentences were
always of religious bearing. They were mainly *Berakot*,
blessings, especially those that form part of the morning and evening prayers and of the grace after meals.
"Blessed be the All-Merciful, the Lord of bread,
blessed be He, who giveth food to all beings," is to-day,

300

as it was four hundred years ago, the form of grace used by the Jewish children in Poland.[22] The morning devotion consisted of two biblical verses: "Hear, O Israel, the Lord is our God, the Lord is One," and "Moses commanded us the Torah as the inheritance of the congregation of Jacob", to which the rhymed couplet was added: "To the Torah I shall ever faithful be; For this may God Almighty grant His help to me." As the child rose from bed with the Shema' upon his lips, so he went to bed proclaiming his belief in the One God. To the recital of the Shema' before retiring was added the following verse from Psalm thirty-one: "Into Thine hand I commend my spirit; Thou hast redeemed me, O Lord, Thou God of Truth."

A child of three or four years cannot be expected to understand the import of prayers, even when couched in the vernacular. Religious feeling comes into play much later in life. It was an advantage from this point of view that the prayers were put into Hebrew, a language removed from daily concerns. In this somewhat strange guise they appeal to the intellect of the child as well as to his fancy. The alien garb makes them sink into the child's mind as a concrete, almost tangible entity, a vessel to be retained until the proper content comes to hand to be poured into it. The language of familiar intercourse is too fluid to fulfil this pedagogic purpose. For the same reason Hebrew was used for the civil speeches of polite society first impressed upon a child. *Berukim ha-Yoshebim*, "Blessed be ye who are present here," was the greeting extended by a child entering a room in which the company was seated at the table, and on leaving he was expected to say, *Bireshutekem*, "with your permission."[23]

The ceremonials of the Jewish religion early caught the fancy of the impressionable child, and kept him fascinated. Having outgrown his baby clothes, the little fellow was given the "prayer-square," the *Arba'-Kanfot*, as part of his first boy's suit. With two such tangible reminders he was in no danger of forgetting his double dignity as a lord of creation and a son of the chosen people. "Shaking" the Lulab on Sukkot, waving little flags on Simhat Torah, filching the *Afikomen* from the Seder table, and, last but not least, the consumption of delicate butter cookies on Shebuot— these and many others of the lighter ceremonial acts and customs prepared the child admirably for the more serious instruction in the *Heder*, which was begun when he was five years old.

The Heder! In the face of the misunderstandings with which friend and foe alike have treated it in modern times, it is difficult to speak calmly of this, one of the greatest institutions of post-biblical Judaism. Surely a defense is out of place when applied to a system still in use now, though its beginnings are lost in the obscurity of the days when Rome was a tiny Italian republic and Alexandria not yet founded. It is also obvious that a creation of the epoch of the Scribes in Palestine could not persist unchanged in Spain in the heyday of Greek-Arabic culture, and to expect the New York of the twentieth century to accept without change the Lublin Heder of the sixteenth would be as irrational as to judge the Polish Heder at its best by the form and constitution it has adopted in our day. It is one thing to judge a system or institution in its corruption and quite another thing to measure the worth and true design of its first founders. All educational institutions must die which do not directly and conspicuously promote either the spiritual or material interests of men. Without an inspiring idea and aim, an institution is dying, if not dead, though to the eye of sense it may seem still to live. Evolution is not the only factor that enters into an estimate of historical development. Degeneration is an equally important aspect, especially with a people like the Jews, whose fortunes have often been forced into unnatural channels by the violent hands of an unsympathetic world. All human works are exposed to vicissitude and decay, and the Heder in the lapse of more than two thousand years has furnished many an instance of that general law.

The Heder in Poland at the period in which Jewish culture was at its height was neither a public nor a private school. It was an institution supervised by the communal authorities, but managed in detail by private individuals. The choice of the teacher lay with the parents, and the teacher was at liberty to accept and reject pupils as he saw fit, but the community reserved the right to pass upon the number of pupils, the curriculum, the schedule, and other particulars regarding the plan of instruction. The school regulations in force in the Jewish community of Cracow in 1551, the oldest of their kind known, contain various points of

interest²⁴. A teacher of elementary pupils was not
permitted to have more than forty children in his class,
and a teacher of Talmud not more than twenty, and
for these numbers each of them was required to employ
two assistants.

A generation later, the same community adopted
rules fixing the salary of the teachers, because, it is
said, "their demands are so exorbitant that many are
not able to satisfy them²⁵." To understand this, it
must be borne in mind that though the community
maintained a free school, the Talmud Torah, parents
availed themselves of it only in extreme cases of
poverty. "Though you have to secure the means by
begging, be sure to provide for the instruction of your
sons and daughters in the Torah," is a dying father's
admonition to his children in his last will and testament dated 1357²⁶. The poorest of the poor sent their
children to the free Talmud Torah; the average poor
denied themselves food and raiment and paid for the
schooling of their boys and girls. This explains why
communal ordinances as well as decisions by eminent
rabbis concern themselves with the times when tuition
fees fell due. Rabbi Solomon Loria decides that half
the stipulated remuneration must be paid the teacher
in advance, to enable him to maintain his establishment decently²⁷. In spite of the authority of Loria, his
view does not seem to have prevailed, for the teachers,
it appears, were paid at the end of the month²⁸. By
this arrangement the New Moon Day was a holiday,
not only for the pupils, who were not required to
return to the Heder for the afternoon session, but also

304

for the teachers who, in addition to their salaries, would sometimes receive "Rosh Hodesh money," a small free-will offering, from their patrons.²⁹ To prevent sordid competition among teachers, which might have left some of them without school and pupils at the end of a month, it was strictly prohibited to change teachers during the term, and teachers, on the other hand, were not permitted to go about seeking patronage between terms. Parents were expected to decide upon their future action regarding the placing of their children uninfluenced by those financially interested in their decision.³⁰

The child's first day at Heder may be said to have been the most impressive one in his life, and the ceremonies introducing the boy to school are very significant of the Jewish attitude toward education in general and religious education in particular.

On Pentecost, the feast commemorative of the giving of the Torah on Sinai, the boy of five began his career at school. Neatly attired, he was put in the care of a member of the community distinguished for piety and scholarship, with whom he went to the synagogue at break of day. There he was met by the teacher, who took him in his charge and began to instruct him. He was handed a slate on which the Hebrew alphabet was written forward and backward, and, besides, the following three verses: "The law commanded us by Moses is the inheritance of the Congregation of Jacob", "And the Lord called unto Moses, and spake unto him out of the tent of meeting, saying," and "May the Torah be my daily calling, and God Almighty my helper," the last from the prayers for children. The first lesson consisted in making the pupil repeat the names of the letters after the teacher. The slate was smeared with honey, which the child licked from the letters, to taste the sweetness of the Torah, as it were. Then the boy was given a cake baked by the innocent hands of a virgin, on which several verses from the Prophets and Psalms were traced: "And He said unto me, Son of man, cause thy belly to eat, and fill thy bowels with this roll that I give thee. Then did I eat it; and it was in my mouth as honey for sweetness;" "The Lord God hath given me the tongue of them that are taught, that I should know how to sustain with words him that is weary; He wakeneth morning by morning, He wakeneth mine ear to hear as they that are taught. The Lord God hath opened mine ear, and I was not rebellious, neither turned away backward." Moreover the cake bore eight verses from Psalm one hundred and nineteen, all of them proclaiming the praise of the Torah. The following verses were inscribed on an egg: "From all my teachers have I learned wisdom" and "How sweet are Thy words unto my taste! Yea, sweeter than honey to my mouth!" All these verses on the cake and on the egg the teacher read and the young neophyte pronounced them after him, and at the end of the lesson the boy was given the cake and the egg, and apples and other fruit besides. Then he was taken on a walk along the banks of a stream, because the Torah is likened unto water: "As water rests not in elevated places, but flows downward and gathers in the lowlands, so the Torah resides only with the humble and modest, not with the proud and presumptuous."

The final ceremonies took place in the house of the parents of the boy. In his honor they prepared a banquet, at which he was greeted by the assembled guests with the words: "May God enlighten thine eyes with His Torah[31]."

Peculiar as these customs may seem, they reveal clearly what the ideals were that filled the mind of the father at the moment of devoting his son to the service of the Lord. It was not the yoke of the law that he sought to impose upon the lad. He endeavored to inspire him with the conviction that the Law of God is lovely, so that when he attained to discretion, he would keep it and observe it with all his heart. Primary instruction was therefore arranged with a view to giving the child a knowledge of the Hebrew text of the Bible and of the prayers, together with their translation into the vernacular. The Bible itself was put into the hands of the Jewish child, and it was the Bible that shaped and moulded his heart and mind.

Hebrew reading was the earliest subject in the course of study in the Heder. The alphabet was put on large charts, first in the usual order, from Alef to Taw, and again in the reverse order, from Taw to Alef; then with vowels and again without vowels. The charts contained also a few Bible verses. To enliven the drudgery of alphabet learning, the children were taught not merely the names of the letters, but also the meaning of the names, of their form, and their position, a method not unlike that of the modern picture book. This practical way of teaching appealed both to the fancy and the intellect. Alef-Bet—the child was told—means, "learn wisdom" (the Hebrew for learn is *Alef* and Bet reminds one of *Binah* "wisdom"); Gimel-Dalet, "be kind" (*Gomel* in Hebrew to be kind) "to the poor" (*Dal*). In a similar manner the forms of the letters were made to live in the fancy of the child. The foot of the Gimel, he was taught, is turned in the direction of the following letter, Dalet, to remind us that one should be kind-hearted and look for the needy to render them assistance. The Tet has its head hidden—turned inside—and a crown thereon so that we may know that the charitable hand must not be seen if we aspire to receive the crown of glory from God for our kind actions. The Shin has three branches but no root to indicate that falsehood—in Hebrew *Sheker*, the initial letter of which is Shin—never takes root. One leg of the Taw is broken to teach us that he who desires to devote himself to the study of the Torah—which word begins with a Taw—must be ready to have his feet bruised by his wanderings to the houses of study. And finally, as the leg of this letter is bent, so must the student of the Torah bend his pride[32]. Other explanations of the alphabet aim to make the child remember the sounds. "Tell the child," says an author of the sixteenth century[33], "that the Bet has its mouth open, and the Pe—mouth in Hebrew—has its mouth closed." The pedagogue thus conveyed to the learner not only the difference in the appearance of these two letters, but also the difference in the position of the lips in pronouncing them, and to this day the Kamez, the long a, is described in the Heder as the Patah with a beard.

The next step was to the prayer-book, which became the text-book for reading as soon as the boy was able to put letters together into words As it was a cherished purpose to have the child say the prayers by himself as soon as possible, no attention was paid to their meaning, until he could read them fluently, on the principle that a child was first to be religiously active, and religious thinking would follow as his intelligence developed with years. Moreover, the prayers not being composed in the classical Hebrew, it was thought advisable to defer effective instruction in the Hebrew language until the study of the Bible could be begun. The third Book of Moses was chosen as the first subject of instruction in the Bible—the principle here being, the law of Israel before the history of Israel.[34] After a part of Leviticus had been taken, the instructor devoted himself to teaching as much of each week's Pentateuch portion as the pupil's time and capacity permitted. The disadvantage of this practice was that the beginner, unable to manage the whole portion, acquired the Pentateuch in fragments. On the other hand, it must be remembered that to teach Hebrew grammar was at this stage as little the intention as to convey the historical content of the Scriptures or their theological interpretation. The aim for the moment was to enable the learner to acquire an extensive Hebrew vocabulary. With only this in view, it was not long before a boy of even average ability could easily be made to go through the week's portion in season.

A clear notion of the methods of Bible instruction in vogue in the sixteenth and seventeenth centuries may be gained from two works entitled, *Baër* (or *Beër*) *Mosheh*, and *Lekah Tob*, composed by Rabbi Moses Saertels, and printed at Prague in 1604–5. The author himself tells us that it was his purpose to perpetuate in print the traditional translation and explanation of the Bible. This being the case, it does not astonish us to find the regulations of the Jewish community of Cracow[35] making it obligatory upon teachers to use Rabbi Moses Saertels' books. From a comparison with the Bible Commentary by Rashi it appears that they depend upon it throughout. Virtually they are an introduction to Rashi, whose Commentary was the text-book given to the pupil after he had mastered a part of the Bible.

Another subject in the primary classes of the Heder was writing, both the square characters and the script, the latter, the so-called Juedisch-Deutsch, being used in correspondence. If we mention, besides, arithmetic from addition to division, and the outlines of Hebrew etymology, we have exhausted the curriculum of the primary Heder or, as the Jewish expression goes, the work of the *Melamed Dardake*, the primary teacher.

At the age of about ten the boy passed from the primary Heder to its higher division, the Talmud Heder, in which all subjects of study gave way to the Talmud, and henceforth he devoted himself to it exclusively. The Melamed Dardake surrendered him to the Talmud teacher, and in his charge he remained until he was able to enter the *Yeshibah*, the talmudic high school.

Different as the course of studies and the method of teaching were in the Heder from those in the modern school, the two institutions depart still further from each other in the life their respective pupils led and still lead. Life in the Heder was arranged with more than due regard for individuality. Not only was the Heder, as we have seen, a private institution in which the parents were given the opportunity of choosing the teacher with a view to their children's needs and gifts, but the teaching also was personal in character. Restricted as the number of pupils was, they were nevertheless divided into *Kitot*, sections.[36] The teacher usually occupied himself with no more than four children at a time. In this way a close personal relation could grow up between master and pupil. It was practically impossible to deceive a teacher by palming off work on him done by others at home. Instruction, especially in the Talmud, was discursive, and the cadence or, better, the sing-song, of a talmudic sentence sufficed to indicate whether or not the little Talmudist understood it. The result was that in many cases the teacher came to take a vital personal interest in the pupils. With pleasure and pride he would observe the progress of his boys, and no greater joy could come to him than to be caught napping by one of them who urged a difficult objection to some talmudic statement, which the teacher was not prepared to answer on the spot. As the whole system purposed the training of the intellect, a "good scholar" in the Heder meant only a mentally

well-endowed pupil. Qualities other than intellectual
did not count. "A mischievous boy has a good head"
is the Jewish way of saying that a bright boy is privileged to indulge in pranks in the Heder.

As a rule the teachers were mild enough in meting
out punishment. Some of their gentleness may perhaps
be set to the account of self-interest. They may have
feared to lose paying pupils through over-great severity.
One of the teachers describes the dilemma in which he
and his confreres were often placed, in the following
graphic words: "When a teacher flogs one of his
pupils, he bursts into tears, goes home to his father,
and complains tearfully. The father gets angry, and
the boy is encouraged to complain to his mother, too.
She, in her affection for her son, incites the father
against the teacher, who, she says, has come within an
ace of killing the boy, and she calls him a fool. Naturally, the father is wrought up against the teacher, and
seeks to engage him in a quarrel, etc., etc.[37]"

The Melamed (teacher) was certainly more humane
and gentle than most of the masters of the English
schools, who till very recently ruled as tyrants. We
may be quite sure that he was not the brute pictured
by the morbid imagination of certain *Maskilim*, whose
animus against the Heder is probably to be sought in a
hatred of the deeply Jewish atmosphere that prevailed
there, and that too in spite of the lack of explicit
religious instruction in the modern sense. The Heder
would have refused to tolerate long-winded definitions
of the being and existence of God, and the little Talmud pupil would not have suppressed his whence and

his what, his *Minna hanne Mille* and his *May ka mashma lan*. The Jewish martyrs and saints were not raised in the hot-house atmosphere of religion spread by the catechism, and it is hardly an accident that the desire for religious text-books did not manifest itself until Judaism was being forced into the four walls of the synagogue. Previous to that time Jewish literature, rich as it was, had no such book to show except a single one composed at the end of the sixteenth century, which is modelled after the catechism used by the Catholic clergy. The author of this book was said to have become a convert to Christianity, which is not true, but it seems as if he laid himself open to such accusations by writing a catechism.[38] The Jewish religion is not a religious arithmetic. It does not permit the idea to usurp the place of the spirit. From the first the Jew has felt that reality is not abstract but individual. Religion to be a vital influence must be lived, not taught, and this condition was fulfilled in the Heder. The whole life there was religiously Jewish, for though the Jewish school aimed first and foremost to cultivate the mind, the other point of view was never lost sight of, that "the fear of God is the beginning of wisdom." The teachings of the Prophets and the lives of the sages were not abstractions to the Heder boys, but flesh and bone realities. Rabbi Akiba's persistence, through which the water carrier became the most celebrated scholar of his day, his devotion to his wife Rachel, and his martyr's death, were not mere incidents in the biography of a hero dead fifteen hundred years. They formed the history of an old and tried

friend whose acts and opinions left an indelible impression upon the child's mind. The Melamed, on the
other hand, was not a critical historian. He did not
differentiate history from fable. The gnat that was
said to have gnawed the brain of Titus was as historical
to him as the destruction of the Temple by the same
Titus. And yet he did more for the preservation of
Jewish nationalism than all the well-turned phrases of
modern orators when, on the day preceding Tish'ah
be-Ab, in a voice choked with tears, he read to his
pupils the *Hurban*, the talmudic narrative recounting the details of the catastrophe that overtook Israel
in the year seventy and again in one hundred and
thirty-three.

As history was disregarded in the Heder, so ethics as
such did not appear in the curriculum. There was no
need to give moral instruction directly. The study of
the Talmud and of rabbinical literature took the place
of the best conceivable manual of ethics. It compelled
the student to think profoundly and assimilate actively
what suited the needs of his nature in the ample
wealth of moral teachings scattered throughout this
literature. The pupil was not called upon to compose
his face solemnly while moral exhortations were poured
down upon his devoted head. In the regular course of
studies the Talmud offered him ethical observations of
fundamental importance, while ostensibly propound-
ing an intricate judicial question which requires fine
dialectical reasoning. The transition from the legal
element to the ethical in the discussion of the Talmud
is almost imperceptible; sometimes the inter-relation

314

between them is so close that the dividing line cannot be discerned. Accordingly, the intellectual interest of the student was not interrupted. "Let thy yea be yea, and thy nay, nay," for instance, is the last link in a long chain of complicated discussions on the legal character of a deposit[39], and the conclusion meant nothing to the student who had not followed the devious reasoning understandingly and constructively.

Nor was the imagination of the child left to starve. How could it, with the numberless stories the Talmud contains about the life and deeds of the great in Israel! Take, for example, the very sentence just quoted: "Let thy yea be yea, and thy nay, nay." As an illustration of it, we are told concerning Rabbi Safra that he was negotiating a sale. The would-be purchaser happened to approach Rabbi Safra and spoke to him about the transaction at the moment when the rabbi was engaged in reciting the Shema'. Not noticing that the rabbi was praying, he made him an offer. Rabbi Safra naturally would not interrupt his prayer. With a gesture he tried to convey to the purchaser that he did not wish to be disturbed. Misunderstanding the import of the gesture, he offered a higher price. At the end of his devotions Rabbi Safra accepted the first price. He would not profit by the other's mistake, for he had silently given his assent to the lower offer.[40]

Again, could there be a more impressive way of teaching children the Jewish view of the treatment of animals than through the suffering of the Patriarch Rabbi Judah, the compiler of the Mishnah? A calf, the Talmud tells us, about to be led to the shambles, took

315

refuge with Rabbi Judah, and hid its head in his mantle, entreating help. "Go," said Rabbi Judah, "for this thou wast created." Thereupon it was said in heaven: "Because he showed no mercy, no mercy shall be shown to him," and suffering was decreed for him. One day his maid-servant wanted to pluck out a nest of young weasels which she found in his house and cast them out to perish. "Leave them in peace," said Rabbi Judah, "it is said of God, 'His tender mercies are over all His works'." Then it was said in heaven: "Because he showed mercy, mercy shall be shown to him," and his pain ceased forthwith.[41] To develop the feeling for which Jewish tenderness more than fifteen hundred years ago coined the significant expression, *Za'ar Ba'ale Hayyim*, this naive story was more effective than many a preachment on our duty to the brute creation. The Heder boy, whose sole aim was to search out and know the teachings of the ancients, derived his ideals from those whose lives interested him in the measure in which he entered into their ideals.

The Heder life must not be thought of as a life of serious tasks only. The boys had more opportunity to play tricks there than in a modern school. Games and youthful merriment were quite compatible with the big Talmud folios. The Heder decidedly had its gay side. On the whole, its life may be said to have been less rule-bound than life in a modern school. To begin with, the chief spur to study was the expectation of reward rather than the fear of punishment. Following in the footsteps of old Jewish authorities of high standing, a popular book of the beginning of the seventeenth century has this to say of the bringing up of children: "One should always teach a child in pleasant ways. First give him fruit, or sugar, or honey cake, and later small coins. Then he should be promised clothes as a present, always making the reward appropriate to his intelligence and his years. Then tell him, if he will study diligently he may expect a large dowry when he marries; and later he should be told that if he will study diligently he will be ordained and will officiate as a rabbi. He must be urged on until the boy himself realizes that he must study because it is the will of God.[42]" The directions to teachers are of similar tenor, and it was the general habit of teachers to attract the children by kindness. To this very day it is the custom, as it was hundreds of years ago, for the teacher to throw sweets or a few coins on the alphabet chart when the child has his first lesson at school, saying at the same time: "An angel has thrown this down for you because you are so good[43]." In some congregations the teachers used to prepare a treat for the children on Hamishah 'Asar be-Shebat, and on Lag ba-'Omer, when no school sessions were held.

The teacher had neither time nor disposition to play games with the children. His place was taken by his assistant, the "Behelfer," who called for the children at their homes and took them back after school hours, and one of whose duties it was to provide for the entertainment and recreation of his charges. The Behelfer was the one who carved the wooden swords for Tish'ah be-Ab and manufactured the flags for Simhat Torah. If the boys were well-behaved, he allowed them to be present while he made his preparations for the Purim play, in which he took the part of Mordecai or Haman or even, at a pinch, of Esther. The big boys, who had outgrown the services of the Behelfer, did not scorn to buy his good-will, sometimes with hard cash. In the first place, it was important to be in his good graces, else he might betray their pranks to the teacher. Besides, his active help could not always be dispensed with. In summer he was the swimming master, and in winter he taught the boys how to skate, the two most delightful forms of amusement known to Heder boys. But even such neutral and secular interests lying at the periphery of Heder life did not escape its genuinely Jewish atmosphere. The boys did not hesitate to call a certain figure on the ice the "*Wa-Yomer David* run," because it was executed in the same position as is adopted in the saying of the prayer in question, with the head resting on the arm. In addition to all these accomplishments, the Behelfer was an adept in making the Drehdel[44], and this game, known to the Greeks, Romans and Germans, was also given a Jewish aspect. It was played only on Hanukkah, but then most vigorously. The sections of the class not actively engaged with the teacher played it in the intervals between lessons during the Hanukkah days, behind the teacher's back, of course. Its connection with Hanukkah was established by interpreting the letters on its four sides as the initial letters of the sentence, *Nes gadol hayah sham,* "A great miracle was done there."

And, in fact, a great miracle *was* done there! The

wonderful salvation of Israel was wrought *there*, in the Heder! Goethe advises us "always to oppose the great masses produced by the historical process of the ages to the perversities of the fleeting hour as they arise." According to this, the perversities that result when individual observations are over-emphasized and ephemeral fashions followed, ought to be opposed by the Jewish school as it was developed in the course of twenty centuries and more. An important and profound lesson will be derived, which the Talmud expresses in the words: "He who says, Nothing exists for me but the Jewish religion, not even the Jewish religion exists for him."[45] Although the Jewish school was the nursery of all the manifold aspects of the Jewish spirit, yet it brought forth not only heroes of the intellect, but religious geniuses as well. If hitherto the Jews have put no pictures of saints in the synagogue, it has not been for lack of them, else they might long ago have resorted to the device of borrowing them from the other nations. It was because the Jews met their ideal saint outside of the synagogue as well as inside. He was a thinking and an acting saint no less than a praying saint.

The most significant truth to be learned from the long history of Jewish education remains to be mentioned. All true culture issues from a unified *Weltanschauung*, from a decided view of life and men and the world, and in the last resort the value of culture depends upon the help it gives us in acquiring and formulating such a *Weltanschauung*. If Jewish education is to resume its old place and significance in Jewish life, it must cease to be the supernumerary

adjunct of a person or a cause. It must again be an
independent institution, fulfilling its task autono-
mously. It must be, as it was, the focus of Jewish life,
of the Jewish intellect, and of the Jewish religion.

THE NAME OF THE RABBINICAL SCHOOLS AND ASSEMBLIES IN BABYLON

By JACOB Z. LAUTERBACH, Hebrew Union College.

THE NAME כלה *Kallah* used to designate the talmudic
schools in Babylon, as well as the regular half yearly assemblies of the Babylonian Jewish teachers, has been the subject of considerable discussion among Jewish scholars. Various
theories about the origin amd meaning of this name have been
advanced, but, to my mind, none of them offers a satisfactory
explanation of the meaning of the name and why it was chosen
as a designation for these schools and assemblies. There are
especially two important facts which must be taken into consideration when seeking to determine the meaning of this peculiar name. Any theory about the meaning of this name which,
does not take into account these two facts must be rejected as
unsatisfactory. The one of these two facts is that the name is
used to designate not only the assemblies and schools, as a whole,
but also, as in the name ריש כלה a smaller group within the school
or a part of the assembly. This fact certainly refutes the theories
which consider the name *Kallah* as derived from an Arabic
word, meaning university or assembly.[1] For the name desig-
nating the university as a whole could not, unless accompanied
by some qualifying or restrictive term, be used as a designation
for a part of the university. This fact also speaks against the
theory which would explain the meaning of the name Kallah
as indicating the manner in which the members of the larger
assembly were seated.[2]

[1] Kohut, Aruk completum s. v. and Halper in Jewish Quarterly Review
n. s. IV p. 546. Kohut also suggests a Persian word meaning "crown" or
"wreath". But as S. Krauss (השלח XLIII, i (Jerusalem 1924) p. 369ff.
rightly remarks, why should they have chosen a word from a foreign language
instead of from the Hebrew or the Aramaic used by them.

[2] J. N. Epstein in J. Q. R. n. s. XII p. 369ff. and also Kohut l. c. Ac-
211

321

The other fact to be considered is that the name was used only in Babylon and applied to Babylonian schools or assemblies exclusively.[3] This disproves the theory that the name Kallah, meaning bride, was given to the assembly of the teachers of the Torah, because the Torah itself is figuratively called Israel's bride. The idea that the Torah is like a bride to Israel was

cording to this theory it remains unexplained why the name was כלא and not כלילא. The same may be said against the theory of Krauss (l. c.), according to which the name should have been כללא or כלל but not כלה.

[3] The theory suggested by Rappoport (Kobak's Jeshurun VII p. 64) and accepted by Harkavy (Studien u. Mittheilungen IV, Berlin 1887, p. 377) that רישי כלי in the prayer יקום פורקן designates Palestinian teachers is not correct. It derives its main and sole support from the fact that in that prayer, as it is found in the printed editions the רישי כלי are mentioned before the רישי גלותא and רישי מתיבתא. Hence it is argued, these רישי כלי must have been Palestinian teachers who would be given precedence to Babylonian authorities. But aside from the fact pointed out by Kobak (l. c. compare Baer, Abodat Israel (Rödelheim 1901) p. 229) that in some manuscripts the order of this prayer is somewhat different and the רישי כלי are not mentioned at all, it would be strange indeed to postulate on the ground of this one very doubtful allusion that the Palestinian teachers were called רישי כלי considering that no other reference to Palestinian Reshe Kallah can be found (comp. S. Poznanski, Studien zur Gaonäischen Epoche I (Warsaw 1909) p. 48, note 6). It would seem more likely to assume that the origin of this prayer dates from the time when the Babylonian schools were called only by the name כלה. The prayer then contained only לרישי כלי ולרישי גלותא referring to the heads of the schools and the exilarchs. Later on after the schools had been converted into Yeshibot and the heads of the schools were called רישי מתיבתא the phrase in the prayer was also changed and it read לרישי מתיבתא ולרישי גלי, as indeed found in the manuscripts referred to by Baer (l. c. the form ולרישי גלי is corrupt from ולרישי גלותא see Kobak l. c.). Some copyists by mistake put in both forms לרישי כלי ולרישי גלותא לרישי מתיבתא ולרישי גלותא. Then finding that the words ולרישי גלותא occurred twice they struck them out from the place where they occurred for the second time, i. e., after לרישי מתיבתא and thus there was left the form of the prayer as found in the printed editions.

expressed in Palestine[4] before any of the Babylonian institutions designated by the name Kallah were established. Now, if this figurative designation of the Torah could have caused rabbinical schools or assemblies to be called by the name *Kallah* the Palestinian schools would likewise have been so designated and Palestinian sources would not have persistently avoided using this name for a rabbinical assembly.

The fact that the name כלה is applied exclusively to Babylonian schools or assemblies certainly justifies the assumption that the Babylonian schools or assemblies, so designated, were, in their beginnings at least, somewhat different in character from the Palestinian schools or assemblies. There must have been some peculiar feature in the organization or constitution of the Babylonian schools and assemblies which made it impossible for their founders or organizers to call them right from the beginning by the name ישיבה which at that time was used in Palestine to designate rabbinical schools and assemblies. This distinctive feature which marked the difference between the Palestinian *Yeshibot* and the Babylonian schools or assemblies is most likely indicated in the peculiar name כלה which was the original name of the Babylonian schools and which to a certain extent was retained by them even after they were put on a par with the Palestinian schools and also designated by the name ישיבה or מתיבתא. It seems to me, therefore, that it is altogether wrong, when seeking to ascertain the significance of the name כלה to begin with a consideration of the etymological meaning of the word in Hebrew or in any cognate language. The proper method would be to start from the other end, that is, to begin with an inquiry into the origin of the institutions, so named, and of the circumstances accompanying their organization to find out whether and how any distinctive feature in their constitution or any peculiar circumstance accompanying their organization is indicated in this special name given to them.[5]

---

[4] See Sifre Deut. 345 and b. Pesaḥim 49b where it is found in a Baraita recited by R. Ḥiyya.

[5] Krauss (l. c.) is the only one who follows this method, but his theory is too far fetched. Besides, as already pointed out (above note 2) he fails to

It is generally conceded that the beginning of these Babylonian schools and assemblies dates from the time of Rab and
Samuel in the first half of the third century c. e.   Without considering here the question to what extent the study of the Torah
had been cultivated in Babylon prior to the time of Rab and
Samuel, it may be safely stated that these two scholars were
the founders of schools for the study of the Torah and the organizers of the assemblies which were called by the name כלה.
Sherira Gaon in his letter (Neubauer M. J. Chr. I, p. 27) plainly
tells us that while they studied the Torah in Babylon they did
not have up to the time of Rab and Samuel academies such as
existed in Palestine,[6] because it was thought that such academies

explain why the name given to these schools was כלה and not כללא if the name
was to indicate the method of study according to כללים, introduced by Rab.
Furthermore, this method of study which Rab is alleged to have learned from
Ḥiyya could not have been the distinctive feature of the Babylonian schools.
It must have been pursued also by the sons of Ḥiyya who lived and worked
in Palestine.   Why then was no Palestinian school ever called by the name
כלה supposed to indicate the method of study according to כללים.

⁶ואף על פי כן היו מרביצין תורה הכא וחוו להו ראשי גליות מבית דוד אבל ראשי מתיבתא
וסנהדרין לא הוות בהון דהדא מילתא קא אמרין דלא הוו אלא מן הסקום אשר יבחר יי ועד
דאפטר רבי בריש גלותא הוו נהגין בבבל ולא בראשי מתיבתא ונשיאים דאינון ראשי סנהדרין
בארץ ישראל.

The same is also stated by R. Nathan in his report (Neubauer M. J. chr.
II p. 77) where he says בתחלה בימי רב שהיה סוף תנאים ותחלת אמוראים לא היתה
עדיין ישיבה בבבל וכו'.   Halevi, Dorot Harishonim IIa (Frankfurt a. M.
1901) p. 404ff. is absolutely unjustified in considering the report of R. Nathan
as based merely upon a misunderstanding of Sherira's words.   There is no
actual disagreement between Sherira and R. Nathan as to the time when
the Yeshibot in Babylon were organized.   Only R. Nathan is more explicit
in stating that during the life time of Rab there was not yet in Babylon any
ישיבה of the kind of the Palestinian academies.   But this is exactly what,
according to Halevi himself (ibidem p. 165ff) Sherira also tells us.   Especially
if we assume with Halevi (p. 406–7) that with the statement ועד דאיפטר רבי
Sherira refers to the grandson of Judah Ha-Nasi, the Patriarch Judah II,
who was also called Rabbi.   For while we have no definite report as to the
date of the latter's death, he must have died a few years after Rab, though

which were considered as authoritative as the Sanhedrin or as taking the place of the Sanhedrin could be organized only in Palestine.[7] The members of such an academy or ישיבה were ordained teachers or זקנים and at its head there was always an

we cannot go as far as Graetz (Geschichte IV, 4th edition, p. 448) putting the death of Judah II as late as 270 c. e. Of course, one cannot accept Halevi's theory that Rab went to Babylon in the days of Judah II (comp. Hoffman in Zeitschrift fur Hebräische Bibliographie V, 1901 p. 105). Rab went to Babylon in the days of Judah ha-Nasi who, according to Hoffman (ibidem p. 101) died about 217 c. e. And if we give to his son Gamaliel IV about 15 or 16 years in the office of the presidency and to Judah II about 20 or 21 years then the latter died about 254, about seven years after the death of Rab. Accordingly both Nathan and Sherira tell us that during the life of Rab (and according to Sherira about seven years later till the death of Judah II, comp. Sherira's statement, p. 29–30, that R. Huna became Rosh Yeshibah only after the death of Samuel, that is, seven years after Rab's death), there was no authoritative academy in Babylon, though there were schools for the study of the Torah. And when Sherira (ibidem p. 29) in speaking of the schools of Rab and Samuel uses the expression והויין להו לרב ושמואל תרתין מתיבתא he does not contradict himself, and we need not with Rappoport accuse him of consciously aiming at antedating the origin of the Babylonian academies (comp. Halevi ibidem p. 165). Being used to call the schools by the name מתיבתא, he unconsciously applies a later terminology to earlier conditions. The same is to be said about the passages in the Talmud. (b. Gittin 6a and Kiddushin 65b. see below note 17).

[7] Sherira alludes to Mishnah Sanhedrin XI, 2. The Sanhedrin had its seat in the Temple and it was believed that all authoritative teachings must come from the place where the Divine presence was manifested כל דרישה שאתה דורש לא יהיו אלא בשכנו של מקום (b. Sanhedrin 11b and 87a). In the course of time with the wanderings of the Sanhedrin, the whole of Jerusalem, instead of the Hall in the Temple was declared to be the fit place for the authoritative Sanhedrin, then, the entire country of Palestine was declared the proper place for the Sanhedrin and the authoritative ישיבות which took the place of the Sanhedrin. But the countries outside of Palestine where the Divine presence did not manifest itself שאין השכינה עלית בחוצה לארץ (Mekilta Pisḥa I, Friedmann Ib) were not considered as בשכנו של מקום, hence not qualified for the seat of the authoritative Sanhedrin.

ordained teacher, a זקן יושב בישיבה an elder who presided over the academy. Babylon, however, was lacking in such ordained teachers, since ordination or סמיכה could be obtained only in Palestine.[8] Under these circumstances, then, when Rab and Samuel were about to establish their schools they could not think of organizing an authoritative assembly or an academy of the kind of the Palestinian academies or assemblies, since there were no ordained teachers in Babylon who could form such a ישיבה. And Rab and Samuel themselves were not fully ordained teachers. For even Rab[9] had not received the full ordination such as would give him the right to be a זקן יושב בישיבה, presiding over an authoritative academy. Accordingly, even Rab organized his school or assembly not as an authoritattive Sanhedrin or a pretentious ישיבה but merely as an association of students or a study group. These gatherings of students or study groups could not well be called by the name ישיבה or מתיבתא since they were not of the same authoritative character as the Palestinian ישיבות. They had to be designated by a name suitable for such study groups and indicating that they were composed of unordained teachers and did not claim to be authoritative assemblies. Now we find that even in Palestine those students who were not yet ordained formed such study groups or student associations. They were called by a special name to distinguish them from the regular members of the academy who were already ordained teachers and were called זקנים. The name for these student groups of unordained teachers was כנסת, in the plural כנסיות, and the members of such a group were called בני כנסת. Thus we find in M. Bekorot V, 5 students of such a class are designated as בני כנסת in contradistinction to a fully ordained teacher who is called מומחה.[10] Likewise in

---

[8] אין סמיכה בחוצה לארץ b. Sanhedrin 14a.

[9] Comp. b. Sanhedrin 5ab and p. Ḥagigah I, 8 (76c) and Nedarim X, 10 (42b). As to Samuel, see b.B.M. 85b-86a, comp. however, Z. Frankel מבוא הירושלם p. 124b.

[10] The Mishnah reads as follows:
בכור שנסמת עינו שנקטעה ידו שנשברה רגלו הרי זה ישחט על פי שלשה בני כנסת ר' יוסי אומר אפילו יש שם עשרים ושלשה לא ישחט אלא על פי מומחה.

326

Ḥullin 51a we are told of a certain Palestinian teacher by the name of עוירא who claimed to have been in charge of such student groups in Palestine under the supervision of Rabbi,[11] מפטיר כנסיות לעילא מרבי רבה (comp. the commentaries of R. Gershom and Rashi ad. loc). This also shows that even in Palestine students who were not yet ordained, and therefore could not be members of the academy, were organized into special groups called כנסיות. These groups, no doubt, were of different grades or classes, one more advanced than the other. This seems to be evident from the Mishnah Sanhedrin IV, 4 where three such groups of students,[12] one more advanced than the other, are mentioned as sitting with the Sanhedrin, and in case of need, one of the first and most advanced group was selected for ordination to be made a full member of the ישבה or Sanhedrin.

It was this form of organization that Rab brought from Palestine and introduced in Babylon. He gathered around himself students and organized them into special groups called כנסיות. And even the most advanced among them or the teachers whom he may have found in Babylon and who associated with him in the task of studying and teaching the Torah, organized themselves into such a group only and were called by the name כנסת, since they were not ordained and

---

It is evident that בני כנסת (this is the correct reading, comp. R. Gershom's commentary to Bekorot 36b. Mishnah edition Naples 1492 and Lowe, The Mishnah on which the Palestinian Talmud rest, Cambridge 1883. Our editions have הכנסת) does not mean ignorant members of the synagogue, but students who know the law but have not received the full ordination and are not yet called חכמים (see Rashi ad loc). They may decide this question, since for such a case it is not required to have the full authority, as R. Gershom ad loc. explains it דלא בעינן מומחין גמורין. And the מומחה with whom they are contrasted is one who has received the full ordination, comp. Maimonides, Yad Bekorot III, i רשות. סומחה שנתן לו הנשיא בארץ ישראל רשות. Rab who, as we have seen, did not have such an ordination would therefore have been regarded merely as one of the בני כנסת.

[11] This Rabbi could not have been Judah ha-Nasi I, it must refer to Judah II. It may also be that רבי רבה here means simply "my great teacher" and Avira merely refers to his teacher R. Ami.

[12] In the Mishnah they are called שורות, for each group occupied a special row of seats.

therefore assumed the name by which a group of unordained students in Palestine was designated. But since the mere term כנסת "organization" or "assembly" did not in itself indicate the purpose of the organization, it was deemed neces- sary to add a phrase descriptive of the character and purpose of the organization. This additional phrase was לומדי התורה or in Aramaic, לומדי אורייתא "students of the Torah". The full name of these study groups or student organizations was therefore כ'נסת ל'ומדי ה'תורה which in abbreviated form, using only the initial letters was כלה or in the Aramaic form כ'נסת ל'ומדי א'ורייתא abbreviated כלא.[13] The smallest of these groups con- sisted of ten members, probably because these study groups would also hold their religious service in the very place where they assembled for study.[14] Hence it became the rule not to start such a study circle or not to hold a meeting of such a group with less than ten members.[15] Each group had its leader who was called ריש כלה "the head of the group", or ראש לבני כלה (b. Berakot 57a)[16] And the head of all the groups and classes that constituted a school or were in one locality was also called ריש כלה, since he was the head of the various groups of students of the Torah in that place ריש כנסיות לומדי התורה. Likewise during the months of assembly, Adar and Elul, when all the teachers and students assembled together, the teacher who pre- sided over the assembly was originally also called not by the title ראש ישיבה but by the name ריש כלה, since he was then presiding over, or the head of all the groups of students ריש כנסיות לומדי התורה. And these two months which were the time for a general assembly for all the students זמן כ'נסיה ל'כל

---

[13] In this form it is found in the Responsa of the Geonim. ed. Harkavy p. 76 and 146 and Ginzberg Geonica II p. 283.

[14] Comp. b. Berakot 8a and 30b.

[15] שאין פותחין בכלה פחות מעשרה b. B.B. 12a.

[16] The members of such a group were called בני כלה (b. B.K. 113a) which corresponds to the בני כנסת of the Mishnah. Of course, some of these groups were more advanced and others less advanced. The latter were called כלי זוטרי "Junior Groups". Sheeltot to ברכה No. 165, (Wilna 1867) p. 80a. In the Talmud we have no express mention of כלי זוטרי. But b. Sukkah 26a כדטעים בר בי רב ועייל לכלה probably refers to such a junior group attended by a young student.

219 THE NAME OF THE RABBINICAL SCHOOLS &C.

ה'לומדים were also called the days of the Kallah יומי כלה (b. M.K. 16a).

Thus originated the name כלה an abbreviation of כ'נסת ל'ומדי ה'תורה by which the Babylonian schools and assemblies at the time of their establishment or reorganization in the days of Rab and Samuel were designated. This designation was chosen by the Babylonian teachers themselves who at that time felt that they could not call their schools or assemblies by the name ישיבה, since the teachers of these schools and the members of these assemblies were not fully ordained teachers.

In the course of time, however, the Babylonians became more ambitious for their schools. They appreciated the high standard of learning that prevailed in their schools and respected the great authority of their teachers even though the latter lacked the formal recognition of authority by the act of ordination. They claimed for their schools equal standing with those of Palestine. They began to call their schools ישיבות, the name by which the Palestinian academies were called, and even considered them, like the latter, a sort of Sanhedrin.

We have no express statement in the Talmud as to the time when this change in the attitude of the Babylonians with respect to their schools took place. Certain indications, however, would lead us to assume that it took place soon after the death of Rab. In the first place, we find that the school at Sura founded by Rab was during his lifetime called merely "the school of Rab" בי רב, and, to my knowledge, is nowhere in the Talmud designated as ישיבה or מתיבתא.[17] The same school, however, under R. Huna, Rab's successor, is already designated as ישיבה or in Aramaic מתיבתא (b. Ketubot 106a).[18] And even the Palestinians are said to have so designated it.

[17] When in discussing the reason for a difference of opinion between Rab and Samuel later Talmudic teachers refer to the existence of schools in the time of Rab and Samuel and mention them as מתיבתא (b. Gittin 6a) they merely use a later nomenclature for earlier times. The same is also the case when Rab and his school is said by some later teachers to have been called בי דינא רבה which is the Aramaic for בית דין הגדול (b. Kiddushin 65b).

[18] כי הוו קיימי רבנן מסתיבתא דרב הונא תמצי נלימייהו הוה סליק אבקא וכסי ליה ליומא ואמרי במערבא קמו ליה מסתיבתא דרב הונא בבלאה.

The abuse to which the ordination in Palestine has been subjected under the patriarch Judah II, a younger contemporary of Rab, which went so far as to enable unworthy candidates to obtain the ordination for money (p. Bikkurim III, 3 (65d) and b. Sanhedrin 7b),[19] may have indirectly helped to bring about the change in the attitude of the Babylonians with respect to their schools.

The Babylonians must have lost a great deal of their former respect for the ordination after the latter became purchaseable. They must have felt that the lack of such an ordination on the part of their own teachers did not detract from their real authority. And we can well believe that even some Palestinian teachers, well aware of the fact that not all of those who have received ordination have also acquired the necessary knowledge and real authority, would not hesitate to designate the school of R. Huna as מתיבתא even though it was composed of unordained teachers. Furthermore, the saying in p. Nedarim VII, 13 (40a) to the effect that a small group of students in Palestine is dearer to God than a great Sanhedrin outside of Palestine,[20] although apparently disapproving of the pretentious claim of the Babylonians that their schools were, like the Palestinian Yeshibot, of the character of a Sanhedrin, clearly points to the fact that already in the third century such claims had been made on behalf of the Babylonian schools.

While all these indications might in themselves not be sufficient to prove convincingly that after the death of Rab, when the school at Sura came under the leadership of R. Huna, it was organized and designated as a Yeshibah, they certainly lend strong support to R. Nathan's report to this effect. And R. Nathan in his report (Neubauer M. J. Chr. II p. 77) expressly

[19] See Graetz, Geschichte IV, 4th Edition, p. 227 and 452; Weiss, Dor. III p. 60 and comp. my article on Ordination, in Jewish Encyclopedia IX, p. 429 ff.

[20] חביבה עלי כת קטנה שבארץ ישראל יותר מסנהדרין גדולה שבחוצה לארץ.
We have no other proof that already in Amoraic times the Babylonian academies claimed the character of a Sanhedrin. Considering, however, that in Geonic times the Academies were considered like a Sanhedrin, we are justified in assuming that this was not an altogether new claim originating in Geonic times.

tells us that after Rab had died they organized the school of Sura as a Yeshibah of the kind of the Palestinian Yeshibot, and its head R. Huna, assumed the title of ראש ישיבה.[21] At any rate, we have no reason to doubt this explicit report of R. Nathan.

But even after they reorganized their schools along the lines of the Palestinian academies and designated them as Yeshibot, the Babylonians did not entirely abandon the older practice of having various student groups, each one called כנסת לומדי החורה or abbreviated כלה. On the contrary, in their schools they retained these student groups, since in so doing their schools became the exact counterpart of the Palestinian academies in which, as we have seen, there were besides the regular members of the academy groups of students called כנסיות.

We therefore find that even after the time of R. Huna there were in the Babylonian schools, various groups of students, each one presided over by a teacher called ריש כלה who was a regular member of the academy, occupying a distinguished position of some high rank but subordinate to the head of the academy or the ראש ישיבה.[22]

ולאחר שנפטר רב עשו ישיבה בבבל על דרך ארץ ישראל והיא ישיבת סורא ומלך בה [21] רב הונא פ' שנה והוא היה הראשון לכל מי שהיה ראש ישיבה בבבל.

[22] Thus we find that R. Naḥman b. Isaac occupied the position of ריש כלה in Pumbedita (b. B.B. 22a). This, no doubt was during the time when Raba was head of the school of Pumbedita. For after the death of Raba when R. Naḥman succeeded him as the head of the school he was probably called ריש מתיבתא. Even if we assume with Ginzberg (Geonica I. p. 46ff) that in Geonic times the head of the Pumbedita academy was called merely ריש כלה and not by the title Gaon, we have no proof that in Amoraic times also the head of the Pumbedita academy had merely the title ריש כלה and not ריש מתיבתא. Likewise, R. Samuel the son of R. Abahu tells us that his father R. Abahu occupied the position of ריש כלה in Pumbedita under Rafram (Ḥullin 49a). But nowhere do we find that the ריש כלה was superior to the ריש מתיבתא. Halper (l. c. p. 545) is not correct in assuming that the saying in b. Berakot 57a tends to prove that in Amoraic times the ריש כלה was higher in rank than the ריש מתיבתא. Rashi's interpretation of the saying is quite correct. Especially if we assume that already in later Amoraic times the head of a group of ten regular members of the Academy was called ריש כלה then a forest of big trees could well have been taken symbolically to indicate a group of prominent scholars. Halper's other suggestion, however, that outside of

Thus it developed that the name כלה came to be used as a designation for the general assemblies in the months of Adar and Elul when the members of the academy met together with all the groups of students connected with them or under their supervision, since these assemblies were really a כ'ניסה ל'כל ה'לימדים. It was also applied as a designation for parts of the school or for certain groups belonging to the academy.[23] But very rarely was the name used as a designation for the academy proper or for the school as a whole.[24]   After the latter had been organized like the Palestinian academies, the name given to them was the same by which the Palestinian academies were called, that is, ישיבה or מתיבתא.

the Geonic academies there may have been heads of independent schools called Reshe Kallah, merits consideration.

[23] In the course of time, however, a change seems to have taken place in the use of the title ריש כלה. In Amoraic times, at least in the earlier Amoraic times (see preceding note) the כלה consisted of a group of students who were not yet regular members of the academy and only the head of the group the ריש כלה was a member of the academy.   But in Geonic times, and possibly already in the later Amoraic period, the כלה was composed of a group of ten regular members of the academy who together with their head, the ריש כלה, formed part of the Sanhedrin. See Nathan's report (op. cit. p. 87).

[24] Thus in Menaḥot 82b in the saying בתרביצא אמרי וכי דבר הלמד בהיקש חוזר ומלמד בהיקש בכלה לא איתמר according to the reading of the Aruk (see Aruk completum s. v. תרבץ our editions have בכללא איתמר which no doubt was by mistake contracted from (בכל' לא איתמר) the term כלה seems to designate the academy proper (comp. Kohut l. c. and Epstein l. c. p. 270). Likewise, if Ginsberg's theory is correct that the head of the Pumbedita academy had merely the title ריש כלה, then כלה designated the entire academy. Comp. also Epstein l. c. p. 371 note 72.

OUTDOOR TEACHING IN TALMUDIC TIMES*

S. Krauss

The subject of teaching under the open sky in talmudic times was first discussed by me as long ago as 1911[1] and referred to again in my ' Talmudische Archäologie.'[2] A. Büchler in his turn discussed this subject in a special paper under the title, ' Learning and Teaching in the Open Air in Palestine.'[3] May I now, after so many years, return to it again in order to offer new evidence of this practice and extend my inquiry to cover both Palestine and Babylonia.

The starting point of my investigation was the expression, *Kerem be-Yabneh*, the seat of Jokhanan b. Zakkai's academy, or, according to others, of his Court (Beth-Din). Mentioned several times in the talmudic sources in such contexts as the following : " when scholars[4] gathered in the vineyard of Yabneh," or " I heard in the vineyard of Yabneh . . .," or, " this question was raised in the vineyard of Yabneh,"[5] the expression has been taken to be a metaphor for a " corona, circle of scholars." It should, however, be taken literally, as referring to a real vineyard in Yabneh in which scholars used to assemble. This is evidenced by the passage in ' Cant. Rabba ' :[6]

> Again, it happened that the scholars of Israel held council[7] in the vineyard of Yabneh. Were they in a real vineyard ? In fact, the Sinedrion is meant, in which scholars sat in rows like trees in a vineyard, and [grouped like soldiers] round their standards.[8]

Similarly, we read in " T. Y. Berakhoth," IV, 7 : " The students of the academy were seated in rows like [trees in] a vineyard." If there is any doubt as to whether " vineyard " is used here as a metaphor, the following statement would seem to be conclusive : " When the scholars in Yabneh entered[9] the vineyard . . ."[10] Nobody can enter an imaginary vineyard.

The reason why the scholars in Yabneh assembled in a vineyard is evident : in the hot Palestinian climate they required a shaded place and this was provided by the vineyard. Büchler dealt very exhaustively with the whole question of open air study and quoted instances of the shades of buildings being used for this purpose in the warm season. Jokhanan b. Zakkai taught in Jerusalem in the shade of the Temple walls.[11] The prophets of old used to address the people on the Temple Mount or even in the shade of the Temple

---

* Based on a lecture delivered at Jews' College (London).

[1] *Die Versammlungsstätten der Talmudgelehrten* in I. LEVY's *Festschrift*.   [2] III 205.

[3] *JQR, NS* IV 485-491. Shortly before his death, BÜCHLER published a study under the title, קדוש עם ראשי על מסע, in *Dissertationes in honorem* DR. EDUARD MAHLER, Budapest, 1937, 379-405, which contains a wealth of information about scholastic life in Palestine. The subject of teaching in the open air is, however, not mentioned at all.

[4] חכמים.

[5] All the sources are collected by S. KLEIN, *Sepher ha-Yishshubh*, Jerusalem, 5899 [1939], p. 754.

[6] VIII, 11 ; cpr. also VIII, 13.   [7] נמנו.   [8] שורות שורות דגלים דגלים.

[9] משנכנסו. In the phrase, ארבעה נכנסו לפרדס in T. B. Hagigah, 14b, the verb " entered " is obviously a metaphor, just as is the expression " Pardes."

[10] *Tosefta Eduyoth I* ed. ZUCKERMANDEL, 454.

[11] *T. Y. 'Abodah Zara* III, 43b ; *T. B. Pesachim*, 25a. Rashi explains aptly : " The Temple walls were very high and projected their shadow over a wide area." His second explanation that " the disciples were so numerous that no school building in the town could contain them," seems to me to be less relevant.

82

Gates.[1] It should be remembered that in ancient times, city gates were buildings of some depth.[2] In Talmudic times these buildings, called *Bet-sha'ar* (Gatehouses),[3] usually terminated in an " exedra " which served as a meeting place for scholars and their audiences. Gatehouses of private buildings, like that of R. Joshua's house where four of his disciples sat for a discussion[4], and even a pigeon house in the courtyard[5], afforded a conveniently shaded meeting place in hot weather. Market places in towns[6] were a customary meeting place for open air studies and also for disputations between " philosophers " (Christian scholars) and the rabbis.

Büchler's views are thus in accordance with mine, except in the following point. In a quotation from the lost ' Yelamdenu ' on Cant. viii 13, reported by the 'Arukh[7], it is stated that " scholars and their disciples[8] used to sit *genuniyoth, genuniyoth*," which I explained as meaning, " small garden " (hortulus).[9] The figure of speech is analogous to *shuroth, shuroth*, and in Mark vi, 39-40, we have a similar instance of reiteration of the noun : "And he [Jesus] commanded them [the disciples] to make all sit down by companies upon the green grass. And they sat down in ranks (πρασιαί πρασιαί), by hundreds, and by fifties." The Greek corresponds perhaps to ערוגות ערוגות.

My explanation was resisted by Büchler who argued that, " the mere fact that the plain word *baggannim* of the text in Cant. viii 13, was not retained without any change of interpretation shows that *genuniyoth* does not mean gardens." He further contended : " Nor can it be said without strain in Hebrew that scholars sit like small gardens ; in the plain prose of an agadah an adverbial accusative denoting place must not be assumed." Finally, he derived the word *genuniyoth* from the root, *gnn*, " to cover," and explained the passage in ' Yelamdenu ' as referring to " the company sitting under the *ḥuppah* (shade)."[10] On this, it may be observed that it does not much matter whether we use *gan* or its diminutive ; the notion of " garden " is conveyed in either case. Further, *genuniyoth* is an adverbial accusative denoting not place, but " the manner of sitting," and agadah is not always " plain prose."[11] Büchler's assumption that the passage in ' Yelamdenu ' refers to *ḥuppoth* can hardly be granted. It is difficult to imagine that the masters and their disciples would erect *ḥuppoth* before engaging in study when to sit down in " gardens " required no preparations.

For the custom of teaching in open fields, the halakhah in ' Menaḥoth,' X 9 offers a significant illustration. According to this halakhah, the biblical injunction (Lev. xxiii 10), that the harvesting of barley should not begin

---

[1] Jer. VII 1.   [2] cp. Jer. XXXIX 4 : " the gate betwixt the two walls."

[3] See my *Talm. Archáol.* I 366. The Halakha distinguishes such gatehouses from the " door house " of private buildings ; see T. Y. '*Erubin.* VIII 1, 25a ; T. B. '*Er.* 75b.

[4] *Tos. Berakhoth.* IV, 18 (*ed. cit.* p. 10).   [5] *Ibidem*, IV, 16 (and·parallels).

[6] For example, Sepphoris ; see *Midrash Tannaim*, ed. HOFFMANN, p. 262.

[7] *Sub voc.* גן (ed. Venice, 53a ; ed. KOHUT II 315). The full passage is given in Büchler's and my articles and·also in GRÜNHUT, *Sepher ha-Liqqutim*, V 130a, and in I. Löw, *Flora der Juden*, IV 256, where my explanation is accepted, but Büchler's view is not quoted.

[8] חברין (literally : " colleagues ").

[9] In my article, *A Misunderstood Word*, *JQR, NS*, IV 111-114.

[10] *JQR, NS.* IV 490. Büchler quotes עתיד הקב״ה לעשות צל וחומות (*Lev. R.* XXV 2) in support of his interpretation of *ḥuppah* as " shade." But in this passage *ẓel*=" shade " is distinguished from *ḥuppah*. For the definition of *ḥuppah* see my article *Ḥuppath Ḥatanim* in '*Oẓar ha-Ḥayim* XII.

[11] cpr. the expressions, שורות שורות and כתות כתות (T. B. *Ber.* 63b, quoted by BÜCHLER), used in agadic passages.

before a sheaf ('*Omer*) had been offered to the Sanctuary on the second evening of Passover, might be suspended and the harvest anticipated for one of the following reasons : either because a later harvest would damage the crop, or, because space was needed for celebrating in the open field the mourning rite, called ברכת רחבה or, finally, because a clear field was required for the students who had no other convenient place for study and who would, otherwise, be idle (מפני ביטול בית המדרש). The study of Torah, in the view of the Rabbis, came before all other commandments. This halakhah clearly implies that study in the open field was customary.

A still more striking instance can be adduced from T. B. Sab. 127a :

> Rabba said in R. Ḥiyya's name : it occurred once that Rabbi went to a certain place on the Sabbath and found that it was too small for his [numerous] disciples. He went out to the field and found it covered with sheaves.[1] Thereupon Rabbi made clear the whole field [on a Sabbath !].

In another version of the same story following immediately upon the first one, it is R. Ḥiyya and his disciples who are the protagonists in this incident. In the Talmud, it is explained that Rabbi (the Nasi) did not clear the field himself, but ordered his disciples to do it.

Again, in T.B. 'Erubin, 34b, it is told that when soldiers occupied all the houses in Nehardea, the seat of the renowned academy in Babylonia, R. Naḥman, the head of the academy, ordered his disciples to go out into the fields and bend down the reeds in order that they might on the following day be able to sit down on the ground for the purpose of study.

Teaching in the market square is referred to in T. B. Mo'ed Qatan 16a, where it is related that " Rabbi " forbade the disciples to study in the market square.[2] But R. Ḥiyya flouted this order and taught his two nephews, Rab and Rabba bar R. Huna[3], in the market square (of Sepphoris ?). Rabbi's prohibition was certainly caused by political circumstances, but R. Ḥiyya, apparently considered that these circumstances did not justify a breach of the custom. He was severely reprimanded for his disobedience.

Finally, in one instance from Babylonia, we find a reference to study out of doors on the banks of a river. In T. B. Horayoth 12a, we read that R. Meshersheya gave to his sons the advice : "When you study, do it near flowing water[4], for as water spreads so may your learning spread."[5]

S. KRAUSS.

Cambridge.

---

[1] שומרים.

[2] בשוק. This may also mean, " in the streets."

[3] See *Rashi ad loc.*

[4] על נהרא דמיא.

[5] In the *Universal Jewish Encyclopedia* I 65, *sub voc.* "Academia" a picture is reproduced with the following description : "Ancient academies : Outdoor teaching as practised in Palestine and Babylonia during the Talmudic period. Neither teacher nor pupil carries notebooks, as all lessons were committed to memory. The lesson was a discourse, after which the pupils asked questions or engaged in discussion." Unfortunately, the source from which the picture was taken is not indicated, nor is any reference made in the body of the article to the particular method of teaching illustrated in the picture.

LEARNING AND TEACHING IN THE OPEN AIR IN PALESTINE

A. Büchler

In the current volumeof this Review, p. 111 ff., Professor Krauss, in his note on the word נינוית, incidentally refers to the question whether the rabbis of Talmudic times studied and taught in the open air. For his evidence, he quotes his full article in Lewy's *Festschrift* on the vineyard in Jamnia, and his *Archaeologie*, III, 205. As neither this work, nor the article mentioned dealt with the general question, I may be permitted to refer again to the very instructive information in Talmudic sources on studying in the open air, and to discuss here a few pertinent statements which may assist students of Palestinian archaeology in solving the interesting problem concerning the vineyard in Jamnia.

R. Joḥanan b. Zakkai taught in Jerusalem on the Temple mount in the shade of the walls of the Temple.[1] One of his former fellow-students in Hillel's school, Jonathan b. 'Uzziel, must also have studied in the open air; for it is reported (Sukkah 28 a) that, when he was learning Torah, every bird flying over him was burnt by the heavenly fire surrounding him.[2] On the steps of the Temple mount, ben-Zoma was once so greatly absorbed in mystical thoughts that he did not greet R. Joshua b. Ḥananiah.[3] In the gate of R. Joshua's house, four of his disciples sat and discussed some questions (Tos. Berakot IV, 18); and R. Tarfon and his disciples sat in the shade of a dove-cot in Jamnia discussing a biblical subject.[4] R. Jose b. Ḥalaftha sat

[1] Pesaḥim 26 a; p. 'Abodah zarah III, 43 b, l. 66.

[2] See Bacher, *Agada der Tannaiten*, I, 124, 1.

[3] Baraita in Ḥagigah 15 a; Tos. II, 5; p. II, 77 a, b; Genes. rab. 2. 4.

[4] Tos. Berakot IV, 16; Mekhilta on Exod. 14. 22, p. 31 b; Midr. Psalms LXXVI, § 2.

in the market (of Sepphoris), and expounded to a matrona and her husband a detail referring to the messianic times.[5]   R. Eleazar b. Pedath studied in the lower market of Sepphoris, while his cloak lay in the upper market ('Erubin 54 b) ; as there were trees planted in that market,[6] he may have sat under one of them. . R. Judah b. R. Jannai was so greatly absorbed in his study that he did not notice that his cloak had slipped (from his shoulders) ; when his disciples drew his attention to it, he pointed to a serpent guarding his cloak (p. Berakot V, 9 a, l. 47).   R. Jannai studied in the gate of Sepphoris.[7]   R. Simeon b. Lakish studied outside the gate of Tiberias.[8]

Naturally, the scholars studied in the open air only during the warm season, and, as the sun often shone hot, sat in the shade of buildings or more probably of trees.   There were in Palestine many kinds of shady trees,[9] some of which were fully

[5] Midrash Tannaim, ed. Hoffmann, p. 262.

[6] Tos. Kil'aim I, 4 ; p. I, 27 a, l. 38.

[7] Genes. rab. 10. 7 ; Num. rab. 18. 22 ; Kohel. rab. 9, 5 ; Bacher, *Paläst. Amoräer*, I, 37, 3.

[8] Genes. rab. 34. 15 ; Kohel. rab. 3. 9 ; p. Berakot V, 9 a, l. 45 ; Bacher, *Paläst. Amoräer*, I, 346, 5.   In Midrash ha-Gadol. on Deut. 18. 14 R. Jannai and R. Johanan sat in the gate of Tiberias, when two astrologers also sat there.   In the first passage אילטים is explained to mean a grove, which would be a more suitable place for study than the gate of a city.   See also Makkot 19 b according to Rashi's version : R. Ḥanina and R. Hoshaiah were sitting at the entrance of Jerusalem, and raised a halakic question ; see also Rabbinowicz.

[9] The Bible incidentally refers to the apple-tree in Cant. 2. 3 ; 8. 5 ; the oak and poplar in Hosea 4. 13 ; the terebinth, under which a prophet sat, in 1 Kings 13. 14 ; Ezek. 6. 13 ; the olive-tree in Hosea 14, 7 ; Jer. 11. 16 ; Psalms 52. 10 ; 92. 11 ; the cedar-tree in Ezek. 17. 23 ; 31. 3 ; the fir-tree (ברוש) in Hosea 14. 9.   No reference is found to the shade of the fig-tree and of the vine ; but Midr. Cant. 2. 13 points to the breadth of the foliage of the fig-tree, and in Pesikt. rab. XLI, 172 b, R. Ḥanina b. Papa says that its branches spread in all directions.   A vine was sometimes trained over a trellis (Krauss, II, 229) and gave very pleasant shade.   As to the shade of the apple-tree, there are contradictory statements.   R. Jose b. Zimra in Cant. r. 2. 3, Pesikt. 103 a, says that in the heat all flee from the apple-tree, for it has no shade ; on the other hand in a passage of the Midr. Jelamdenu in

covered with leaves already in Adar (March–April).[10]   Once when
R. Joḥanan b. Zakkai and his favourite disciple Eleazar b. 'Arach
were on the way, and the latter offered to expound to the master
a detail of mystical philosophy, R. Joḥanan dismounted from his
ass and, with his companion, sat down on a stone under an
olive-tree, and soon all the trees joined in praises for R. Eleazar's
exposition.[11]   During the religious persecutions, R. Akiba once
taught and expounded the law at his table under an olive-tree.[12]
R. Jonathan b. Eleazar (of Sepphoris) was once, in the summer,
sitting under a fig-tree; when he noticed the flow of juice from
the ripe figs, he called his disciples and showed them the wonderful blessing.[13]   In these instances individual teachers and
exceptional circumstances prove nothing for the studying or
teaching of the rabbis under trees.   But different is the case
of R. Hyrkanos, probably the son of R. Eliezer,[14] who had in
Kefar-'etam the act of חליצה performed under a terebinth;[15]

Jellinek's בית המדרש VI, 82, § 27, it is the last refuge in a garden where
no other shady tree is planted.   In Pesaḥim 111 a R. Isaac refers to the
danger of sleeping under a solitary palm-tree, and in Midr. Psalms 92. 10
R. Isaac b. Adda points out that the shade of the palm-tree is far away from
the tree, meaning the shade of the crown.   As to the shade of the juniper
under which Elijah sat in 1 Kings 19. 4; Midr. Psalms 120. 4, and the
kikayon in Jonah 4. 10, see the commentators.

[10] In p. Rosh ha-Shanah II, 58 a, l. 22, it is stated that in the month of
Adar it is so warm that an ox would like to strip his hide in the shade of a
fig-tree.   In the parallel in b. Sanhedrin 18 b: 'In Adar, in the morning an ox
would die from cold, at noon he would lie down in the shade of a fig-tree and
strip his hide.'   The leaves withered after a hundred days, Tos. Shebiit IV, 20.

[11] Ḥagigah 14 b; Tos. II, 1; p. II, 77 a, l. 59.

[12] מסכת כלה in Coronel's חמשה קונטרסים, p. 19 a; Derek ereṣ XI,
5, 6; Epstein, מקדמוניות היהודים, p. 115.

[13] Tanḥuma תצוה 13, Buber 10.   Buber refers to a parallel in והזהיר
p. 100 b, which adds : · To be in the shade and protected from the sun.'   In
p. Pesaḥim VII, 20 b, l. 1, R. Iddi reports a similar incident without mentioning
any name.   In Shabbat I, 56 b R. Naḥman b. Isaac sat under a palm-tree and
studied.

[14] Shabbat 147 a; Sanhedrin 68 a; Menaḥot 35 a; Sotah III, 19 a, l. 6.

[15] Jebamot XII, 6; the Cambridge Mishnah reads כפר עכו, pal. כפר
איכום.

338

for this shows that he taught and judged in the open air under a tree.[16] R. Ḥiyya b. Abba and his colleagues, according to some R. Jose b. Ḥalaftha and his colleagues, according to others R. Akiba and his colleagues, were sitting under a fig-tree and studying; when they saw that the owner of the tree came early every morning and picked figs, they thought that he suspected them of eating his figs, and they moved to another place.[17] The most characteristic passage, however, is Cant. rab. 4. 4, § 6, where R. Aḥa, in interpreting Cant. 4. 3, says : כפלח הרמון רקתך, הריקן שבסנהדרין רצוף תורה כרמון הזה, ואין צריך לומר מבער לצמתך על היושבין תחת הזית ותחת הגפן והתאנה ועוסקין בדברי תורה 'the weakest member of the Synhedrion is as full of learning as the pomegranate (is full with seeds) ; but even more so those sitting under the olive-tree, and under the vine, and under the fig-tree, and studying Torah '.[18]   About the middle of the fourth century, it must accordingly have been the general custom of the scholars to study under trees, and, as R. Ḥiyya's case shows, not merely of individual teachers, but of whole schools.   Though late, yet historically very instructive, is the agadic statement in Seder Eliahu IX (Friedmann, p. 50) that Deborah went and sat under a palm-tree and taught Torah publicly.   Though based on Judges 4. 5, it would not have been said that she taught in public under a palm-tree, if the custom had not still been general in the times of the author.   This is further evident from the statement in the same passage, לא היו תלמידי חכמים בישראל אלא כחצי דיקל בלבד, 'that in Deborah's time there were not more scholars than about half a palm-tree'.   For this very strange measure presupposes that the scholars of the time, as a rule many, were studying under trees ; [19]

---

[16] Cf. Judges 4. 5 ; 1 Sam. 14. 2 ; 22. 6.

[17] p. Berakot II, 5 c, l. 9 ; Genes. rab. LXII, 2 ; Cant. rab. 6 2, 2.

[18] According to the climax, the men studying under the trees were the excellent members of the Synhedrion.   R. Samuel Jafé refers the first group to the scholars attending the meetings of the Synhedrion without being yet members (Sanhedrin IV, 4), and the second group to the members.

[19] Friedmann in his note refers to Megillah 14 a where MSS. in Rabbinowicz read : מה תמר זה צלו מועט אף תלמידי חכמים שבאותו הדור

339

the palm-tree, which offered no shade of any extent, was only mentioned because the verse spoke of such a tree.[20]

As to the great school in Jamnia, the frequent כרם שביבנה, the vineyard in Jamnia, naturally suggests that the school met during the warm and dry season in an orchard next to a building required for the rainy months. In addition, a Baraita in Baba meṣi‘a 59 b, which seems to have escaped the attention of scholars dealing with the school buildings, gives, in spite of the miracles reported, noteworthy information. In the heated discussion of the scholars of the *bet-din* in Jamnia, which led up to the exclusion of R. Eliezer b. Hyrkanos from the school, this scholar said to the assembly: ' If the decision is according to my view, this carob-tree shall prove it '; and the carob-tree was uprooted (and carried off) a hundred yards. When the rabbis refused to accept the proof derived from the carob-tree, R. Eliezer said: ' If the decision is according to my view, the canal shall prove it ', and the canal flowed backwards. When the rabbis refused to accept the proof derived from the canal, R. Eliezer said: ' The walls of the school shall prove it '; and the walls of the school inclined to fall. When R. Joshua rebuked them, they did not collapse, nor stand erect; and they are still standing in the same position. The order in which R. Eliezer calls on his witnesses shows that the discussion took place in the open air, in a garden or a field with a carob-tree and a water-canal, and that close by stood a school-house with strongly built walls.[21] If

מועטין היו, as the shade of the palm-tree is little so the number of scholars in Deborah's time were few.

[20] Also R. Judah b. Ilai's statement in Cant. rab. 6. 9, § 2 (cf. Friedmann's Pesikt. rab. p. 198 a), is to be considered as evidence. He refers the sixty queens in Cant. 6. 9 to the sixty חבורות, companies of righteous men who sit in the garden of Eden under the tree of life and study the Torah ; and the eighty concubines are eighty companies of average men who study the Torah outside the tree of life ; and the girls without number refer to students innumerable.

[21] According to the parallel account in p. Mo'ed Ḳaṭan III, 81 d, l. 9, the pillars of the house of meeting (= the school) were on that occasion shaken ; but a little earlier in the report the carob-tree belonged to R. Eliezer's

further details were known, 'the vineyard in Jamnia' would be proved as an extensive orchard under the shady trees of which the rabbis sat in the summer and discussed all questions.

Comparing with this the passage from the Midrash Jelamdenu discussed by Professor Krauss, היושבת בגנים חברים, כשם שחברים יושבין גנוניות גנוניות ועוסקים בתורה אני יורד אצלם ואני מקשיב לקולם ושומע, we would be inclined to find here a reference to scholars sitting in gardens and studying. But the mere fact that the plain word בגנים of the text in Cant. 8. 13 was not retained without any change or interpretation shows that גנוניות does not mean gardens. Nor can it be said without strain in Hebrew that scholars sit like small gardens; in the plain prose of an agadah an adverbial accusative denoting place must not be assumed. Kohut seems to be right in suggesting from the context and from the parallel in Cant. rab. 8. 13, 2 as the meaning of גנוניות 'company', 'assembly'; but his derivation of the word from κοινωνία seems unlikely. What is wanted here is a synonym of כת or חבורה, as used in the statement of R. Tanḥum b. R. Ḥiyya of Kefar-'Akko in Berakot 63 b, עשו כתות כתות ועסקו בתורה לפי שאין התורה נקנית אלא בחבורה 'form groups and study Torah, for this can only be acquired in company'. גנונית which was used only on account of גנים in the verse, seems to be identical with or similar to גנון used as interpretation of גן in Cant. rab. 1. 3, 2 (יבוא דודי לגנו, לגינונו (Lev. r. 9. 8, Pesikt. r. V, 18 a), 5. 1, 1 באתי לגני לגנוני (Pesikt. 1 a), meaning a cover, a shade overhead, just as סוכה and צל, and as חֻפֶּה in Isaiah 4. 5; and גנונית probably meant the company sitting under the חֻפֶּה and waiting, as the בני חפה in Tos. Berakot II, 10; Tos. Shabbat XVII, 4; p. Ḥagigah II, 77 a, l. 59; b. Sukkah 25 b, 26 a; p. II, 53 a, l. 21, 'for God as the bridegroom to come to the bower'. As חֻפָּה was even in Talmudic times used still for a shade,[22] foliage under which the scholars were sitting could be

private house. The details are in favour of the Baraitḥa in the Babylonian Talmud.

[22] R. Ḥiyya b. Abba in Lev. rab. 25. 2, says: עתיד הקב"ה כעשות צל וחופות לבעלי המצות אצל בני תורה בגן עדן, God will make for charitable men in the garden of Eden a shade and bowers next to the scholars. He took

called נגונא.[23] If this interpretation is right, the passage is an additional proof for the studying of scholars in groups in the shade of trees.

A. Büchler.

London.

the idea from his master R. Johanan who said, in Baba bathra 75 a, that God will once make seven bowers for every righteous man, as He had, according to R. Hama b. Haninah, made for Adam ten bowers in the garden of Eden (also in Lev. rab. 20. 2; Pesikt. rab. XXXI, 145 a); see *Monatsschrift f. G. u. W. d. J.*, XLIX (1905), 18 ff.

[23] Compare Lev. rab. 24. 7 where Deut. 23. 15 כי יי אלהיך מתהלך בקרב מחניך להצילך is explained by הֵגֵן, to protect, shade overhead, as by the foliage of a tree, להנן עליך להיות צל על ראשו. In Mekhiltha on Exod. 13. 21, p. 25 a, it is explained that God rewarded Abraham's words to the angels in Gen. 18. 4 to lean under the tree, by spreading over his descendants seven clouds; in both cases it was shade overhead. See also 4 Ezra 1. 20; Midr. Threni r. 1. 17; Psalms 42. 4.

EDUCATIONAL INSTITUTIONS AND PROBLEMS DURING THE TALMUDIC AGE

MOSHE ABERBACH

Baltimore Hebrew College, Baltimore, Md.

I

On the Meaning of בית אולפנא

THE Targum Jonathan to II Kings 22:14, translates והיא יושבת
בירושלם במשנה ("Now she, viz., the prophetess Huldah, dwelt in
Jerusalem in the second quarter") by והיא יתבא בירושלם בבית אולפנא
("Now she dwelt in Jerusalem in the house of instruction").[1] That
בית אולפנא signifies some sort of school or college is certain. The
rendering of משנה by בית אולפנא would appear to indicate that in the
talmudic age the בית אולפנא was an institution where the Mishnah was
taught, i. e., a secondary school, in contrast to the בית ספר, an elementary school, where the curriculum was confined to the study of Scriptures.[2] However, before jumping to any definite conclusion, we have
to consider the context of the verse in question, which relates that the
prophetess Huldah dwelt in Jerusalem in the מִשְׁנֶה. Granted the premise that משנה must refer to a school, the Targum Jonathan could
have rendered it only by a term denoting a college for adults; for
while Huldah could conceivably have been assumed to have attended
college lectures and discussions like an early prototype of Beruriah,[3]
she could hardly have been imagined in a Mishnah school for children
aged ten to fifteen.[4]

The precise meaning of בית אולפנא can best be determined by discovering the exact shade of the meaning of אולפנא or its shorter form
אולפן in passages where these terms are not used too vaguely. One

---

[1] Significantly, both A.V. and R.V. follow the rendering of Targum Jonathan
by translating משנה as "college." The American-Jewish version renders: "second
quarter" —, which is certainly more correct, since משנה is known to have been the
name of a section of Jerusalem; cf. Zeph. 1:10.

[2] Cf. Y. Meg. III, 1, 73d; Y. Ket. XIII, 1, 35c; Lam. R., Proem 12; ibid., 11,
2, 4; Pesiq. R.K. XV, 121b: בית ספר למקרא.

[3] On Beruriah, cf. The Jewish Encyclopedia III, 109–10, s.v. Beruriah.

[4] Cf. M. Avoth V, 21: בן עשר למשנה .... בן חמש עשרה לתלמוד.

107

such midrashic passage would seem to provide some slight — but far
from conclusive — evidence that אולפן was an oral tradition identifiable with the Mishnah. We are told that when the Patriarch, R.
Judah II, was enraged against Jose of Maon, R. Simeon ben Lakish
tried to pacify him by pointing out that Jose was after all a scholar
who deserved respect and gentle treatment on account of his learning.
"Does he then know anything of the words of the Torah?" asked
R. Judah. "Yes," replied R. Simeon. "Has he received instruction
(אולפן)?" the Patriarch continued his inquiries. Again R. Simeon gave
an affirmative reply. Finally, R. Judah asked: "And if I question
him (viz., on the law), will he be able to answer?" To this, too, R.
Simeon was able to give a positive reply.[5]

The three questions put by the Patriarch may conceivably allude
to Scripture, Mishnah and general religious law — the last perhaps
even to talmudic dialectics. One could, accordingly, infer that, if the
אולפן of the second question referred to Mishnah, a בית אולפנא would
be an ordinary Mishnah school. This interpretation is, however, by
no means certain. R. Judah's second question could mean, "Was he
given instruction (viz., by competent teachers)?" — in contradistinction to autodidactic study. Even if we retain our original interpretation, it is not evident that the instruction in Mishnah, which Jose
received, was necessarily of the kind provided in secondary schools
for young teen-age pupils. He could have been taught the Mishnah
in a higher institution of learning designed for senior students, some
of whom did not enjoy the advantages of an adequate education in
their childhood.[6] No definite conclusion can, therefore, be derived
from this passage.

The identification of בית אולפנא with a Mishnah school of the
usual type is not borne out by other passages which, on the contrary,
point to a college for adult students. Thus, the Targum Onkelos to
Genesis XXV, 27b reads: ויעקב גבר שלים משמש בית אולפנא — "But
Jacob was a perfect man who ministered at the בית אולפנא." Clearly,
the reference here must be to a higher institute of learning for adult
students such as Jacob — "a perfect man" — is supposed to have been.

---

[5] Cf. Gen. R. LXXX, 1 (edit. J. Theodor II, 952): אמר ליה: ... אמר ליה: ויודע הוא בדברי
תורה כלום? אמר ליה: הין. אמר ליה: ואולפן קביל? אמר ליה: הין. ואי שאילנא ליה מנייב? אמר ליה:
הן.

[6] Note that even such outstanding scholars as R. Eliezer and R. Akiba commenced their elementary education only when they had reached full manhood;
cf. Avoth-R.N., Version I, ch. 6; Version II, chs. 12–13, (edit. Schechter 15 a–b);
B. Ket. 62b–63a; Ned. 50a; Gen. R. XLII, 1 (edit. Theodor I, 397–98); Tanḥ.
לך לך 10, (edit. Buber 34a–b).

Again, in the Talmud Yerushalmi, two Amoraim, R. Jonah and R. Jose, are reported to have said: "Let us drop discussion (אולפנה) and return to the Mishnah."[7] Here, אולפנה, so far from being identical with Mishnah, stands in sharp contrast to it. Its meaning appears to be dialectical discussion, i. e., Talmud.[8] It follows, therefore, that בית אולפנא cannot be a Mishnah (i. e., secondary) school, but an institution specializing in talmudic studies or — in other words — in dialectical discussions.

No less significant is another passage in the Talmud Yerushalmi where an unmistakable distinction is drawn between the expert in talmudic dialectics called רבה דאולפנה and the Mishnah (or Baraita) expert known as רבה דמתניתא:[9]

"Which is greater (i. e., more reliable)? The Mishnah master or the Gemara master?"[10] From this it must appear evident that the בית אולפנא cannot possibly be a secondary Mishnah school. It must in all probability have been a college for talmudic dialectics.

Lastly, we have a somewhat enigmatic passage in the Midrash, which also seems to indicate that the בית אולפנא was a higher institution of learning rather than a secondary school. Expounding Ecclesiastes 4:6, R. Yiẓḥak stated that "Better is he who studies Halakhoth[11] and hermeneutics, and is conversant with them, than he who studies Halakhoth, hermeneutics and Talmud,[12] and is not conversant with them; but . . . . it is his ambition to be acclaimed a scholar of traditional law" (בר אולפן).[13]

The interpretation of this passage is somewhat doubtful. If Halakhoth alludes to the Mishnah, we must assume Talmud to be equivalent to Gemara, i. e., the dialectical discussions of the Amoraim. The בר אולפן would, accordingly, be one who has progressed well

---

[7] Y. Ber. VI, 5, 10c: נישבוק אולפנה וניתי לן למתניתה. In this case, as the context shows, מתניתה actually corresponds to a statement in the Tosephta; cf. T. Ber. V, 12. The fact that אולפנה is here spelt with a ה at the end instead of the more usual א — is of no significance. Similar spelling changes are quite frequent in the Palestinian Talmud, e. g., עקיבה instead of עקיבא.

[8] Cf. Pnei Moshe to Y. Ber. ad loc.: נניח סברת אמוראין שהן בעלי התלמוד.

[9] Cf. Weiss, Dor. III, 49: . . . מצאנו שגדולי החכמים אשר ידם רב להם בידיעת המשניות היו מכונים בתואר הכבוד ,רבה דמתניתא' . . . חכמים אשר היו נפלאים במעשה ההויות ובטשא ומתן התלמודי . . . הם אשר ידם אמונה במעשה התלמוד היו נקראים בשם ,רבה דאולפנה'.

[10] Y. Yev. IV, 11, 6b: ?רבה דמתניתא, רבה דאולפנה? הידינו רבה; cf. P'nei Moshe's comment ad loc.: ?מי הוא הגדול . . . הרב של הברייתא או של הגמרא? על מי לסמוך?

[11] Apparently, the laws contained in the Mishnah; cf. Soncino Midrash Leviticus R. III, 1 (Vol. IV, p. 34).

[12] Cf. ibid. "Used here apparently in the sense of dialectics."

[13] Lev. R. III, 1: טוב מי ששונה הלכות ומדות ורניל בהם ממי שהוא שונה הלכות ומדות ותלמוד ואינו רניל בהם, אלא . . . רעותיה דמתקרי בר אולפן.

345

beyond the stage of ordinary Mishnah-text studies. Consequently, בית אולפן or בית אולפנא would necessarily refer to a college for adult students specializing in talmudic dialectics. If, on the other hand, the term *Halakhoth* is strictly limited to religious laws without any connection with the text of the Mishnah, then we must grant that *Talmud* in this context most probably refers to Mishnah. The בר אולפן would, accordingly, be a Mishnah scholar — albeit an advanced, adult scholar. Consequently, the בית אולפנא might well have been a Mishnah or secondary school. In support of this, one might cite the fact that the בית תלמוד does in fact often designate a Mishnah school.[14]

As against that, it is, however, significant that there is at least one midrashic passage which clearly distinguishes between the Mishnah school on the one hand and the Talmud school on the other. In every synagogue in Jerusalem, we are told, there was "a school for Scripture, a school for Talmud and a school for Mishnah."[15] Even if we reject the words "and a school for Mishnah" as a late addition to a text repeatedly cited without these words in the Palestinian Talmud and the Midrashim,[16] we should still be at a loss to explain how an ambitious adult student aiming at the honorific title of בר אולפן could attain his object merely through the study of the Mishnah text — a subject taught to school children from the age of ten onwards.[17] A thorough study of the Mishnah was inconceivable without talmudic dialectics, and the coveted title of בר אולפן must be presumed to have been conferred only on one who was adept at Gemara rather than exclusively at Mishnah.

While the evidence at our disposal may not be absolutely conclusive, it nonetheless appears almost certain that the בית אולפנא was an institution for higher studies for adults rather than a Mishnah school for teen-age boys. The terminological confusion may have arisen out of the different uses of the words תלמוד and בית תלמוד (to which the בית אולפנא is evidently related) in different periods and contexts. The original בית תלמוד must have been essentially a place where the Mishnah was intensively studied and discussed by senior students. Only on this assumption can we explain the use of the word תלמוד in reference to what we are expressly told was a Mishnah

---

[14] Cf. Y. Meg. III, 1, 73d; Y. Ket. XIII, 1, 35c; Lam. R. Proem 12; *ibid*. II, 2, 4; Pesiq. R.K. XV, 121b: ... ומ׳ח תלמוד למשנה.

[15] Cf. L. Ginzberg, Genizah Studies I, 261–62: בית ספר למקרא ובית ספר לתלמוד ובית ספר למשנה.

[16] See above, note 14.

[17] See above, note 14.

school.[18] As for the secondary school for young teen-agers, it was also styled בית תלמוד, partly because it served as a preparatory school for the real talmudic college, and partly because it had this in common with the talmudic college that both based their curriculum on the Mishnah. It was, therefore, not altogether illogical to refer occasionally to both institutions by the same name, notwithstanding their considerable differences in method, standard and attainments.

There is thus no contradiction between the *Talmud* in בית תלמוד למשנה, which undoubtedly refers to the secondary Mishnah school for teen-agers, and the *Talmud*, the study of which enabled one to be styled בר אולפן, and which must consequently have been — as we are often told[19] — a more advanced subject based upon, but by no means identical with, the Mishnah. We may, therefore, conclude that the בית אולפנא was a high institute of learning, the graduates of which were styled ברי אולפן in recognition of the fact that they had immersed themselves in talmudic dialectics.

II

SEATING ARRANGEMENTS IN THE PALESTINIAN AND BABYLONIAN
ACADEMIES DURING THE TALMUDIC AGE

Schools and colleges in ancient Palestine and Babylonia were generally poorly equipped and frequently almost devoid of furniture.[1] Students would often sit on the bare floor[2] or on stones, which sometimes had a deleterious effect on their health.[3] Masters, too, occasionally sat on stones,[4] and during times of economic stress they might even have to bring some seat-substitute from home. Thus, R. Judah bar Ilai,

---

[18] See above, note 14.
[19] Cf., e. g., M. Avoth V, 21: בן חמש עשרה לתלמוד ... בן עשר למשנה. בן עשר למשנה; cf. Mekhilta, Introduction, edit. Friedmann, p. XXXIV: כל המקרא, ובתר כן מה? ששה סדרים. ואח'כ .... תלמוד.
[1] Cf. S. Krauss, Talmudische Archäologie III, 206. It is noteworthy that Hellenistic schools were better furnished, including armchairs for the masters, benches or backless wooden stools, with cushions, for assistant-masters and students, and a high reading-desk for recitations; cf. H. I. Marrou, *A History of Education in Antiquity,* p. 145; J. K. Freeman, *Schools of Hellas,* pp. 83–84.
[2] Cf. S. Krauss, *ad loc.* See below.
[3] Cf. Y. Beẓah I, 6, 60c: 'R. Ishmael be-rabbi said: "The stones on which we used to sit in our youth waged war with us (i. e., harmed our health) in our old age." ' In Babylonia, stone plates were sometimes used as seats, and Rab had to warn his disciples not to sit on the outer stone plates of the college conducted by the Babylonian Amora, Asi, because they were cold (cf. *ad loc.*).
[4] E. g., R. Eliezer ben Hyrcanus, cf. Cant. R. I, 3, 1.

who flourished in the difficult period following the Hadrianic persecution and was exceptionally poverty-stricken,[5] used to carry a jug
on his shoulders to the House of Study, where he would use it as a
seat.[6] R. Simeon ben Yoḥai, R. Judah's contemporary, would bring
a basket for the same purpose.[7] Both of them considered the act of
carrying these seat-substitutes as a work of honor, inasmuch as it
enabled them to avoid having to squat on the floor.[8]

For junior disciples, as well as school children, seating on the bare
dusty floor was generally the rule.[9] There they would sit, probably
in a crosslegged position, holding their scrolls, when studying the
Bible, between their knees.[10] As early as the first half of the second
century B. C. E., Jose ben Joezer advised his disciples to transform
their homes into meeting places for the Sages and to "sit amid the
dust of their feet, while imbibing their words with thirst."[11] In the
first century C. E., the Apostle of the Gentiles proudly recalled that
he had sat at the feet of Rabban Gamaliel I[12] — an expression which
has since become a proverbial metaphor for studying under somebody's direction.

The talmudic tradition, on the other hand, records that up to the
time of Rabban Gamaliel I, the study of the Torah was carried on in a
standing posture only, but after his death "illness" — or feebleness —
descended upon the world, so that it became necessary to sit while
studying the law.[13]

Evidently this is a reference to somewhat informal "peripatetic"

---

[5] Cf. Ned. 49b.
[6] *Ibid.*   [7] *Ibid.*
[8] *Ibid.* See also Rashi *ad loc.*
[9] Krauss (Talm. Arch. III, 206) and apparently also Jastrow (Talmud Dictionary *s.v.* ספסל, p. 1015, col. 2) maintain that there were special benches for the
use of school children — open frames serving also as footrests for those behind.
They refer to Tosephta Kelim Bathra I, 11, where, however, only "school-teachers'
benches" are mentioned. This is rightly interpreted by Ebner (*Elementary Education
in Ancient Israel*, p. 66) as benches for the use of the teachers to impress their
authority upon their pupils. Since even older students often sat on the ground
(see below), it is hardly likely that young students would have been provided with
benches. Moreover, in view of the economic conditions prevailing in Palestine
during the talmudic period, the provision of benches for a substantial number of
school children would have been economically prohibitive.
[10] Cf. Avoth-de-R. Nathan, Version I, ch. 8, (edit. Schechter 19a).
[11] M. Avoth I, 4. While other interpretations of והוי מתאבק בעפר רגליהם are
possible (cf. Obadiah of Bertinoro and Rashi *ad loc.*; cf. also Soncino Talmud,
Avoth p. 3, n. 8; Goldschmidt, *Der Babylonische Talmud*, Avoth, *ad loc.*, p. 1151,
n. 4), the one adopted here is the most probable.
[12] Acts XXII, 3.
[13] Cf. Megillah 21a.

schools.existing in the pre-talmudic age.[14] However, after the destruction of the Second Commonwealth — if not earlier — standing during study was unusual except when the student was given individual instruction[15] or was delivering a discourse or a sermon either in the synagogue or at college before his master and fellow students. Senior disciples who distinguished themselves on such occasions would be congratulated with the words: "You have been worthy of saying it standing; may you be worthy of saying it sitting"[16] — a privilege reserved for a recognized master.

M. Kossowsky has made a good case for the assumption that new students had to stand at the back of the lecture-hall before being promoted to one of the rear benches.[17] In support of this, he cites — inter alia — the occasional retort, "I have ministered unto (i. e., studied under) Rabbi N. standing longer than you did sitting."[18] This, he believes, indicates that the freshman student was not permitted to take a seat at the academy and had to remain standing during lectures during the early period of his studies. We are, indeed, told of those "who were standing behind the fence" at the academy of Javneh,[19] though this is hardly conclusive, since they may well have been occasional auditors rather than regular students.

There is, however, a major difficulty militating against this theory. Since halakhic discussions in the talmudic age would often continue for many hours at a time, it is highly improbable that students would be required to stand on their feet day after day when they might just as well have sat on the ground. In fact, while we are informed about promotion from the floor to the benches of the lecture-hall,[20] there is no record of any promotion from a standing place "behind the fence" to a seat in the academy.

It therefore appears to me that the expression שמשתי עומדות[21] or שמשתי בעמידה[22] refers literally to "attendance upon scholars" (שמש תלמידי חכמים), including the performance of menial duties, which was generally required of students,[23] especially freshmen, just as apprentices

---

[14] For a detailed discussion of this tradition, cf. J.Q.R., Vol. LII, No. 2 (Oct. 1961), pp. 168–74.
[15] Cf. Morris, *The Jewish School*, p. 64.
[16] Cf. Y. Hor. III, 7, 48c; Gen. R., (edit. Theodor, p. 1262 [ויח, 98, 11]).
[17] Cf. Samuel K. Mirsky Jubilee Volume, p. 322.
[18] *Op. cit.*, p. 313; cf. Y. Ḥag. III, 1, 78d; Y. Shab. X, 5, 12c.
[19] Y. Ber. IV, 1, 7d; Y. Ta'an. IV, 1, 67d.
[20] Cf. Bavli B.M. 84b.
[21] Cf. Y. Ḥag. III, 1, 78d; Y. Shab. X, 5, 12c.
[22] Cf. B. Ḥul. 54a.
[23] Cf. B. Ber. 7b; 47b; Keth. 96a; Shab. 40b, *et al.*

would be expected to perform menial services for their masters.[24]
Such duties of attendance upon scholars would gradually diminish
as the student advanced in the *Yeshivah* and became a senior, ultimately rising perhaps to the position of *Talmid Ḥaver* — a junior
colleague of his masters. During the early period of his studies, the
young scholar would have to stand near his master — especially, one
may assume, during mealtimes — ready to serve his teacher's needs.
After a while, the student would be permitted to sit, while continuing occasionally to minister to his master. The claim to have
ministered standing longer than someone else sitting need not be
taken, as is done by Kossowsky,[25] as insulting. It may simply mean
that the student concerned had spent a longer period of his life serving
his master and attending to him than someone else did in ordinary
study under the same master. The expression לשמש would thus be
used in a double sense — ministering and studying —, and may have
been deliberately chosen as a word-play.

There is a good deal of evidence that sitting on the ground rather
than standing (during lectures) was the normal practice for junior
students[26] and, occasionally, for senior ones, too. Thus, we are expressly informed that Simeon of Timnah,[27] who flourished in the
first half of the second century C. E., used to sit on the ground before
R. Eliezer, R. Joshua and R. Akiba, although he himself was a distinguished scholar — albeit unordained — as well as a great linguist.[28]
The scholars who sat in three rows in front of the Sanhedrin in
Javneh — and possibly also in Jerusalem[29] — were apparently also
seated on the floor.[30] In the second half of the second century C. E.,
R. Eliezer ben R. Simeon and the youthful Rabbi Judah the Patriarch
were seated on the ground during lectures, though they were tem-
porarily promoted to the benches.[31] Even in the lecture-halls of major
academies, including the college of R. Judah the Patriarch, the

[24] Cf. B. Shab. 78a (see Rashi *ad loc.*); Giṭṭ. 58a (end); Deut. R. III, 4, ed. S.
Liebermann, p. 85.

[25] *Op. cit.*, p. 323.

[26] Cf. B. Ber. 28b: "Seat your children between the knees of scholars." Note
also the frequent expression, "A disciple who is sitting before his master" (B. Shab.
30b; Sanh. 6b; Ḥul. 6a).

[27] So according to S. Klein, ארץ יהודה, pp. 152, 155. The usual rendering, "The
Temanite," is possible — there was a place by the name of Teman in Judaea (cf.
Klein, *op. cit.* p. 199) — but on the whole less probable.

[28] Cf. B. Sanh. 17b.

[29] Seating arrangements at Javneh may have been modelled on those obtaining
at the Sanhedrin of Jerusalem.

[30] Cf. Rashi to M. Sanh. IV, 4 (Bavli *ibid.* 36b, end).

[31] Cf. B. B.M. 84b.

students often had to sit on the floor, and — except for privileged individuals — latecomers were not supposed to "step over the heads of the holy people."[32]

The practice of sitting on the ground during study continued in the amoraic age. We are, for example, told in a Midrash that students would strain their necks to see their masters during lectures.[33] This can be understood only on the assumption that the disciples squatted on the ground at the feet of their teacher who, in turn, sat on a bench or a couch, so that they had to strain their necks to see his face.

This necessity of sitting on the floor during lectures, *which was presumably due to lack of furniture,* came to be considered a virtue per se, so that even senior disciples were not supposed to sit on a couch, chair or bench, even if such a seating accommodation was available, but were to squat on the ground in trembling, awe and dread.[34]

Not everybody agreed with this extreme view, which was strongly contested by the third-century Amora, R. Abbahu, who maintained that a master must not sit on a couch while his pupil was seated on the ground.[35] They should either both sit on the ground or both on a couch,[36] and there must be no distinction, even as the Almighty had made no distinction between Himself and Moses when He had told him, "Stand then here by Me" (Deut. 5:28).

It was in line with this idealistic egalitarianism that R. Abbahu presented King David, in aggadic fashion, as a master who had never sat on pillows or cushions during lectures, but on the ground just like his disciples.[37] R. Abbahu's extreme idealism was, however, not universally accepted, and his own master, R. Joḥanan, was reported — perhaps with some exaggeration — to have sat on seven cushions during his lectures[38] — a degree of comfort which was certainly not shared by his students. According to R. Abbahu's fanciful interpretation, Ira the Jairite[39] — traditionally regarded as David's teacher[40] — had likewise taught his disciples propped up on pillows and cushions.[41] David's alleged refusal to follow his master's example[42] was, it seems,

[32] Cf. B. Yevamoth 105b; Meg. 27b; Soṭ. 39a; Sanh. 7b.
[33] Cf. Cant. R. I, 10, 2.
[34] Cf. Avoth de — Rabbi Nathan, Version I, ch. 6, ed. Schechter 14a.
[35] Cf. B. Meg. 21a.
[36] So according to Rashi, *ad loc.*
[37] Cf. B. Mo'ed Qaṭan 16b.
[38] Cf. B. Bava Qamma 117a.
[39] Cf. II Sam. 20, 26.
[40] Cf. Targum *ad loc.*; B. 'Eruv. 63a; Num. R. III, 2; Cant. R. I, 2, 1.
[41] Cf. B. Mo'ed Qaṭan 16b.
[42] *Ibid.*

designed to serve as an *apologia* for R. Abbahu's own failure to follow the practice of his teacher, R. Joḥanan.

Some two centuries before the age of R. Abbahu, teachers would sometimes waive the customary distinction between themselves and their senior disciples. This appears to have been done not so much during lectures as on social occasions, which were, however, liable to be devoted to halakhic discussions, thus becoming informal study sessions. For example, we find the aged R. Dosa ben Hyrcanus seating R. Joshua, R. Eleazar ben Azariah and R. Akiba, who had come to consult him on a halakhic problem, on golden (or gilded) couches.[43] Several decades later, we learn that for distinguished disciples benches would be specially made or obtained.[44] They would thus be promoted to the position of junior master or fellow — probably that known as *Talmid Ḥaver*.[45]

For the majority of students, however, seats on benches were normally not available. To ease, therefore, the discomfort of sitting on the ground, mats were sometimes spread on the floor.[46] Among Joshua's merits, which gained him the leadership of Israel, was said to have been his assiduity in spreading the mats on the floor of Moses' "House of Assembly" (i. e., House of Study).[47] Needless to say, this would-be historical analogy faithfully reflects the conditions prevailing in the *Yeshivah* during the talmudic age.

In winter, when the cold floor or stones on which students would sit, caused additional discomfort,[48] they would "soil" their garments by spreading them on the ground and sitting on them[49] — a practice which may have been customary at other seasons of the year, too. In cold rooms, students might also have to cover their legs and knees with their cloaks in order to keep themselves warm. During the time of R. Judah bar Ilai when, following the disastrous Bar Kokhba rising and the Hadrianic persecution, economic conditions had become desperate, as many as six students would sometimes have to share one such cloak during their studies.[50]

Seating arrangements at schools and colleges were, it seems,

[43] Cf. B. Yevamoth 16a.

[44] Cf. B. B.M. 84b.

[45] Cf., e. g., B. Bava Bathra 158b; Y. *ibid.*, IX, 12, 17a; Y. Shekalim III, I, 47b.

[46] Cf. B. Ber. 25a. Mats were also used at home in lieu of chairs, at any rate among the poor who could not afford proper furniture, cf. B. Ned. 50a.

[47] Cf. Num. R. XXI, 14. Although this is a late Midrash, it probably reflects conditions in the earlier talmudic period, too.

[48] See above, n. 3.

[49] Cf. Derekh Er. Zuṭa, ch. I., beginning.

[50] Cf. B. Sanh. 20a.

modelled on those customary at the Sanhedrin of Javneh, where members were seated in semicircular rows — "like a half of a circular threshing floor, so that they might all see one another."[51] Facing the rabbis and judges of the Sanhedrin, were three rows of disciples — in effect, trainee judges — who would take over whenever vacancies occurred.[52] Seating in colleges must have been along similar lines; for it was considered of special importance for students to be able to see their master. "When you sit before your master," disciples were advised, "look at his mouth, for it is written, 'But thine eyes shall see thy teacher' (Isa. 30:20)."[53] Rabbi Judah the Patriarch, who prided himself on his keen intellect, which he attributed to the fact that he had been one of R. Meir's minor disciples, being seated behind his back,[54] nevertheless regretted not having sat face to face with that great teacher; for in that case, he thought, his intellect would have been even keener.[55]

This case indicates what is also known from other sources, namely, that students were seated in accordance with their intellectual attainments. The more brilliant disciples were seated in the front rows, while the less intelligent were consigned to the back seats.[56] At the Sanhedrin or High Court of Javneh, promotion from the three disciples' rows to the judges' benches was in accordance with a detailed rota, the disciples being seated in the form of a queue, so that promotion for one meant that all those who were behind him were moved one seat forward.[57]

A similar system also obtained in the colleges. Thus, in the third century C. E., the Amora Rab Kahana left his native Babylonia for Palestine, where he was seated in the first row of senior disciples and rabbis who attended R. Joḥanan's lectures. Rab Kahana had, however, been instructed by his teacher Rab not to participate in the

---

[51] Cf. M. Sanh. IV, 3. School children would likewise sit in semicircular rows, especially in synagogues; cf. Cant. R. VI, 11, 1; cf. Ebner, *Elementary Education in Ancient Israel During the Tannaitic Period*, pp. 66 f.

[52] *Ibid.* IV, 4. Cf. also Y. Ber. IV, 1, 7d and Y. Taan. IV, 1, 67d, on the scholars of Javneh who were seated in rows like the rows of a vineyard.

[53] Cf. B. Hor. 12a; Kerit. 6a.

[54] Kossowsky, *op. cit.*, pp. 323 f., derives from this case the assumption that there were rows of disciples behind the teacher. On the whole, it seems more likely that the semicircular rows of students were occasionally overcrowded, so that at any rate those who sat at the extreme ends of the last row were slightly behind the master.

[55] Cf. B. 'Eruvin 13b; Y. Beẓah V, 2, 63a.

[56] Cf. B. Bava Bathra 120a; Kossowsky, *op. cit.*, p. 316.

[57] Cf. M. Sanh. IV, 4; B. Sanh. 37a.

discussions for seven years, so that R. Joḥanan assumed that the silent Babylonian could not be much of a scholar. He was, accordingly, moved back from the front row until he was finally seated at the very end. At last he decided to make use of his keen dialectical powers, and before long he was again in the front row.[58]

Junior, as well as less scholarly disciples, occupied the rear benches, being promoted only when they had either distinguished themselves in halakhic debates or after years of diligent study and attendance on their teachers. Thus, R. Joḥanan, the most outstanding scholar in third-century Palestine, related himself that in his student days he had been sitting seventeen rows behind Rab at Rabbi Judah the Patriarch's academy, and while Rab and the Patriarch were exchanging fiery halakhic arguments, he (R. Joḥanan) had been unable to follow.[59]

That college seating arrangements primarily reflected the intellectual capacities of the students is also indicated in the legend concerning Moses' visit to R. Akiba's academy. Seating himself behind eight rows of disciples, Moses, according to the legend, was ill at ease, being quite unable to follow the arguments of master and students.[60] While the story is legendary or didactic in character, its background is quite authentic, reflecting as it does the intellectual distinctions as between "front benchers" and "back benchers."

Social distinctions based on intellectual attainments were also reflected in the system of promotion from a floor seat to a college bench wherever such "luxurious" furniture was available — as at Rabban Gamaliel II's academy at Javneh where there were eighty or, according to another tradition, three hundred benches — many more being added after the Patriarch's deposition.[61] Previously, we are told Rabban Gamaliel II had done his best to restrict admission to the Academy[62] — hence the large number of auditors who "were standing behind the fence."[63] The Patriarch's successor, Rabban Simeon ben

---

[58] Cf. B. Bava Qamma 117a.

[59] Cf. B. Ḥul. 137b.

[60] Cf. B. Menaḥoth 29b.

[61] Cf. Y. Ber. IV, 1, 7d; Y. Ta'an. IV, 1, 67d; B. Ber. 28a. In the fourth century, we hear of benches in the college of Bar Ulla, though the outer benches, which were exposed to the vagaries of the weather, tended to be cold, and students had to be warned not to use them; cf. Y. Beẓah I, 6, 60c. The benches were apparently arranged morning and evening, sometimes by a leading disciple, no doubt in order to preserve the precise order of seating, which would be thrown out-of-gear if the benches were disarranged; cf. Num. R. XXI, 14. See also n. 47.

[62] Cf. B. Ber. 28a.

[63] Cf. Y. Ber. IV, 1, 7d; Y. Ta'an. IV, 1, 67d.

Gamaliel, seems to have followed a similar trend of restricting Academy seats to proven scholars, while senior disciples, including his own son — who later became Rabbi Judah the Patriarch — were seated on the floor.[64] When Judah and his fellow student, R. Eleazer ben R. Simeon, distinguished themselves in halakhic discussions, they were promoted to bench seats, which had to be specially made for them[65] — evidently because no vacancies were available and promotion was normally granted only when a vacancy occurred through the death or emigration of an incumbent seat holder.

At this point, Rabban Simeon ben Gamaliel intervened, insisting that his son be demoted to a floor seat, allegedly to avoid the ubiquitous evil eye. R. Eleazer, too, was demoted, officially for the same reason. The latter did not, however, appreciate this concern for his welfare, but, infuriated by his demotion, he assumed an attitude of hostility towards R. Judah, who had been indirectly responsible for what he regarded as an affront to his social position at the academy.[66]

There is every reason to believe that "the evil eye" in this context was a thinly disguised jealousy, which often attended acts of promotion to a college seat. Rabban Simeon ben Gamaliel's attitude and motivation are clearly shown in his statement elsewhere that "no seat promotion takes place without people complaining about him[67] saying, 'Why was this man given a seat while another man was not given a seat?' "[68] It was because of the envy and jealousy attending promotion, especially when the lucky candidate happened to be the Patriarch's son, that Rabban Simeon ben Gamaliel decided to demote his son rather than risk the evil gossip of envious students.

In this context, the emphasis placed on "knowing one's proper place" at the Sanhedrin and in colleges is noteworthy.[69] It is no accident that in the list of forty-eight distinctions necessary for the acquisition of learning, "recognizing one's (proper) place" and "rejoicing in one's lot" are placed in juxtaposition.[70] For the "Disciples of the Wise" were only human and tended to be jealous of those who had the good fortune of being advanced to a bench seat or to the

[64] Cf. B. B.M. 84b.
[65] *Ibid.*
[66] *Ibid.*
[67] The reference is obscure. It may refer either to the student who was promoted or to the head of the Yeshivah for preferring one disciple, while ignoring another. The latter interpretation is adopted by Kossowsky, *op. cit.*, p. 316.
[68] Sifre, Deut. 13, ed. Friedmann, p. 68a.
[69] Cf. M. Sanh. IV, 4; Avoth VI, 6.
[70] Avoth *ibid.*; cf. Kossowsky, *ad loc.*

front row in the Yeshivah. It was therefore necessary to exhort students to know their proper place and be satisfied with it.[71]

While no doubt the attainment of truth and clarification of the Law were the primary objectives of study, the disciples — and sometimes even the masters — were not unmindful of the social ambitions of intellectual combat. Promotion and demotion deeply affected both students and teachers whose sole ambition was frequently a seat of honor in the House of Study. Thus, Rab Kahana regarded his demotion from the first to the seventh bench as a punishment of such severity that he felt absolved from the promise he had given to Rab not to put any questions to R. Joḥanan.[72] The latter, discovering that the Babylonian was not a "fox" but a "lion" — a sharpwitted scholar who could defeat R. Joḥanan in argument —, humbled himself by descending from his seven-cushion seat to the floor. Yet, this self-inflicted humiliation mortified him so deeply that he morbidly imagined that Rab Kahana was laughing at his (R. Joḥanan's) intellectual discomfiture.[73]

Allowing for certain legendary features in this story, it is clear that "the war of the Torah,"[74] which resulted in improved or worsened seating facilities, was fought with the utmost seriousness by students and teachers alike who, having renounced the pleasures and glories of this world, devoted their efforts and concentrated their ambitions on advancement and pre-eminence within the "four cubits of the Halakhah."[75]

[71] Cf. Kossowsky, *ad loc.*
[72] Cf. B. Bava Qamma 117a.
[73] *Ibid.*
[74] Cf., e. g., B. Meg. 15b; cf. also B. Ber. 4a for the expressive phrase, "humiliating someone in (disputations concerning) Halakhah."
[75] Cf. B. Ber. 8a.

A PHILOSOPHICAL SESSION IN A TANNAITE ACADEMY

By JUDAH GOLDIN*

Commenting on the verse[1] which reports the devastation of Jerusalem by Nabuzaradan, that 'he burnt the house of the Lord, and the king's house; and all the houses of Jerusalem, even every great man's house,' וראת כל, בית גדול,[2] the Midrash[3] makes the following remark:

> And to what does the clause *every great man's house* refer? That's the academy (*bet midrash*) of Rabban Johanan ben Zakkai. And why is it called *bet gadol* [literally, the house of the great one]? Because there the *shebah* (*shevah*) of the Holy One, blessed be He, was rehearsed, related, recited

— the verb used is *teni*, which means not only to recite but to study and to teach. To translate *shebah* by the neutral word 'praise', is to miss the real intent of the statement. *Shebah* in the present sentence, as in a great many others in talmudic-midrashic literature, is clearly δόξα; and one of the traditional commentators on our midrashic passage has already correctly explained it: in Johanan ben Zakkai's academy they were engaged in the Creation and Merkabah (Chariot) speculations.[4] The parallel passage in the Palestinian Talmud[5] bears him out. Here we do not read *shebah*, but *gedulot*, the Magnificence, and the citation of 4 Regum 8.4 as prooftext ('narra mihi omnia magna-

---

* A slightly longer and more fully documented version of this paper, written in Hebrew, appears in the *Harry A. Wolfson Jubilee Volume*, recently published by the American Academy for Jewish Research. Several notes in the present English version, as well as a brief amplification at the conclusion of the discussion, do not appear in the Hebrew.

[1] 4 Reg. 25.8 f.; cf. Jer. 52.13. While the Vulgate of Jer. *ibid.* does read 'omnem domum magnam' (LXX: πᾶσαν οἰκίαν μεγάλην), in 4 Reg. 25.9 it reads simply 'omnemque domum' (see also LXX *ad loc.* ed. Rahlfs I 750), though in the Hebrew (MT) in both the reading is *bet gadol* (in Jer. *bet ha-gadol*).

[2] This translation is, of course, in accordance with MT; cf. the translation of the Jewish Publication Society.

[3] *Lamentations Rabba*, Petiha 12, ed. Buber 12.

[4] The commentary is *Yefeh 'Anaf* by Samuel ben Isaac Ashkenazi Jaffe of the second half of the sixteenth century (see *Lam. Rab.*, Vilna edition, 3b). Cf. *Encyclopaedia Judaica*, 8.744f. And on *shebah* = *doxa*, cf. also S. Lieberman in G. G. Scholem, *Jewish Gnosticism, Merkabah Mysticism, and Talmudic Tradition* (New York 1960) 123.

[5] J. *Megillah* 3. 1. And note the combination of *gedulah* and *shebah* in *Pesikta de-Rav Kahana*, ed. Buber 41b (but ed. Mandelbaum 76 reads only *gedulato*, and even in the variant readings does not give the Buber reading). *Pesikta Rabbati*, ed. Friedmann 65b reads simply *gedulato*, and the same is true of *Tanhuma Numbers*, ed. Buber 60b,

lia' etc.; LXX: πάντα τὰ μεγάλα)[6] makes the meaning perfectly clear. As
G. Scholem wrote long ago in another connection,[7] 'The term employed:
shivho shel hakadosh barukh hu, signifies not only praise of God — in this
context that would be without any meaning — but glory, δόξα, *shevah* being
the equivalent of the Aramaic word for glory, *shuvha.* The reference, in short,
is not to God's praise but to the vision of His glory.'

Our Midrash, in other words, testifies that in the academy of Johanan ben
Zakkai there were sessions devoted to speculations on the theme of visions
of God's glory. And in fact this should not surprise us, for it is in keeping
with what talmudic literature tells us elsewhere[8] about an exchange between
the great sage and his favorite[9] disciple, Eleazar ben 'Arak — how on one
occasion, when Eleazar discoursed brilliantly on the Merkabah theme, Johanan
could not resist praising him in most superlative terms. 'He rose and kissed
him on his head and exclaimed: Blessed be the Lord, God of Israel, who gave
such a descendant to our father Abraham,' and so on and so forth.[10]

We shall shortly examine more closely this well known encounter of Johanan
and Eleazar ben 'Arak. I have referred to it at this point, however, because
along with our midrashic passage it may serve to suggest something about
the nature of the curriculum (if I may be permitted such a term) in Johanan's
academy. That is to say: it is already evident that in this famous academy
not only were there sessions devoted to the study and development of Halakah,
Law, as talmudic literature abundantly demonstrates, but there were also
sessions devoted to esoteric lore, the kind of speculation that one customarily
associates only with mystics and gnostics, and supposedly shunned by the
talmudic Rabbis. As Scholem proved in some of his most recent publications,[11]
so-called gnostic themes can be traced back to the 'normative' rabbinic
thought of the second century A. D., and even late first century. I hope
in the near future to prove that already *early* in the first half of the first cen-

---

[6] Is this perhaps what lies behind 'magnalia Dei' of Acts 2.11 also, at least in part?
Cf. the commentary by K. Lake and H. J. Cadbury in F. Jackson and K. Lake, *Beginnings
of Christianity* IV (London 1933) 20.

[7] *Major Trends in Jewish Mysticism* (Jerusalem 1941) 65 (paperback ed. New York
1961, p. 66). Note also *The Scroll of the War of the Sons of Light Against the Sons of Darkness*, ed. Y. Yadin, trans., B. and C. Rabin (Oxford 1962) 274f., ' ... GDL 'EL, TŠBWHT
'EL, KBWD 'EL.'

[8] *T. Hagigah* 2.1 (on which see now S. Lieberman, *Tosefta Ki-Fshutah*, New York 1962,
Part V, Order Mo'ed, pp. 1287ff.); *B. Hagigah* 14b; *J. Hagigah* 2.1; *Mekilta Simeon*, ed.
Epstein-Melamed 159.

[9] See further n. 16 *infra.*

[10] For a similar exclamation and enthusiasm in connection with another of his disciples,
see version B of *'Abot de-Rabbi Natan*, ed. S. Schechter (hereafter ARN) p. 32.

[11] See especially the work referred to in n. 4 *supra*, and cf. the review by M. Smith in
Journal of Biblical Literature 80 (1961) 190f.

tury, Pharisaic teachers were aware of theurgic practices, of which at least one sage did not approve, outspokenly.[12] The point is, talmudic sources evidently reveal that in the academy of Johanan ben Zakkai there was more than preoccupation with the Law. This there is no need to belabor. But I would like to suggest that in addition to Halakic studies, in addition to general Haggadic (non-legal) sessions, in addition to concerns with esoteric lore, there were also sessions devoted to the consideration of philosophical questions.

Needless to say, it is not always easy to draw a sharp line between esoteric statements that involve one in metaphysics, and philosophical expositions. But when I speak of philosophical questions in the present study, I have in mind the exploration of ethical problems in the idiom which had become characteristic of Hellenistic philosophical circles, particularly after the period of classical Greek philosophy. As scholars have universally observed, in the Hellenistic period, more and more, ethics came to be central in the preoccupation of philosophers.[13] This does not mean that there was no interest in the other branches of philosophy — physics, or rhetoric, or metaphysics. But as A. D. Nock put it,[14] to quote one historian out of many, ' . . . in the Hellenistic age the philosophic centre of interest became primarily ethical.'

It is with this therefore that we are here concerned when we speak of philosophical questions. But one more preliminary observation before we proceed to analysis of the talmudic texts: I do not seek to blur distinctions, to make of the vineyard of Jamnia an epicurean garden with Hebrew Florilegi, to equate a talmudic epigram lifted out of context with some Greek sentence also uprooted from its natural habitat. The rabbis were not Platos in Hebrew disguise, nor were they students (much less disciples) of Plato. On the other hand, however, especially after the detailed researches of E. Bickerman, Hans Lewy, and S. Lieberman,[15] it is impossible to deny that in the tents of Shem quite a number of Japhet, Hellenistic influences took up residence. That being the case, one may not a priori dismiss the possibility that in a

---

[12] For the present, see ARN 56. I hope to show that the exegesis occurring there is indeed *literal* exegesis.

[13] See, for example, E. Zeller, *Outlines of the History of Greek Philosophy* (New York) 1911) 208: ' . . . in the systems of Hellenistic philosophy ethics and social theory occupy the most prominent positions . . . '

[14] *Conversion* (London 1933) 114.

[15] Merely by way of example (for very many details are scattered throughout the rich and numerous studies of these men) the following may be listed : by E. J. Bickerman, *Der Gott der Makkabäer* (Berlin 1937); *The Maccabees* (New York 1947); 'La chaîne de la tradition pharisienne,' *Revue biblique* 59 (1952), 44ff.; 'The Maxim of Antigonus of Socho,' *Harvard Theological Review* 44 (1951) 153ff.; by Hans Lewy, the collection of essays in *'Olamot Nifgashim* [Heb.] (Jerusalem 1960); by S. Lieberman, *Greek in Jewish Palestine* (New York 1942) and *Hellenism in Jewish Palestine* (New York 1962).

tannaite academy there should be sessions devoted to philosophical problems. Some texts at least suggest otherwise; let us look at them, without more ado. And we shall begin with Johanan ben Zakkai's *favorite* disciple, Eleazar ben 'Arak.[16]

To him, chapter II of *Pirqe 'Abot*[17] attributes the following saying: 'Be diligent in the study of Torah, and know how to answer an Epicurean. Know in whose presence thou art toiling; and faithful is thy taskmaster to pay thee the reward of thy labor.' A typical rabbinic view, one is tempted to say: there is emphasis on the study of Torah, there is opposition to epicureanism, there is affirmation of the doctrine of reward. No doubt. The difficulty is this however: what *exactly* did Eleazar ben 'Arak say? Already in *'Abot de-Rabbi Natan* (hereafter ARN),[18] when Eleazar is quoted, the last clause, 'to pay thee the reward of thy labor,' is omitted, and there is good reason to believe that this clause came to be attached to Eleazar's maxim as a result of its similarity to part of Rabbi Tarfon's maxim cited immediately thereafter in the same chapter of *Pirqe 'Abot.*[19] Not only that, but in *Pirqe 'Abot* Eleazar's term for God appears as 'thy taskmaster,' *ba'al melakteka*, whereas in ARN the term used is 'author of the covenant with thee, thy Confederate,' *ba'al beritka.*[20] Perhaps these are small matters. But more serious is the following: An examination of each of the maxims by Johanan ben Zakkai's disciples cited in the second chapter of *Pirqe 'Abot* reveals that each is made up of three sentences[21] — this is their basic design and stylistic character. On the other hand, if you analyze Eleazar's saying, you discover not three, but four sentences, even if the clause about reward is omitted; thus: (1) Be diligent in the study of Torah; (2) Know how to answer an Epicurean; (3) Know in whose presence thou art toiling; (4) Faithful is thy taskmaster. ARN is of no help in this regard; actually it complicates matters all the more, for in addition to these sentences it adds still another, to wit, 'Let not one word of the Torah escape thee.'[22]

---

[16] See *Pirqe 'Abot* (hereafter PA) 2.8-9; ARN 58f.; and cf. J. Goldin, *Fathers According to Rabbi Nathan* (New Haven 1955) 74 and n. 13 *ad loc.* And note in particular *Mekilta Simeon* 159.

[17] PA 2.14.   [18] p. 66.

[19] 2.15-16 ; cf. ARN (both versions) 84. See also C. Taylor, *Sayings of the Jewish Fathers* (Cambridge 1897-1900) I 12 (Heb. Text), and II 145.

[20] Cf. Taylor II *ibid.* and A. Marmorstein, *Old Rabbinic Doctrine of God* (Oxford 1927) 78.

[21] And this applies no less to Rabbi Eliezer ben Hyrqanos' saying in 2.10, as D. Hoffmann, *Ha-Mishnah ha-Rishonah* (Berlin 1913) 33, showed. See also n. 84 in J. Goldin, 'The End of Ecclesiastes' in *Studies and Texts* III, ed. A. Altmann (now being published).

[22] This statement does not occur in Version B of ARN *ibid.*; on that version's reading, see the idiom in the citation from Rabbi Ephraim bar Samson in G. Scholem, *Reshit ha-Qabbalah* (Jerusalem-Tel Aviv 1948) 40.

Textual difficulties of this sort can prevent us from ever getting at the substance of an author's statement. But in the present instance we are rather fortunate in having a reading preserved by a large number of Genizah manuscripts in the Cambridge University Library. Here we find the following version of Eleazar's saying — and note that it is indeed composed of three, rather than four, sentences: 'Be diligent to learn how to answer an Epicurean, know in whose presence thou art toiling, and faithful is thy *ba'al berit*.'[23] Not a word, in short, about the study of Torah. And this is unquestionably the correct reading. The expression *lilmod Torah*, to learn or study Torah, is so fixed a stereotype and cliché in rabbinic literature, that one can easily see how Eleazar's saying came to be garbled. Be diligent to study? Surely, said some later transmitter or copyist, Eleazar had in mind studying Torah.[24] No wonder the editor of ARN decided to improve even on this, and added, 'Let not one word of the Torah escape thee.'[25]

Since, however, we are interested in what Eleazar said, and not in what later teachers thought he said, we had best focus on his own words, which are, to repeat: 'Be diligent to learn how to answer an Epicurean, know in whose presence thou art toiling, and faithful is thy taskmaster (or, thy *ba'al berit*).' If we focus on these words we cannot, I believe, fail to recognize that a kind of anti-epicurean polemic is before us, some as-it-were Stoic (I emphasize as-it-were) remark. I insist: this is not to say that Eleazar is a formal member of a Stoic school. All that is intended thus far is to call attention to the fact that if we hear what Eleazar is saying, we shall discern that he is *urging* us to learn how to refute an Epicurean (note his idiom: 'be diligent to learn to refute,' *hewe shaqud lilmod le-hashib*), that he exhorts us to remember that our toils in this world do not go unattended, and that there is one to whom we are subject and He is trustworthy, dependable.

One notion we had best dispose of at the outset, and that is, that talmudic sources use the term *epiqurus* indiscriminately to suggest any kind of heretic or unbeliever.[26] Despite widespread impression to the contrary, the term occurs in the Mishnah only in the *Pirqe 'Abot* passage we have cited and

---

[23] This reading, 'be diligent to learn how to answer an epicurean,' sometimes indeed with the *'et* accusative sign rather than the prefix *lamed*, occurs at least in the following MSS and MS fragments: TS, E 3, 40, 55, 63, 74, 82, 93, 103, 111, 124, 128, 141. Note in fragment No. 40 the interesting reading *she-toṣi'* (rather than *she-tashib*).

[24] One example may be instructive. In Codex Kaufmann of the Mishnah the reading is: 'Be diligent to study (learn) how to answer an epicurean'; and on the margin of the MS someone has noted that the word 'Torah' should be inserted after 'learn'!

[25] Perhaps it is this editor in fact who is responsible for that word 'Torah' getting into the text.

[26] Cf. R. Marcus in his note d *ad* Josephus, *Antiquities* 10.281 (Loeb Classics; Josephus VI 313).

once more, also in an old Mishnah,[27] which incidentally describes the points of difference on dogmatic issues between Pharisees and Sadducees. 'The following have no share in the 'olam ha-ba', the World to come (or, Age to come): He who says, there will be no resurrection, Torah was not revealed, and Epiqurus' i.e., an Epicurean — note especially that the text reads, (an) Epiqurus, not the Epicurean; note further, that in all the best MSS and editions, the transliteration of the word is excellent, אפיקורוס, not אפיקור [28] as in many later indifferent appearances of the term. Except for these two places the word does not appear anywhere else in the Mishnah — all other appearances of the term in the Mishnah, as one may learn even by consulting Kasovsky's *Concordance*,[29] are untrustworthy. In the Mishnah, then, the word has not yet been worn thin by frequent usage. All of which is simply meant to underscore, that it is wisest not to water down Eleazar's remark, and if he said an Epicurean, he meant just that. Very likely he had not non-Jewish, but Jewish Epicureans in mind. But he very likely did have in mind such Jews as had become epicurean more or less in outlook, not just any heretic at all.

To be sure, by the latter half of the second century, as would appear from Lucian's 'Alexander the False Prophet,' the term Epicurean seems to have become a dirty word, one can frighten audiences with it[30] although they might not know what the term meant really, somewhat like the word 'communist' in some circles today. But that Eleazar was using Epicurean in a slovenly name-calling manner is most unlikely. Observe, he does not say, Beware (*hewe zahir*) of an Epiqurus — an idiom so congenial to *Pirqe 'Abot*.[31] What he says is, Be *shaqud*, diligent, *lilmod*, to study, to learn, *le-hashib*, to reply, to refute. He is speaking of serious refutation of the Epicurean, and like a Stoic insists that there is a trustworthy God before whom we engage in our toiling.[32]

We are now in a position, I believe, to understand part of the story of Rabban Johanan's enthusiasm over his disciple's brilliant Merkabah discourse.

---

[27] *Sanhedrin* 10.1, and for the correct reading and the implications thereof cf. J. Goldin in *Proceedings, American Academy for Jewish Research* 27 (1958) 49, and notes *ad loc.*

[28] And though the copyist of the Version B manuscript for S. Schechter's edition of ARN 66 recorded אפיקורס I personally checked Vatican MS heb. 303, and found the reading to be definitely אפיקורוס.

[29] C. Y. Kasovsky, *Thesaurus Mishnae* [Heb.] (Jerusalem 1956) I 261. And note its *single* appearance in the Tosefta, *Sanhedrin* 13.5.

[30] Cf. ed. M. Harmon (in Loeb Classics, IV 175ff.).

[31] See for example PA 1.9, 11; 2.1, 3, 10, 13; 4.13.

[32] Cf. R. D. Hicks, *Stoic and Epicurean* (New York 1910) 304: 'The Epicureans were never tired of arguing against the conception of God as either Creator or Providence ... On these points their chief antagonists were the Stoics ...

The talmudic sources relate that when Eleazar finished speaking, his master not only kissed him and exclaimed 'Blessed be the Lord, God of Israel, who gave such a descendant to our father Abraham,' but went on as follows:

> There are some who teach, interpret (*doresh*) becomingly, but do not practice, do not carry out, becomingly; there are some who practice what is becoming, but do not teach becomingly. But Eleazar ben 'Arak teaches becomingly and practices becomingly. How fortunate you are, O father Abraham (et cetera).

'Practices what he preaches,' *na'eh doresh we-na'eh meqayyem*, has become so familiar an expression in Hebrew, that occasionally one imagines that it occurs frequently in the classical sources. The fact is, it occurs only in one other context. When, it is reported, the bachelor Ben 'Azzai held forth on one occasion, on the importance of the first biblical commandment, to be fruitful and to multiply, his colleague Eleazar ben Azariah rejoined stingingly:

> Things are well said when they come from the mouths of those who put them to practice, *na'im debarim ke-she-hen yoṣ'in mi-pi 'oṣehen*. There are some who teach becomingly and practice becomingly. Ben 'Azzai teaches becomingly but does not practice becomingly.[33]

Or as we might put it, he *talks* a good line. Now, in this context Eleazar's rejoinder is perfectly intelligible. But what can that remark mean in the story of Eleazar ben 'Arak's Merkabah discourse in the presence of Johanan ben Zakkai? What practice, ill or otherwise, would be at issue? That when Johanan warned him that esoteric subjects are not discussed in public, Eleazar assented? As the texts read, it is no wonder commentators (e. g. the *Maharsha*)[34] have had difficulty with that sentence. What meaning can *na'eh meqayyem* have here, even if *na'eh doresh* does apply to a brilliant discourse?

It is a Hellenistic source which furnishes the answer to this question. Diogenes Laertius says that when the Athenians honored Zeno, the founder of the Stoic school, among other things this is what they said of him:[35]

> ... Zeno of Citium ... has for many years been ... exhorting to virtue and temperance those of the youth who come to him to be taught, directing them to what is best, affording to all in his own conduct a pattern for imitation in perfect consistency with his teaching (παράδειγμα τὸν ἴδιον βίον ἐκθεὶς ἅπασιν ἀκόλουθον ὄντα τοῖς λόγοις οἷς διελέγετο). [36]

And so, 'practices what he preaches' is a *topos*, a way of complimenting pure and simple. And since I wrote the paragraph above, S. Lieberman has

---

[33] *T. Yebamot* 8.4 (and see S. Lieberman, *Tosefeth Rishonim* [Jerusalem 1938] II 22); cf. *B. Yebamot* 63b and *Genesis Rabba* 34, ed. Theodor-Albeck 326f.

[34] I.e., Rabbi Samuel Edels (1555-1631), the author of impressive talmudic *novellae*. His comment occurs *ad B. Hagigah* 14b.

[35] Diog. Laert. 7.10-11 (ed. Hicks in Loeb Classics, II 121, whose translation I am using).

[36] On the genuineness of the decree see Hicks' reference *loc. cit.* 120.

graciously sent me in private communication, two or three additional examples, one of them by the way from Plutarch (*Moralia* 1033ᵃ seq.), in which *Stoics* are criticized for not living, conducting themselves, as they themselves teach. One cannot help therefore recalling what Lucian writes of the philosophers in his *Menippus*:[37] τοὺς γὰρ αὐτοὺς τούτους εὕρισκον ἐπιτηρῶν ἐναντιώτατα τοῖς αὐτῶν λόγοις ἐπιτηδεύοντας.

It may be no more than a coincidence that Eleazar ben 'Arak should be praised by his teacher as the founder of the Stoics was praised. And I certainly do not intend to press this too hard. Let us therefore get on with our sources. We read:[38] When Johanan ben Zakkai's son died, his five famous disciples came to comfort him. Each one made the earnest effort, Eliezer ben Hyrqanos, Joshua ben Hananiah, Jose the Priest, Simeon ben Nathanel, and Eleazar ben 'Arak. But all of them, except the last, failed. As Johanan put it to each one in turn, as each finished his little homily, 'Is it not enough that I grieve over my own, that you remind me of the grief of' others? But when Eleazar appeared, the outcome was different. As soon as he appeared, Johanan knew he would be comforted, and in fact he was. And here is what Eleazar had said and what proved to be the genuine consolation:

> I shall tell thee a parable: to what may this be likened? To a man with whom the king deposited some object. Every single day the man would weep and cry out, saying: 'Woe unto me! When shall I be quit of this trust in peace?' Thou too, master, thou hadst a son: he studied the Torah, the Prophets, the Holy Writings,[39] he studied Mishnah, Halakah, and Haggadah, and he departed from the world without sin. And thou shouldst be comforted when thou hast returned thy trust unimpaired.

Now, this notion of the soul of one's beloved held in trust is not unknown in rabbinic sources; it is especially· familiar in the anecdote of the death of Rabbi Me'ir's sons.[40] It occurs also in non-rabbinic sources,[41] and I would like to cite a relevant passage from Philo (*de Abrahamo* 44)[42] who in praising Abraham says:

> ... I will speak of one [merit] which concerns the death of his wife, in which his conduct should not be passed over in silence. When he had lost his life-long partner ... when sorrow was making itself ready to wrestle with his soul, he grappled with it, as in the arena, and prevailed. He gave strength and high courage to the natural antagonist of passion, reason,

---

[37] *Men.* 5 (in Loeb Classics, IV 82).

[38] ARN 58f.

[39] The correct reading of the text is preserved in Israel ibn Al-Nakawa, *Menorat Ha-Maor,* ed. H. G. Enclow (New York 1929-32) III 523.

[40] *Midrash Mishle,* ed. Buber 108-9.

[41] See for example Sapientia 15.8, 16, and especially Josephus, *Wars* 3.8.5.

[42] I am using Colson's translation (Loeb Classics, VI 125ff.).

which he had taken as his counsellor throughout his life and now particularly was determined to obey. ... The advice was that he should not grieve over-bitterly as at an utterly new and unheard-of misfortune, nor yet assume an indifference as though nothing painful had occurred, but choose the mean rather than the extremes and aim at moderation of feeling, not resent that nature should be paid the debt which is its due, but quietly and gently lighten the blow..

The testimonies for this are to be found in the holy books ... They show that after weeping for a little over the corpse he quickly rose up from it, holding further mourning to be out of keeping with wisdom, which taught him that death is not the extinction of the soul but its separation and detachment from the body and its return to the place whence it came ; and it came, as was shown in the story of creation, from God. *And, as no reasonable person would chafe at repaying a debt or deposit (χρέος ἢ παραχαταθήχην) to him who had proffered it, so too he must not fret when nature took back her own, but accept the inevitable with equanimity.*

The passage, as is clear, reverberates with Stoic echoes.[43] 'Never say about anything,' Epictetus tells us,[44] '"I have lost it," but only "I have given it back." Is your child dead? It has been given back (ἀπεδόθη). Is your wife dead? She has been given back.' Interesting enough, when Tarn comes to summarize Stoic teaching, even he chooses as one of its distinctive emphases, 'the Stoic will not grieve for his son's death.'[45]

Once again perhaps it may be wise to repeat the note of caution already struck. It does not *necessarily* follow from all we have thus far explored, that without the Stoics the talmudic Fathers could not have arrived at the idea of the soul as a deposit — though I must say, even Ps. 30.6 (MT 31.6), 'In manus tuas commendo spiritum meum,' does not *altogether* suggest the idea to the tannaite midrash, the *Mekilta*,[46] which cites the verse as prooftext for the statement that 'all souls are in the hand of Him by whose utterance the world came into being.' In the companion midrash, *Mekilta of R. Simeon*,[47] the idea is not even given the benefit of this prooftext: the verse isn't cited at all ! Be that as it may, even a novice knows that it is fake scholarship to declare that there is necessary dependence simply because one finds

---

[43] See also Colson's note, *loc. cit.* 598f. Cf. Philo's *Quaestiones*, ed. R. Marcus (Loeb Classics) I 350-52.

[44] *Encheiridion* 11, ed. W. A. Oldfather (Loeb Classics) II 491.

[45] *Hellenistic Civilization* (London 1936) 299. In *Republic* 10, 603, Plato also says that the good man will not mourn excessively over the loss of his son; but though he gives several reasons for this, he does not speak of the soul as a deposit or trust.

[46] Ed. J. Z. Lauterbach II 67. St. Augustine on that verse does not speak of this either. Note that primarily the verse recalls to him its use in Luke 23.46, and hence he underscores 'Audiamus vocem Domini,' cf. *Enarrationes in Psalmos* ad loc. (ed. Dekkers and Fraipont, CCL 38 [1956] 199). Cf. St. Jerome on Ps, 145.4 (MT 146.4) (ed. Morin, CCL 78.324).

[47] Ed. Epstein-Melamed 95.

similarity of ideas. But, firstly, similarity should be recognized if it exists, even if there may be no dependence. Secondly, however, there is a detail that must be introduced in this connection.

Josephus cannot be depended on either when he protests *pro vita sua* or — and it is this which concerns us here — when he describes sects in Jewish Palestine as though they were Greek schools of thought. This has been underscored so frequently by so many scholars that it would be childish to ignore their remarks. And yet, even if we grant that it is grotesque to look upon Pharisees, Sadducees, and Essenes as though they were imitation Greek schools, perhaps we may learn something from the particular form of absurdity of which the author is guilty. It is instructive that, when Josephus describes the Pharisees, of all schools, he chooses the Stoics to compare them with: 'the Pharisees, a sect having points of resemblance to that which the Greeks call the Stoic school.'[48] The statement is not to be dismissed cavalierly: observe how carefully he has expressed himself, 'a sect having points of resemblance,' ἡ παραπλήσιός ἐστι. That Josephus is capable of giving an accurate characterization of a Greek school, we know from his observations on the Epicureans:[49]

> It therefore seems to me, in view of the things foretold by Daniel, that they are very far from holding a true opinion who declare that God takes no thought for human affairs. For if it were the case that *the world goes by some automatism* (εἰ συνέβαινεν αὐτοματισμῷ τινι τὸν κόσμον διάγειν)[50], we should not have seen all these things happen in accordance with his prophecy.

Josephus may be stretching a point, and more than a point, when he feels he has to. But he is undoubtedly registering something real about the Pharisees — they *were* affected by a Stoic climate; and as Tarn has written:[51] 'The philosophy of the Hellenistic world was the Stoic; all else was secondary.' Jewish Palestine was not immune to this.

Such at least is the climate of notions around Eleazar ben 'Arak, Johanan ben Zakkai's favorite disciple of whom the text says: 'Happy the disciple whose master praises him and testifies to his gifts!'[52] And if we keep this climate in mind we shall understand a famous block of passages in *Pirqe 'Abot* (hereafter PA), often cited, but perhaps not sufficiently appreciated.

---

[48] *Vita* 2, end, ed. Thackeray 7.

[49] *Antiquities* 10, end, ed. R. Marcus (Loeb Classics) VI 313.

[50] See also S. Lieberman, 'How Much Greek in Jewish Palestine,' in *Studies and Texts* I, ed. A. Altmann (Cambridge, Mass. 1963) 130. By the way, rabbinic sources reflect also an awareness of the fact that as regards Providence and belief in God, there are varieties of views; cf. *Sifre* Deut. 329, ed. Finkelstein 379 and *Midrash Tannaim* 202.

[51] *Op. cit.* 290. And regarding semitic influences on Stoic thought, cf. Rostovtzeff, *Social and Economic History of the Hellenistic World* (Oxford 1941) 1426 n. 232.

[52] Cf. Goldin, *Fathers ... Nathan* 74, and note *ad loc.*

When the second chapter of PA resumes the chain of tradition which is the basic scheme of the first chapter, it quite properly introduces Johanan ben Zakkai with the customary formula. 'Rabban Johanan ben Zakkai took over from Hillel and Shammai.'[53] Then, as is the practice of PA, it quotes his saying. Since the editor is eager to show that that chain of tradition, whose first link was forged with Moses at Sinai,[54] was not broken even after Johanan ben Zakkai — though in his day the Temple had been destroyed[55] — he proceeds to introduce the five famous disciples of Johanan, and to quote *their* sayings. But as everyone knows, this introduction is not quite like all the previous introductions. Before the editor quotes these men, he first informs us how Johanan used to describe them.[56] Even after that he does not quote the disciples; before the editor gets down to their sentences he introduces a long conversation piece, a section recording an exchange between Johanan and his disciples.[57] Only after all this does he transmit their sayings. Nothing like this, description[58] or conversation, occurs anywhere else in PA.

The insertion of a description of the disciples is easily explainable. Since the editor is eager to assert that despite the national, the political and institutional, disaster, the destruction of the Jerusalem Temple, the Pharisaic chain of tradition remained unbroken, we can appreciate why he feels he ought to report the master's own testimony regarding the stature of his disciples. These were no ordinary disciples, no run of the mill sages. Eliezer ben Hyrqanos was 'a plastered cistern which loses not a drop. Joshua — Happy is she who gave birth to him. Jose — A saint. Simeon ben Nathanel — Fears sin. Eleazar ben 'Arak — Ever flowing stream.' I wish I could understand specifically each of these compliments — they are obviously intended to suggest something extraordinary; and perhaps to have called Eliezer ben Hyrqanos 'a plastered cistern which loses not a drop,' was more or less what Zeno meant when he compared his successor Cleanthes 'to hard waxen tablets which are difficult to write upon, but retain the characters written upon them.'[59] But, as I say, while it is not the practice of PA otherwise to include such data regarding the other sages, in the case of the five disciples of Johanan the motive is understandable. But why, after he has introduced them so handsomely, does not the editor begin to quote them, as he does with all other sages? Why before quoting their sayings does he insert the long conversation, especially in a treatise where no other give-and-take is presented,

---

[53] PA 2.8; cf. the idiom in 1.3, 4, 6, 8, 10, 12.   [54] PA 1.1.

[55] See the story in Goldin, *Fathers* ... *Nathan* 35ff.

[56] PA 2.8.   [57] 2.9.

[58] On the other hand, see how the compiler of Version A of ARN (ch. 18) pp. 66-69 was led by this to draw up additional material (but not of a master describing *disciples*, but of a sage describing his teachers and predecessors, and a sage describing other sages).

[59] Diogenes Laertius 7.37 (II 149).

halakic *or* haggadic? And since this is not the only question raised by the long passage, perhaps it would be wise to quote it, so that we may see vividly what the problems are:[60]

> Rabban Johanan said to them: Go forth and see which is the right way to which a man should cleave.
>> Rabbi Eliezer replied: A liberal eye.
>> Rabbi Joshua replied: A good companion.
>> Rabbi Jose replied: A good neighbor.
>> Rabbi Simeon replied: Foresight.
>> Rabbi Eleazar replied: Goodheartedness.
> Said Rabban Johanan ben Zakkai to them: I prefer the answer of Eleazar ben 'Arak, for in his words your words are included.
> Rabban Johanan said to them: Go forth and see which is the evil way which a man should shun.
>> Rabbi Eliezer replied: A grudging eye.
>> Rabbi Joshua replied: An evil companion.
>> Rabbi Jose replied: An evil neighbor.
>> Rabbi Simeon replied: Borrowing and not repaying; for he that borrows from man is as one who borrows from God, blessed be He, as it is said, 'The wicked man borrows and does not repay, but the just man shows mercy and gives' (Ps. 36.21; MT 37.21).[61]
>> Rabbi Eleazar replied: Meanheartedness.
> Said Rabban Johanan to them: I prefer the answer of Eleazar ben 'Arak, for in his words your words are included.

There it is, a conversation (as I said) unlike anything else in PA, and only after it has been reported, are we offered the sayings of these sages. As one reads it, not only must he ask, what in the world is it doing here, but he cannot escape at least two other questions. First, what are these men talking about? True, their master had asked them about the right way, or course, to which a person ought to cling, and they had offered their replies. But is it not fantastic that these men, the best disciples Johanan ben Zakkai had—Johanan ben Zakkai who had been quoted a paragraph or so before[62] as the author of the saying, 'If thou hast wrought much in the study of Torah take no credit to thyself, for to this end wast thou created,' and as ARN added,[63] 'for men (*haberiyot*) were created only on condition that they study Torah' — is it not fantastic that, when the best disciples of such a master, leading sages in Israel, are asked about the right course to which a man should cleave, not even one of them suggests in his answer something connected with Torah?

---

[60] PA 2.9; for the translation cf. J. Goldin, *Living Talmud: the Wisdom of the Fathers* (Chicago 1958) 99.

[61] With St. Augustine's comment on this verse, 'Quid si pauper est' etc. (CCL 38.355f.), cf. ARN 48 and 57, and Maimonides' Code, *Mishneh Torah*, Sefer Zera'im, Hilkot Matnot 'Aniyyim X (and note X,4).   [62] PA 2.8.

[63] p. 58; and see also Version B of ARN, 66.

Jewish sages without a word about the Torah? Second, what is the meaning of asking first about the right way and then about the evil way, and then the answers which are simply the negation of the former affirmations? What have I learned from the second conversation that I did not already learn from the first one?

That the ancients already found ths passage something of a serious problem is evident from the way it is preserved in ARN.[64] To give only a couple of examples: In PA Johanan had asked, which is the right way to which a man should cleave. In ARN, his question appears as, 'Which is the good way to which a man should cleave, *so that through it he might enter the world to come?* . . . Which is the evil way which a man should shun, *so that he might enter the world to come?*' In other words, 'the world to come' has suddenly made an entrance. Or again: In PA, to the first question Rabbi Jose had replied, A good neighbor, and to the second question, An evil neighbor. In ARN on the other hand, he seems to have grown a little more garrulous in his answers. To the first question he replies, 'A good neighbor, a good impulse (*yeṣer ṭob*), and a good wife'; to the second, 'An evil neighbor, an evil impulse, and an evil wife.'[65] These are not the only variants; study of the parallel passages will reveal interesting variants in Eleazar ben 'Arak's answer too.

The answers of the disciples are far from clear, but if we wish to capture something of the meaning of this exchange between Johanan and his disciples, it is terribly important to listen to his question with utmost attention. Johanan did not ask a trivial question, nor did he express himself carelessly. He asked about the way to which a man should 'cleave,' *dabaq.* Properly to feel the force of this verb *dabaq*, one might compare Johanan's question with the almost identical — *almost* but not entirely — question later raised by Judah the Prince, the redactor of the Mishnah, also quoted in the second chapter of PA — indeed he is the first sage cited there.[66] Judah asks: 'Which is the right course that a man ought to *choose* (*she-yabor*) for himself?' But Johanan speaks not just of choice, but of *cleaving.* That the Hebrew sources take the verb *dabaq*, cleave, very seriously, can be demonstrated by a number of texts. The biblical verse (Deut. 11.22) exhorts, 'to love the Lord your God, to walk in all His ways, and to cleave (προσκολλᾶσθαι) unto him (*adhaerentes ei*).' At which the tannaite midrash, the *Sifre*, exclaims:[67] 'But how is it possible for a human being to ascend on high and cleave to the Fire?' Even in Scripture the verb *dabaq* has a fervor to it; here is Jeremiah (13.11) expressing himself: 'For as the girdle cleaveth (*yidbaq ha-'ezor*, κολλᾶται) to the

---

[64] p.58.   [65] And note the reading of Version B, 59.
[66] PA 2.1, beginning; cf. Version B of ARN, 70.
[67] *Ad* Deut. 49. ed. Finkelstein 114.

loins of a man, so have I caused to cleave unto Me (*hidbaqti'elai, ἐκόλλησα*) the whole house of Israel and the whole house of Judah, saith the Lord.' (*Sicut enim adhaeret lumbare ad lumbos viri, sic agglutinavi mihi omnem domum Juda, dicit Dominus.*) That the Midrash is fully sensitive to this verse can be seen in the Tanhuma comment on Lev. 19.2:[68] 'Be ye holy! Why? For I am holy, for it is said, "As the girdle cleaveth to the loins of a man," etc.' 'Let him kiss me with the kisses of his mouth' (*Osculetur me osculo oris sui*), says the poet of Canticles (Cant. 1.1, MT 1.2); and the Midrash in its homiletical pun explains, '*Let Him kiss me*, let Him cause me to cleave to Him (*yishaqeni, yadbqeni*).'[69]

So long as we are lingering over the word *dabaq*, 'cleave,' I hope it is not out of place to call attention to one more point, especially for the benefit of Hebraists. According to our sources, both PA and ARN, the question Johanan asked was: What is the way (or, course) to which a man should cleave (איזוהי דרך .... שידבק בה האדם)? In other words, he is speaking of *cleaving to a way*. But though *dabaq* is not a rare word in Scripture, nowhere does such an expression occur — and not only in Scripture, but at least for the time being, in none of the documents from the Dead Sea. A man cleaves to his wife,[70] the tongue cleaves to the roof of the mouth,[71] one cleaves to the truth and good deeds and the testimonies of the Lord,[72] curses cleave to a man,[73] and Ps. 62.9 (MT 63.9) offers even 'My soul cleaveth unto Thee' (*Adhaesit anima mea post te*), literally, after thee, דבקה נפשי אחריך (cf.LXX 62.9, ἐκολλήθη ἡ ψυχή μου ὀπίσω σου);as we have seen, there are those who cleave

---

[68] Ed. Buber, III 37b.

[69] *Canticles Rabba* 1.2, 6. For the pun on the verb *nashaq ad loc.* see the commentators. On the intensity of the expression in Cant. see also Origen's Commentary (Origen, *The Song of Songs, Commentary and Homilies*, trans. R. P. Lawson [Ancient Christian Writers 26; London 1957] 60): 'But, since the age is almost ended and His own presence is not granted me, and I see only His ministers ascending and descending upon me, because of this I pour out my petition to Thee, the Father of my Spouse, beseeching Thee to have compassion at last upon my love, and to send Him, that He may now no longer speak to me only by His servants the angels and the prophets, but may come Himself, directly, and kiss me with the kisses of His mouth — that is to say, may pour the words of His mouth into mine, that I may hear Him speak Himself, and see Him teaching. The kisses are Christ's, which He bestows on His Church when at His coming, being present in the flesh, He in His own person spoke to her the words of faith and love and peace, according to the promise of Isaias who, when sent beforehand to the Bride, had said (cf. Isa. 33.22): *Not a messenger, nor an angel, but the Lord Himself shall save us.*' Cf. also S. Lieberman, *Yemenite Midrashim* (Jerusalem 1940) 14.

[70] Cf. Gen. 2.24.   [71] Ps. 136.6 (MT 137.6).

[72] *Dead Sea Scrolls* II 2: *Manual of Discipline*, ed. M. Burrows (New Haven 1951) Plate I, line 5; *Thanksgiving Scroll*, ed. J. Licht (Jerusalem 1957) 202; Ps. 118.31 (MT 119.31).

[73] *Dead Sea Scrolls* II, Plate II, lines 15 f.; *Zadokite Documents*, ed. C. Rabin (Oxford 1958) 5.

to the Lord (cf. Deut. 4.4; LXX, Ὑμεῖς δὲ οἱ προσκείμενοι [!] κυρίῳ, Vos autem qui adhaeretis Domino Deo vestri). But nowhere else will one find this combination דבק בדרך — nowhere else, that is, except in a statement of old exegetes whom the tannaite sources call Doreshe Reshumot or Doreshe Haggadot. Lauterbach once called them the Allegorical Interpreters.[74] Be that as it may, the exegesis of these anonymous teachers is of a figurative-speculative kind. And it is in one of their comments, preserved in the tannaite Sifre[75] that the following occurs: 'If it is your wish to recognize (acknowledge?) Him at whose utterance the world came into being,[76] study Haggadah — for thus you come to recognize God and cleave to His ways' ומדבק בדרליו.

The term dabaq then is no ordinary term, and it was no ordinary question Johanan asked, and the give-and-take with his disciples was no ordinary conversation. The idiom reveals a certain intensiveness, a certain fervor, and this is the telling thing. It is the idiom which suddenly summons up remembrances of a mood and a tone of voice which were current in Hellenist circles. As Nock wrote three decades ago:[77]

... this idea [that devotion to philosophy would make a difference in a man's life] was not thought of as a matter of purely intellectual conviction. The philosopher commonly said not 'Follow my arguments one by one, check and control them to the best of your ability; truth should be dearer than Plato to you,' but 'Look at this picture which I paint, and can you resist its attractions? Can you refuse a hearing to the legitimate rhetoric which I address to you in the name of virtue?' Even Epicurus says in an argument, 'Do not be deceived, men, or led astray: do not fall. There is no natural fellowship between reasonable beings. Believe me, those who express the other view deceive you and argue you out of what is right. Epictetus, II, 19, 34 also employs the same appeal, Believe me, and counters opponents by arguments which appeal to the heart and not to the head. Inside the schools, at least inside the academic school, there was an atmosphere of hard thinking, of which something survives in the various commentaries on Aristotle. Yet even in the schools this was overcast by tradition and loyalty. ... The philosophy which addressed itself to the world at large was a dogmatic philosophy seeking to save souls.

---

[74] See J. Z. Lauterbach, 'The Ancient Jewish Allegorists in Talmud and Midrash' in Jewish Quarterly Review N. S. 1 (1910-11) 291-333, 503-31.

[75] Ad Deut. loc. cit., and note ibid. the variant readings in the critical apparatus.

[76] Literally, 'Him who spake and the world (ha-ʿolam) came to be.' I would like to call special attention to the variants 'The Holy One, blessed be He' and 'thy Creator' recorded by Finkelstein, ad loc. (I neglected to do this in the Hebrew version of this study), for if these doreshe haggadot are pre-70 A.D., they did not use ha-ʿolam for 'world'. See my note 39 in 'Of Change and Adaptation in Judaism' in History of Religions, 4 (Chicago 1965) 283.

[77] Conversion 181. And see also H. I. Marrou, History of Education in Antiquity (New York 1956) 206.

This is the mood of our PA passage, and this is the mood of Johanan's question, which I believe can almost be rendered in the words from Diogenes Laertius, τί πράττων ἄριστα βιώσεται.[78] It was then a philosophical question Johanan asked; and first he asked which is the right way, and then which is the evil way. In other words, what is he doing? He formulates his question first in the positive, then in the negative, one way and its opposite. And when his disciples replied, as we saw, they did the same thing (to Simeon's answer we shall get shortly), one way and its opposite: liberal eye, grudging eye (עין טובה, עין רעה); good companion, evil companion; good neighbor, evil neighbor; goodheartedness, meanheartedness (leb tob, leb ra').

It will now be instructive to review the summary of Stoic teaching drawn up by Diogenes Laertius[79] (of which Hicks says,[80] by the way, 'the summary of Stoic doctrine in Book VII (39-160) is comprehensive and trustworthy'):

> Amongst *the virtues* (τῶν δ'ἀρετῶν) some are primary, some are subordinate to these. The following are the primary: wisdom, courage, justice, temperance. Particular virtues are magnanimity, continence, endurance, presence of mind, good counsel.
>
> Similarly, *of vices* (τῶν κακιῶν) some are primary, others subordinate: e. g., folly, cowardice, injustice, profligacy are accounted primary; but incontinence, stupidity, ill-advisedness subordinate. Further, many hold that *the vices* are forms of ignorance of those things whereof the *corresponding virtues* are the knowledge. . . .
>
> Another particular definition *of good* which they give is 'the natural perfection of a rational being *qua* rational.' To this answers virtue and, as being partakes in virtue, virtuous acts and good men; also its supervening accessories, joy and gladness and the like. So *with evils*: either they are vices, folly, cowardice, injustice, and the like; or things which partake of vice, including vicious acts and wicked persons as well as their accompaniments, despair, moroseness, and the like.
>
> Again, *some goods* (τῶν ἀγαθῶν) are goods of the mind, and others external, while some are neither mental nor external. The former include the virtues and virtuous acts; external goods are such as having a good country or a good friend, and the prosperity of such. Whereas to be good and happy oneself is of the class of goods neither mental nor external. Similarly of *things evil* (τῶν κακῶν) some are mental evils, namely, vices and vicious actions; others are outward evils, as to have a foolish country or a foolish friend and the unhappiness of such; other evils again are neither mental nor outward, e. g., to be yourself bad and unhappy.
>
> Again, *goods* (τῶν ἀγαθῶν) are either of the nature of ends or they are the means to these ends, or they are at the same time ends and means.

---

[78] 7.2 (Loeb Classics II, 110). And cf. Marrou, *op. cit.* 209: 'The more the Graeco-Roman period advances, the more important the moral aspect becomes, until it is the essential if not the only object of the philosopher's speculation and activity and whole life.'

[79] 7.92 ff (II 199 ff., Hicks' translation)

[80] In his introduction, p. xx.

A friend and the advantages derived from him are means to good, whereas confidence, high-spirit, liberty, delight, gladness, freedom from pain, and every virtuous act are of the nature of ends.

The virtues (they say) are goods of the nature at once of ends and of means. On the one hand, in so far as they cause happiness they are means, and on the other hand, insofar as they make it complete, and so are themselves part of it, they are ends. Similarly *of evils* (τῶν κακῶν) some are of the nature of ends and some of means, while others are at once both means and ends. Your enemy and the harm he does you are means; consternation, abasement, slavery, gloom, despair, excess of grief, and every vicious action are of the nature of ends. Vices are evil both as ends and as means, since insofar as they cause misery they are means, but insofar as they make it complete, so that they become part of it, they are ends. . . .

. . . . *Of the beautiful* (τοῦ καλοῦ) there are (they say) four species, namely, what is just, courageous, orderly and wise. . . . Similarly there are four species *of the base or ugly* (τοῦ αἰσχροῦ), namely, what is unjust, cowardly, disorderly, and unwise. . . .

Goods ('Αγαθά) comprise the virtues of prudence, justice, courage, temperance, and the rest; while the opposites of these are *evils* (κακά), namely, folly, injustice, and the rest.[81] . . . *To benefit* (ὠφελεῖν) is to set in motion or sustain in accordance with virtue; whereas *to harm* (βλάπτειν) is to set in motion or sustain in accordance with vice. . . .

. . . Things of the *preferred class* (προηγμένα) are those which have positive value, *e. g.* amongst mental qualities, natural ability, skill, moral improvement, and the like; among bodily qualities, life, health, strength, good condition, soundness of organs, beauty, and so forth; and in the sphere of external things, wealth, fame, noble birth, and the like. To the class of *things 'rejected'* (ἀποπροηγμένα) belong, of mental qualities, lack of ability, want of skill, and the like; among bodily qualities, death, disease, weakness, being out of condition, mutilation, ugliness, and the like; in the sphere of external things, poverty, ignominy, low birth, and so forth. . . . [82]

Again, *of things preferred* some are preferred for their own sake, some for the sake of something else, and others again both for their own sake and for the sake of something else. . . . And similarly with the class of *things rejected* under the contrary heads. . . .

Befitting acts (καθήκοντα)[83] are all those which reason prevails with us to do; and this is the case with honoring one's parents, brothers and country, and intercourse with friends. *Unbefitting, or contrary to duty* (παρὰ τὸ καθῆκον) are all acts that reason deprecates, *e. g.* to neglect one's

---

[81] Since at this point Diogenes presents also the view of those who believe that in addition to the good and evil, there is also the neutral, he adds that neutral (neither good nor evil) 'are all those things which neither benefit nor harm a man: such as life, health . . . and the like. This Hecato affirms in his *De fine* book vii,' etc. Cf. Diogenes on Plato in 3.102 (H 365-66).

[82] Here too Diogenes adds: 'But again there are things belonging to neither class; such are not preferred, neither are they rejected.' Cf. preceding note.

[83] Cf. Diogenes 7.108: 'Zeno was the first to use this term καθῆκον of conduct'; and see Hicks' note *ad loc.*

parents, to be indifferent to one's brothers, not to agree with friends, to disregard the interests of one's country, and so forth . . . [84]

Surely this is enough, more than enough. The summary of Stoic ethics has manifestly been drawn up along a certain line, first the positive, then the negative, first in terms of the good and then immediately thereafter in terms of the evil. I am in no position to say whether this pattern or idiom is unique to the Stoics, especially when I recall some sections in the *Republic,* for example;[85] and I would indeed be grateful to classicists if they could inform me whether such a style is characteristic of study and discussion in Hellenistic schools generally. But it is impressive, is it not, that only in Diogenes' summary of *Stoic* teaching, and in no other summary of his (including the long presentation of Epicurean teaching),[86] is this style so distinct. Whatever else one may wish to conclude, this at least seems to me legitimate — that in Stoic circles defining and discussing were carried on in this style, first the one term, and then its opposite.

And this is precisely the form of the give-and-take between Johanan and his disciples, first the good course, and then the evil course. It is a philosophical *façon de parler* Johanan is using. And since it was a philosophical question he had asked, as we saw earlier in our analysis of the idiom of his question, his disciples answered him in the philosophical way, first the positive, then the negative. Since it was a philosophical question, his disciples answered in characteristic philosophical terms — and that is why not one of them even bothered to refer to Torah. And since it was an important session, though nothing like it occurs elsewhere in the treatise, the editor of PA preserved the record of it, put it down right after he had recounted the praises of the disciples — but before he cites their sayings. It is as though the editor were asserting: You see, not only did their master Johanan testify to the greatness of these men, but here is a transcript of a very significant session conducted in their academy. Only after all this does the editor begin to cite them — and significantly enough, these sayings are introduced by the very formula he had used in introducing the Men of the Great Assembly, the first spokesmen of the Oral Torah: 'and they said three things.'[87]

One more point, and then we shall arrive at the conclusion. We noted that the disciples had replied to Johanan's questions first positively, and

---

[84] Cf. notes 81-82 *supra.*

[85] Cf. 3.400; 4.442-43; and compare especially 8-9 with the earlier books. See also Diogenes on Plato, 3.103ff. (II 367f.).

[86] '. . . Book X is made up largely of extracts from the writings of Epicurus, by far the most precious thing preserved in this collection of odds and ends' (Hicks in his Introduction, p. xx).

[87] Cf. PA 1.1 and 2.10, ARN 59, and see C. Taylor, *Sayings of the Jewish Fathers* II 144 (and the duplication is *not* to be preferred).

then negatively: 'Liberal eye, grudging eye; good companion, evil companion; good neighbor, evil neighbor; goodheartedness, meanheartedness.' So the answers of four of the disciples. But what of the reply by Simeon ben Nathanel? To the first question, what is the good course, he had replied, 'Foresight'; to the second question, what is the evil course, he had replied, 'Borrowing and not repaying.' Many a commentator has insisted, and probably correctly, that since the other four replies were in the fixed form of Johanan's question, of positive and negative, the same must no doubt be true of Simeon's reply. This stands to reason. But one thing we surely cannot fail to recognize:

> But speaking of this very thing, justice, are we to affirm thus without qualification that it is truth-telling and *paying back what one has received* from anyone . . . ? I mean, for example, . . . if one took over weapons from a friend who was in his right mind and then the lender should go mad and demand them back, that we ought not to return them in that case and that he who did so return them would not be acting justly. . . . Then this is not the definition of justice: to tell the truth and return what one has received.
>
> 'Nay, but it is, Socrates,' said Polemarchus breaking in, 'if indeed we are to put any faith in Simonides' . . .
>
> 'Tell me, then, . . . what is it that you affirm that Simonides says, and rightly says about justice.' 'That it is just,' he replied, 'to render to each his due (ὅτι ... τὸ τὰ ὀφειλόμενα ἑκάστῳ ἀποδιδόναι δίκαιόν ἐστι). In saying this I think he speaks well.'
>
> 'I must admit,' said I, 'that it is not easy to disbelieve Simonides. For he is a wise and inspired man. . . . '[88]

To be sure, Socrates is being ironic, but Simonides' definition was, as we know, the current and generally accepted one. As Shorey remarks in his note: 'Owing to the rarity of banks "reddere depositum" was throughout antiquity the typical instance of just conduct.' And see also what Shorey cites as regards Stoic terminology.[89]

At least therefore in one of his answers, Simeon is echoing the kind of opinion that one overheard in the schools of the larger world outside the rabbinic academy. And perhaps 'foresight' is, as some commentators suggest, the opposite of *reddere depositum*.[90]

* * *

---

[88] Plato, *Republic* 1, 331D-E, ed. P. Shorey (Loeb Classics I 20f.); cf. Diogenes Laertius 3.83 (I 351).

[89] p. 22 note a. And cf. the citation from Stobaeus (ἀπονεμητική τῆς ἀξίας ἑκάστῳ) and the note in A. C. Pearson, *The Fragments of Zeno and Cleanthes* (London 1891) 175.

[90] See, e.g., *Midrash Shemuel* of Samuel ben Isaac of Uçeda (XVI cent.) (New York 5705 [1935]) 71f. Interestingly enough, in B. Tamid 32a 'foresight' is the answer given by the elders (sages) of the south to Alexander the Great!

What does all this add up to? In a sense, not very much. We certainly
have no evidence that the Palestinian Jewish sages read Plato or Zeno, much
less studied them. But one result seems to me inescapable: living in the
Hellenistic-Roman world the Tannaim could not remain unaffected by that
world. It is not simply a matter of loan words; it is something much more
profound. Not only did the Palestinian sages appropriate the terminology
for some hermeneutic rules from the Hellenistic rhetors,[91] but inside the
bet ha-midrash, the rabbinic academy, apparently one did take up from time
to time philosophical questions, and one did attempt to answer these questions
in the current philosophical idiom. Study of the Law of course remained
paramount. But along with such activity went an awareness, at least in the
School of Johanan ben Zakkai, of the subject and style popular in intellectual
circles generally.

One thing should not mislead us. The fact that in a number of stories the
philosophos is bested in his encounter with the rabbi,[92] indicates nothing more
than a typically recurring popular attitude: anything they can do, we can
do better. This is not anti-philosophy as such; indeed, there is in such
stories a distinct acknowledgment that among the Gentiles the wisest
are the philosophers; but of course the *hakam* is superior since he is a master of the Torah.[93] Such stories are in spirit and intent like those anec-

---

[91] See on this the important researches of S. Lieberman, *Hellenism in Jewish Palestine*
28-114.

[92] E.g., *Genesis Rabba* 1.9, ed. Theodor-Albeck 8. Note indeed the subject of their discussion: was Creation *ex nihilo* or not?

[93] See the real note of respect in the story told in *Derek 'Eres, Pirqe Ben 'Azzai*, Ch. 3,
3, ed. Higger 183 ff. (and note the literature he cites on 184f.).
The statement by Rabbi Abba bar Kahana (*Gen. R.* 65.19, p. 734, and parallels) that
the greatest philosophers among the nations of the world were Balaam and Oenomaus of
Gadara cannot seriously illuminate what was or was not known by first-century Tannaim, particularly before the destruction of the Temple in 70 A. D. (see below n. 95): Abba bar Kahana
is a third generation Amora (in other words, late *III* cent. and early *IV* cent. A. D.)! Certainly Rabbi Me'ir (the second-century Tanna) in his relationships with Oenomaus is down-
right warm (see briefly on this *Jewish Encyclopedia*, 9.386). But much, much more to
the point (and perhaps therefore I would do well not to sound so condescending towards
Abba bar Kahana and his information): In the second century to have regarded
Oenomaus as nothing less than outstanding is the very reverse of being philosophically
not knowledgable; see for example the discussion on the Cynics — their influence and
their intellectual-spiritual role — in S. Dill, *Roman Society from Nero to Marcus Aurelius* (London 1904) 359 ff., and particularly the references in his notes. As for some
early Christians (cf. Dill 361), for Jewish Sages, too, much in what Cynics preached would
be a joy indeed. Observe, for example, Dill (and his references!) 363: '[The Cynics] were
probably the purest monotheists that classical antiquity produced. ... The most fear-
less and trenchant assailant of the popular theology among the Cynics was Oenomaus of
Gadara, in the reign of Hadrian. Oenomaus rejected, with the frankest scorn, the anthro-
pomorphic fables of heathenism. In **particular,** he directed his fiercest attacks against the

dotes in the first chapter of the Midrash on Lamentations where an Athenian, in other words, one universally reputed to be particularly clever, is outwitted by Jerusalemites, and even by youngsters of Jerusalem.[94] In no way do such stories demonstrate that philosophy, and the current manner of discussing what was generally regarded as philosophical questions, were repugnant to the talmudic sages and therefore were excluded from the rabbinic academy. Whether professional philosophers would have been impressed by the level or range of philosophical discussion inside the rabbinic academy is beside the point: it would be like asking what a Kant would think of various courses offered by many collegiate departments of philosophy. No one is suggesting that the talmudic sages were technical philosophers. But the popular terms and ethical themes of dominant Hellenistic philosophical speculations were not alien at least to the circle around Johanan ben Zakkai. He and his disciples did not shun either the subject or the style.[95] Their place of meeting was of course the *bet ha-midrash*, but inside it they found the spaciousness for the study of Scripture and the study of Mishnah, the dialectic of Law and the contemplation of mystic lore, the engagement with the dogmas of Revelation and the deliberations of philosophy.

Yale University.

----

revival of that faith in oracles and divination which was a marked characteristic of the Antonine age.' And more to the same effect on p. 364 (let alone p. 361, 'With rare exceptions, such as *Oenomaus of Gadara* [my italics] they seldom committed their ideas to writing'). So then, R. Me'ir — of the Antonine age! — is really up to what this effective philosopher is deeply concerned with; the Tanna need not at all be presumed to be ignorant of the ideas of the popular philosopher. Questions like, Is Oenomaus of the stature of a Plato or Aristotle in the history of philosophy, have nothing to do with the case; cf. above, p. 3 and notes ad loc. and pp. 19. Surely Seneca was no philosophical illiterate; and what does he say of Demetrius? '*Vir meo judicio magnus etiamsi maximis comparetur*' (quoted by Dill 362)! (Quintilian's stricture, 10.1.128, Loeb Classics IV 73, that 'Seneca had many excellent qualities, a quick and fertile intelligence with great industry and wide knowledge, though as regards the last quality he was often led into error by those whom he had entrusted with the task of investigating certain subjects on his behalf,' is hardly a disqualification in our present context. One: apparently Seneca was prepared to accept his assistants' judgments. Two: at least we can discover what his assistants regarded as intellectually respectable. And this is surely relevant to our immediate study.)

Finally, to speak of Balaam as a philosopher clearly reflects not a discrediting of philosophy, but a more than average respect for it — for not only is Balaam the recipient of divine revelations recorded in Scripture, but he is likened to Moses for the Gentiles: cf. *Sifre Deut.* 357 on Deut. 34.10, ed. Finkelstein 430, *Midrash Tannaim* 227. There is even a tradition that, like other eminent personages, Balaam was born circumcised, ARN 12.

[94] *Lamentations Rabba* on Lam. 1:1; cf. ed. Buber 23b ff.

[95] That the give-and-take recorded in PA 2.9 took place before Johanan withdrew to Jamnia is clear from an analysis of the sources; see also G. Alon, *Studies in Jewish History* [Heb.] I (Tel Aviv 1957) 261f. (and the text, *ibid.* should be corrected when it speaks of Eleazar ben Azariah, to Eleazar ben 'Arak).